Chamulas in the World of the Sun

There are no things greater
than economic investment.

Zapotec Tribes There are no things greater
than

She had long brown hair

The Destruction of the First Creation in a Rain of Boiling Water
(See Text 41)

Chamulas in the World of the Sun

Time and Space in a Maya Oral Tradition

Gary H. Gossen

WAVELAND
PRESS, INC.
Prospect Heights, Illinois

For information about this book, write or call:

Waveland Press, Inc.
P.O. Box 400
Prospect Heights, Illinois 60070
(312) 634-0081

The cover illustration is an original Chamula drawing of a courting scene — the subject of many Chamula narratives.

To the memory of my grandparents
Gerhardt and Marie Gossen
and
David and Maude Hamilton

who taught me their understanding of tradition
in wonderful summers on their farms on the
Kansas prairie

Preface

Ethics and Aesthetics are One and the Same.

—L. Wittgenstein

This book is about the oral tradition and cosmology of the Chamula Indians of Mexico. It is based on fifteen months of field research in Chamula, a Tzotzil-speaking Maya community in the state of Chiapas in southern Mexico. My aim is to present the oral tradition of a contemporary Maya community as a complete information system. That is, all genres as defined by the Chamulas are considered, both in themselves and in relation to the rest of the community's verbal behavior and to its world view. Such a broad sweep is necessary because language is both the means and the manifestation of knowledge about the world. Within each society the specialized knowledge and linguistic forms contained in an oral tradition are always related to the rest of that society's language, cosmology, and social behavior. Too often, however, oral tradition has been treated in piecemeal fashion, as in a collection of sayings, an appendix of myth texts, a corpus of tales stripped of their cultural contexts of meaning or performance, or a catalogue of motifs and tale types. Yet people in traditional nonliterate societies ordinarily learn and use a full complement of genres in their respective oral traditions. To describe these genres holistically is a major goal of this book.

To consider the whole of an oral tradition in addition to its parts requires a contextual orientation to the data. Thus, the function of genres within the social fabric must be explored. Yet folklorists and anthropologists have had a traditional liking for the study of oral tradition as "item" or isolated text, rather than as "event" or the performance of texts within specific cultural contexts. They have shown a preference for what Edmund Leach called butterfly collecting. This orientation, while valuable in providing a reservoir of reference material, nevertheless implies that oral tradition is marginal to the mainstream of social life, that it is what A. Irving Hallowell called a "floating segment of culture." This is an unfortunate view, for in many traditional societies, oral tradition is as important for the maintenance of the social order as are kinship systems and social organization. To borrow a phrase from Dell Hymes, oral tradition should be considered a part of the "ethnography of speaking."

A holistic, contextual approach to traditional verbal behavior requires great caution in the use of Western terminology, for such behavior is as variable as is human culture. Even the term "folklore" is so ambiguous that to anthropologists and folklorists it means quite different things. The word may exclude gossip, for example, on the ground that it has not yet stood the test of time, yet today's gossip may be tomorrow's traditional narrative. Terms like "verbal art," "oral literature," and "oral narrative" present similar problems in that they may be interpreted by the Westerner to include traditional prose and poetry but to exclude such forms of verbal behavior as punning games. Such imprecise labels are avoided whenever possible in this study. Experience shows that the segment of cultural behavior to which they variously refer is not uniform in content from culture to culture. Some cultures, like those of Polynesia, stress the role of reporting genealogical history in traditional verbal behavior. Others, like the Siriono of Bolivia, have minimal interest in cosmological or etiological explanations and absolutely no interest in genealogical history. Still others, like the tribes of the Northwest Coast of North America, emphasize the verbatim recitation of mythical precedents for ritual organization and ritual action. In parts of central Africa, "minor" genres such as the proverb figure prominently, on a par with etiological narratives and genealogical history. A useful term that describes the whole of the verbal aesthetic tradition in all cultures without an ethnocentric bias is the expression "oral tradition," which emphasizes the process of oral transmission while allowing for each culture's particular tradition.

In order to identify the forms and genres that belong to the oral tradition of a particular culture, folk taxonomies are of considerable help. They consistently demonstrate that Western genre labels do not correspond precisely to folk genre labels. In any major collection project, therefore, an initial step should be to elicit the folk taxonomies, which enable the investigator to ask relevant questions of informants about all important genres and may suggest further useful areas of exploration.

Once a collection has been obtained, a model must be constructed for interpreting and understanding the texts as they operate in the real social milieu. The model should attempt to describe a whole oral tradition in terms that generalize and abstract the immense amount of diverse empirical data without ignoring the fact that models do not have an autonomy of their own, that they refer at all times to what people do, say, and think. As Edmund Leach observed in relation to myth: "Myths for me are simply one way of describing certain types of human behavior; the anthropologists' jargon and his use of structural models are other devices for describing the same types of human behavior. In sociological analysis we need to make frequent use of these alternative languages, but we must always remember that a descriptive device can never have an autonomy of its own. However abstract my representations, my concern is always with the material world of human behavior, never with metaphysics or systems of ideas as such." One purpose of this book is to offer an alternative analytical language that takes into account the general sociological nature of the data on oral aesthetic forms as well as concrete data on a specific oral tradition.

In anthropological and folklore studies it has been the

custom to approach oral tradition with analytical methods and theories that were developed for other aspects of human behavior. "Folklore theory," the poor stepsister of the humanities and the social sciences, has never really stood on its own feet. One does a "Freudian analysis" or tries a "psychoanalytic interpretation" of a folktale. One seeks for archetypes, origins, migrations, and distributions of motifs and tale types by the historical-geographical method. One prepares a "Durkheimian sociological analysis" or a "Malinowskian functional analysis" or a "Lévi-Straussian structural analysis" of one fragment of the oral tradition of a people. There is a sadness in these methods, not only because they are in a sense "on loan," but also because they approach oral aesthetic forms as though their fundamental nature were everywhere the same, in need only of the right general paradigm to become universally intelligible. Yet oral traditions are as diverse as cultures. Herein lies the need for a model that allows a specific oral tradition to speak for itself, in its own categories of meaning, without ignoring the general social character of all oral symbolic media.

Oral tradition—like art, language, religion, philosophy, law, and other symbolic systems—serves as an evaluative and expressive domain. These aspects of social life constitute what Talcott Parsons has called "patterns of orientations to problems of meaning." Symbolic systems provide in their respective codes, implicitly and explicitly, the cultural guidelines of form, sense, and meaning that give order to a potentially chaotic world. To borrow from Clifford Geertz, they are models of and for the community's ethos. Ethics and aesthetics should therefore be approached as logically identical, for both phenomena derive from and reflect the very construction of the moral universe. They do not simply support each other as separate, functionally related entities but provide slightly different symbolic representations of the same thing. Again to quote Edmund Leach, "Logically, aesthetics and ethics are identical. If we are to understand the ethical rules of a society, it is the aesthetics we must study."

Leach implies that aesthetics, as part of a system of communication, may be structured in such a way that it can be translated into other codes of ideal categories. But in order to translate the diverse aspects of oral tradition into other codes, one must attempt to find a conceptual "common denominator" or metalanguage for considering such diverse phenomena as narrative setting, social control, linguistic style, textual content, and folk genre categories. With such a metalanguage, it would be possible to analyze the place of oral tradition in the social system; that is, as one of several superordinate codes of rules and values.

The fundamental components of a community's world view, specifically its categories of time and space, provide one useful conceptual metalanguage for a contextual analysis of oral tradition. For one reason, cosmology and oral tradition are alike in that both contain assumed public knowledge about the nature of order. In nearly all societies, concepts of time and space provide the underpinnings for the way in which the moral universe is supposed to behave. In a specific culture these fundamental axes—time and space—are shared with other culture-specific notions about order. An obvious example is the connection between religion and cosmology or myth and cosmology. Myth, of course, is only a fraction of traditional verbal behavior. If a whole oral tradition is viewed as a systematically organized reservoir of normative information, the isomorphic features or structural "resonances" of cosmology should be apparent throughout the content and organization of that tradition. It is such a structural chord that I am seeking in this book.

In calling this relationship "structural," I am not using the term in its global, nonempirical sense, as in French structuralism. By "structure" I mean an isomorphic feature of a specific cultural system that has generality and replicability. By "isomorphic feature" I mean an aspect of organization that is shared by two or more domains. The most useful metalanguage for dealing with isomorphic features of oral tradition in relation to the rest of society is provided by culture-specific concepts of time and space. These concepts have generality in that they may refer simultaneously to aspects of culture as diverse as ethnocentrism and demographic patterns, poetry and history, social organization and cosmology, witchcraft and sacred geography. They also provide replicability, for people can talk substantively and consistently about concepts of time and space. For all kinds of texts it is possible to elicit native criticism and exegesis that are readily translatable into temporal and spatial data. People can report when and where the events in a narrative happened; how many lines a song verse should have; where it should be sung and how often; and even where and when it was given to the people, as in their narratives of creation of the social order. They can tell where and when witches perform their antisocial acts, or how many times they must say a formula backward in order to gain the desired results. They can talk about the evolution of the present moral order, as in myth, or about last week's challenge to the moral order, as in gossip about a murder. All of these may be considered as substantive data about oral tradition, and they are for the most part replicable. One might elicit the same data tomorrow, barring idiosyncratic differences in informants. This combination of utility for eliciting substantive supporting information about texts and for identifying points of structural similarity with other aspects of culture is what makes time and space an appropriate metalanguage for the holistic study of an oral tradition. Cosmology, therefore, is used in this book as a language for reporting and analyzing another language, the reservoir of information in Chamula oral tradition.

I began this project in the summer of 1965, and wife and I did the major portion of the field work in 1968 and 1969. My research in Chiapas was undertaken at the suggestion of Evon Z. Vogt, whose advice and warm encouragement were instrumental in seeing this book, as well as the dissertation on which it is based, to completion. To him go my very special thanks. The Harvard Chiapas Project, founded by Professor Vogt in 1957 as a continuing center for the study of ethnography and culture change in the Chiapas Highlands, provided the reservoir of ethnographic and linguistic data that made possible my more specialized research.

I was supported in the field by research funds from a
National Science Foundation Cooperative Predoctoral Fellowship, a National Institutes of Mental Health Predoctoral
Fellowship, and a National Institutes of Mental Health Research Grant. The Research Committee at the University of
California at Santa Cruz supported me during the summer of
1971, when I wrote the final draft of this book, and provided a generous subsidy for publication of the Appendix.

Several persons here and in Mexico gave invaluable help
at various stages of the research. I am especially grateful to
Evon Z. Vogt, Gordon R. Willey, Douglas Oliver, David
Maybury-Lewis, Alan Dundes, Munro S. Edmonson, Alfonso
Villa Rojas, Thomas O. Beidelman, James Clifton, Pierre
Maranda, Elli Köngäs Maranda, Richard Bauman, M. Kirk
Endicott, James J. Fox, Keith Kernan, Roger D. Abrahams,
Victoria R. Bricker, Robert Laughlin, John Halverson,
Robert Da Matta, Michelle Rosaldo, George Collier, Shelley
Errington, Joseph Silverman, Robert Wasserstrom, David
Margolin, Jan and Diane Rus, Judy Merkel, Frank and
Joan Harrison, Thomas Rohlen, and Triloki Pandey.

The local community in San Cristóbal de las Casas was
also warm and hospitable. Gertrudis Duby de Blom, long
a friend and patron of Chiapas anthropological research,
kindly made available her library and photographic collection. Manuel Castellanos, Director of the Oficina de Asuntos
Indígenas, and Armando Aguirre T., the resident anthropologist at the Centro Coordinador Tzotzil-Tzeltal of the Instituto Nacional Indigenista, were extremely generous with
their time and knowledge, as were Prudencio Moscoso,
Leopoldo Velasco, Alejandro García, Ernesto Ramos, and
Vicente Reyes.

In Chamula itself our debts of hospitality and gratitude
are considerable. Above all, I wish to thank the ex-President-
es Juan Gómez Oso, Pascual López Calixto, Salvador Gómez
Oso, and Salvador López Castellanos; Salvador Guzmán
Bakbolom; Salvador López Calixto; Marian López Calixto;
Manuel López Calixto; Juan Méndez Tzotzek; Manuel Mén-
dez Tzotzek; Mateo Méndez Tzotzek; and Salvador López
Sethol. They welcomed us into their homes and ceremonies

and taught us their language and customs as patiently as they might have taught their own children. Because of us, they also suffered occasional harrassment and ridicule. For this I hope they can forgive us, finding satisfaction in the fact that they have imparted a small part of their rich oral tradition to sympathetic ears.

To my sister-in-law, Elizabeth Adam, I extend warm thanks for her help over several months in Chiapas. To my uncle, Dale Hamilton, I am grateful for the months of hospitality and peace on his farm in Kansas, where we did the preliminary organization and analysis of the data. Thanks are also due to Queenie McClain, Karen Dalman, and Janet Smith for excellent secretarial services, and to Barbara Bernie for assistance in annotating the text abstracts. Finally, I cannot thank adequately my wife Eleanor. From helping me to solve field problems, to editing and typing thousands of pages of text and manuscript, from cooking for a houseful of informants, to doctoring my constant fleabites in the field, she has willingly shared the task of preparing this book.

GHG

Contents

Maps

Figures

Chamula Drawings By Marian López Calixto

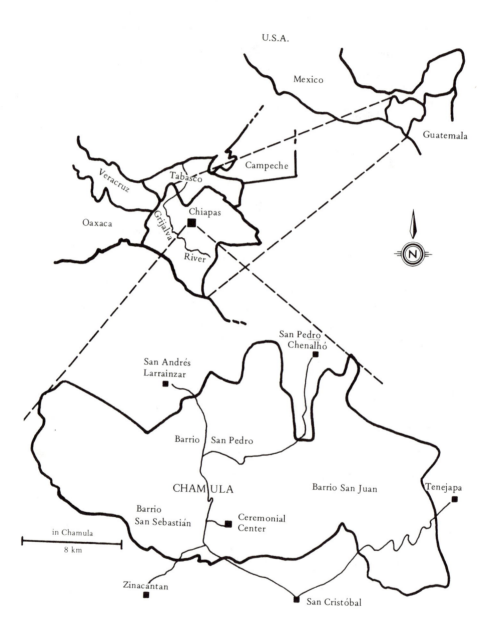

U.S.A.

Mexico

Guatemala

Campeche

Veracruz

Tabasco

Chiapas

Oaxaca

Grijalva

River

San Pedro
Chenalhó

San Andrés
Larrainzar

Barrio San Pedro

CHAMULA

Barrio San Juan

Tenejapa

Barrio
San Sebastián

Ceremonial
Center

in Chamula

8 km

Zinacantan

San Cristóbal

Map 1. Chamula in Chiapas and Mexico

(1) The Community

> Our Lord San Juan saw that the land was better,
> That his sheep would thrive better,
>
> That there were no ants to bite his sheep,
> That there was no strong heat;
>
> For it was not Hot Country,
> The land was good:
>
> His children would prosper,
> His sheep were no longer sad.
> —Salvador Guzmán Bakbolom, Text 115

San Juan Chamula is a predominantly monolingual Tzotzil-speaking *municipio* (municipality) of approximately 40,000 Maya Indians which lies at the top of the oak- and pine-forested Chiapas highlands of southern Mexico (Map 1).[1] It is one of the largest of twenty-one Indian municipios in the state of Chiapas which speak languages belonging to the Tzeltalan group (Tzotzil, Tzeltal, and Tojolabal) of Maya languages (McQuown, 1956: 195; Secretaría de Industria y Comercio, 1963: 25).[2]

Historical Background

Chamula has been a distinct cultural entity since before the time of the Spanish Conquest. The community is a direct heir to many of the traits that characterized pre-Columbian Maya societies, whose artistic and intellectual accomplishments were notable.[3] Chronicles from the time of the Conquest indicate that Chamula was then one of the principal population centers of highland Chiapas (Pozas, 1959: 17). Among the Indian communities of the highlands, Chamula and Huixtan were the last to submit to the will of the conquerors Luis Marín and Francisco de Medina in 1524 (Trens,

1957: 112). In the same year Chamula was given as a large
land grant (*encomienda*) to Bernal Díaz del Castillo. It
survived intact the subsequent centuries of oppressive colonial land and labor exploitation. The efforts of the Dominicans to concentrate the dispersed Chamulas into population
centers (*reducciones*) failed for the most part, as such efforts
did throughout much of Meso-America. Three such reducciones were set up in Chamula around 1550. Although
they were apparently unable to maintain their original con-
centration of population, they continued to function as
subadministrative units for the outlying hamlets that had
been assigned to them. The modern barrios of Chamula, of
which there are three, may be survivals of the Dominicans'
abortive efforts.[4]

The Chamulas participated in a marginal way in the Tzeltal
Rebellion of 1712–1715, which was essentially an extension
of the better-known Indian revolts of Yucatán in the same
period. Chamulas, like other Maya groups in the area, were
expressing frustration and anger at their treatment as debt
slaves and economic pawns of the Spaniards. Independence
from Spain in 1821, followed by Chiapas' brief period as
an independent state (1821–1823) and its decision by popular
referendum in 1824 to become a part of Mexico rather than
of Guatemala, were events that hardly affected Chamula at
all. Patterns of exploitation of Indian labor and production
persisted under new masters, with little change from the
colonial period. These conditions, together with factional
ferment in state and national politics between the Federalists
and Centralists, led indirectly to the so-called Cuzcat Rebellion of 1869–1870. This revitalization movement centered
in Chamula but encompassed all of the Chiapas highlands.
Like the better-known Caste Wars of Yucatán during the
same period, the Chamula revolt sought the return of all
power to the Indians. Symbolizing the syncretistic nature of
the movement was the crucifixion of a Chamula boy on
Good Friday, 1868. The crucifixion reflected both the
Indians' Christian indoctrination and a desire to return to
their pre-Columbian cult of the sun deity. Defense of the
cult led to the amassing of firearms and the formation of an

Indian army of thousands. They terrorized and killed Ladinos (Spanish-speaking mestizos) throughout the highlands, caus-ing a temporary exodus of the population from the area. This culminated in an unsuccessful invasion of San Cristóbal, the local Ladino trade and administrative center, on June 17, 1869. The Indians were not fully subdued until 1870 (Trens, 1957: 177–210).

Under the dictatorship of President Porfirio Díaz (1867–1910), the social injustices that had indirectly caused the Cuzcat Rebellion became still more firmly established on both a local and a national scale. In Chiapas, as throughout Mexico, the most immediate problem for the peasantry and Indians was the lack of sufficient agricultural lands for subsistence. This shortage gave many of them, including hundreds of Chamulas, no alternative but to submit to the yoke of debt slavery on the big haciendas. In spite of the relevance of its ultimate objectives to their destiny, the subsequent Mexican Revolution (1910–1917) did not involve Chamulas or other Indians of the highlands in ways that they understood. Chamulas were recruited for first one side and then the other. They were mistreated by both factions and were typically obliged, at gunpoint, to work as servants and suppliers of food. The eventual victory of General Álvaro Obregón's forces and his troops' occupation of San Cristóbal changed little of relevance to the Chamulas.

Actual redistribution of land to Chamulas under the provisions of the Constitution of 1917 did not begin until 1936, during the presidency of Lázaro Cárdenas. Since then, the area controlled by the municipal government of Chamula increased from 240.61 square kilometers to 364.56 square kilometers in 1968. This increase was made possible through collective land grants (*ejidos*) and confirmations of title on modest de facto holdings. Even with these grants, population density has remained extremely high; in 1960, for example, it was 73.6 persons per square kilometer (Manuel Castellanos, 1969, personal communication). Consequently, significant numbers of Chamulas have moved out of the municipio to ejidos and other types of agricultural colonies located through-out the state of Chiapas.

On the administrative front, significant changes have also taken place since the 1930s. By order of the state office of Indian Affairs (Asuntos Indígenas) in 1937 and 1938, Chamula was required to reform its traditional political hierarchy in two ways. First, the top elective political position, that of presidente or chief magistrate, was no longer to be held by a monolingual elder, as had been the custom, but was to be held by a younger, educated man, bilingual in Spanish and Tzotzil and willing to cooperate with the office of Indian Affairs. Second, the number of scribes (*escribanos*), who were supposed to know Spanish and were assigned to assist monolingual elders in their affairs, was increased from four to eight. The eight new scribes were hand-picked by the director of the office of Asuntos Indígenas for their relatively high level of education, knowledge of Spanish, and promise of cooperation with the Ladino officials. They belonged to the few families who now form the nucleus of the oligarchy that controls Chamula politics.

A third important trend that began in the 1930s and still continues is the opening of truck roads both within Chamula and between its ritual and administrative hub (henceforth called Chamula Ceremonial Center) and those of other Indian communities and San Cristóbal. The construction began in 1936 and has vastly increased the quantity and ease of inter-municipio trade. Although the Pan-American Highway between San Cristóbal and Tuxtla, completed in 1950, does not pass through Chamula, it has also opened up a fast, relatively cheap network of transportation for Chamulas. They use the highway to go by truck to the Pacific lowlands, where they work as day laborers on the coffee plantations and in cornfields belonging to Zinacantecos or other Chamulas.

Finally, El Centro Coordinador Tzotzil-Tzeltal, a national agency organized in 1950, has had a significant role in certain aspects of recent change. Its goals have been those of "teaching the Indians to become literate in Spanish, bringing modern medicine and new agricultural crops and technology into the Indian communities, integrating them into the national life by building roads to hitherto isolated villages, and generally improving their economic situation vis-a-vis

the local Ladinos" (Vogt, 1969: 30). This agency's projects
in Chamula have included a clinic, several agricultural demon-
strations, and over thirty primary schools (first four grades)
located throughout the municipio. However, Chamula is not
a showplace of the center's achievements in the highlands,
for although the center has emphasized the need for its
services in densely populated and impoverished Chamula,
local cooperation has been moderate to poor.

In summary, Chamula throughout much of its history has
been the home of a large group of land-poor Indians, among
whom unrest has been common. As a self-conscious Indian
municipio, it has few rivals in all of the Chiapas highlands. It
permits no Spanish-speaking Mexicans to live permanently
or to hold property within its boundaries, except one family,
that of the Mexican secretary who directs their dealings with
state and national governments. Overnight stays on a semi-
regular basis are permitted only for Ladino schoolteachers,
the Ladino priest (who is required to stay in the ceremonial
center and was temporarily banished for not doing so in
December of 1969), and a doctor who occasionally visits the
clinic, a service provied by the National Bureau of Indian
Affairs (Instituto Nacional Indigenista). Any other non-
Chamulas must get specific permission from municipal
authorities to remain there overnight. While Chamulas are
quite conscious of their identity as a municipio, their own
municipal territory cannot contain all of them. Chamulas
are found living and working in substantial numbers throughout the state. However, Chamulas who leave their home
municipio temporarily or permanently tend generally not to
become acculturated; nor do they cease to speak Tzotzil,
for sufficient numbers work and relocate together to make
it possible to maintain a microcosm of normal Chamula life.
Wherever they go, they return to Chamula for fiestas, for
Chamula Ceremonial Center is the hub of their moral universe,
smišik banamil, the "navel of the earth."

Land and Economy

Chamulas live on a cool highland plateau. Only a few
hamlets lie on the northern escarpment, which drops off to

warmer regions. The climate is relatively pleasant the year round. The summer rainy season (May to October) is generally cool, with many overcast days and foggy mornings. The winter dry season (November to April) has the annual temperature extremes. Heavy frosts are common from November to February, and the hottest season falls in late April, just before the onset of the rainy season.

Chamula straddles the highest reaches of the state of Chiapas. The highest mountain in the Chiapas highlands, Cerro de Tzontevitz (2,900 meters), lies within Chamula's borders. Chamula ceremonial center, which has a very small permanent population, lies at an elevation of approximately 2,300 meters, which is about average for the whole municipio. The great majority of Chamulas live in hamlets that are scattered on ridges or in small basins across their eroded mountain plateau. The exhausted red soil contrasts with the deep green of the remaining pine and oak forests on the edges of the basins, which the Indians have stripped over the centuries. Slash and burn maize agriculture follows the destruction of the forests, which are exploited for numerous wood-based industries, such as charcoal and furniture, and for firewood. In many regions of the municipio, the slash-and-burn shifting agricultural cycle has been accelerated to such an extent that the land cannot recover. The thin cover of grass that remains on the stripped land is used as sheep pasture until overgrazing turns such areas into eroded expanses of sterile earth. The entire municipio as seen in aerial photographs looks like a mosaic of various stages in the cycle from forest to wasteland.[5]

The subsistence base is the ancient American trinity of maize, squash, and beans, supplemented significantly by cabbage and potatoes. A small flock of sheep (six to fifteen head) is kept by nearly all households to provide the wool for their own clothing and some surplus that can be sold for cash. Mutton, however, is never eaten. Chickens and turkeys provide a small cash income from egg production and are consumed during festivals and curing ceremonies. Domestic rabbits are also kept by many families. Candles, lamp oil, ribbons, chile, salt, sugar, and coffee are purchased in San

Cristóbal or from other Indian traders. Many of these staples come from the tropical lowlands, as do many of the Chamulas' most important ritual goods. Such goods include tobacco in the form of cigarettes; tallow and paraffin for candles; brown sugar, which is the main ingredient of an illegally manufactured crude rum liquor, a ritual *sine qua non*; fresh sugar cane, from which is made a kind of beer; pine resin incense; and many tropical plants used for religious decorations. Some of these substances must be present for celebration of any ritual transaction.

A small amount of cash or surplus agricultural produce is necessary for obtaining these goods. Only a few rich families in each hamlet have sufficient land both for their own food production and for cash-producing surplus crops. This situation presents several alternatives, which Chamulas can use separately or in combination to overcome the problem of inadequate maize production at home. They can work on the lowland coffee plantations or in nearby San Cristóbal for several months every year to earn cash to buy the food that their small land parcels do not produce. They can rent land in other parts of the highlands or in the lowlands in order to grow sufficient maize for their own use and for payment to their workers, with perhaps some surplus remaining to sell for cash. Alternatively, they can hire themselves out as field hands to some other Indian who rents the land. Their wages will nearly always be paid in maize. They can remain in Chamula and engage in economic specialization, such as ceramics, carpentry, liquor-distilling, and flower-growing, which do not require a large land base.[6] If none of these alternatives is feasible or desirable, and if the person is not wealthy, he can emigrate to the Mexican government's "New Centers of Population," which are usually granted as ejido lands. At present, the lands available under this relocation program lie relatively far from Chamula and often far even from the highlands. Thus, Chamula's independent spirit and ideals of separatism do not reflect an economic reality. Chamulas are bound inextricably to the economic fortunes of the state of Chiapas. Their beautiful mountain home remains essentially a spiritual home, a fact that constitutes a basic assumption in their world view. Regardless of the exploitation and scorn that they encounter outside their municipio, the moral universe, exclusively Chamula, awaits them on their return.

Social Groupings and Settlement Patterns

The Ceremonial Center

The Chamula settlement pattern generally follows that of the ancient Maya: dispersed patrilineal hamlets that contain the majority of the population, with a relatively unpopulated ceremonial center (see Bullard, 1960). The center contains, in addition to rental housing for ritual officials, most of the sacred places that figure prominently in various rituals through-out the year (Map 2). The ceremonial center also contains, within the central San Juan Church, what is believed to be the actual center of the universe or "navel of the earth."

The Barrio

The barrio is the next most inclusive social grouping below the municipio. The three barrios are the chief components in the religious and political organization of the municipio. Religious and political officials, henceforth called cargo-holders (from the Spanish *cargo*, meaning "office" or "res-ponsibility"), always enter the official hierarchy as representa-tives of their barrios, and ritual procedure constantly emphasizes the tripartite composition of religious and politi-cal organization. Barrio affiliation is carried in the patriline as are one's surname and whole social identity. This affiliation does not usually change in an individual's lifetime, although in certain instances it may. The barrio does not ideally func-tion as an endogamous group, although this is usually the case. The barrio's most important function lies on the ritual and administrative level.

The Cemetery Group

Between the hamlet and the barrio is what may be called the cemetery group. It consists of two to eight hamlets, usually from the same barrio, which customarily bury their dead in the same cemetery. The hamlets that bury their dead

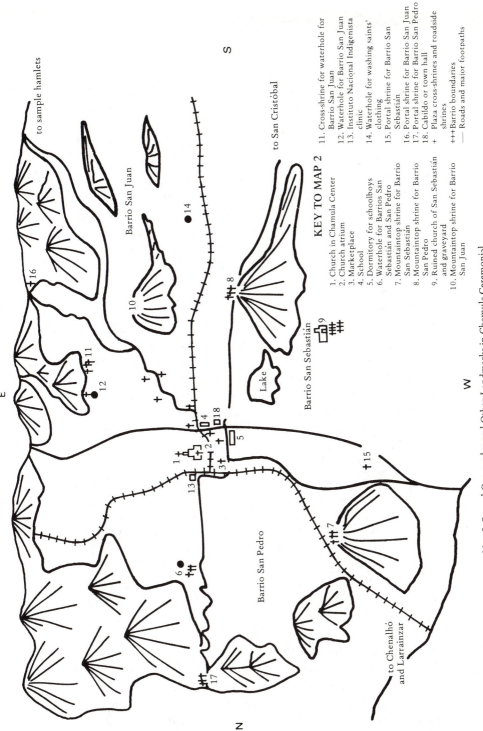

KEY TO MAP 2

1. Church in Chamula Center
2. Church atrium
3. Marketplace
4. School
5. Dormitory for schoolboys
6. Waterhole for Barrios San Sebastián and San Pedro
7. Mountaintop shrine for Barrio San Sebastián
8. Mountaintop shrine for Barrio San Pedro
9. Ruined church of San Sebastián and graveyard
10. Mountaintop shrine for Barrio San Juan
11. Cross-shrine for waterhole for Barrio San Juan
12. Waterhole for Barrio San Juan
13. Instituto Nacional Indigenista clinic
14. Waterhole for washing saints' clothing
15. Portal shrine for Barrio San Sebastián
16. Portal shrine for Barrio San Juan
17. Portal shrine for Barrio San Pedro
18. Cabildo or town hall
+ Plaza cross-shrines and roadside shrines
+ + Barrio boundaries
— Roads and major footpaths

to sample hamlets

Barrio San Juan

Barrio San Sebastián

Lake

Barrio San Pedro

to Chenalhó and Larraínzar

to San Cristóbal

N

E

S

W

Map 2. Sacred Geography and Other Landmarks in Chamula Ceremonial Center

together and celebrate the Festival of the Dead (All Saints'
Day) together in the same cemetery feel a closeness to one
another which is reinforced by the fact that most of their
consanguineal, affinal, and ritual kinship relationships are
restricted to the same few hamlets. This means not that
hamlets are exogamous units, but that when a man cannot
find a spouse (who must have a different patronymic from
his) in his own hamlet, it is more than likely that he will find
her in the nearby hamlets with which his family already has
traditional ties of ritual kinship or simply a long acquaint-
ance. This special relationship of neighboring hamlets is
nowhere manifested more clearly than in the cemetery.

The Hamlet
In general, the hamlet is the smallest social group that
identifies an individual's geographic origin in terms which
will be understood by most adult Chamulas. It is also the
second largest subdivision of the municipio for administrative and representational purposes. In 1968, there were only
seventy-six "official" hamlets within the municipio, but on
a map that Chamula informants and I constructed with the
aid of aerial photographs, we were able to locate 109 "traditional" hamlets, which still exist unofficially as significant
population units for most Chamulas.

The hamlet is ideally described by Chamulas as a group of
people who had a common ancestor, yet all recognize that
this is rarely the case. The maximum length of generational
memory, even among the strongest patrilines, seems to be
five generations, and descent group disputes and consequent
splits have changed so many surnames and redirected affections that residents of a single hamlet would not necessarily
recognize a common ancestor. Chamula hamlets differ from
those in nearby Zinacantan in that they are usually neither
demographically nor socially isolated; nor do they tend to
be so strongly endogamous (Vogt, 1969: 148–149). For most
domestic units in Chamula, some of their relationship systems
(consanguineal, affinal, and compadrazgo) reach outside
the hamlet, carrying with them economic and social ties
that in other communities tend to remain within the hamlet.

The Waterhole Group

Within each hamlet there are usually several waterhole groups. They consist of families who jointly maintain and use a single water supply. Because of the area's karst topography and internal drainage, waterholes in most hamlets have a very limited distribution. Strong descent groups tend ordinarily to control the rights to their use, because they clean them and sponsor ceremonies in honor of the earth gods at the beginning of the rainy season each year to guarantee the water supply.

The waterhole group generally consists of a major patrilineal descent group and adhering weaker (poorer) groups, not necessarily related, who together use and maintain a single water supply. The waterhole group is usually an exogamous unit, but only to the extent that the same patronymic is represented. Some waterholes, even those controlled by powerful groups, dry up in the dry season. All must then either go to unowned sources or, less commonly, pay for seasonal rights to a waterhole that still has water, provided the controlling families will admit them as users. In sum, the waterhole group is a unit of economic, social, and political solidarity that has its simplest behavioral expression during the rainy season when most existing waterholes have an adequate water supply.

The Patrilineage or Sna

In Chamula, there is a descent line-based social unit that lies between the waterhole group and the domestic group as a form of social integration. Evon Vogt coined the term *sna* (literally, "his or her house" in Tzotzil) to refer to this patrilineal group in neighboring Zinacantan. It consists of two or more patrilocal domestic units that form a localized descent line. Vogt's description of the sna also applies to Chamulas' patrilineage: "the *sna* is thus an extension of the patrilocally extended domestic group . . . Genealogical connections can be traced in these localized patrilineages . . . The members of a patrilineage live on adjacent lands which they have inherited from their ancestors. A patrilineage possesses some jural authority, in that important decisions for lineage members are made by senior males" (Vogt, 1969: 140).

Membership in the patrilineage is made explicit several times a year by participation of the domestic units in certain rituals. The most important of these is the Holy Cross ceremony in May, whose purpose is to encourage the earth gods to guarantee a dependable water supply and good crops. It is in this setting that patrilineages usually assert themselves as dominant or submissive. Generally the strength of a patrilineage depends on its land base.

The Domestic Group

The patrilocal domestic group is the smallest social group to which Chamulas belong. This unit consists of kinsmen who live together in a single house or house compound and share a single maize supply and a single ritual shrine (an outdoor altar located in the patio of one of the houses). The domestic group is the scene of most everyday social interaction and economic cooperation and has the greatest responsibility for socialization of the young. It, with the sna or patrilineage, is also the group that performs or sponsors the life crisis and domestic rituals associated with Chamula life. The rituals pertaining to birth, baptism, marriage, and burial are sponsored by the domestic unit and its extension, the patrilineage. In the Chamula ceremonial center, Catholic ritual is required for baptism and optional for marriage, but birth and burial do not involve the official church at all. Curing ceremonies, performed by shamans, are also sponsored and financed by the domestic unit. Certain annual festivals, such as the Holy Cross Festival in May and the Feast of the Dead in October, involve major ritual activity within the domestic unit and the patrilineage. Incidental ceremonies such as maize field blessings also take place within the domestic unit, although they may also involve the larger patrilineage.[7]

Political and Religious Organization

Four groups of officials conduct the political and religious life of Chamula. The first is an "elective" municipal body,

the Ayuntamiento Constitucional, which is prescribed by
Mexican law and officially governs Chamula. Although mock
elections are held to choose the members of the Ayuntamiento, its six positions are filled by appointees approved by
the ruling oligarchy of powerful families and past cargoholders. Terms for these officials, who should be bilingual,
are for three years. The head of the Ayuntamiento Constitucional is the presidente municipal or chief magistrate. He
has responsibility for the entire political hierarchy and serves
as the chief arbiter in court cases.

The presidente is simultaneously head of the traditional
civil hierarchy, called the Ayuntamiento Regional. This
second group of officials constitutes the effective governing
body of Chamula affairs. It is responsible for legal, financial,
and disciplinary matters, as well as for public works. It
comprises sixty-three officials, mostly monolingual in Tzotzil,
who travel from their respective hamlets to live in the ceremonial center during their one-year terms. They are served
by a small group of bilingual young men called "escribanos"
or scribes, whose appointments are for indefinite terms.
Officials enter the hierarchy as representatives of their respective barrios and are ranked according to the prestige and
financial responsibility of their position, or cargo. They rule
by sacred authority, symbolized by the silver-tipped staff
that they carry.

A third group of officials, forming the religious hierarchy,
sponsors public and private ceremonial activities in honor of
the saints. It also coordinates its own activities with those of
the civil hierarchy. All the religious cargos (of which there
were sixty-one in 1968) cost a great deal of money and time
to perform and are therefore extremely prestigious. The
positions are in fact ranked in terms of such costs. High-status
positions, such as pasión (Spanish for "passion") and nichim
(Tzotzil for "flower")—charged with maintaining cults to the
sun and moon deities—cost as much as 20,000 pesos (over
U.S. $1,500) and must be requested as much as fifteen years
in advance. Somewhat lower status is attached to the positions of mayordomo (Spanish for "overseer") and alférez
(Spanish for "standard-bearer")—who sponsor the cults of the

saints and of their sacred objects, respectively. Like political officials, religious cargoholders assume office as representatives of their barrios and must maintain an official residence in the ceremonial center. With the exception of the pasión and nichim positions, which last for two years, the other cargos in the religious hierarchy are for one year.

There is a fourth group, which includes officials who do not have any kind of corporate organization. Included are nearly eighty positions, of mixed nature, tenure, financial cost, and prestige. They generally share the features of not requiring an official residence in the ceremonial center and not requiring constant ritual involvement throughout the year. Some women occupy positions in this group, whereas the three other groups have no female officials. Also included are four positions, with probable pre-Columbian antecedents, which have life tenure and are passed in the patriline from father to son.

Great effort is made by the decision-making network to appoint men from all of the hamlets in the municipio in order to achieve more equal representation through the years. The existence of most offices in triplicate, corresponding to the three barrios, expresses this ideal of corporate representation. It is important because past cargoholders are expected to represent and carry out the wishes of the central political and religious organization on the grass-roots level. The nature of repeated participation in the cargo system is extremely complex. People tend to follow either a religious or a political career, with joint participation generally restricted to the higher status levels. For the most part, officials make an effort to serve in a single position for three terms, thus identifying themselves with that position as an elder. Moreover, the opportunity to hold high-status cargos tends to be open only to certain influential families, which suggests a kind of social stratification in the community. Regardless of the status of a cargo position, however, it should be performed with religious commitment, for it is a genuine service to the community. If cargos were not assumed and performed properly, people believe, the community would collapse under the wrath of angry gods and saints. The com-

munity responsibility vested in these officials is graphically
expressed in the language that is used with reference to
cargo performance. When one speaks of serving in the cargo
system, he uses the verb *kuč*, which means "to carry" or
"to bear (as a burden)." Individuals "bear" the financial and
ritual load of a religious or political office for a year or
more, in which way they gain the esteem of the community
and the gods. They actively help the gods to maintain the
temporal order. This is not unlike the ancient Maya concept
of the deities, who were believed to carry the various temporal
cycles on their backs through their appointed times (Thompson, 1960: 59; Bricker, 1966: 360–363).

Chamula shamans (*h ʔiloletik* or "seers") are also specialists in matters of cyclical time. Much of their ability to
cure is thought to derive from their capacity to understand
and control matters of human destiny. The length of each
human life is predetermined at birth by the sun-Christ deity.
At that time he lights candles of different length in the sky,
corresponding to the assigned lifespans of different individuals. As long as the candle burns, the individual and his
animal soul companion live. When it goes out, they die. The
word for this candle (*ʔora*) is the same as one of the general
words that refer to time. The word *ʔora* (perhaps related
to the Spanish *hora*, "hour" or "time") also means destiny.
Related to this concept is the belief that individuals have
animal soul companions, also given by the sun deity at birth,
who share their human counterparts' physical and spiritual
destinies. These animals live in two special corrals, one in a
sacred mountain and the other in the sky, and are cared
for by San Jerónimo (St. Jerome). They range from jaguars
and coyotes for rich and powerful people, to oppossums
and squirrels for poor and humble people. Shamans as well as
prestigious cargoholders need powerful animal soul companions in order to perform their tasks in the human community. Hundreds of shamans work at the hamlet level as
curing specialists, guarding the health—that is, time or
destiny—of their clients. The shamans learn their trade by
dream, revelation and apprenticeship. They are not formally
organized or ranked, but work individually on a cash or

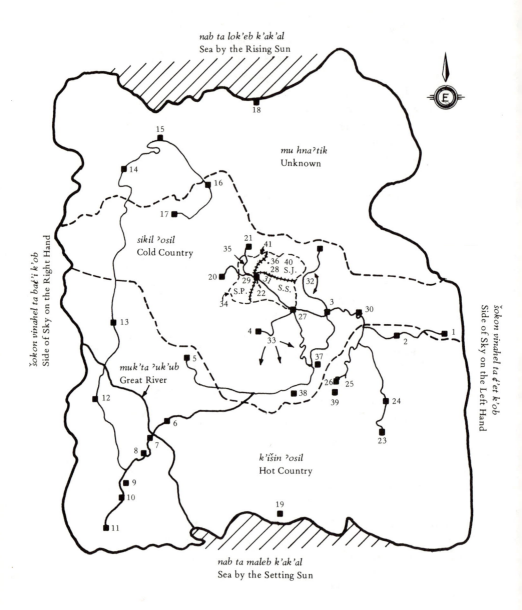

nab ta lok'eb k'ak'al
Sea by the Rising Sun

mu hna²tik
Unknown

sikil ²osil
Cold Country

šokon vinahel ta bat'i k'ob
Side of Sky on the Right Hand

šokon vinahel ta t'et k'ob
Side of Sky on the Left Hand

muk'ta ²uk'ub
Great River

k'išin ²osil
Hot Country

nab ta maleb k'ak'al
Sea by the Setting Sun

Map 3. A Chamula Map of the World, by Marian López Calixto. Orientation—east up—follows the original.

—— Major roads
— — Major regional boundary
----- Chamula municipal boundary
+++ Internal Chamula barrio
boundary

1. Guatemala
2. Comitán, a Ladino town south of San Cristóbal and near the Guatemalan border
3. San Cristóbal, a Ladino town and the principal trading center of the highland area
4. Zinacantan, a Tzotzil-speaking municipio adjacent to Chamula. Many Chamulas work in the lowland maize fields rented by Zinacantecos and thus have greater contact with them than with other indigenous groups
5. Simojovel
6. Chiapa de Corzo, a lowland Ladino town on the Pan American Highway, west of the highlands and just east of the Grijalva River
7. Grijalva River bridge on Pan American Highway near Tuxtla Gutiérrez
8. Tuxtla Gutiérrez, capital of the state of Chiapas
9. Arriaga, a lowland Ladino town on the way to the coffee plantations
10. Huixtla, a lowland Ladino town in the region of the coffee plantations
11. Tapachula, the principal Ladino town in southwestern Chiapas, also near the coffee plantations
12. Puebla
13. Mexico City
14. England
15. United States
16. Campeche, capital of Mexican state of the same name
17. Mérida, capital of Mexican state of the same name
18. Place where the sun comes up from the Sea by the Rising Sun
19. Place where the sun sinks into the Sea by the Setting Sun
20. Larrainzar, a Tzotzil-speaking municipio northwest of Chamula
21. Chenalhó, a Tzotzil-speaking municipio north of Chamula
22. Chamula Ceremonial Center
23. Pujiltik, a Ladino town in Hot Country
24. Suyitán, a Ladino town in Hot Country
25. Venustiano Carranza, a lowland Ladino and Indian town that is an important source of shamans and witches. Nearby is a sacred mountain.
26. Lansavitz, a sacred mountain used for Chamula rain-making ritual
27. Oshyoket, a sacred mountain overlooking the valley of Zinacantan
28. Calvario San Juan, a sacred mountain near Chamula Center
29. Calvario San Pedro, a sacred mountain near Chamula Ceremonial Center
30. Teopisca, a Ladino town on the Pan American Highway toward Comitán
31. Calvario San Sebastián, a sacred mountain near Chamula Ceremonial Center
32. San Cristóbal Mountains, separating the municipios of San Cristóbal and Chamula
33. Zinacantan Mountains, separating Zinacantan Ceremonial Center from the Pan American Highway
34. Chamula boundary
35. Sacred waterhole for Chamula barrios of San Pedro and San Sebastián
36. Sacred waterhole for Chamula barrio of San Juan
37. Nachih, a hamlet of Zinacantan located on the Pan American Highway
38. Nabenchauk, a hamlet of Zinacantan located on the Pan American Highway
39. Mispia, a sacred mountain used for Chamula rain-making ritual
40. Tzontevitz, a sacred mountain in Chamula and dwelling place of the patron saint San Juan, of earth gods, and of the Chamula soul animals
41. Ojovitz, a sacred mountain in Chamula and home of earth gods

barter basis. Personal illnesses of the soul, misfortunes incurred by an animal soul companion, injury by witchcraft, and misfortune caused by the wrath of the earth gods are the most frequent kinds of problems dealt with by shamans. They also officiate at preventive rituals at the hamlet and patrilineage levels. In sum, Chamula political, religious, and shamanistic activities strive to maintain order in a moral universe that is continually threatened by men and supernaturals alike.

Cosmology: The Categories of Space

Most basic to Chamula spatial orientation is the belief that they live at the center of the earth, *smišik banamil,* or "the navel of the earth." They believe that their centrality on the square earth-island, combined with the high elevation of their land in the Chiapas highlands, gives them a special relationship with the sun, the principal deity, which no other Indian or mestizo community can hope to match. Consequently, they view their home municipio as the only truly safe and virtuous place on earth. As social and physical distances increase, danger lurks more threateningly. The edges of the earth are populated by demons, strange human beings, and wild animals. From there can be seen the terrifying spectacle of the sun and moon deities plunging into and emerging from the seas every day on their respective vertical circuits around the island universe.

A drawing by a Chamula illustrates the spatial relationships subscribed to by many Chamulas. (Map 3). I asked a young Chamula, eighteen years old, who had attended school for five years, to draw Chamula as it lay within *skotol banamil,* "all of the earth." I requested a numbered code for place names. On the map, Chamula is centrally located on the square island-earth and also looms enormous in the context of the whole earth. Moreover, Chamula is the only municipio mentioned in the key that has a boundary. Even the barrios are given, which shows the ideal tripartite division of the municipio. The world is divided into five major regions: Chamula, *hlumaltik,* "our land"; Cold Country, *sikil ʔosil,* which includes most of the Chiapas highlands, parts of which are known to Chamulas through work and travel; Hot Country, *k'iśin ʔosil*, including the Pacific lowlands and the Grijalva River valley, partially known by most Chamula men from day labor there on coffee plantations and in rental cornfields; the Unknown, *mu hnaʔtik,* "we don't know," which includes places on the earth about which Chamulas may have heard but to which they have not been and do not wish to go; and the seas, *nabetik*, which surround the earth and provide points of articulation between the earth and the two vertical parts of the cosmos, the underworld, *lahebal*, and the sky, *vinahel*.

In a larger version of this map, I measured the relative distances between selected places that covered the whole range of the artist's familiarity, from his home to places he had only heard about. The measuring was done in standard units marked on a thread. Analysis of these distances suggested that the degree of social similarity definitely served as a criterion for representing relative distances. In his representation the artist consistently brought distant Chamula hamlets closer to home than they actually were. Conversely, he pushed places occupied by non-Chamulas outward toward the margins of the universe to the degree that he considered them to be dissimilar from Chamulas.[8] In effect, the only uniformly predictable, familiar, and "near" places to Chamula —in a conceptual sense—are those areas where Chamulas customarily live, work, and travel. The center of this moral universe is their own ceremonial center.

Within their own municipio, space is further divided and evaluated according to several criteria. First, they distinguish between ordinary space and sacred space. Sacred spaces can potentially be used for ritual action. This means that language, gestures, objects, and attitudes associated with sacred places are directed to supernatural beings or are meant to please them. Ordinary places, in contrast, are simply the settings for everyday social transactions and economic activities.

In addition to the distinctions between ritual and nonritual space, Chamulas divide their municipal territory into three other spatial categories: woods, *teʔtik*, including all areas

uninhabited by people or unused by people on a regular basis;
cleared land, *hamalaltik*, particularly that used for agricultural
and pastoral purposes; and houses, *naetik*, which also include
gardens and other buildings in the residential compound.
No one of these spatial categories forms the exclusive domain
of either ritual or nonritual space. Ritual behavior may occur
equally as well in the woods (as in caves and at waterholes),
in the fields (as in maize-blessing ceremonies), and in the
house (as in house shrine and curing ceremonies). In other
words, sacred space may transcend the other spatial categories. The ceremonial center, for example, which is the
symbolic focus of Chamula ritual activity, contains segments
of all three other categories of space. It also contains symbols
of all of the important social groups of Chamula. As such, it
can be considered a kind of controllable microcosm of the
whole spatial universe (Map 2).

Chamulas believe that the earth is an inclined island,
which is higher in the east than in the west. This belief is
supported by Chamula experience of the outside world.
Men frequently go south and west to the nearby lowlands of
the Grijalva River valley to work on coffee plantations.
Although this tropical lowland area is relatively close to their
cool highland home, its elevation is spectacularly lower than
that of Chamula. In other words, the drop-off to the south
and west is dramatic; to the north and east there is no immediate drop-off, only a continuation of small highland valleys
and basins. Significantly, Moss Mountain (Tzontevitz), the
highest in the central Chiapas highlands and the most sacred
of all mountains to Chamulas, lies both to the east of the
ceremonial center and within Barrio San Juan, which is the
highest ranking of the three barrios. Chamulas have few
economic reasons to travel extensively to the north and east
beyond their own boundary. This is not the case with the
lowland south and west, which are relatively well known to
most Chamula men. Economic activity, travel, social organization, and topography, therefore, support the prevailing
belief that the earth-island is generally high in the east and
low in the west. This view is reflected in the Tzotzil words
that are sometimes used to designate these directions: *ta*

ʔak'ol ("above" or "up") means east; *ta ʔolon* ("below or "down") means west.[9]

Chamulas believe that the earth is laced with caves and tunnels which eventually reach its edges. These limestone caves and passages are believed to provide channels for the drainage of the highlands. Chamulas also believe that the earthlords, who live in the mountain caves, provide all forms of precipitation, including the accompanying clouds, lightning, and thunder. These beliefs are supported by the fact that the central Chiapas highlands are in fact a karst-type limestone area in which internal drainage is extremely important. Only earthlords, snakes (which are the familiars and alternate forms of the earthlords), and demons inhabit the internal cave networks of the earth. Hence, they are associated with dampness, darkness, and lowness.

The earth is the middle of three major horizontal layers of the Chamula universe. The sky and the underworld make up the remainder. Three layers, which informants draw as concentric domes, make up the sky. The first and smallest dome is the only level of the sky that is visible to most human beings. Yet it has no substance of its own; its visible phenomena are actually an intense penetration of what is happening on the upper two levels. The stars, the moon (conceptually equivalent to the Virgin Mary, *hmeʔtik* or "Our Mother"), and minor constellations travel in the second level. The sun (conceptually equivalent to Christ, *htotik* or "Our Father"), Saint Jerome, the guardian of animal souls, and major (bright) constellations reside and travel in the third level. The heat and brilliance of the sun's head are so great that they penetrate the two inferior layers of the sky. Thus, it is only the sun's face and head which we perceive on earth; his entire body would be visible on the third level.

The underworld is the dwelling place of the dead and is characterized by inversions of many kinds. When it is dark on earth, it is light in the underworld, while the sun is traveling that part of his circular path around the earth. Conversely, night in the underworld occurs during the daytime on earth. There is no proper food in the underworld. The dead eat charred food and flies in place of normal food. The dead

must also refrain from sexual intercourse. With these exceptions, life in the underworld is much like life on earth.
People do not suffer there, with the exception of those who
have murdered or committed suicide. These are burned by
the sun as he travels his circuit in the underworld during the
earth's night. The underworld is also the point from which
the universe is supported. Opinions vary on the nature of this
support, but most Chamulas think that either a single earthbearer carries the universe on his back, or four earthbearers
support the universe at the intercardinal points.

The whole cosmological system is bounded and held
together by the circular paths of the sun and the moon, who
are the principal deities in the Chamula pantheon (Fig. 1).
Each day they pass by the eastern and western edges of the
earth on their trips to the sky and the underworld. These
deities effectively represent most of the fundamental assumptions made by Chamulas about order, for they define both
temporal and spatial categories that are critical for the
maintenance of life.

Cosmology: The Categories of Time

It is impossible to consider Chamula categories of space
without considering the complementary notions of time. This
is the case because the sun deity not only delimits the spatial
extent of the universe but also determines fundamental
temporal units (days, seasons, and solar years) by the duration
and position of his path. It was the sun who established
order on the earth. He did so in progressive stages, three times
creating a world, or creation, and then destroying it because
the people had behaved improperly. Only the Fourth Creation, which includes the present, has been successful.

The four creations provide the largest cyclical temporal
units that Chamulas recognize.[10] These creations can also be
said to succeed each other in a linear sense, for the events of
later creations are not mere repetitions of earlier creations.
The creations tend to have an orthogenetic, cumulative
development. That is, each creation has been progressively
better and more satisfying to the Creator than that which

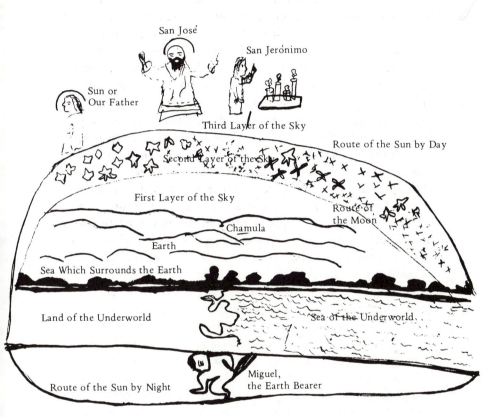

Figure 1. A Chamula Chart of the Universe, By Marian López Calixto

preceded it. In this sense, the four-part creation cycle forms a whole that is greater than the sum of its parts. In each of the first three creations of the universe, the Creator failed to achieve his ideal for mankind and destroyed his abortive efforts. Although Chamulas believe the present Fourth Creation to be his most successful effort so far, they also know that it is full of evil and ever in danger of destruction; hence, they are concerned to defend it from bad behavior and evil people. The length of the four creations is uncertain. Opinions regarding the antiquity of the First Creation vary from 300 to 80,000 years. The Fourth Creation never is said to begin more than 400 years ago and may, according to some informants, have begun a mere 120 years ago, which is the maximum limit of genealogical memory. Variations are similar for the Second and Third Creations. Therefore, not even an average of the opinions of all informants would yield a significant figure for the absolute age of the creations. The point is simply that they succeed each other chronologically as relative periods of time.

Within the present Fourth Creation, several other sets of temporal categories are operative. The life cycle is usually marked by ritual observances at birth, baptism, marriage, and death. Between birth and baptism, a period varying from one month to two years, a child is called a monkey (*maš*) for he has no name. The monkey association with the unbaptized child is explained by the presence of monkeys on earth in the First Creation, before human culture in its correct form had appeared. The monkey people did asocial things, such as eating their own unnamed children at puberty. Hence, the giving of a name at baptism has considerable symbolic significance in bringing the child closer to the realm of social behavior. From baptism to death, the individual life cycle symbolizes the progress of the generations of ancestors toward the present. In other words, many symbolic aspects of ontogeny—the individual life cycle—recapitulate mythological phylogeny. This perspective helps to explain some of the deference given in Chamula society to elders, who are thought to have absorbed much of the respected knowledge of past generations.

Although past generations are esteemed, genealogical memory is relatively shallow, reaching a maximum of five generations in powerful descent lines and two generations in ordinary descent lines. An old man may remember events and kinsmen covering sixty to eighty years of his own lifetime and, by hearsay, perhaps sixty to eighty years of his father's, grandfathers', and great-grandfathers' times. That total, 120–150 years, is the extreme upper limit of Chamula generational and historical memory. Formal records are kept in the ceremonial center by years in the Gregorian calendar, but these data are known by only a handful of politically prominent Chamulas and affect the lives of average persons in no significant way. Past time is most meaningful if it is treated in relation either to generations of known lineages or to significant natural and human events. The future is important only in that important cargo positions may be requested as many as fifteen years in advance, but no more. There is some fear of millenial destruction of the universe by earthquakes in the year 2000, but this prospect, for Chamulas, is properly a matter of cyclical time and not lineal time.

The most commonly used units of chronological time in the Fourth Creation are actually not units at all but natural and historical points of reference. However, no more than about 150 years can be subdivided by these historical landmarks. Beyond this point, Chamulas claim that they have no reason to talk about the chronology of the past. This boundary appears to mark the effective borderline between events of human (Chamula) experience and events involving their early ancestors and the gods. The landmarks of the Fourth Creation are fairly standard in that they had a consistent relation to one another for most Chamulas with whom I worked. The individual dates have little or no meaning; it is the relative order of events that counts. Important temporal landmarks are:

The Time of Father Miguel Hidalgo (*yora pale mikel*), 1812–1825, The Wars of Independence.
The Time of the War of Pedro Díaz Cuzcat or the War of Galindo (*yora leto yuʔun kuskat* or *leto yuʔun kalinto*),

1865–1869. A nativistic movement centering in Chamula; the Chiapas extension of the Yucatec Caste Wars.

The Time of the Ash (*yora tan*), 1903. The eruption and widespread ashfall of a volcano near Tapachula.

The Time of the War of Pajarito (*yora leto yuʔun paharito*), 1910–1911. Chamula rebellion and civil conflict that occurred when Chamulas were pitted against Tuxtla by the Bishop of San Cristóbal.

The Time of the War of Carranza (*yora leto yuʔun karansa*), 1912–1920. The Mexican Revolution.

The Time of the Fever (*yora kʾakʾal čamel*), 1918. The influenza epidemic of 1918.

The Time of the Closed Church (*yora makbil čʾulna*), 1934–1936. The religious persecution and anticlerical policy that occurred under the administration of President Lázaro Cárdenas. During this time the Chamula religious organization operated in secrecy.

The Time When Elders No Longer Had High Positions in Municipal Government (*yora čʾabal ša moletik ta kavilto*), 1937–1941. The order given by the San Cristóbal Office of Indian Affairs requiring youth, literarcy, knowledge of Spanish, and an attitude of cooperation between municipal authorities and their assistants.

The Time When They Built the Road to Tuxtla (*yora melčah be ta tušta*), 1946–1950. Construction of the section of the Pan American Highway between San Cristóbal and Tuxtla Gutiérrez, the capital of the state. Many Chamulas were employed in this project.

Events more recent than 1950 have not been sifted by tradition for consistent use as temporal landmarks. A serious drought in the early 1960s will probably become a point of reference in the future, but it is still too early for any certainty.

Chamulas make constant reference to different units of cyclical time. Time is for the Chamulas as much of an obsession as it was for the Ancient Mayas. The most important Ancient Maya cycle that survives in Chamula is the solar

calendar of 365 days, composed of eighteen months of
twenty days and one month of five days. It is conceived by
the Chamulas to represent a natural cycle: the oscillation of
the position of the rising and setting sun from the extreme
south on December 26 (1 *d'un*) to the extreme north and
back again to the south. The Chamula calendar is more
closely timed to the solstices than is the Gregorian calendar.
However, Chamulas do not allow for leap year in their
reckoning. They use their calendar extensively to indicate the
correct days for activities in the agricultural cycle. Festival
days are also reckoned by it but are checked with the Catholic
festival calendar, which is used by religious officials. Most
Chamula men know the calendar by memory and have no
need to consult a graphic form of it.

The one representation of the solar calendar that I have
actually seen is an irregular, rectangular tablet of wood about
one foot wide by two feet long, made from a discarded piece
of door. In the house from which it came, the calendar tablet
was hanging from a nail at the foot of a bedstead. The
individual days are tallied by vertical charcoal marks, about
one-fourth inch wide and one inch long, reading from left to
right. The twentieth and final day of each month is marked
by a thickened charcoal mark, half an inch wide, suggesting
that, conceived spatially, the days pile up or accumulate
during the progression of the month. This concept is not
unlike that of the cargoholders carrying the burden of public
service or of the Ancient Maya gods carrying the burden of
time for their respective cycles. The metaphor of cumulative
time as a burden finds further expression in the fact that the
calendar is renewed each day by darkening or reapplying
the charcoal mark pertaining to the date of that particular
day. In this way, the calendar should ideally receive a new
coat of charcoal each year, thus increasing its burden.

The Catholic calendar determines the dates of the important festival cycle each year. An annual publication called
Calendario del más antiguo Galván is the calendar-almanac
used by religious officials and scribes to set up the correct
ceremonial year. Although people often know the dates
of the festivals according to the months of the aboriginal

calendar, it does not determine the date of celebration in any way. The only ritual activity that is still controlled by units of the aboriginal calendar is the flower-changing ceremony, which should be performed by all of the religious cargo-holders at intervals of twenty days, corresponding to the beginning of each of the traditional eighteen months. Beyond this private cargo ritual, the Catholic calendar sets the schedule for the ceremonial year.

The festival cycle is the annual round that is used with greatest frequency as a popular reference for time. All adult Chamulas can locate precisely or generally any day of the year with reference to days before, during, or after a festival. These festivals mark the high point of recreation for the laity and the period of most intense ritual activity for the religious cargoholders. Although each festival is associated with a specific saint or saints and is the principal responsibility of certain cargoholders, all alféreces and mayordomos are expected to participate each time. The major festivals last three days, with the exception of the Festival of Games in February, which lasts five days. Most festivals reach a climax on the final day with a procession of the images of the saints. Minor saints' days do not usually involve public ritual; their celebration occurs in the homes of the relevant cargoholders and in the church.[11]

The seasonal cycle provides still another temporal and symbolic reference for Chamulas, the most striking feature being the alternation between rainy and dry seasons. The dry season generally lasts from the beginning of November through April, the rainy season from May to the end of October, with a little dry season in July and August.

Many other minor cycles are used to refer to time. The maize agricultural cycle, for example, provides more than ten terms for talking about the time of year. There are nearly thirty terms referring to the time of day, which are descriptive rather than numerical. At least eight terms refer to the phases of the moon. The Chamulas also recognize regular cycles of several constellations and separate planets. The quality of predictability separates them from the heavenly bodies that are not perceived to move. In the case of the planets and constellations, as with the sun and moon, their predictable cyclical motion through space measures the passing of time.

The Time-Space Principle

A unitary principle of time-space appears to underlie the Chamula view of order in the moral universe, as in aesthetics. Chamulas were fond of asking my wife or me the question, "Do people bite and eat one another in your country?" Surprised, we would usually answer, "Of course not. Do people bite and eat each other here?" They would roar with laughter at our stupid question and then usually answer, "Well, no, but the first people did." Only after participating in many of these seemingly absurd exchanges did the problem begin to make sense. I soon learned that the United States (*slumal hrinko*) lay in the outer, if not totally unknown, reaches of relative distance on earth. It followed as night the day that great social distance also pushed back the level of relative time, so that asocial behavior eliminated long ago in Chamula (such as infanticide and cannibalistic consumption of one's own children) might easily still occur at the outer limits of the universe. In other words, rule-governed behavior seemed to function on a sliding scale, which decreased on both a temporal and a spatial axis away from the present and away from Chamula. Furthermore, because we had white skin, light eyes and hair, it was not uncommon for the Chamulas to ask us if we had earth gods or saints as kinsmen, for the sacred and the asocial seemed to be identified with similar levels on a time-space continuum.

In other words, asocial behavior is relegated to socially distant and ambiguous categories of time and space to the degree that the actions differ from proper Chamula behavior. Good, or social, behavior exists in its purest form in the ritual setting, in the "navel" of the moral universe contained by the limits of Chamula custom. Good behavior in the present is therefore associated with places close to home. The forces of good and evil continue to compete at the most distant reaches of the universe, where the sun and moon deities make their daily treks about the earth. Solar and lunar eclipses remind Chamulas that the demons occasionally overcome the forces of order, even in the deities' own territory. The places between Chamula and the distant sacred domains of the deities are even more dangerous because they are unknown and therefore ambiguous in the classificatory system. This is why it is credible to Chamulas that the betwixt-and-between spatial category contains beings who are still suspended in the precultural barbarism that they—the Chamulas—have ideally superceded. Bad, or asocial, behavior ought to have disappeared during the chaotic and chastening march of the Chamula ancestors through the first three creations toward the present social order. Yet Chamulas acknowledge that the ideal has not been fully realized. They realize that even in their own midst, as well as in the world around them, hundreds of forces exist that might destroy the social order and send mankind back to the chaos of distant time and space. This fact constitutes the prime dilemma of Chamula thought.

Thus, a single principle—the cohesion of complementary values of space and time—appears to function as a fundamental order-giving concept in Chamula associational thinking, symbolism, and cosmology. Time and space form a single structural primordial reality to modern Chamulas.[12] For them, as for their Ancient Maya forbears, time and space are a unitary concept whose primary referent is the sun deity.[13]

The Sun As the First Principle of Order

A primary and irreducible symbol of Chamula thinking and symbolism is the sun, "Our Father," *htotik*. In the concept of the sun, most units of lineal, cyclical, and generational time are implied at once, as are the spatial limits and subdivisions of the universe, vertical and horizontal. Most of the other deities (with the important exception of earthlords) and all men are related lineally or spiritually to the sun-creator, who is the son of the moon. Day and night, the yearly agricultural and religious cycles, the seasons, the divisions of the day, most plants and animals, the stars, and the constellations—all are the work of the creator, the life-force itself. Only demons, monkeys, and Jews preceded and were hostile to the coming of order. These forces killed the sun early in the First Creation and forced him to ascend into the heavens, where he provided heat, light, life, and order. It is significant that the Tzotzil words for day (*k'ak'al*) and fiesta (*k'in*), which provide fundamental time references for Chamulas, are directly related, respectively, to the Tzotzil word for fire (*k'ok'*) and to the Proto-Maya word for time, sun, and deity (*kinh*). Moreover, one of the several names for the sun-creator is *htotik k'ak'al*, or "Our Father Heat (Day)."

The fundamental spatial divisions of the universe, its cardinal directions, are derived from the relative positions of the sun on his east-west path across the heavens:

East: *lok'eb k'ak'al*, "emergent heat (day)"
West: *maleb k'ak'al*, "waning heat (day)"
North: *šokon vinahel ta baȼ'i k'ob*, "the side of the sky on the right hand"
South: *šokon vinahel ta ȼ'et k'ob*, "the side of the sky on the left hand"

The principal temporal divisions of each day are also described in terms of the relative position of the sun on his path across the heavens. For example, "in the afternoon" is generally expressed in Tzotzil as *ta mal k'ak'al*, "in the waning heat (day)." "In the mid-morning" is expressed as *štoy ša k'ak'al*, "the heat (day) is rising now." Temporal divisions of the year are expressed most frequently in terms of the fiesta cycle. One can specify almost any day in the year by referring to stages of, or to days before or after, one of the more than thirty religious fiestas that are celebrated annually in Chamula. In referring to a certain day in relation to the fiesta cycle, for example, one could say *sk'an to ʔošib k'ak'al ta k'in san huan* ("It is three days until the fiesta of San Juan"). Although this statement is usually understood as translated here, the relationship and similarity of words (*k'ok'*, "fire," and *k'ak'al*, "heat" or "day"; *k'in*, "fiesta," and *k'išin*, "hot") in the concepts is such that it is possible to understand the sentence as, "three daily cycles of heat before a major (religious) cycle of heat." These few examples suggest that the sun and its life-giving heat determine the basic categories of temporal and spatial order.

The Sun and the Primacy of the Right Hand

Chamula cosmological symbolism has as its primary orientation the point of view of the sun as it emerges on the eastern horizon each day, facing "his" universe, with north on his right hand and south on his left hand. This orientation helps to explain the derivation of the descriptive terms for north ("the side of the sky on the right hand") and south ("the side of the sky on the left hand"). Furthermore, the adjective "right" (*baȼ'i*) is positively evaluated in innumerable words and idioms in Tzotzil. By extension, it means "actual," "very," "true," or "the most representative," as in *baȼ'i k'op* ("Tzotzil"), which may be translated literally as "the true language," or in *baȼ'i k'ob* ("right hand"), which may also be read as the "real hand" or "true hand." North is on the right hand of the sun-creator as he traverses the sky. This placement appears to be related to the belief that north is a direction of good omen and virtue. Chamulas often express this view as, *mas lek sk'an yo ʔnton ta baȼ'i k'ob li htotike,* or, "Our Father's heart prefers the right hand way."

The fundamental orientation to the right also clarifies Chamula ritual treatment of space. In the first place, religious cargoholders themselves possess an aspect of deity in that they share with the sun and the saints (the sun's kinsmen) the responsibility and the burden of maintaining the social order. While acquiring for themselves a sacred aspect through exemplary behavior and language, as well as through constant use of sacred symbols and objects such as rum, incense, candles, fireworks, and cigarettes, most of which have actual or metaphoric qualities of heat, they metaphorically follow the sun's pattern of motion by moving to their own right through any ritual space in front of them. Thus, there is an overwhelming tendency of almost all Chamula ritual motion to follow a counterclockwise pattern. This direction is the horizontal equivalent of the sun's daily vertical path across the heavens from east to west.

This transformation of the sun's path according to Chamula premises could be derived by imagining oneself facing the universe from the eastern horizon, as the sun does each morning, and "turning" the vertical solar orbit to the right so that it lay flat on the earth. I should emphasize that no Chamula ever stated the derivation so simply. However, informants consistently said that east is the sun's position at *šlok' htotik* ("the sun appears" or "dawn"); north is the horizontal equivalent to the sun's vertical position at *ʔolol k'ak'al* ("half heat," "half-day," or "noon"); west is *šbat htotik* ("the sun departs" or "sundown"); and south is the horizontal equivalent to the sun's vertical position at *ʔolol ʔak'obal* ("half-night" or "midnight"). This horizontal transformation allows cargo officials to "move as the sun moves," thereby restating symbolically both the temporal and spatial cycles for which the sun is responsible. Thus the beginning of any ritual (counterclockwise) circuit becomes the "conceptual east." North in this system becomes the horizontal equivalent of the point of "maximum heat" of the sun at noon at the zenith of his orbit; west and south also follow the solar circuit. As a result, the cardinal direction north shares with the east the sign of good omen and positive orientation, while west and south are generally negative in the cosmological system (Fig. 2).

The positive symbolic value of the north may also derive from Chamulas' awareness of the fact that the apparent position of the rising sun shifts northward on the eastern horizon during the increasingly longer days between the vernal equinox and the summer solstice. This period is also associated with the first rains of the wet season (in early May) and with the beginning (also in late April or early May) of the annual growing cycle for highland crops. South, in contrast, is associated with night and the underworld in the daily cycle. South is also associated with the time of shortening days, from the autumnal equinox to the winter solstice, which marks the end of the growing season and the beginning of killing frosts and death in the annual solar cycle. These characteristics help to explain why the south is negatively regarded in some respects, for it represents both night and frost, dry weather and the nonproductive agricultural season. West represents incipient death in the life cycle and twilight

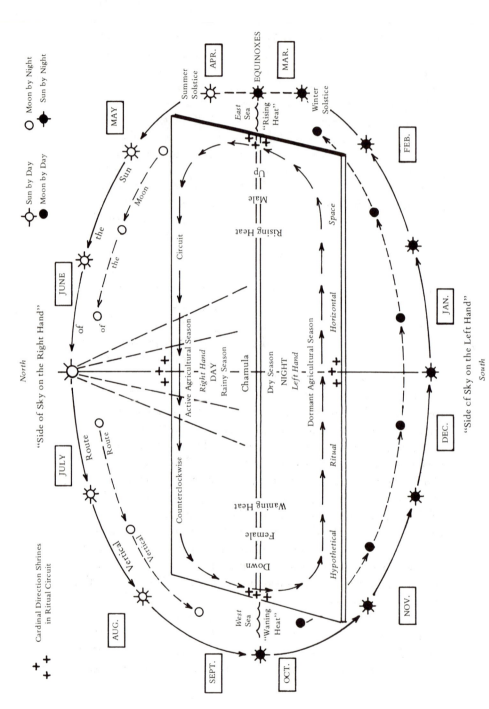

Figure 2. Some Category Relationships in Chamula Cosmology, Show ing Spatial and Temporal Equivalents

in the daily cycle, as well as the period between the summer solstice and the autumnal equinox. The fact that the inter-cardinal direction southeast is the first point in the spatio-temporal symbolic scheme to represent an "upswing" or emergence of the sun from the negative nadir (south) of the system may be important in explaining why the southeast is frequently an alternate to the east as the initial position in ritual circuits and positions of ritual personnel.

Ritual circuits, therefore, carry a great deal more information than would appear at first glance. They proceed counter-clockwise because that direction is the logical horizontal equivalent of the annual solar cycle and the daily solar cycle. Even though circumstances may not allow all individual circuits to begin in the actual east or southeast, the principles of the right hand and counterclockwise motion appear to serve as ritual surrogates for the eastern solar orientation and the solar cycle. Any initial ritual location can thus become "conceptual east." In this way men are better able to base their ritual orientation on the first principle of life itself, which is the sun.

The Primacy of "Up"

The primacy of the sun as giver of order implies still another symbolic discrimination: the primacy of "up" over "down." Cosmologically, increasing height and goodness are associated with the rising sun; decreasing height and threat are associated with the setting sun. Moreover, the eastern part of the earth is believed to be tilted upward (*ta ʾak'ol*), and the western part downward (*ta ʾolon*). Living in what they believe to be the highest place on the earth, therefore, Chamulas as a group are at a point closer to the sun when at its zenith of potency and heat (at noon) than is any other Indian or Ladino community with which they are acquainted. Furthermore, Tzontevitz, the sacred mountain that lies in the highest-ranking of the three barrios, besides being the highest peak in the central highlands, is also the home of their patron saint San Juan. Chamulas therefore enjoy an especially close relationship with the sun in a physical and metaphorical sense. This position also places the predominantly Indian highlands in a more desirable, or closer, relationship with the sun than the predominantly Ladino lowlands. This factor is related to the Chamula view of social and ethnic distance, in which the highlands are generally considered to be less dangerous and less asocial than the lowlands.

In the ritual setting, the primacy of "up" is expressed metaphorically by the positions of saints in relation to human beings. Habitually they ride on litters and sit on platforms that raise them above the level of men. Cargo-holders who serve them thereby achieve the elevation of goodness, virtue, and prestige. For alféreces, the religious cargoholders who have charge of saints' objects, particularly their banners and clothing, this ritual height is expressed by special pole and branch towers, fifteen feet high, which are constructed at their homes when they leave office. A representative of the alférez then sits in the tower, symboliz-ing the new heights of the desirable that have been achieved by the outgoing official during his year in office. In so doing, he has helped the sun to maintain order and thus partakes of the sun's good, rising aspect.

Related to the rising aspect of ritual cycles is the impor-tance of head over feet. Heads and faces of images of saints receive a great amount of attention in ritual action and symbolism, the reason being that the head is the source of their heat and power. An example is a ritual sequence that focuses on the sacred flagpole tips, which the pasión celebrates in honor of the sun deity at the Festival of Games in Feb-ruary. The tips symbolize the head and halo of the sun and, by extension, the whole concept of the sun. It is significant that this ritual sequence, which is the major annual ceremony in honor of the sun deity, occurs in February, a time of drought, frost, and agricultural dormancy, but also a time for the commencement of the upswing of the solar cycle from its nadir in the symbolic system (Fig. 2).

The Primacy of Heat

The importance of heat is ever present in Chamula life, from daily household activity to ritual settings. The daily round of Chamula domestic life centers on the hearth, which lies near the center of the dirt floor of nearly all Chamula houses. The working day usually begins and ends around the fire, men and boys sitting and eating to the right of the hearth (from the point of view of one facing the interior from the door), women and girls to the left of the hearth. Furthermore, men in this patrifocal society always sit on tiny chairs, which raise them above the cold, feminine ground, and wear sandals, which separate them from the ground and complement their masculine heat. Women, in contrast, customarily sit on the ground and always go barefooted, which symbolically gives them direct contact with the cold, feminine earth. Coldness, femininity, and lowness were prior to heat, masculinity, and height in the mythological account of the coming of order. The male sun was born from the womb of the female moon and was then killed by the forces of evil and darkness (the demons and Jews). This in turn allowed him to rise into the sky as the life-giving source of order.

The very words for time are related to heat, in that the sun symbolizes the source of earthly heat as he does nearly all other aspects of cosmological order. Days, fiesta intervals, seasons, and years are all measured by increasing and decreasing cycles of heat. The opposite of order is symbolized by the cold darkness in which the demons, Jews, and monkeys lived before the forced ascension of the sun into the sky. The life cycle is conceived as a cycle of increasing heat from a cold beginning. A baby has a dangerously cold aspect. This is reflected in the term *maš* ("monkey"), which refers to an unbaptized child. A child acquires steadily increasing heat with baptism and sexual maturity. The heat of the life cycle reaches a high level with social maturity, which is expressed by marriage and reproduction. The acquisition of heat may be carried further through a cargo or shamanistic career. Life and death are also elementary expressions of the hot-cold syndrome of Chamula values. Life crisis rituals and cargo initiations include symbols of both life (hot and integrative) and death (cold and disjunctive). Heat and cold are also fundamental categories in the bewildering complexity that characterizes the Chamula theory of illness. In nearly all these domains (with the exception of some illnesses, of which a hot-cold disequilibrium is a cause), increasing heat expresses the divine, order-giving will of the sun himself.

Ritual language and ritual substances also have the quality of heat, actual or metaphoric. Redundant poetic style in prayers, songs, and ritual formulas is said to reflect the "heat of the heart." Similarly, tobacco, rum, incense, candles, and fireworks generate or emit heat. Furthermore, the raw materials for these substances are believed to be of lowland, tropical origin. Resin for incense, beef tallow and wax for candles, the ingredients for gunpowder, sugarcane for rum, and tobacco for cigarettes, do in fact come from, or at least through, the lowlands. Their tropical origin expresses a paradox in Chamula thinking about the world. Although the highlands are closer than the lowlands to the sun in a vertical sense, the climate of the highlands is actually much colder than is that of the lowlands. It may actually be the ambiguous quality of the lowlands (physically hot, which is symbolically good, yet socially distant, which is dangerous) that makes them a logical source for sacred symbols and substances. Sacred symbols typically partake of two contrasting domains (such as Christ being the son of God and of man). The point of intersection creates an emotion-laden betwixt-and-between category, which often has both sacred and taboo qualities (see Douglas, 1966). The importance of the lowlands as a source of ritual goods may place it in this category. The picture is complemented by the fact that many Chamulas are economically dependent in many ways on the lowlands.

The Primacy of Light

It follows from the sun's primordial force in Chamula symbolism that light also represents the desirable and the good. This characteristic has precedent in the cosmogonic moment when the sun ascended into the sky, creating the categories of temporal and spatial order. Light and heat were the first manifestations of the new order. Light has many other aspects, among which is the ability to penetrate. This quality is shared by the cargoholders and shamans with the deities, all of whom are thought to have penetrating, all-seeing vision. Chamula men and boys customarily wear white wool tunics, while women and girls generally wear brown and

black wool skirts and blouses. The days and seasons are
generally imbued with positive significance according to their
increasing proportion of light. The logical inverse of this
principle is expressed in the Festival of the Dead, which takes
place on November 1, at the beginning of the cold, dry
season and at a time of decreasing proportion of light to
darkness each day. The ritual focuses on a meal that is prepared and served to the dead in the middle of the night.
Similarly, funerals involve, among other things, nocturnal
ritual sequences and the consumption of charred maize
kernels (not cooked before charring) and black tortillas
(made with a bluish-black variety of maize).

　　Another important light-dark syndrome occurs at Christmas, just after the winter solstice, when the sun begins to
renew its strength. The climax ritual of the birth of Christ
(which is also the birth of the sun) consists in Chamula of a
midnight torchlight procession around the church atrium on
December 24. In this ritual an image of the Virgen del
Rosario is carried around the atrium, preceded by the image
of the Christ child. The female image is carried by widowed
women who wear white shawls; the Christ child is carried
by the male sacristán and his assistants. This is the only time
in the ritual year (except for the immediately preceding
posadas, a pre-Christmas ritual of Catholic origin, beginning
December 16) in which a single female religious figure is
carried around the atrium in procession. It is also the only
time in the ritual year in which an equal number of male and
female images (one each) participates in the procession.
Usually there are more male images than female images in
these processions. Furthermore, it is the only time in the
ritual year in which the saints' procession occurs at night,
precisely at midnight; the other processions occur slightly
before noon or just at noon. These reversals in the Christmas
ritual make cosmological sense because they occur at a time
of the year when the nights are longest, when frost has
already killed most plant life, and when the sun has just
been ritually reborn. The forces of light will prevail as the
sun grows up and the days increase in length in proportion to
night. The gradually lengthening days, as a result of the sun's

longer presence, will bring heat and a new growing season for the sun's body, which is maize, the most basic and sacred of all Chamula foods.

The Primacy of Maleness

The sun gave mankind maize from his body. This is reflected in a ritual term, *šohobal*, which is frequently used in reference to maize foods. It means "radiance" or "halo of the sun." According to Chamula mythology, maize (which is "hot" in the hot-cold scheme of food evaluation) came from a piece of the sun's groin (not his penis) and included a part of his pubic hair, which is the silk of the ear of the maize. The moon only gave potatoes (her breast milk) and beans (her necklace). The contrast is great, for maize is the staple of the Chamula diet; potatoes and beans are less important items. The relationship is analogous to that between the male and female principles in this patrifocal society. Maleness receives ritual primacy; the female principle complements it. In the beginning, the moon bore the sun as her child, but soon afterward he asserted his authority over his mother in innumerable ways. Among other tricks, the sun blinded his mother with hot water while they were taking a sweat bath together, which explains the moon's lesser radiance and her tendency (according to Chamula belief) to follow behind the sun in the sky at a point in her circular path on the second level of the sky that is nearly always just opposite the sun's position in his path on the third level. Furthermore, the moon has the responsibility of leaving a breakfast of maize gruel for the sun each morning at the eastern horizon. In sum, her relationship to her son is like that of the female principle to the male principle in Chamula life: submission within a larger sphere of economic interdependence.

The primacy of maleness is expressed symbolically in nearly all ritual proceedings, for women have no official cargo positions. They do have special ritual tasks, but these do not count in the cargo system. All wives of cargoholders receive the title of their husbands, prefixed by "mother" (*me?*), suggesting a ritual relationship of male and female like that which prevails between the sun and the moon. The primacy of maleness has other expressions. In general, right, counterclockwise motion is associated with male saints; left, clockwise motion is associated with female saints. This contrast is expressed in the distribution of both sitting and working space within Chamula houses. The space to the right of the front door of a house interior is for male sitting, eating, and working; the space to the left of the front door is the female sitting, eating, and working space. Such a pattern prevails in nearly all of the Chamula homes that I saw, but applies only to the times of day in which both sexes are present, particularly at mealtimes. At other times during the day, women customarily work throughout the house interior. The pattern does not seem to apply to sleeping positions in the household.

In a similar manner, the male-right/female-left rule applies to the permanent positions of all female saints and major male saints in the Chamula church. The female saints reside on the left side (south) of the church, from the point of view of the patron saint San Juan, who stands above the altar in the center of the east end of the church. Whereas there are no female saints on the male side (north), there are a few unimportant male saints on the female side (south). An oil painting of hell (a very dark one, which has never been cleaned), the cross of the dead Christ, and the baptistery, all of which are negative objects within the symbolic scheme, are also found in the most negative, female part of the church, the southwestern corner. The opposite, northeastern corner of the church is the most positive, masculine part of the church. This corner lies to the patron saint's immediate right. Lining the north and east walls are, first, images of Christ (the sun), and then, images of the major male saints. These positions appear to be microcosmic representations of the categories of Chamula cosmology and cosmogony, for north was on the sun's right hand when he rose into the heavens in the east, just as the north is on San Juan's and Christ's right hand in the Chamula church.

When processions take place at the climax of major fiestas in honor of male saints, the male saints march out of the church and around the atrium to the right (counterclockwise). Female saints, in contrast, march out to the left (clockwise) around the atrium, meet at the halfway point (the west entrance to the atrium), and bow to each of the male saints in sequence. The female saints then reverse their direction and line up behind the last male saint. They march around the last 180 degrees of the circuit behind the male saints, but this time in counterclockwise movement, which is associated with the male principle. The female saints thus "capitulate" symbolically to the male principle and follow the male saints as the moon follows the sun and Chamula women follow their husbands. At minor fiestas in honor of male saints and at major fiestas in honor of female saints, the two sexes do not march in opposite directions. The female saints simply follow the male saints all around the atrium in the male, counterclockwise direction.

Temporally, there are yet other ways in which maleness asserts its primacy. The fiesta cycle, for example, does not honor a single major female saint during the half-year between the winter and summer solstices, a time that is experiencing increasing atmospheric heat and lengthening of days in proportion to nights. This is the time of the two most important fiestas in the annual cycle: the Festival of Games, in honor of the sun, in February; and the fiesta of San Juan, on June 21–24. In the latter half of the year, four major female saints are honored by fiestas—Santa Rosa and La Virgen de la Asunción, both in August; la Virgen del Rosario, in October; and La Virgen de Guadalupe, in December—but these are not so important nor so well attended as those that occur in the male half of the year.

The distribution of major female saints in the annual fiesta cycle parallels certain aspects of the female principle in each day. Half of the day, from midnight to noon (the time of the sun's increasing heat as it rises from the depth of the underworld to the zenith of the heavens), is believed to be the time of the sun's influence over the female principle, thus causing women to behave properly and morally during these hours. From noon to midnight (the times of waning heat), women are believed to be more prone to commit adultery and to do evil in general, for they are at that time under the influence of the demon (*pukuh*). This belief has mythical precedent in the fact that it was the demon (not the sun) who originally taught the first woman (not the first man) to have sexual intercourse. Hence, Chamulas believe that men, like the sun, have had to assume the major ritual responsibility for guaranteeing moral order and stability.

The Primacy of the Senior Principle

Another symbolic pattern that seems to follow from the sun's primacy is the primacy of "senior" over "junior" in the classificatory system. The sun is the senior (*bankilal*) kinsman of all the other saints except the Virgin and San José, who were prior to the sun (Christ) and are sometimes difficult for Chamulas to classify. The senior-junior (*bankilal-ʔiċ'inal*) relationship is used in evaluating rank in many domains, from siblings to animal soul companions, cargoholders, and topographical features. In this Chamula evaluative system, relative age, size, distance, strength, wealth, or one of many other criteria may be applied to the ranking of a closed domain of objects or individuals, as is the case also in nearby Zinacantan (Vogt, 1969: 238–245)

The primacy of "senior" over "junior" has a background of time-space associations that contributes to its strength as a ritual principle. "Senior" is first of all prior to "junior" in the rather fuzzy genealogy of the deities. Senior aspects therefore have priority over junior aspects in ritual expressions of the social order. Spatially interpreted, this means that senior personnel usually stand or sit to the right, from their own point of view, of junior personnel. Female counterparts (usually wives) of these officials stand still further to the left or behind the male cargo officials. Whether or not they are formally placed by ritual position, individuals receive drinks and other ritual sacraments in equal portions according to the principle of the most senior first, the most junior last. The male principle, seniority, and high-ranking cargo positions take precedence over the female principle, youth, and low-ranking cargo positions. Any ritual group, then, can be ranked according to the primacy of the senior principle.

To confuse matters, the most senior official hardly ever

moves in the front position of a group that is traversing a ritual circuit. In fact, he usually brings up the rear of the group. This positioning, however, is not a paradox but derives from the fact that cargoholders share certain attributes of deities, particularly the sun himself, as they traverse ritual circuits in a counterclockwise direction. If the conceptual east is the point of orientation and beginning for a ritual circuit, then it follows that the member of the party who has greatest "heat," which is a fundamental attribute of the sun symbol of the east, should remain closest to the source of that heat. The simple spatial rule is that "like remains close to like," and nearly every time this places the most senior official at the end of a procession. Although this pattern seems to prevail almost without exception in groups of male cargoholders, it does not hold for women, who customarily follow men in daily life and in ritual processions as well. Since men in this patrifocal society outrank women for most purposes, one might assume that, according to the pattern of seniors last, women would precede men. The opposite is in fact the case because the female principle is both logically prior to patrifocal order (the female moon gave birth to the male sun) and subordinate (junior) to patrifocal order (the precocious sun blinded his mother and began to give her orders shortly after his birth). This dual attribute of the female principle may also be expressed in the ritual sequence in which female saints begin moving to their own left (clockwise) and then line up behind the male saints, joining them to complete a counterclockwise (male) circuit.

The seniority–east association also makes intelligible such diverse spatial patterns as the seating order at ritual meals and the distribution of candles at shamanistic curing rituals. In the case of the ritual table, the most senior-ranking members of the group sit closest to the conceptual east in the cosmological microcosm and the most junior members sit closest to the conceptual west. Similarly, the household cross-shrine, which serves as the point of orientation in shamanistic rituals, appears to serve as the conceptual east. The many required sizes of candles are always arranged (except in cases of witchcraft rituals) so that the most "senior" candles (white, largest, longest-burning, and most expensive) are lined up closest to the conceptual east and the most "junior" ones, toward the conceptual west. I use the term "conceptual" because it is sometimes not physically possible to begin sequences or to place shrines in the position of true east. However, time-space symbolic equivalents, which appear to be assumed knowledge for most Chamulas, can make almost any situation ritually effective if the correct relationships are maintained.

Microcosm and Multivocality

The most effective symbols imply a great deal at once. The sun, the giver and maintainer of order, is such a symbol in Chamula thought. No Chamula ritual passes without innumerable references, in language and action, to patterns whose precedent is found in the cosmogonic moment of the sun's ascent into the heavens. Everything accompanying that event is now fixed in Chamula custom and belief, for that moment provided the necessary spatial and temporal categories for an orderly social existence. The ritual task is to restate what is essential about this event in the most economical form possible. Because relatively few words and actions must encapsulate its essence, the sun symbolism is important for its "multivocality," to borrow a useful term (V. Turner, 1967: 50). For example, a microcosmic action, such as the movement of personnel through ritual space, takes its meaning from the universe, the macrocosm of the sun. The primacy of the right hand and masculinity, the cycles of heat in the day and the year, the point of view of the eastern horizon, counterclockwise motion, the highly redundant ritual language—all join to recreate the past in the present and to narrow the limits of the universe to a manageable size within the sacred precincts of the ceremonial center. The procession of religious images around the atrium of the church at the climax of each major fiesta recreates the cosmogonic moment of the coming of the first light, the first heat, the first maize— the coming of order itself. Moreover, the procession occurs at noon, when the sun is at the zenith of the heavens, giving maximum heat to the center of the universe. The ritual states not a part, but all of this at once.

(2) The Nature and Types of Chamula
Verbal Behavior

Don't you see that long ago Spanish was the
first language which Our Lord gave to
the people?
There was but one language;

That was the language that all had to learn,
For Our Lord gave the Ladinos souls before
he gave them to us.

When he changed the languages,
The people began to divide;

They spread out everywhere,
Some to the rising sun, some to the setting
sun;

Those who went together had the same
language;
Separately they departed, those who spoke
the same tongue.

Otherwise they would not have understood
each other;
That is why we became separate, those of us
who speak the true language, Tzotzil.
—Shun Méndez Tzotzek, Text 103

A bewildering number of processes,
abstractions, and things can be glossed under the word *k'op*,
which refers to nearly all forms of verbal behavior, including
oral tradition. In its substantive form alone, *k'op* can mean
"word," "language," "argument," "war," "subject," "topic,"
"speech," "problem," "dispute," "court case," or "traditional verbal lore."[1] Chamulas recognize that the correct use
of language (that is, the Chamula dialect of Tzotzil) distinguishes them not only from nonhumans but also from their
distant ancestors, from their present Tzotzil- and Tzeltal-
speaking neighbors, and from Ladinos and tourists. In the
distant past, no one could speak, which is one reason that
people were destroyed at the end of the First and Second
Creations. Then, while the sun deity was still walking on the
earth, people finally learned to speak (Spanish), and all

people everywhere understood each other. Later, the nations
and municipios were divided because they had begun to
quarrel. Language was changed so that people would learn to
live together peacefully in smaller groups. Separate languages
then came to be the distinguishing traits of social groups.
This is still true in the highlands, where not only costume but
also various dialects of Tzotzil or Tzeltal immediately distinguish the Indian communities from one another. Chamulas
even recognize dialect differences within their own municipio,
particularly between the barrios of San Pedro and San Juan.
Moreover, historical points of reference, such as the rebellions
of 1869 and 1911, are remembered in Chamula texts as
being times when the learning of new prayers, creeds, and
words was made obligatory by one of the contending sides.
Language, then, in the present as in the past, is an important
criterion by which Chamulas distinguish both separate social
groups and specific kinds of attitude and behavior within
those groups. In other words, the labels for kinds of verbal
behavior are, like kin terms, tags for different kinds of
interaction.

Oral Tradition As Distinct from Language

The first break in the Chamula folk taxonomy of language
(*k'op*) distinguishes three general classes: "ordinary or conversational language" (*lo'il k'op*); "language for people whose
hearts are heated" (*k'op sventa šk'išnah yo'nton yu'un li
kirsanoe*); and "pure words" or "oral tradition" (*puru k'op*).
Ordinary language is restricted in use only by the dictates
of everyday social situations, and by the grammar or intelli-
gibility of the utterance. It is believed to be totally idiosyncratic and without noteworthiness in style, form, content or
setting; it is everyday language. Pure words, in contrast,
include all of the stable genres that comprise Chamula oral
tradition; they have formal and contextual constraints of
many kinds. Chamulas view pure words as "closed" in
certain respects and ordinary language as "open," for the
latter can be used freely for other kinds of communication;
pure words are "bound" in that they are destined to be

performed only in specific social settings. Besides these two major types of verbal behavior, there are several forms that Chamulas do not classify either as ordinary language or as pure words. These marginal or intermediate forms are called language for people whose hearts are heated. They might also be called "inspired language," as the heat metaphor implies in Tzotzil, because they utilize stylistic devices which reflect heightened emotion, that is, heat, on the part of the speaker. The content of the marginal forms, however, is not predictable. Thus, they are neither completely idiosyncratic (open), as is ordinary language, nor completely predictable (closed), as are pure words. The marginal forms include children's improvised songs, children's improvised games, court speech, oratory for cargoholders, and emotional or bad language (Fig. 3).

The intermediate class of language for people whose hearts are heated introduces a crucial theme of Chamula native criticism of language. The heat metaphor, which derives primarily from the Sun/Christ symbolism in Chamula cosmology, implies an excited, emotional attitude on the part of the speaker. The "heated heart" marks a departure from mundane, ordinary language. It implies the beginning of a continuum of intensity of verbal interaction with accompanying stylistic features. Running through this category and through all the genres of pure words is a continuum of stylistic redundancy that Chamulas associate with rising spiritual heat, the "heat of the heart." In its elementary form spiritual heat simply involves a repetition of words and phrases. It begins in the marginal genres by expressing elevated, excited, but not necessarily religious attitudes on the part of the speaker and eventually forms the stylistic base (in parallel couplets) of formal ritual language, which is a part of pure words. Thus, increasing heat provides a kind of metaphoric transition to the attitude and style of pure words, which contain the stable genres of Chamula oral tradition. To recapitulate, ordinary language is cold in this evaluation scheme because it does not have constraints of form, content, and context. As one moves through the taxonomy, beginning with language for people whose hearts are heated

and moving into pure words, progressively more heat of the
heart is required for good performance and verbal control
because the speaker is under progressively more constraints
of style, content, form, and setting. The implication is that
pure words are only one part of a continuum of linguistic
attitudes and styles. The elementary forms are found outside
the domain of pure words.

Within pure words, time association is the most important
criterion in distinguishing the secular forms ("recent words,"
or *ʔač' k'op,* associated with the present, Fourth Creation)
from forms having greater ritual and etiological significance
("ancient words" or *ʔantivo k'op*). Recent words include
narratives of the Fourth Creation, games, and a large group
of humorous genres called frivolous language. These generally
assume the present social order and defend it informally. In
the opinion of informants, these genres first evolved in and
are associated with cosmic time like the present. Furthermore, their spatial associations and secular behavioral settings
are close to home. Not having the accumulated spiritual heat
of four creations, the genres of recent words are viewed by
Chamulas as being somewhat colder than ancient words.
Ancient words first evolved in and refer to events of the
three creations that preceded the present one. Having been
in existence for all of cosmic time, they are the hottest of all
the forms of verbal behavior in terms of spiritual heat. With
the exception of true ancient narratives, which may be told
at any time the information in them is necessary, all of the
genres of ancient words are associated with ritual settings.
In addition to true ancient narrative, ancient words include:
language for rendering holy, prayer, and song.

In sum, pure words differ considerably from ordinary
language in Chamula because of the heavy emphasis on their
predictable, traditional aspect. Chamulas take the oral aspect
for granted. Although the line between ordinary language
and the fixed, stable genres is fuzzy, as attested by the
marginal forms of language for people whose hearts are
heated, the joint presence of predictable content and formal
features in genres that are associated with specific behavior
settings distinguishes what Chamulas consider to be traditional

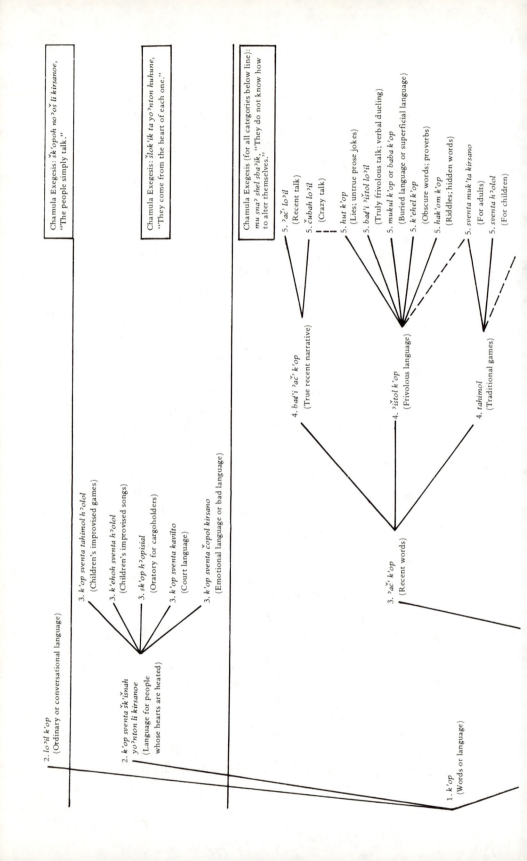

Chamula Exegesis: *šk'opoh no'oš li kirsanoe,* "The people simply talk."

Chamula Exegesis: *šlok'ik ta yo'nton huhune,* "They come from the heart of each one."

Chamula Exegesis (for all categories below line): *mu sna' šhel sba'ik,* "They do not know how to alter themselves."

5. *'ač' lo'il* (Recent talk)

5. *čubah lo'il* (Crazy talk)

5. *hut k'op* (Lies; untrue prose jokes)

5. *bat'i 'ištol lo'il* (Truly frivolous talk; verbal dueling)

5. *mukul k'op or baba k'op* (Buried language or superficial language)

5. *k'ehel k'op* (Obscure words; proverbs)

5. *hak'om k'op* (Riddles; hidden words)

5. *sventa muk'ta kirsano* (For adults)

5. *sventa h'olol* (For children)

3. *k'op sventa tahimol h'olol* (Children's improvised games)

3. *k'ehoh sventa h'olol* (Children's improvised songs)

3. *sk'op h'opisial* (Oratory for cargoholders)

3. *k'op sventa kavilto* (Court language)

3. *k'op sventa copol kirsano* (Emotional language or bad language)

2. *lo'il k'op* (Ordinary or conversational language)

2. *k'op sventa šk'išnah yo'nton li kirsanoe* (Language for people whose hearts are heated)

4. *bat'i 'ač' k'op* (True recent narrative)

4. *'ištol k'op* (Frivolous language)

4. *tahimol* (Traditional games)

3. *'ač' k'op* (Recent words)

1. *k'op* (Words or language)

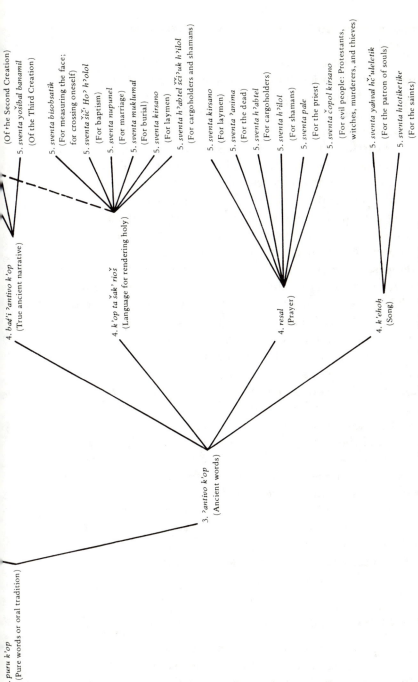

Figure 3. A Folk Taxonomy of Chamula Verbal Behavior. All Tzotzil genres are given in the singular; English glosses are either singular or plural. Dotted Lines indicate overlapping categories.

verbal behavior both from ordinary language and from marginal genres.

Some examples will clarify the criteria that distinguish the three supercategories. What we would call "gossip" is in Chamula a form of pure words because it reports a single event in a predictable way in a predictable setting. It is not, in theory, idiosyncratic or original, as is language for people whose hearts are heated. Gossip is classified as true recent narrative, a genre of pure words, for it is a significant segment of information, known by several people and potentially available to everyone, which is told in a familiar narrative style in a predictable setting. Ideally, the information is passed on as a whole. For example, the gossip among women at a waterhole about the presidente's oration to the Chamulas at the past Festival of San Juan is true recent narrative, a form of pure words, whereas the oration itself is not, because no one knew exactly what the presidente was going to say, only how he would say it and where. This is the reason that oratory for cargoholders is classed as language for people whose hearts are heated. In a similar manner, statements of defendants, plaintiffs, and officials at a court hearing do not belong to pure words, even though the elaborate formulas used for such speech are highly stylized, often resembling ritual language. However, tomorrow's gossip about the outcome of the court case will be true recent narrative, a genre of pure words. A similar situation occurs with regard to emotional language, which belongs to the class of language for people whose hearts are heated. At its highest pitch, the language of anger rings extraordinarily poetic in its use of traditional metaphor and cadence, yet it is by no means considered a performance of pure words unless a murder or the like ensues, which would make the event worthy of retelling as true recent narrative.

The Genres of Verbal Behavior

A complete taxonomy of Chamula folk genres (Fig. 3) was elicited at intervals over a period of one year essentially from six male informants ranging in age from eighteen to sixty years. These same informants provided the majority of the texts that are included as genre examples and as an appendix in this book. Five informants came from two contiguous hamlets; the sixth lived in the nearby ceremonial center. They were selected from this limited territory so that it would be possible to control for spatial data in their texts. Both formal question frames and informal discussion were used to elicit the categories of the taxonomy. The two methods were complementary in that formal interviewing (for example, "How many kinds of—would you say there are?") produced a taxonomy and genre labels that could be used informally to identify and talk about types of texts after they had been recorded or transcribed. A typical question asked countless times was, "Is this a—?"

The taxonomy was useful in that it provided explicit native genre labels for organizing the collection of texts and also helped to assure a more comprehensive coverage of the forms of verbal behavior recognized by Chamulas. The taxonomy also provided needed security and efficiency in developing a specific Tzotzil vocabulary for working with information that the Chamulas took for granted. Just as important as the taxonomy itself were the clues it suggested for useful kinds of supporting information that might be collected for all texts. Specifically, since time association appeared to be the principal attribute that distinguished between the two subcategories of pure words (recent words and ancient words), it occurred to me early in the field work that temporal attributes of the genres might provide a key to understanding the whole of verbal behavior as it related to other aspects of Chamula life and thought. Since I also knew from the interviewing that spatial categories originally determined temporal categories and that time past remained alive at the edges of the universe, I decided to elicit temporal and spatial data for all texts, in addition to basic informant and contextual data. Thus, the design of the field work depended in large part on the initial information that was obtained from the taxonomy.[2]

In some cases I interviewed the same informants more than once at different times during the year, using different techniques. I hoped to discover from this repetition which categories continued to be significant over time and under different circumstances. Although in some instances I was also able to ask female informants about certain forms of verbal behavior, the taxonomy reflects a definitely male bias. Interviews and recording sessions with women were hard to arrange because I was both male and foreign. The taxonomy also gives less than a true picture of the informants' responses because space does not allow for discussion of the fine points of disagreement among them. For example, Mateo Méndez Tzotzek, aged sixty, had a mind for the concrete, and when I asked him how many kinds of ancient words there were, he answered: "Well, there's the story about rabbit and coyote, and the one about Our Lord and the trees that disappeared, and the one about the boy who was helped by the jaguar when his grandmother punished him," and so on. Others, asked the same question, typically gave the four genres of ancient words that are recorded as fourth level taxa in Figure 3. Mateo, however, did not follow this classification. He simply proceeded to give examples of one kind (true ancient narrative) of ancient words. In other words, he entered discussion of the taxonomy at a more detailed, or lower, level than the others. Because he was the only one of the six with whom I worked who classified in this way, his responses are not recorded at the fourth and fifth levels of the scheme. This omission does not imply that his method was not valid or that it did not occur with some frequency; the other scheme simply occurred with more frequency.

The taxonomic scheme represents fairly general agreement on the first, second, and third levels. The fourth and fifth levels were not given as consistently by all informants. If fewer than half of the six principal informants named a category, it was not included in the scheme. No effort was made to describe the taxonomy as a grid of uniform or symmetrical criteria and distinctive features, for such a scheme would have distorted the Chamulas' view of it. For example, time is a relevant criterion for distinguishing between recent words and ancient words on the third category level. For other categories at the same level of the

taxonomy, place of performance is a distinguishing feature
(as in court language). For still others at the same level,
performer of the genre is the relevant descriptive or distinctive
feature (as in children's improvised games). Therefore,
although the term "level" is used here in reference to the
scheme, it does not suggest any kind of basic "componential"
or "deep" structure. Levels are used only as descriptive
conventions.

Charles Frake observed that folk taxonomies tend to be
most richly differentiated in those areas of a classificatory
domain that have the greatest number of distinct social
contexts (1961: 121). The present taxonomy, however
approximate, reflects such foci in Chamula daily life. One
could have little doubt, after living in Chamula homes and
attending their festivals, that frivolous language, prayer, and
language for rendering holy are the genres that occur most
frequently and in the greatest number of contexts. This does
not mean that those three genres are more important than
others, but it does show that the taxonomy branches most
extensively where the alternative settings for that kind of
verbal behavior are most numerous. This richness is apparent
in the relatively large number of fifth-level subcategories for
those three genres.

The fourth- and fifth-level categories throughout the
taxonomy do not necessarily occur in mutually exclusive
settings. For example, appropriate prayer, song, and language
for rendering holy are frequently performed at the same time
by different personnel in a single ritual setting. During rest
periods at the same ritual setting, all participants are likely to
be joking among themselves in truly frivolous language and
cursing tourists in emotional language.

(3) The Marginal Genres

They emerge from the heart of each speaker.
—Marian López Calixto

The marginal genres belonging to language for people whose hearts are heated represent the beginning of a continuum of restriction as to form, content, and setting in Chamula verbal behavior. These forms are more stylized than ordinary language, but they are not yet pure words. To understand what is almost but not quite pure words, is to clarify the nature of pure words themselves. In the Chamula taxonomy of marginal genres, however diverse their specific behavior settings, they all occur in moments of heightened emotion. This type of verbal behavior is distinguished from ordinary language in that "people's hearts are heated" (*šk'išnah yo ʔnton yu ʔun li kirsano ʔe*). In the Chamula value system, heat has great positive value, for that which is "hot" is strong, mature, and life-giving. Yet heat is also dangerous when abused or uncontrolled, as drunken behavior demonstrates. The symbolic essence of heat is the sun deity, which is also the supreme marker of cyclical time and order. Thus, it follows that cyclical patterning and repetition of phrases, metaphors, words, and ideas characterize nearly all verbal statements about the social order. It might be said that human social order depends on repetition of rule-governed behavior as communicated and understood through language.

Repetition and mastery of the use of language, furthermore, signal a child's successful socialization as well as the adult's mastery of cultural specialties. Repetition stands out as a distinctive feature of the marginal genres. Speakers are excited, their hearts are hot, yet it is not known beforehand just what the speakers will say. Herein lies the critical difference which, according to Chamulas, excludes these genres from the stable genres that comprise pure words. The marginal genres have the redundant features of form and style that characterize the whole oral tradition, yet their content still comes from "within each one" (*šlok' ta huhune*); their content is thus original rather than having come intact from another source or another person. This explains why the marginal kinds of speech, from the Chamula point of view, are neither ordinary speech nor pure words but fall somewhere in between. Moreover, the kinds of situations dealt with by these genres are either learning processes (as in children's games), challenges to the social order (as in bad language), or efforts to rectify the social order (as in court cases and oration).

Children's Improvised Games

Children's improvised games (*k'op sventa tahimol h'olol*) are not traditional, for Chamula adults describe them as being improvised by children as they play: "Each child decides it according to what his heart wants" (*ta snop huhun 'olol ȼ'akal k'usi sk'an yo'nton*). To the outside observer, however, these games do not seem to be strictly improvised, for they utilize formulas and subject matter that vary only slightly from one play group or individual to the next. Yet for the most part they do not have predefined rules or roles. Since the subject matter of these games is mostly an imitation of adult behavior, the model of the adult role is usually the sole basis for rules. Played by both boys and girls from about three to twelve, these games are not joint recreation. The strict sexual division of labor in adult life is reflected in the children's game groups. For example, little boys imitate the festival roles of cargoholders, while little girls mold and fire play ceramic pots. The following example illustrates both the nature of the imitation and the language used. The information came from personal observation of the game and also from an informant's text about the game.

Fire bull

The game of fire bull (*vakaš k'ok'*) is played with a hollow wire frame in the shape of a bull on which powder charges can be placed in series, beginning with the tail and ending with the horns. Before and during many of the saints' festivals several of these are burned. Characteristically, one man stoops over with the metal and papier-mâché frame on his shoulders and the charges are lighted. The bull (the man carrying the frame) bucks, kicks, and runs clockwise (the direction that is symbolically subordinate to counterclockwise movement) around the cross in the middle of the church atrium. He is both preceded and pursued by a cowboy (*vakero*) or roper (*šokavan*). The cowboy, dressed in a clown suit, carries a cape and dances in front of and behind the bull, like a bullfighter swinging his cape to bait the bull. The cowboy also carries a lasso, which he tries to throw over the bull's head. The baiting of the bull is considered to be good entertainment, but it also has symbolic significance. Beef is among the hottest of foods in the hot-cold syndrome. It is typically served to ritual personnel at high points of festivals. Therefore, the alférez who sponsors the festival symbolically "gives off heat" for the well-being of the festival by purchasing the charges and sponsoring the bull-baiting game. Laymen, however, consider the game's primary significance to be entertainment. Its religious value remains implicit. Little boys imitate this aspect of festivals with great enthusiasm in their play. It is, in fact, a public game with rules in its original context.

In the imitation of this particular game that I witnessed, three boys were involved. Two of them were four years old and the other, five. The boys were playing in a pasture near some older girls who were watching sheep. The time was mid-July, approximately two weeks after the festival of San Juan, at which they may have seen the game performed in Chamula Ceremonial Center. The older boy played the bull.

The two younger boys played the two clowns. The only prop used was a dry branch, which covered the bull's back and head and provided the horns. The two clowns had no props and simply chased the bull, yelling *vaka, vaka, vaka* ("bull, bull, bull").[1] The bull pretended to chase them and charged, moving them in a clockwise circle, somewhat like the festival characters' behavior. While being pursued, the boys also tried to rope the bull with an imaginary cord. Following is a segment of the dialogue that occurred during the game. At this point, the bull had just begun to chase the clowns:

Clown 1:
    vaka, vaka, vaka,
    The bull, the bull, the bull.
        tal me vakaš k'ok'.
        The fire bull came.

    hatavan me,
    Run away!
        hatavan me.
        Run away!

    čuk o me ta č'ohon.
    Tie him up with the rope.
        čuk o me ta č'ohon ʔun.
        Tie him up with the rope.[2]

Clown 2 (has a rope):
    veno, bat ša.
    Okay, he got away.
        bat ša.
        He got away.

Clown 1:
    šoka ʔo me.
    Rope him!
        šoka ʔo me.
        Rope him!

Clown 2:
    mu stak'.
    I can't!
        mu stak'.
        I can't!

ta šlučvan.
He's charging!
   ta šlučvan.
   He's charging!

Clown 1:
mu šaši? yu?un.
Don't be afraid of him.

šoka ?o.
Rope him!
   šoka ?o.
   Rope him!

Clown 2:
lok'an.
Get out of the way!
   lok'an.
   Get out of the way!

na? mu ščik'ot.
I don't know if I'll make it.

?a lik'ak' ša.
Oh, I got burned!
   ?a lik'ak' ša.
   Oh, I got burned!

(He is burned from the exploding charges.)

?ay.
Oh!
   ?ay.
   Oh!

lah ša šlučun, ti mu vakaš k'ok'.
He just charged me, that damned fire bull.

Bull (making charging noises):
?uha.
   ?uha.

?uhe.
   ?uhe.

Clown 2 (to bull):
k'alal čalučvane, mu me ¢o¢uk šalučvan ?un.
When you charge, don't charge so hard.

Bull:
  veno, mo'oh ša.
  Okay, I won't from now on.
  (With this, they begin to repeat the same sequence.)

The most salient characteristic of the language used is
verbatim repetition of phrases. Also, the bull does not speak
until the very end of the dialogue. Just before the end, he
makes appropriate snorting noises. The contrast between the
clowns' normal dialogue and the bull's minimal verbal participation illustrates the effort made in improvised children's
play to imitate both cultural (with language) and noncultural
(without language) behavior as closely as possible, while
always emphasizing the difference between the two. The
socializing function of improvised games probably explains
in part why repetition and imitation are so crucial to them.
Children literally learn ideal patterns of behavior by struc-
turing their verbal and physical play on such patterns, and in
highly redundant fashion.

Children's Improvised Songs

Children's improvised songs (*k'ehoh sventa h'olol*) are
another aspect of play that parents claim not to teach their
offspring. As such, these songs are not traditional, according
to the Chamulas, because children are thought to dream them
up of their own accord. The only performances of this kind
of song that I have personally heard seemed to be improvisa-
tions, for the children, when asked, could not remember
what they had just sung. Neither could they give the names
of the songs. "Only a song" (*k'ehoh no'oš*), they would say.
Adults say that children's songs do not count as true song
because they change according to the children's whims and
interests.
  The melodies used for these songs are traditional, owing
to the fact that children hear religious music at home and in
many ritual settings. Traditional religious melodies appear to
be the only ones that children hear with any frequency in

Chamula. There are no data, for instance, to indicate that
Chamula mothers sing lullabies to their children. Children's
songs probably serve, then, as means of learning what constitutes traditional song. Perhaps because of this imperfect
imitation, children's improvised songs are considered by
Chamulas to be like their improvised games. They also
resemble children's games in that repetition of phrases is
extremely important.

Children's songs are unlike their improvised games,
however, in that they are usually sung individually and not
in groups. Sometimes they are sung or hummed absent-
mindedly as children walk along the road while doing an
errand for their parents or while playing alone. The subject
matter in the songs varies from religious phrases to economic
activities, such as hoeing or planting. These themes are
probably explained by the narrative content of adult religious
music, which serves as a model. Many of the genuine adult
songs narrate ritual activities, as in the song, "We are washing
San Juan's clothing."

The following example shows the diversity of content that
can occur in a single child's song. The boy who sang it was
the five-year-old cousin of one of my informants, who
recorded the text one afternoon at his house in Peteh hamlet.
He heard his cousin talking and singing to himself as he
struck a skinny cat with a stick. The cat, my informant
assumed, suggested the jaguar theme, for domestic cats are
playfully referred to as jaguars.

Sung:
ʔiii ʔiii ʔiii ʔiii.
   laaa laaa laaa laaa.

natik ʔane bolom ʔa,
Your tail is long, jaguar,
   natik ʔavič'ak bolom ʔa.
   Your claws are long, jaguar.

ta šibat, ta šibat,
I'm going to go, I'm going to go,
   ta šibat ta vinahel sventa lek ʔoy li koʔnton.
   I'm going to go to the sky so that I will be happy.

Spoken (yelling to his older brother):
ʔay, pašku, ta šahk'an, yuʔun lek šanaʔ
Oh, Pascual, I want you, because you know so well how,
šačanubtasun ta ʔak'ot ʔun.
to teach me to dance.

Sung (imitating stationary adult dancing steps):
haaa haaa haaa.
laaa laaa laaa.

pinto čon ʔun bi,
Spotted animal,
pinto bolom ʔun bi,
Spotted jaguar,
haaa laaa liii laaa laa.

Spoken:
li voʔne li hč'ulele pepen,
My soul companion is a butterfly,
yuʔun ta šivil ta ʔik' tahmek.
because I fly around a lot in the air.

Sung:
laaa laaa laaa aaa.

yahvalel banamile,
Lord of the earth,
yahvalel vinahel bi,
Lord of the heavens,

yahvalel ʔosil ʔun,
Lord of the land,
yahvalel teʔtik ʔay.
Lord of the woods.

yaaa yaaa yaaa.
ʔuhaaa haaa haaa bi.
laaa laaa laaa.

natik ʔak'ob, ʔok'il ʔun,
Your paws are long, coyote,
natik ʔavakan teʔtikal čihʔun,
Your legs are long, deer.

č'iš č'iš ʔavisim, bolom ʔun.
Your whiskers are standing on end, jaguar.

k'učaʔal ta šak'elun bi.
Why are you looking at me?

yu?un nan hč'ulelot ?unbi.
Perhaps you are my soul companion.

hooo laaa laaa laaa.

muk'ta vinik,
Great man,
  muk'ta ?an¢ ?unbi.
  Great woman.

lorenso, vinik ?unbi,
Lawrence, the man,
  lorenso kašlan ?un.
  Lawrence the Ladino.

ruuu ruuu ruuu uuu uuu.
  ruuu ruuu ruuu uuu uuu.

htotik ?unbi,
Our Lord,
  hme?tik ?unbi.
  Our Lady.

This is, technically speaking, a child's mixture of themes from saints' songs (the last part) and soul companion songs (the first part), larded with fantasy. Because this text is a child's experiment, it is imperfect from the Chamula point of view and therefore is not true song. One reason that adults exclude children's improvised song is that true song is ideally used only in ritual contexts. This ideal is constantly abused by the adults themselves, who use religious music in numerous secular contexts. Thus, the crucial difference appears to be that adults know the right tunes to go with the right words; children do not. Furthermore, most children cannot play the instruments (harp and guitar) that should accompany true song. Therefore, even though children use the correct melody (form) with improvised words (content), adults do not accept the combination as legitimate song, for it is jumbled, incomplete, and is not performed in the proper setting. The text just given actually contains several correct lines from a true song, called "Jaguar Animal" (*bolom čon*), but adults would still disqualify it as song, noting the child's frivolous attitude and careless combination of traditional and improvised words.

An important linguistic component of the above text is
the child's experimentation with metaphoric couplets, which
are the stylistic building blocks of all the formal genres of
ancient words. The following couplet has a structure like
thousands that exist in the more formal genres: same syntax
in two lines, with a one-word synonym substitution in the
second line:

pinto čon un bi
Spotted animal,
    pinto bolom un bi
    Spotted jaguar.

However imperfect from the point of view of adults, the
song text above poses one of the crucial questions of Chamula
life: what is the identity of one's animal soul companion?
The boy's thoughts on this question range from a butterfly
to a jaguar. His thinking is naïve and somewhat presumptuous,
for only shamans are supposed to know such information for
certain. Moreover, it is foolish to suggest that he, a mere
child, might have an animal soul companion as powerful as the
jaguar, who is thought by Chamulas to attend only rich and
powerful adults. Nevertheless, it seems fitting that in this
approximation of a correct song the singer asks some of the
questions that are essential to the process of socialization.
The beginning of the life cycle sets the stage for the beginning
of an inquiry into the normative order of society. Not sur-
prisingly, the initial inquiry is made with only an imperfect
mastery of the oral tradition.

Oratory for Cargoholders

Oratory for cargoholders (*sk'op sventa h'opisialetik*)
remains marginal to the main body of oral tradition because
the cargoholders who use this genre to address crowds at
festivals are not constrained by tradition with regard to what
they say. They improvise as the situation dictates. Only the
style of speech, which is loaded with repetition and metaphor,
and its public setting distinguish oratory from ordinary

speech. Although oratory may occur in other settings of
Chamula life, the most common forms are formal, public,
political proclamations and announcements from the kiosk
in the church atrium during festivals. Political proclamations
are also given from the top of a concrete bench near the
town hall. These speeches are surrounded by no ritual proceedings. The speaker, usually the presidente, simply climbs
up in the kiosk or on top of the bench and shouts through
a megaphone or battery-operated public address system. The
festival setting per se is irrelevant to what is usually a secular
message concerning such matters as tax levies or ejido grants.
Rather, it is the drawing power of the festival, assembling
listeners in one place, that makes it the prime time for
political oration and other cargoholders' announcements.

The following example comes from the oration of the
presidente to the people of Chamula on October 6, 1967
(the day of the festival of the Virgen del Rosario), advising
them that a new town hall would have to be built. This is
not a verbatim transcription of the oration but an informant's rendition from memory of what he heard. Although the
words are no doubt slightly different from those that the
presidente actually spoke, the style is nevertheless faithful to
the usual pattern of delivery. Its persuasiveness befits the
most prestigious civil official, who has a great amount of
spiritual heat and, in all probability, a powerful tropical
jaguar as an animal soul companion. This particular speech
was given over a battery-operated loudspeaker at the old
town hall.

> k'elavil li kavilto lee.
> Look at the town hall over there.
>> mu ša štun.
>> It's no longer any good.
>
> toh mol ša.
> It's already very old.
>> k'alal ta šak' li Hoʔe hutene, šʔečʼ tahmek.
>> When it rains a little bit, it leaks a lot.
>
> ta la štʼuših vuntak.
> The papers get wet.

li sekretaryoe mu la šuʔ čʔabteh k'alal šak' li Hoʔ hutene.
The secretary can't work when it rains a little bit.

ʔaʔ liyalbe baʔyel.
He was the one who told me first.
  mu ta holuk htuk, moʔoh.
  It didn't occur to me alone, no indeed.

pere ʔečan yaluk li sekretaryo ta šʔoč li kaviltoe.
But it happened that the secretary said that the town hall
    was leaking.
  mu yuʔunukuk ta shut ʔečal, yuʔun ta hkil htuk ʔeke.
  He certainly didn't lie on that account, for I saw it too.

ʔeč ʔo šal, čaʔabolahik, ta hmel¢antik ti hkaviltotike.
Therefore, please, let us build our town hall.
  čaʔabolahik čavak'ik lahuneb sčaʔvinik pešu, huhun
    vinik.
  Please agree to give thirty pesos, each of you.

pere haʔto ta ʔač' ʔavil čavak'ik ti tak'ine.
But not until next year are you to give any money.
  ta ʔorae, moʔoh to.
  Not now, not yet.

k'alal mi mel¢ah kuʔuntik ti hkaviltotik, šuʔ šihʔačinahotik
When we have our town hall erected, we can protect our-
    te ta yolon k'alal šak' li Hoʔe.
    selves there beneath it when it rains.
  ʔeč štok mu yuʔunuk ta šk'aʔ.
  Neither will it rot.

ta ʔora, puru tak'in ta šak'betik li steʔeltake.
Now, it is only money that will give it its framework.
  te ta škom ta kalab, hničʔnabik.
  There it will remain for our offspring, for our sons.

veno, mi lavaʔik ʔakotolik, huntotak, hunmeʔtak,
Well, have you all understood, uncles, aunts, older brothers,
    bankiltak, ʔan¢etik, ¢ebetik, keremetik.
    women, girls, and boys?
  mu me ščʔay ʔavoʔntonik ti ta šavak'ik.
  Do not let your hearts forget that you are to contribute.

šanaʔik me.
You know about it.
  mu me ščʔay ʔaholik.
  Don't forget about it.

Note the stylized repetition, such as "our offspring, our sons" and "uncles, aunts, older brothers, women, girls, and boys." Certain patterns of parallel syntax also occur. Furthermore, key ideas are repeated consecutively, usually in pairs, in slightly different syntax. Still another stylistic feature of the speech to indicate heightened emotion, "a heated heart," on the part of the speaker is the careful use of the whole plural verb form, a grammatical formality which does not occur regularly in ordinary language. When it does occur, it is used for special emphasis or emotion, for Chamula Tzotzil does not require consistency in noun and verb number in a single sentence. If a plural subject is understood, it is not necessary to match it with a plural verb. Both, in fact, may be stated singuarly, and listeners will understand that the plural meaning is intended. But formal speech, such as oratory, requires the correct use of plural nouns, pronouns, and verbs. An example may be cited from the above text (plural endings are in italics):

ʔeč ʔo šal čaʔabolah*ik* ta hmel¢an*tik* ti hkavilto*tike*.
Therefore please (plural) let us build our town hall.

Oratory, therefore, amounts to a specialized kind of emotional speech in Chamula. For this reason Chamulas consider it to be marginal to the principal genres of oral tradition. However, like the other marginal genres, it contains important linguistic styles that are canonized in the genres of pure words.

Court Language

The whole matter of Chamula law is too complex to attempt to give a thorough ethnographic background.[3] This discussion of court language (*k'op sventa kavilto*) is therefore restricted to the nature of language used at trials and hearings. Local authority is responsible for resolving most traditional legal matters, in both minor disputes and criminal cases. Therefore, major political officials have as one of their major functions the interpretation of local common law and sometimes of state and national law. The municipal officials whose task it is to hear and solve court cases are the presidente, the juez, and the highest-ranking alcaldes. The presidente has the highest rank in this group, and it is the function of the juez (from Spanish for "judge") and alcalde (from Spanish for "mayor") to advise the presidente in settling court disputes. They also substitute for him in his absence. Some members of this group sit seven days a week for approximately eight hours a day, listening to the plaintiffs and defendants as they personally present their cases. In the exceptional cases in which an intermediary takes a case to court for someone else, it is strictly by personal arrangement. Most court cases ultimately involve direct confrontation between plaintiff and defendant before the authorities at the town hall.

Court speech is marginal to the genres of oral tradition because, although one usually knows beforehand how people in court will speak, one does not know the content of their statements. Court speech, in other words, is improvised as the situation demands. The only constants are style of speech and the court setting. As with all of the marginal genres, semantic and syntactic repetition is an essential stylistic component.

The case from which the following example was taken involved sheep theft, a common but extremely serious offense. Prior to the hearing, the plaintiff had found her sheep in the hands of the thief. The mayores had brought the thief and his mother to the town hall with the stolen sheep, where I saw the hearing June 1968. The text is taken from notes made by a Chamula assistant and by me:

Owner of sheep:
   ʔulbat, huntot peserente.
   I have come, Uncle Presidente.

Presidente:
   laʔ me.
   Come forward, then.

Owner:
   lital me hk'oponot, huntot peserentee.
   I came to talk to you, Uncle Presidente.

Presidente:
> k'usi čaval.
> What's on your mind?

Owner:
> muyuk, huntot peserente, k'us ʔelanil čispasbe li hkuȼ'e
> Nothing, Uncle Presidente, but what my kinsmen did
>> li k'alal la hyelk'anbun ti hčihe bat ščon k'alal ta
>> to me when they stole my sheep and went to sell
>> hobel.
>> them in San Cristóbal.

> ba k'elavil mu ʔečeʔuk ta hut ke.
> Go to see for yourself that I am not lying.
>> le vaʔal ta čikina ščiʔuk li hčihe.
>> There they are standing at the corner of the house
>> with my sheep.

Presidente:
> bu ʔoy.
> Where are they?

> *(He sees the thief and his mother standing nearby and speaks to them.)*

> k'usi šapas liʔ ne, čiʔiltak.
> What are you doing there, countrymen?

Thief:
> č'abal.
> Nothing.

Presidente:
> k'us ta ʔavuʔun li čih ne.
> Are the sheep yours?

Thief:
> č'abal.
> No.

Presidente:
> laʔ me čae.
> Come over here then.

Thief:
> šuʔuk.
> All right.

> *(He steps up to the presidente.)*

Presidente:
k'u ča?al ?eč šapas šavelk'an ti čihe.
Why did you do such a thing as rob sheep?
    k'uča?al mu ša?abteh.
    Why don't you work?

vinikot mu yu?unuk ?an¢ukot.
You're a man and not a woman.
    k'uča?al mu šasa? ?abtel.
    Why don't you get a job?

keremot to.
You're young yet.
    mu yu?unuk molukot ša.
    It's not as if you were an old man already.

buč'u la hyalbot čavelk'an čih.
Who told you to rob the sheep?
    mi ?ame?.
    Was it your mother?
        ?o mi ?ahol la hyal.
        Or did you decide to do it yourself?

Thief:
č'abal.
No.
    č'abal.
    No.

*(The presidente questions him further, but he does not
say who suggested it.)*

Presidente (to the thief's mother):
mi Ho?ot lavalbe mantal la ?avol ta šbat čih ta
Was it you who ordered your son to go thieving sheep
        ?ak'obaltike.
        at night?

Mother:
Ho?on nan.
Yes, it was probably I.
    hna? un bi.
    I admit it.

Ho?on la hkalbe, batikik ta ?elek' čih ba hčontikik
I told him, "Let's go to rob sheep and sell them in
        ta hobel.
        San Cristóbal.

hk'eltikik mi šč'am, škut li kole.
Let's see if they'll lend them," I said to my son.

mu hna⁷ k'usi tal ta hol.
I don't know why it occurred to me.
⁷a⁷ li čubahun.
I must be crazy.
⁷o no⁷oš.
That's the only reason.

(The presidente extracts more confessions and then speaks to the mother again.)

Presidente:
⁷eč štok mu ⁷a⁷uk to sba velta čavelk'anik čihe.
This is not the first time you have stolen sheep.
⁷oy ša shayibuk velta ⁷elk'anik.
Many times already you have stolen.

šavelk'an ti čihe.
You steal sheep.
šavelk'an ti ⁷alak'e
You steal chickens.
šavelk'an ti ⁷isak'.
You steal potatoes.
šavelk'an ti ma⁷ile.
You steal squash.
šavelk'an ti k'u⁷ile.
You steal clothing.
šavelk'an ti ⁷itahe.
You steal cabbages.
šavelk'an ti tuluk'e.
You steal turkeys.
skotol k'usi šavelk'an.
You steal anything.

⁷a⁷ ša no⁷oš muyuk bu šavelk'anbe li sbek' yat li
The only thing you don't steal from people are their
kirsano⁷etik;
testicles;
⁷a⁷ no⁷oš čalo⁷e.
And those you only eat.

(The woman, terribly shamed, looks down, as does her son. They are sentenced to a week in jail with hard labor —he, carrying stones; she, sweeping up rubbish—at the end of which time they must pay a fine of 300 pesos.)

Note that court speech is not only formal and emotional, with much redundancy, but is also structured to shame the offenders publicly. Many Chamulas believe that the most important aspect of the punishment dealt out by officials consists of public shame. Shame is the more bitter if it is brought to public attention repeatedly. The court style facilitates such repetition:

> šavelk'an ti čihe.
> You steal sheep.
>   šavelk'an ti ʔalak'e.
>   You steal chickens.
>   šavelk'an ti ʔisak'e. . .
>   You steal potatoes. . .

The repeated syntax, with one-word substitutions, is related to the metaphoric couplet. It serves as an intensifier of the message, ultimately accusing the woman of oral-genital contact, which is disapproved of by Chamulas as animal-like. The words are a metaphoric culmination of the animal-like qualities of her habitual thievery, which have been stated in parallel syntax nine times.

Emotional or Bad Language

The category of emotional language overlaps with the other marginal genres and also with ordinary language. The Tzotzil expression for this kind of talk, *k'op sventa čopol kirsano* or "language for bad people," gives a negative evaluation of language that is spontaneous and immediate. It implies that speech which is more fixed with regard to form and content is viewed more positively. The heat metaphor helps to clarify this evaluation. In Chamula terminology, emotional or "bad" language is produced by the "heating up of one's head or heart." For religious purposes, this increment of heat is desirable; but in everyday affairs, the "heating up one's head or heart" usually occurs in response to some sort of inter-personal conflict. It is for this reason that Chamulas refer to emotional language as bad language.

The following example of this kind of verbal behavior

comes from a case of elopement that occurred in May 1968. The dialogue was taken from a text written by an informant. A boy and a girl decided that they would begin living together without going through the traditional petitioning ceremonies in which the boy's relatives beg the girl's father to allow her to marry and to set a bride-price. Early one morning when it was still dark, the angry father of the girl went to the new house of the girl and her lover. He banged on the door, but his daughter's friend pretended that he did not know what her father wanted:

> *Lover:*
> k'usi mantal.
> What do you want?
> buč'u?ot.
> Who are you?
> > mu šakohtikin.
> > I don't know you.

> *Father:*
> vo?on, hihodelačinkaro.
> It's me, you son of a whore.
> k'uča?al lavik'bun talel ti h¢ebe, kabron.
> Why did you lure my daughter away from me, you bastard?
> > mi mu vinikukot, šaman ti ?an¢e, penteho.
> > If you were a man, you would buy a woman, damned coward.

> čak'an ?avahnil, pere moton čak'an.
> You want a wife, but as a gift you want her.
> > kabron, mu šak'an, kabron, mu šak'an šaman.
> > You don't want to, bastard, you don't want to buy her.

> lok'an tal ta ?ora, mi šak'an, kabron.
> Come out here right now, if you will, you bastard.

> *Lover:*
> šu?uk. čilok' tal.
> All right. I'll come out.

> *Father (as he beats up the boy):*
> hihodelačinkaro.
> Son of a whore.

ʔayavaʔi la ʔatot ne, kabron.
Pay attention to your father-in-law, bastard.

Lover:
ti ʔay. taʔloʔun.
Oh! That's enough!
taʔloʔun.
That's enough!

Father:
komo ke taʔloʔ
What do you mean "That's enough"?

(He continues to beat him.)

ʔayavaʔi la ʔatot, kabron.
Pay attention to your father-in-law, bastard.
k'učaʔal šavelk'an talel ti h¢ebe, kabron.
Why did you steal my daughter, you bastard?

Lover:
pere k'elavil, huntotik.
But look here, uncle.
k'učaʔal čamahun ʔep tahmek.
Why do you hit me so much.

ʔa ta ʔa¢ebe čisk'an tahmek.
The fact is that your daughter desires me very much.
liʔ ša ʔoy ta hnae.
She's already here at my house.

pere li Hoʔot ne čaʔilin ʔun.
But you are mad at me.
pere k'usi škutik ʔun.
But what is there to fight about?

la ʔa¢eb ne liʔ ša ʔoy ta hna.
Your daughter is already here at my house.
ʔa lek ta htoh ta ʔa¢ebe.
It's better for me to pay for your daughter.

mu šavutun tahmek.
Don't scold me so much.
ʔalbun kaʔi, k'uši ta htoh ta ʔa¢ebe.
Tell me, how much shall I pay for your daughter?

Father:
pere k'učaʔal mu labat ta hna ʔak'oponun čaʔe.
But why didn't you go to my house to talk to me
    about it?

Lover:
    muyuk bu ši?ay bu ti hna?oh yu?un ča?iline.
    I didn't go for I knew very well that you would get
        angry.
    ?eč o šal te no?oš litalkutik šči?uk ta ?anič'one.
    That's why I simply came here with your daughter.

(They settle on a bride-price, and both parties come out
more or less satisfied.)

This example shows moments of emotional discourse
mixed with regular discourse. One of the key features of
emotional speech is redundancy. In fact, degree and kind of
redundancy serve as the most important axes of stylistic
variation in the whole of Chamula oral tradition. Three kinds
usually characterize emotional language and all of the other
marginal genres. The first is simple repetition, that is, repetition of the same word or phrase in moments of stress. It
may be repeated from two to five or six times. An example
from the above text would be the expression of surrender:

    tal?lo?un.
    That's enough!
      ta?lo?un.
      That's enough!

The second kind of repetition is nonparallel repetition, which
implies that neither exact words nor sentence structure are
repeated. Only the idea of the sentence is restated for
emphasis. An example from the text is the father's original
cursing of the girl's lover, in which the reason for the father's
wrath is stated consecutively in four different ways:

    k'uča?al lavik'bun talel ti h¢ebe, kabron.
    Why did you lure my daughter away from me, you bastard?
      mi mu vinikukot šaman ti ?an¢e, penteho.
      If you were a man you would buy a woman, damned
        coward.
    čak'an ?avahnil, pere moton šak'an.
    You want a wife, but as a gift you want her.
      mu šak'an, kabron, mu šak'an šaman.
      You don't want to, bastard, you don't want to buy her.

The third kind of repetition, parallel repetition, consists of repeated syntax with one- and two-word substitutions. These three kinds of redundancy may be viewed as elementary structures lying at the informal end of a continuum of stylistic variation running through the whole of Chamula oral tradition.

(4) True Recent Narrative

"Why is it that my milpa won't grow?
   It has gone to ruin," said the bad man.

So it was that he became very poor.
   The worthless man simply went to San
      Cristóbal to beg for alms.

It was the doing of the bad lizard,
   For it is not proper for us to kill lizards,
   Who are the patrons of the maize plants,
   Who are the patrons of the bean plants . . .

So my father told me.
                              —Marian López Calixto, Text 13

The main body of Chamula oral tradition as Chamulas recognize it falls within the category of pure words. Of its two main subdivisions, the one known as recent words is associated with the present, or the Fourth Creation. It in turn has three subcategories, one of which is true recent narrative. The word *bad'i*, which is attached to the root *ʔač' k'op* to make up this generic name, in fact means more than "true." Its meanings include "primary," "actual," "essential," "very," and "principal." Therefore, this category might just as well be translated "the principal kind of recent words."

The events reported in true recent narrative are believed to be recent in a rather ambiguous way. For some informants, "recent" means that the events have happened in their own lifetimes. For others, "recent" means that the events have happened sometime since people came to be as they are now. In other words, the time covered may go back only to their own childhood, to the time of their grandfathers, or as far back as a few hundred years. A more inclusive temporal dimension than absolute years for the events of true recent narrative is the Chamulas' cyclical time unit of the Fourth Creation. That which is possible in the present distinguishes

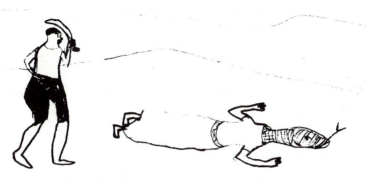

A Man Encounters the Daughter of an Earth God
(See Text 73)

the content of these narrative events from the content of the
other narrative genre, true ancient narrative, which reports
events that, although true, happened in a time radically
unlike the present.

Recent Talk and Crazy Talk

True recent narrative includes two categories: "recent
talk" (*ʔač' lo ʔil*) and "crazy talk" (*čubah lo ʔil*), which are
distinguished from each other by whether or not they are
funny. Recent talk generally includes recent folk history,
gossip, legend, and some folktales. Crazy talk generally
includes prose jokes and funny stories. Having heard both
genres performed in context, however, I must report that
Chamulas' formal distinction between humorous and non-
humorous does not always apply. In fact, recent talk may be
just as funny as crazy talk. Perhaps the explanation lies in
the fact that these two subgenres share an important content
feature: both deal with normative transgressions, threats
to and abuses against the established order. Either they report
the consequences of such transgressions, or they warn of
those consequences. In nearby Zinacantan, Victoria Bricker

(1968: 52–54) noted that normative deviance provides one of the most common topics for humor. It is not surprising, therefore, that the neighboring Chamulas group humorous narratives with subgenres of true recent narratives and of frivolous language.[1] All of these genres—in fact, nearly all genres of recent words—share an almost obsessive concern for underlining and inculcating norms.

Settings for Performance

Chamula does not emphasize any special physical setting as most appropriate for the telling of true recent narrative. They can be told at home, in the cornfields, while traveling, or during leisure time. It has already been noted by Robert Laughlin (1962: 51), Evon Vogt (1969: 307), and Victoria Bricker (1968: 118–120) that the neighboring Zinacanteco Tzotzil-speakers are not raconteurs of the same kind as the Indians of the North American Northwest Coast and Southwest. This is also true of Chamula. An anthropologist can, in fact, spend weeks or even months living with Chamulas and traveling with them without hearing a single tale or item of folk history. I discovered, after inquiring about specific contexts of tale-telling, that the Chamulas' practical bent carries over from their social relations into their tale-telling. Just as one does not visit a Chamula home without specific business to transact, one does not tell narratives without a reason. I know of no such experience in Chamula as a tale-telling session for amusement alone. Tales are nearly always told for a specific purpose, either as supporting evidence or in explanation. For instance, if the weather is getting very dry and the maize plants are shriveling, in discussing the threat of drought, someone might refer to similar circumstances that led to drought and famine in another year. In like manner, if a man sees a drunk losing part of his clothing at a festival, he might turn to a friend and ask if he had heard how the Protestants not only take off their clothing publicly but also dance naked and have sexual intercourse on the altar as part of their religious observance. In other words, there is an appropriate social setting for telling these narratives. The time is right when the information in them is relevant or necessary. And these circumstances can occur nearly anywhere that Chamulas live, work, or travel.

Truth As a Defining Attribute

For an event to be singled out for retelling several times is sufficient for it to qualify as true recent narrative. If an event has cohesiveness as a true, meaningful piece of information worthy of passing on as a unit, then it belongs to this genre. Chamulas place little value either on verbatim repetition of the narrative or on the addition of embellishments. They simply repeat stories as they can remember them. Narratives belonging to this genre are, by definition, true accounts. Therefore, the criterion of truth or falsehood does not ordinarily enter into conscious consideration in retelling or listening to them. I made no effort to test the empirical truth of events in the narratives, such as Jan Vansina did in his research on a Central African oral tradition (1965). I was concerned with truth or falseness only as Chamulas value these qualities as criteria for evaluating their narratives. And as far as they are concerned, true recent narratives are indeed true reports. As the individual's interests and personality vary, the specific content of the tales he tells also varies, yet he tells them as the truth and expects that they will be accepted as such.

Ownership and Knowledge of Narratives

No one owns tales as such. Some narratives refer back to events that are of interest or significance only to certain lineages or certain hamlets, but even these are not owned by those whom they concern most directly. Nor is there any standard means, as through visions, dreams, or purchase, by which one learns narratives. There are a few very recent tales that report the visions of particular shamans and the travels of their souls, yet after numerous retellings this information ceases to be identified with them alone. From the Chamula point of view, the very existence of true recent narratives assumes public access to the information they carry. In practice, however, different hamlets, descent groups, and economic specialists have varying access to what is, ideally, "common knowledge." That which everyone knows in one hamlet may be unknown and perhaps irrelevant to people in another hamlet. For example, recent narrative events of concern to potters in one hamlet will probably not be very interesting to charcoal manufacturers in a neighboring hamlet. As such, no hamlet has narratives that are exactly the same as those of any other hamlet. In this sense, no hamlet can be expected to yield a sample of narratives that is truly typical of the municipio. Nor is the tradition static with regard to time. Every day potentially removes or adds narratives to the corpus of events that are currently being passed on as true recent narratives. Therefore, no collection, however extensive, can claim to be complete.

No sex, age, or occupational group has particular rights to tell or listen to true recent narratives, nor is any group formally excluded from telling or hearing these narratives. There is a tendency, however, for groups to be sexually segregated by division of labor at optimal times for telling these stories. Women tell narratives of this kind while weaving or getting water together, as events suggest the subject matter. Men usually tell these tales while working together in the fields, traveling by foot, or resting in the evening when they are working on coffee plantations in the lowlands. Such separation, however, is by no means the rule, for I have heard examples of true recent narrative as mealtime conversation in Chamula homes, at which time all members of the domestic group are usually present. Not only is this genre unrestricted as to place of performance, audience, or teller, but no restrictions on subject matter apply. Although particularly ribald passages are supposed to make women ashamed, they hear and giggle about them all the same.

Style, Form, and Content

The style of these narratives varies a great deal from one story to the next and from one performer to the next. Generally, however, true recent narratives have fewer restrictions regarding style, form, and content than has any other genre of pure words. The style varies from the conversational, with few cases of repetition, to the somewhat formal, with consistent patterning in dyadic constructions, as in the example below. The form of the narrative is the discourse, describing a set of recent events that make up a meaningful whole. The content, though ideally unrestricted, does not usually include events or characters considered by Chamulas to belong to a time radically unlike the present. No feature of the content of the genre stands out so strikingly as its concern with cases of normative deviation. Apparently there is little worth noting in recent events that stays within the established norms and permitted limits of variation. To win a place in true recent narrative, the natural or social phenomenon must shake the status quo. Occasionally, positive changes in the established order are remembered, but it is much more likely that misfortunes and threats to the social order will enter the oral tradition as true recent narrative.

A few narrative conventions are required of a good storyteller. There are several phrases that are commonly used in true narrative of both types, ancient and recent, and much less frequently in ordinary speech. For the most part they serve as conjunctions, fillers, or pauses between phrases and indicate that the discourse will continue. They also allow intervals of time during which listeners may express some emotion or pleasure, approval, amusement, disapproval, or surprise. Examples of such narrative conjunctions from true recent narrative texts are:

va?un, "well, then"
    Example: va?un lek ša ša?i ti ?an¢ ?une.
           Well, then, the woman was already happy.
?ora ?un, "and now (then)"
    Example: ?ora ?un tal ša ti mu pukuh ?une.
           And then the awful demon approached.
?ora tana ?un, "and right now (then)"
    Example: ?ora tana ?un ti ?an¢e ha? no?oš
           And right then the women did nothing more
           puru tak'in la yič'.
           than receive money.

k'elavil ʔun, "look here," "pay attention," "get this"
    Example: veno, k'elavil ʔun.
        Well, get this.
            ti šinolan ʔan¢ bat ša šči'uk s¢'iʔ.
            The Ladina woman went away with her dog.

k'elavil tana liʔune, "get this right now"
    Example: k'elavil tana liʔune.
        Get this right now.
            ʔoy ša lekil kirsano ta banamil.
            There were already good people on earth.

ti voʔne ʔune or *ʔa li voʔne,* "long ago"
    Example: ti voʔne ʔune, makal to ti banamil.
        Long ago, the land was still uncleared.

A Text: "The Deer Hunters"

"The Deer Hunters" (Text 16), a complete text in this genre, was elicited from Salvador Guzmán Bakbolom, age thirty. Salvador heard the story for the first time in the Hot Country, where he was working on a coffee plantation. He was told it by a man about his same age who was working with him. One afternoon they were talking in the plantation's sleeping quarters about how nice it would be to buy a new rifle to go hunting. They decided that with the money they would earn that season at the coffee plantation, they would buy rifles on the way home to the highlands. His friend suggested that they hunt deer on a mountain located in Ranchu hamlet in Chamula, where he had heard that there were many deer but that they were hard to shoot. Some of his friends had tried to kill them, but failed. The text then enlarges on that particular hunting trip, in a style that clearly employs dual semantic units, as shown by indentation, but does not employ parallel syntactic units:[2]

vaʔi, ti hnu¢olaheletik bat snu¢ik teʔtikalčih ta svi¢al ranč
u.
Well, the hunters went to hunt deer on Ranchu Mountain.
    yuʔun la te ʔeč' hun vinik.
    It happened that a man passed by there.

lah la yil ʔoy la teʔtikalčih.
He saw that there were deer on the mountain.

te la ta šveʔ.
There they were feeding.

vaʔiʔun lah la yalbe sčiʔiltak ti vinike.
Well, the man told his friends about it.

    k'elavil čiʔiltakik, mi šak'anike ba hsaʔtik teʔtikalčih.
    "Look here, you guys, do you want to go deer-hunting?

leʔ ta viȼe.
There on the mountain,
    te la hsaʔ ta šveʔ
    There I found them feeding."

mi melel ši la sčiʔiltak ti vinike.
"Is that right?" said the man's friends.

    melel ʔeč škal ši la ti vinike.
    "That's right. I'm telling the truth," said the man.

veno, batik ta ʔora šae ši la sčiʔiltak ti vinike.
"Well, let's go right now, then," said the man's friends.

    vaʔiʔun batik la.
    Well then, they departed.

lah la yičʔikʔel stuk'ik.
They took their guns with them.

    te la tuk' batik ti bu lah yil ti vinike.
    Straight they went to where the man had seen them.

pere k'alal k'otik ti bu ʔoy to teʔtikalčihe, č'abal ša la te.
But when they arrived at the place of the deer, they were
    no longer there.

    ʔoč la saʔik ta teʔtik, pere muʔyuk la.
    They began to search through the woods, but to no avail.

batik la ta k'unk'un tahmek;
They went very slowly;

    ta la saʔikʔel.
    They searched along the way.

šanavik ša la ʔoš hunuk kuarto ʔora.
They had scarcely been walking for fifteen minutes.

    haʔ to la šilik te.
    Then they saw something there.

la staik hun muk'ul čon tahmek sčapoh la sba.
They found a huge snake which had coiled itself up.

    stoyoh la shol.
    It had raised its head.

pero šiʔik ta tahmek ti hnuȼolaheletike.
How terrified the hunters were!

vaʔiʔun ti hnuȼolaheletik muʔyuk ša la bu ti teʔtikalčihe.
Well, then, the hunters didn't stay any longer at the
   place of the deer.
te la sutik talel ti bu ti čone.
They came back from the place of the snake.
   ʔentonse ti hnuȼolaheletik sutik ʔel ta snaik.
   Then the hunters returned to their homes.

pere muʔyuk la bu staik ti teʔtikalčihe.
But they didn't find the deer.
   haʔ noʔoš la staik hun muk'ul čon.
   They only found a huge snake.

ta ʔos la smilik ti cŏne,
They were about to kill the snake,
   pero muʔyuk la bu šuʔ yuʔunik smilel.
   But they didn't succeed in killing it.

haʔ la ti čone ta ʔoš šbit ta sbaʔik.
The snake was just about to jump upon them.
   lah ša la shitun sba.
   It had already flung itself at them.

ʔentonse, k'alal lah yilik ti lah ša shitun sba ti čone,
Then, when they saw the snake fling itself at them,
   hlikel la bitik batʔel.
   They lost no time in leaping away.

batik k'alal ta snaik.
They went home.
   ti čon te la kom ta teʔtik.
   The snake remained there in the woods.

Time-Space Attributes

   The implicit message of "The Deer Hunters" can be derived
from its ethnographic background. The supernatural qualities
that Chamulas associate with snakes make them very much
afraid of snakes. Some snakes are believed to be transforma-
tions of the earth god. Still others are believed to be kept
as pets by the earth god in his cave in the mountains. Since
the earth god has a very bad disposition, being at times
portrayed as a fat, rich Ladino, and since he is believed to
control rainfall, thunder, and lightening, there is great risk in

making him angry. To provoke his wrath might produce
drought, or might even cause the earth god to buy one's
animal soul companion so as to do it harm and, by extension,
to hurt the human owner. The earth god's domain is the
wooded mountains and nearby caves, precisely where the
hunters in the tale went on their expedition. In all probability, the deer that the hunters were seeking actually
belonged to the earth god. The snake was simply protecting
the earth god's rightful property within his rightful domain.
The message is clear: one should not willfully invade the
domain of the earth god.

The time-space associations of the text express some of the
cosmological principles of Chamula. First, the informant
stated that the event reported had happened nine years ago
and that it had occurred in Chamula in Ranchu hamlet,
located perhaps two kilometers from the sample area. Thus,
there is a cohesion of close spatial associations and very
recent time of occurrence. This nearness brings the events
into the range of credibility for everyday life. Complementing
the close time-space associations is the setting in the woods,
where events can hardly be entirely positive, for the woods,
within the microcosm of Chamula, symbolize lowness,
coldness, darkness, threat, and behavior that is not rule-
governed. Furthermore, they contain caves, which are the
points of articulation between the earth and the underworld.
Caves are also the domain of the earth lords, represented as
socially distant Ladinos, who typically exploit Chamulas
economically and have snakes as familiars. The narrative is
coded, therefore, to remind listeners that even within
Chamula there are boundaries that should not be crossed by
ordinary men.

Another illustration of the cohesion of time-space attributes in true recent narrative is the story called "The
Drought" (Text 79), condensed here:

Long ago, when travelers were going to Santa Catarina
(Pantelhó), they had to take their own water, for it was very
dry in those days. Once their water ran out and they had to
drink their own urine. They reached Santa Catarina and

tried to buy water, but it was so expensive that they sold their goods as soon as possible and started home, again drinking their own urine, for the drought was worse than ever. The reason all the people had to go to Santa Catarina was that there was as yet no market in Chamula. Soon the rains came, and they were devastating. It rained for four days, causing houses and hills to collapse. Some people were trapped in their houses. One child was found dead after several days. He had been trapped in the house and was rotten and wormy. His mother did not bury him but tossed him in a brook, which soon sank into the earth. And from that time to this, there has never been a drought as severe as that one.

Coded into the content here are equal values of time and space. Pantelhó is a Tzotzil-speaking municipio that lies at the edge of the highlands and borders on the Hot Country. It is known but not familiar to most Chamulas. It is therefore both believable and understandable that in such a place Chamulas were forced to perform such an asocial act as drinking their own urine. Furthermore, the time at which the story took place, according to the informant, was about three-hundred years ago, or early in the Fourth Creation. The events of drought and flood might easily recur today. Likewise, the other events—the drinking of urine and the failure to bury the dead child who was wormy—could conceivably recur today. These acts were clearly mistakes but could not really be helped. They also involved unnatural acts of consumption: the drinking of urine and the consumption of the child by worms while he was not yet buried. Although possible in Chamula itself, the events were more at home in a municipio that was socially somewhat distant.

The logic of time-space association also operated in the circumstances that prompted the telling of the narrative. The year 1967 was a very dry season, and all signs indicated that there would not be enough rain in August and September to allow the highland maize to mature. It was then that an old Chamula mentioned to Marian López Calixto (who told me the story) that if it did not rain soon, they might be forced to drink their urine as their ancestors had. In other words, a present threat to the natural and social order prompted

the report of a similarly threatening past event. One unnatural
situation, drought, led to another, the drinking of urine, and
another, the flood, and still others—the collapse of houses, the
burial of the child in its own house, the appearance of worms,
and the parents' failure to bury the child properly. The social
order collapsed completely, in a domino effect. That is,
one asocial situation provoked a whole series of slips. These
events were credible because, among other reasons, the
"correct" time-place associations accompanied the old man's
narrative.

These texts typify the spirit of the genre. The composition
and setting of true recent narrative are far from random.
Chamula assumptions about cosmology and the time-space
principle appear to dictate what must go into a narrative so
as to make it credible and viable. However prosaic the subject
matter of individual texts, these tales as a whole carry a
reservoir of coded information about challenges to and
abuses of order—a topic that is never far from the thoughts
of Chamulas. Whether serious or funny, the abiding concern
of nearly all texts of true recent narrative is the layman's role
in preserving the social and natural order on a day-to-day
basis. The dual constructions that typify the genre's style
give them emphasis through redundancy, which is required
for important information. There are tales of people who kill
their animal souls and die in consequence; of people who
waste maize and thereby provoke the gods to send drought;
of people approached by monsters in unknown parts of
Chamula; of starving Indians who kill animals for food in the
Hot Country and turn into coyotes, thereby bringing the
menace of these animals to the highlands; of people who take
bribes in exchange for information detrimental to Chamula
and subsequently die for their injudicious action; of civil
strife in which the Chamulas kill each other; of national wars
in which all sides hurt Chamulas; and of people who have
sexual relations with animals and are duly punished. In all of
these typical themes, the human element is prime. Although
supernatural beings interact indirectly with humans, their
intervention is rarely creative. In fact, deities actually
threaten to destroy order if people do not solve their own

problems and behave correctly. True recent narratives thus present a kind of catalogue of cases in the human ethical dilemma.

(5) Frivolous Language

> Because laughter aims at correcting, it is
> expedient that the correction should reach as
> great a number of persons as possible. This is
> the reason comic observation instinctively pro-
> ceeds to what is general. It chooses such
> peculiarities as admit to being reproduced,
> and consequently are not indissolubly bound
> up with the individuality of a single person . . .
> peculiarities that are held in common . . . By
> organising laughter, comedy accepts social life
> as a natural environment; it even obeys an
> impulse of social life.
>
> —Henri Bergson, *Laughter*

Frivolous language (*ištol k'op*) is one of
the most richly differentiated genres of Chamula pure words.
This is partly owing to the fact that humor in various forms
occurs in countless everyday settings. Although verbal humor
does not always have a constant form, much of it occurs in
consistent patterns and formulas. Like true recent narrative,
frivolous language assumes the present social order and
maintains a defensive orientation toward it.

In general, verbal behavior that is both funny and constant
in form, setting, and content belongs to the category of
frivolous language. For example, *'ištol*, meaning "toy,"
implies an existing pattern or object that is played with. Set
forms of language (*k'op*) provide the object of play; hence,
the translation of *'ištol k'op* as "frivolous language" or
"toy language." Therefore, everything that is funny is not
necessarily frivolous language. For instance, the humorous
misfortune of a person falling down might be funny to those
who see it, but unless that event acquires a kind of semi-
permanency through the telling and retelling, it will be no
more than a humorous incident.

As in nearby Zinacantan, humor in Chamula is concerned
with norms of behavior and with deviations from them.

Because true recent narrative is also concerned with cases of normative deviation, there is some overlap between these two genres (Fig. 3). Both of them function as informal controls on behavior. True recent narratives represent a kind of reservoir of cases of threat and deviation, which are told only with proper stimulus, that is, in response to a present event for which past illustrative cases are useful. Frivolous language is more fragmentary and spontaneous, and it often occurs without any apparent stimulus. It subsumes at least five subcategories of humorous verbal behavior.[1]

Lies

The subcategory lies (*hut k'op*) within the genre frivolous language overlaps with the subcategory crazy talk (*čubah lo ʔil*) within the genre true recent narrative. The important difference between the two is that lies must not be true; they can be a piece of fantasy or an imaginary anecdote in prose. Crazy talk should be a true humorous prose anecdote. However, although the truth criterion separates these categories formally, in reality they are both funny stories, and it is frequently no more than a matter of opinion whether or not they are true. What they have in common—their reports of the flagrant violation of norms—unites them for all practical purposes. The performance setting of lies and crazy talk may be anywhere, even in a ritual situation, provided that the teller and listeners have the correct joking relationship and do not neglect their duties for the sake of the funny story. Informants indicated that both adults and children may tell and listen to lies, but usually in groups segregated according to age and sex. It seems, however, to be a typically male genre. Although I was told that women joke in lie sessions at the waterhole and elsewhere, neither my wife nor I ever heard a female performance of this subgenre.

The actual purpose of lies, according to informants, is simply for amusement. No deceit is intended, for listeners know from the stylistic and contextual features that they are a kind of tall tale. Lies, however, are not entirely spontaneous. One lies about a certain subject matter in certain ways. Although I was also told that there is a limit to the number of possible lies, that they cannot be generated at will, this is doubtful, for only a slight play on words and a little imagination seem to produce new texts of this genre. However, the genre does have some constant features of content, style and setting. Otherwise, it would probably be classified as marginal to the main body of oral tradition.

One of the principal stylistic constants is verbatim repetition of key suggestive words. This repetition serves as a clue to the listener that the narrative is probably a lie and not straight or true. This feature keeps lies separate from true recent narratives, which, though potentially humorous, are in fact true. Another stylistic feature that distinguishes this genre from true recent narrative is the interweaving of suggestive puns, called "truly frivolous talk," which themselves form another subgenre of frivolous language. Furthermore, lies use nonparallel dyadic structures, a style that is also characteristic of true recent narrative.

The following text illustrates these stylistic features of lies. The setting of the performance was the school in the Chamula Ceremonial Center. Some schoolboys were telling the teacher, who was a non-Chamula speaker of Tzotzil, about a swim in the stream, from which they had just returned. One boy began the report with a story:

> ʔoy hun mol;
> There was a man who was very old;
> > pere molmol tahmek ti mol lae.[2]
> > Very, very old the old man was.
>
> vaʔun, ta sk'ak'alil luneš la ta šbat ta pašyal.
> Well, on Monday he went for a walk.
> > ta stiʔil[2] stiʔil[2] stiʔil[2] la montanya ta šbat ta pašyal ti
> > At the very, very, very edge of the woods the old man
> > > mol laʔe.
> > > went walking.
>
> vaʔun, bat la tahmek ʔun.
> Well, he traveled for a long time.
> > ʔi ʔoy la te la sta hun la s¢eleh, ta ti mol la ʔune.
> > And there he came upon a mound, the old man did.

heč la ti mole ?oy la k'utik si la yič'oh ti mole.
Well, the old man had some things that he had been
     carrying.
    va?un, ?i sk'el la ?eč'el ?un, ti mol la ?une.
    Well, he took a look at them, the old man did.

va?un slok' la spišol ti mol la ?une, sk'el la ?eč'el.
Well, he took off his hat, the old man did, and looked all
     around.
    va?un sk'el la tahmek.
    He looked around a lot.

"pere k'usi le ?e šbak'bun la ta spas ta momoltik tahmek.
"But what can that be that's moving in the grass so much?
    la ti k'usi te la ?oy ta momoltik la ?une."
    Whatever is there in the grass?"

va?un, bat la ba snop ?un.
Well, he was going to think about it.
    sk'el la lek tahmek, ti mole.
    He stared at it, the old man did.

lok' la me talel ?une.
It started to come out.
    tal la k'usi la te ta spas ta momoltik la ?une.
    It was coming, whatever it was that was moving in the
     grass.

va?un, heč, la ti mol la ?un mu la bu ta ši? la ?une.
Well, even so, the old man was not afraid.
    te la va?al ti mol la ?une.
    There he was standing up, that old man.

hec la ti ta šbak' ta momoltik la ?une mu ¢'i? la ?un.
It turned out that what was moving in the grass was a
    damned dog.
    va?un, ši? la ti mol ?une.
    Well, the old man was frightened.

"?ay, pere k'usi ta škak'be tana ?un.
"Oh, what can I throw at it?
    tal ša la ti koyote," ši la ti mole.
    The coyote is coming," said the old man.

?avan la ?un: "?u . . . ?u . . . ?u . . . ha . . . he . . . he . . ."
He shouted: "Uh! . . . Uh! . . . Uh! . . . Ha! . . . Hay! . . . Hay! . . ."
    ši la ti mole.
    said the old man.

va?un, tal la ti ¢'i? la ?une.
Well, the dog kept coming.

heč, la ti mol la ?une mu?yuk la k'usi la yič'oh lae.
Well, it turned out that the old man did not have anything
    with him (to throw).
    "pere k'usi ta škak'be tana ?un" ši la ti mole.
    "But what am I going to throw at him?" said the old
        man.

heč la ti mol la ?un snop la ?un.
So the old man thought about it.
    "mas lek ta šihatav," ši la ti mole.
    "It's better for me to run away," said the old man.

?uy, stambe la hatavel la ?un.
Oh, he continued to flee.
    lik la ta ?anil.
    He began to run.

?i tal la ti ¢'i?e,
And the dog was coming,
    heč la ti mol la ?une lub¢ah ša la ?un.
    So it happened that the old man got tired.

te ša la, smala ti ¢'i?e.
There he was, waiting for the dog.
    ?inopah la talel tahmek ?un.
    He got closer and closer.

ti povre mol la ?une shipbe la snamte?e.
The poor old man threw his walking stick at him.
    likel ta bik'bat ti snamte?e.
    In a second his walking stick was swallowed.

shipbe la šonob štok.
He threw his sandals at him too.
    ?i bik'bat štok ?un.
    And they were swallowed also.

shipbe la spišol štok
He threw his hat at him also.
    ?i bik'bat la štok.
    And it was swallowed too.

?i shipbe la smoral štok,
He threw his carrying bag at him too,
    ?i bik'bat la ?un.
    And it was also swallowed.

"ʔoy, pere k'usi ša yan ta hipbe ša ʔun" ši la ti mole.
"Oh, but what else can I throw at him?" said the old man.
    stenbe la sk'ob ʔun.
    He stuck out his hand.

ti sk'ob la ʔune ʔi bik'bat la ʔun.
His hand was swallowed.
    "bat ša li hk'obe" ši la ti mole.
    "My hand is gone!" said the old man.

heč la ti sk'ob lok' la ʔun ʔa ti mu ¢'iʔ la ʔune,
It happened that his hand came out of the damned dog,
        valk'uh la ʔun ta ye.
        and turned him inside out.
        toʔoš la te ma¢'al ti sk'obe k'alal la snit la lok' ʔel ʔune.
        His hand was still stuck when he withdrew it.

haʔ ša la sbe s¢oʔ la lok' la ti sk'ob la ʔune.
It was his anus that came out with his hand.
        ʔi haʔ la čam ti ¢'iʔ la ʔune.
        And so the dog died.[3]

(The boy—the "old man" of the story—continued by describing in great detail his experiences while bathing.)

The story in the lie is funny, according to informants, because the man tricks the dog that attacks him. Not only does he trick him; he manages to kill him. This shows, Chamulas suggested, that people can conquer natural forces if necessary. The remaining question involves what the story has to do with swimming and bathing, the activities to which the lie is supposedly related. The answer lies in a complicated play on words that is also carried in the lie and which makes the story uproariously funny to Chamulas. The old man in the story refers both to the boy who is bathing naked in the stream and to his penis. The edge of the woods (sti ʔil montanya) in which he is walking also refers to the bank of the stream, since sti ʔil can also mean "bank." Both of these borderline areas (edge of the woods and the stream) are significant in suggesting removal from safe and moral categories of space. The sequence of events bears out the threat, for the encounter amounts to a word-for-word sexual encounter of the naked old man (or boy) with a female dog. All of the things that he "throws" at the dog (except the sandals) are very common punning words which have sexual meanings. The word *pišol* ("hat") refers to the foreskin of the penis; *namte ʔ* ("walking stick"), to the penis; *moral* ("carrying bag"), to the scrotum; and *k'ob* ("hand"), to the penis. The word *k'ob* is also considered a superb punning word on another level, for *k'ob* differs by only a single phoneme shift from *kob,* a verb root meaning "to have sexual intercourse." Likewise, the mouth of the dog, *ye*, can also mean vagina. The fact that the old man cannot remove his "hand" from the dog's "mouth" refers to a well-known problem that dogs have in disengaging themselves after copulation. Therefore, beneath the first meaning lies a second, sexual meaning. Yet even the second is strangely moralistic in that the old man (or boy) impales the dog and kills it for forcing him to become involved in bestiality, something of which Chamulas disapprove very strongly. In a sense, human weakness was turned to victory over acultural behavior, and it all happened, significantly, in the present, and in a symbolically threatening place, the edge of the woods. It is therefore the combination of a good story with proper time-space coding and potential for double entendre and moralistic statement that makes a successful lie.

Truly Frivolous Talk

The subgenre truly frivolous talk (*baȼ'i ʔištol loʔil*), which includes punning and verbal dueling, carries part of the name, *ʔištol* or "frivolous," of the category that immediately subsumes it (*ʔištol k'op*) and in some respects exhibits essential qualities of the higher level taxon. No subgenre of frivolous language occurs more frequently than truly frivolous talk. It is significant that *loʔil* ("talk") and not the more formal *k'op* ("language") describes the subgenre.

Like its affiliated subgenres, truly frivolous talk is mostly unrestricted with regard to physical setting. It can occur virtually anywhere that conversation occurs, provided that the performers have the correct joking relationship. Its performance is officially excluded only from ritual settings, and even at those affairs I have seen cargoholders complete

a prayer and then begin drinking to the happy accompaniment of truly frivolous talk. As with lies, informants said
that there are no official sex or age restrictions as to who
may speak truly frivolous talk to whom and before whom.
My own observations did not support this judgment, however,
for I never heard men speak the genre directly to women.
In fact, I am familiar with only two kinds of mixed sex
performances of truly frivolous talk. One occurs among
siblings below the age of seven or eight. This setting may also
include members of the play group, but residence patterns
usually place kinsmen together in these informal groups.
Even in this mixed-sex setting, the genre is used by the boys
to taunt the girls. Girls are supposed to pretend that they do
not understand the intended meanings, most of which are
sexual puns. A male-female exchange, therefore, does not
actually occur. Boys exchange the loaded words, and girls
listen in. A second mixed-sex setting occurs when bachelor
men joke in groups by themselves with truly frivolous talk
and intentionally speak loud enough to be overheard by
passing women. Although the women may in fact understand
the intended double entendre, they should never giggle or
acknowledge in any way that they have heard the exchange:
to do so would label them as sexually available. I have
heard that adolescent girls and women use truly frivolous
talk to joke among themselves, but neither my wife nor I
heard actual female performance of the genre. We heard
women laugh at suggestive puns in dialogue, but verbal
dueling among females escaped us, if in fact it exists.

Modified forms of truly frivolous talk exist. Any pun,
intended or accidental, that provokes laughter because of
suggestive meanings can be classified as frivolous talk. An
example appears in the discussion of the lie text above.
Any pun or suggestive turn of phrase in ordinary dialogue
can also be classified as frivolous talk. Truly frivolous talk,
however, is far more fixed in form and setting, as the adjective *baď'i*, meaning "real" or "true," indicates.

Truly frivolous talk usually takes place in boys' and men's
groups. To be successful—that is, to extend the verbal duel
to its limits of suggestiveness—the people involved should

have a joking relationship. This means that they must have a
familiar, open kind of interaction. This usually implies the
absence of communication barriers such as age and rank.
Truly frivolous talk is a game in which someone wins and
someone loses. The winner is the one who says the last word
in a series of structured exchanges.[4] The series may include
from two to well over a hundred words and phrases. Prestige
and recognition within the group are the only items actually
to be lost or gained by the outcome of a verbal duel. Consecutive items in the verbal series usually rhyme or vary
from one another by only one or two phonemic shifts.
Suggestive words can also remain constant and enter into
new combinations with other words. As a result, sound and
semantics impose strict limits on what words are appropriate.
A good progression in truly frivolous talk should combine
minimum sound shift from word to word or phrase to phrase
with maximum derogatory or suggestive meaning. Although
truly frivolous talk can supposedly be improvised, informants
agreed that there is a limited number of beginning words, for
which one learns a string of appropriate succeeding words
and phrases. New combinations of sets of exchanges are
probably occurring all the time, just as certain ballad phrases,
such as "never tie your affections to a green growing tree,"
occur in many contexts in the English ballad tradition.
Yet within these sets or sequences, there is strikingly little
variation.

Since space does not allow a comprehensive list of all
words and phrases that can, potentially, be expanded in
exchanges of truly frivolous talk, I have selected an example
which illustrates several aspects of the genre. It was recorded
by an informant, Marian López Calixto, from a performance
by his friends at the Festival of the Dead, October 30 and 31,
1968. The two performers in the text were about seventeen
years old, bachelors and close friends. Their age implies a
special kind of joking relationship, for bachelors and young
married men from the ages of twelve to about thirty-five
are permitted various kinds of public physical contact with
one another. This contact—such as holding hands, putting
their arms around one another's shoulders, occasional grabs

at each other's genitals, and dancing in each other's embrace as couples at festivals—may have covert homosexual significance. Such behavior is extremely common and more often than not provides the kind of setting in which truly frivolous talk occurs. This setting explains some of the prevailing sexual, even homosexual, nuances of the genre.

In the text that follows, the two young men who participated are indicated by the numerals 1 and 2. This text of 65 exchanges was actually only the first part of a very long sequence, which included 145 additional exchanges before one of the players gave up. In all, the original text included 210 exchanges.

Tzotzil	*English*	*Explanation*
1: *k'elun*	Look at me.	A standard initial phrase for truly frivolous talk.
2: *k'el ʔavahnil*	Look at your wife.	That is, I might do as your wife.
1: *helavanik*	Go ahead.	
2: *heč ʔavalik*	That's true, what you say.	
1: *šʔeč' ʔavak'ik*	It happens that you give it to her.	
2: *šʔeč' ʔavok'ik*	It happens that you break it.	That is, break her hymen.
1: *šʔeč' ʔapokik*	It happens that you wash it.	Sexual intercourse is thought of as a scrubbing motion, the sexual fluids being the soap.
2: *šʔeč' ʔapohik*	It happens that you snatch her away.	
1: *šʔeč' ʔanopik*	It happens that you think about it.	
2: *šʔeč' ʔamukik*	It happens that you bury it (in her).	Referring to the penis.

1: šʔeč' ʔapitk'unik ʔavikaḍ	It happens that you put down your load.	That is, relieve yourself sexually.
2: yik' kas	Smell of gas.	Refers to the passing of wind.
1: yik' kas ʔanutiʔ	Smell of gas of your carrying net.	A carrying net is a hemp bag, referring here to the scrotum.
2: poko	Wash it.	That is, wash your scrotum. Also a play on the Spanish *poco*, meaning "small amount," as an insult to the size of the other's scrotum.
1: pok'ok'	Toad.	The scrotum, when swollen, is thought to look like a swollen toad.
2: pok' sat	Swollen face.	An insult, as this is the name for a species of fish. It also refers to the head of the penis.
1: ʔatot	Your father.	That is, your father has a fish face or "your father looks like the head of a penis."
2: ʔatol	Number.	A play on the Spanish *atole*, meaning "maize gruel," a substance that resembles semen.
1: ta šatoy	You lift them up.	Refers to lifting and spreading the female's legs in sexual intercourse.

2: *toyo voʔote*	Lift them up yourself.	
1: *šʋoʔvun ʔahol*	Your head is hatless.	That is, you have an erection.
2: *balom ʔok'es*	The cylindrical trumpet.	Refers to the penis.
1: *sba ʔavok'es*	Your trumpet is on top.	Referring to the sexual act.
2: *hpušk'in*	I double it over.	That is, he rejects the other's penis and will not receive it, or he bends it to hurt the other.
1: *ʔilo*	Let's see it.	Refers to the other's penis.

(At this point, the second boy exhibited himself, as requested, thereby answering the challenge with a gesture. Others standing nearby made playful grabs for his penis, and the exhibitor tried to avoid their hands. He continued by answering the challenge verbally.)

2: *ʔapuro*	Your cigar.	That is, you can put it in your mouth if you like.
1: *ʔavuro*	Your burro.	Another word for penis.
2: *yahval*	Owner or patron.	An insult, insinuating that the protector of the other is a domestic animal, a burro. All humans should have deities and good animal soul companions as protectors. Domestic animals are usually the soul companions only of witches. The word also insults him by suggesting that,

		animal-like, the other person's penis is his owner; he lives for sex alone.
1: *ta šaval*	You say it (I don't).	
2: *ta šavaʔi*	You understand (however).	
1: *ta šabat*	You are getting excited.	That is, you are getting an erection.
2: *ta ša šhat ʔaveš*	Your pants are already ripping.	From the pressure of the erection.
1: *ʔak'bo ʔaviš*	Fuck your older sister.	
2: *ta šak'an hviš*	You desire my older sister.	
1: *ʔilo ʔat*	Look at that penis.	Referring to the other's erection.
2: *batan*	Let's get started.	
1: *ʔaȼ'am*	Salt.	Refers to ejaculated semen.
2: *čak'an*	You want it.	
1: *t'ant'an*	Naked.	
2: *ʔaču ʔ*	Your teat.	
1: *sču ʔ čivo*	The teat of a ewe.	
2: *vovoč'*	Slimy.	Refers to either the woman's or the ewe's saliva-covered breast, or to the penis covered with seminal fluid.
1: *bu ta šʔoč*	Where does it go in?	
2: *bu čaʔoč*	Where do you go in?	
1: *bu ta šk'ot*	Where does it reach to?	
2: *bu ta škom*	Where does it remain?	
1: *bu ta šhom*	Where does it burst?	
2: *bu ta sk'an*	Where is there still room?	

1: *mu sk'an*	There isn't any.	
2: *mu šal*	It doesn't say so.	
1: *mu šhalav*	It doesn't weave.	Refers to the shuttle that is inserted between vertical threads in weaving; a sexual allusion.
2: *mu šanav*	It isn't moving.	An instruction between partners during intercourse.
1: *ʔa mu šonob*	Your damned sandal.	Suggests that the man has inserted his sandal rather than his penis.
2: *ʔašokon*	Your side.	Another order to a sexual partner.
1: *šokol*	Is free.	Completes preceding phrase.
2: *homol*	Hole.	Refers to the vagina.
1: *toh mol*	Is very old.	
2: *toh muk' homol*	The hole is very big.	Imputes femininity to the other speaker.
1: *sbe ʔak'ab*	The path of your urine.	
2: *k'u ʔora čačam*	When are you going to die?	Refers to orgasm.
1: *k'u ʔora čačan*	When are you going to learn?	Refers to inadequate timing during intercourse.
2: *k'u ʔora čak'an*	When do you want it?	
1: *k'u ʔora čaman*	When are you going to buy it?	
2: *manšu*	Tame.	An insult to a sexual partner for being lazy.
1: *mančuk*	So what.	

The sexual theme prevailing throughout this text and in most texts of this subgenre may be explained in part by the fact that norms of sexual behavior for both males and females in Chamula are extremely puritanical at all ages. Premarital chastity and marital fidelity are expected of both men and women. The significance of these norms and the very high frequency of deviation from them is shown by the large number of court cases involving sexual infractions that come daily before the magistrate and his helpers. It is possible that the sexual fantasies and homosexual suggestiveness in truly frivolous talk are reactions to and sublimations of anxieties instilled by the Chamulas' very strict norms for male-female relationships. Children up to six or seven years of age frequently share a sleeping platform with their parents, whose sexual activity therefore proceeds in the children's immediate presence. The preoccupation with sex in Chamula humor may be partially explained by the incompatibility between this candid parental sexual behavior and talk, on the one hand, and the strict rules for premarital chastity on the other. Adding to the sexual stress created by these circumstances is an economic factor—a relatively large brideprice—which keeps most Chamula men from marrying until several years after puberty.

Another point of stress that is verbalized in truly frivolous talk is the brother-in-law relationship. The brothers of a wife are said to resent their brother-in-law, in part because he has purchased and removed a member of the labor force from the localized patriline. So delicate and strained is the brother-in-law relationship that many couples choose to ask the wife's brothers and their wives to become compadres in order to seal the relationship with a more stable and affectionate bond than the affinal one. In the text above, there is frequent reference to the older sister of one of the participants as a potential sexual partner for the other. This suggestion is funny precisely because that relationship is the one implying the greatest amount of conflict if he should, in fact, marry the sister in question. If he should seduce her before marriage, it would be grounds for murder. Joking talk of flaunting sexual norms simply underlines the importance of those norms.

The significance of this subgenre in the whole of Chamula oral tradition is shown by the fact that there are few functions in Chamula at which one does not hear truly frivolous talk in some form or another, however abbreviated. Although it is most typical of bachelors and young married men, even the most sober cargoholders will burst into laughter at a well-timed sequence of truly frivolous talk. Moreover, the genre is extremely important to the socialization process in general and to the learning of the language in particular. Small boys suffer extreme ridicule from older boys who beat them at truly frivolous talk. To know how to speak well and persuasively is greatly valued by Chamulas, and the ability to joke in this genre serves as a fairly dependable index of a man's social maturity, linguistic competence, intelligence, and political potential. One can also assume that a man who jokes well in truly frivolous talk is perfectly familiar with the cultural norms and the range of potential deviation from them. To know what to laugh at and to be able to make others laugh requires a thorough knowledge of social rules. Virtuosity in truly frivolous talk, therefore, indicates an excellent traditional education.

Buried or Superficial Language

This subgenre is like truly frivolous talk and lies in that it depends for its humor on double entendre and normative deviation. Unlike the former two genres, buried language ideally requires a specific behavioral cue for performance. The genre addresses specific normative transgressions and seeks to make the offender realize his error by indirect means. The two names for this genre, buried language (*mukul k'op*) and superficial language (*baba k'op*), describe its spirit quite literally: *mukul* means "buried" and *baba* means "above" or "superficial." The two genre labels are alternative ways of referring to exactly the same kind of verbal behavior. Although "buried language" is used in this discussion, the forms are identical. The speaker uses circumlocution to try to shame the offender into compliance. Ideally, every performance of buried language should have a specific referent situation; yet in practice, the absence of such an immediate referent does not daunt would-be jokers. The genre thus appears in two contexts: as a corrective device and as a theme for joking per se.

Buried language is a prose genre that may occur in combination with other genres of frivolous language. Alone, however, buried language sounds like a set of non sequitur sentences. Only if the referent situation is known do the sentences make any sense to the non-Chamula. For Chamulas themselves, hearing the sentences is sufficient to determine the kind of transgression that is being redressed. Buried language is a kind of cryptic insult. When the recipient gets the point, ideally he should stop doing whatever the speaker is criticizing. That will certainly happen if the speaker is superior to the recipient in rank. If they are of equal rank, the recipient may return the insult in some way or begin a sequence of verbal dueling in truly frivolous talk. Buried language should never be said by inferiors to superiors in rank by sex, age, or cargo status. It can usually be said by superiors to inferiors in any of the various ranks, with one exception: although men are superior to women for most purposes, they should not say buried language to any women other than those with whom they have a joking relationship. The genre is frequently used by elders to correct children in the home and also by boys and girls or men and women in their respective play and work groups. Cargoholders may also use the genre to correct wrongdoers at fiestas.

The following example of buried language was addressed by a fifteen-year-old brother to a younger brother of twelve. The deviation to be redressed was the younger brother's having removed his trousers in preparation for going to bed one evening and then sitting by the fire in such a way that his genitals were visible to all, including his younger and elder sisters. That they might see him exposed was improper for they might be ashamed. The younger brother was also expected to feel shame at being so careless with his personal appearance. For small boys to expose themselves by not wearing trousers underneath their tunics was to be expected; but for an adolescent boy, this was improper. It could also be dangerous, for if a mature boy or young man should accidentally or on purpose expose himself to a single girl, she could report the case to cargo officials as a proposition. This outcome would cause all sorts of legal difficulties, including a possible jail sentence and a fine.

> li šune lek sna? švay ta hobeltik.
> John (the penis) certainly knows how to sleep in the grass
>> (pubic hair).
>> ti šune yu?un mu sk'an bu šbat.
>> The fact is that John doesn't want to go anywhere.
>
> heče te vo¢ol li šune.
> So there John is all huddled up.
>> li šune lek sna? švay ta hobeltik.
>> John certainly knows how to sleep in the grass.
>
> mu sk'an ta šlok'
> He doesn't want to leave.
>> te ?oy, te tik'il ta stas.
>> There he is, there curled up in his nest.
>
> heče te ča?el shol ti šune.
> And John's hair is just all mussed up.
>> puru momoltik te ?oy vo¢ol.
>> There's nothing more than grass there around him.
>
> heče te nihil ta sk'elvan ti šune.
> There John is, head bowed, looking at it.
>> ?oy sik ta ša?i.
>> He's probably cold.
>
> heče te mu¢ul snuk'.
> His neck is just all bent over.
>> heče te sot'ol smoral.
>> His carrying bag is just all wrinkled up.
>
> heč ti smorale toh ?ik' tahmek.
> His carrying bag is just as black as can be.
>> toh pim s¢a¢al ti smorale.
>> The hair of his carrying bag is very thick.
>
> te ?oy sk'ehoh ti smoral ta k'al ?osil ti šune.
> There his carrying bag has hidden itself in John's ravine.
>> nopol te ?oy yiloh sba?ik ti buy yermanoe.
>> Close by there he and his brother (the anus) have seen
>>> each other.

haʔ te bu šlok' talel lume,
It's right there where his land (feces) comes to,
   nopol sȼ'ak ti šune,
   Near John's property line,
      te ta yiʔ bel smulino.
      There at the base of his corn grinder (anus).[5]

At the conclusion of the buried language, the whole house was chuckling, including the recipient. He was so embarrassed that he went outside. When he came back inside, he made an effort to sit so as not to expose himself. In trying to adjust his tunic properly, he was extremely self-conscious and conspicuous, for his family was still watching him and laughing at him.

In the absence of a specific social blunder to which Chamulas can address buried language, one of several loaded words is introduced as a starter. To use the genre as a game rather than an explicit means of correction is more typical of bachelors and young married men than of mature adults or small children. Nubile girls are also said to play games with buried language, although I never heard them myself. Nearly all the words that initiate "unofficial" buried language have sexual connotations. Even so, the normative implication of the genre remains strong, for the exchanges usually verbalize and condemn deviant sexual behavior. The most common base words are *č'umteʔ*, a prickly, pear-shaped vegetable (chayote or *Sechium edule*), which refers to the vagina; *loʔbol*, the common banana and also the plantain, which are the most popular of all phallic symbols; *čoris*, link sausage, also a favorite phallic symbol; and *moton*, literally "gift," which refers to free extramarital or premarital sexual favors, and to passing wind. Whole conversations of what to the non-Chamula listener seems to be straight language can be based on such words. The laughter elicited by these exchanges, however, suggests that superficial meaning does not have much importance.

In the following example, the two male participants were about fourteen years old. Having bought bananas at the market in Chamula Ceremonial Center one Sunday morning, they have just begun to eat them while walking around the plaza:

Boy 1:
mi lah ʔaloʔ ʔaloʔbol ti Hoʔote.
Did you finish eating your banana?

Boy 2:
sk'anto. ʔa li Hoʔote.
Not yet. And yourself?

Boy 1:
ʔa li Hoʔone čʼay li hloʔbole.
I lost my banana.

Boy 2:
bu ʔavak' ʔun.
Where did you leave it?

Boy 1:
veno, ta hsaʔ.
Well, I'll look for it.
kaʔtik mi hta.
Let's see if I find it.

Boy 2:
veno, saʔo.
Look for it then.

Boy 1:
k'usi liʔ
What's this?
ša li hloʔbol ʔune.
Here's my banana.

Boy 2:
buy liʔ.
Where?

(Boy 1 pulls his tunic aside to exhibit the bulge in his trousers.)

Boy 1:
šatale.
Come over.
liʔ ʔoy pahal ti koʔe.
Here it is planted in my groin.

pere hutuk sit.
But it's a little swollen.
šak'elavil.
Come and see.

toh hubem tahmek.
It's really fat.
    ško?olah čak čitom ti kate.
    My penis is just like a pig.

(They both laugh.)

hutuk li motone.
It's just a little gift.

(Boy 1 makes a gesture to take out his penis and show it to his friend, who threatens to grab it. Boy 1 turns away, passes wind, and continues.)

?u. lok' hutuk li motone.
Oh. (Another) little gift came out.

Boy 2:
    ?u pišol šaval.
    Oh, you said "hat?"

Boy 1:
    makal ta ?apišol.
    It's stopped up with your hat.

The text continued with a brief exchange of truly frivolous talk. The transition to that genre was appropriate, for the joking meaning of "hat" is the foreskin. There is also humor in the second boy's implication that the first boy said "hat," when in fact the noise was a fart. This text shows the ease with which one genre provides the transition to another genre within the category of frivolous language. Also significant are the nonlinguistic aspects of the performance, such as gestures and inadvertent events (like passing wind), which accompany and influence the performance of nearly all genres of frivolous language. They suggest that the full context of a performance must be known in order adequately to describe and interpret its meaning.

Obscure Words or Proverbs

Of all the subgenres of frivolous language, this category of obscure words (*k'ehel k'op*) was the most difficult to elicit. In fact, I had spent nearly a year in the field before discover-

ing that a genre similar to the proverb exists with considerable
vitality, although the genre had long been thought to be
unimportant in the aboriginal oral traditions of the Americas
(Dundes, 1967: 58). The reason for its supposed absence
is probably its peculiar linguistic form and obscure context
of performance. In Chamula, the main point of its linguistic
form and social function is not to be obvious in any way;
the more ambiguous it remains to its audience, the better for
those who manage to understand it and the greater the shame
for the social transgressor to whom it is usually addressed.
This quality of obscurity differs from other oral traditions,
such as those of many African societies, in which the proverb
figures prominently in formal aspects of social life, such as
court procedure. By contrast, Chamula tradition uses proverbs
that are "buried in ordinary speech" (*mukul ta tukil k'op*).
Many Chamulas, in fact, simply cannot distinguish obscure
words from ordinary speech as a discrete unit. For these
reasons, the word "proverb", as it is generally understood in
English is an inadequate gloss for *k'ehel k'op*. "Obscure
words," the better gloss, overlaps with several other expressive
domains, such as verbal games, jokes, aphorisms, and insults,
which are often separable in other cultures.

The name of the genre describes its form and function, for
k'ehel means "oblique," "indirect," "cryptic," "hidden,"
"obscure," or "put away." In this respect it is unlike all of
the other genres of frivolous language, which are rather
blatant and obvious. Within their other social contexts,
subtlety is optional. The social context of proverbs, however,
demands subtlety. The genre nevertheless shares with the
other subgenres of frivolous language several characteristics:
it has a generally constant form, possesses humor, functions
as an informal device for social control, and uses puns and
multiple meanings. It is different from the other subgenres in
that it always has a referent or stimulus for performance,
and it must function subtly.

The social situations addressed by obscure words involve
serious deviations from rules that need correcting, but which
cannot be corrected by direct means. Examples of such asocial
behavior are violent drunkenness on the part of cargoholders
and others, fouling public and sacred places, improper dress

for the sexual role, exposure of genitalia, breaking wind, greediness at meals, and urinating on others while drunk. Unless those involved are of equal rank, sex or status, the process of righting or calling attention to these situations by direct means would probably have negative consequences for the speaker. This happens because differences in rank and status make it virtually impossible for certain categories of people to speak directly to other categories of people in Chamula society. The barriers, such as those that exist between men and women who are not kinsmen or between children and their elders, are the more insurmountable when potentially embarrassing topics must be discussed. With the use of obscure words, however, even the most delicate situations can be righted without negative consequences to the speaker.

The content of obscure words, like the social situations addressed by them, is ambiguous. The word *k'ehel* ("obscure") states literally that something is withheld from the listener. Thus, the key to understanding obscure words lies in completing a whole message from the segment given. In this way each conveys and asserts a social rule, not explicitly, but by suggestion and association with its logical opposite in the natural or noncultural domain. To accomplish this elaborate circumlocution, an obscure word states one or at most two of three aspects of a social rule: its assertion, its negation in the realm of nature or noncultural behavior, and an example of an infraction of the rule. An obscure word, therefore, behaves as a logical puzzle. A partially-filled paradigm, the obscure word offers a challenge to an individual's knowledge of Chamula rules and social categories. It gives the transgressor something to think about, but not everything. The meaning remains for him to extract or for bystanders to point out through laughter. The impetus to think in terms of the puzzle it describes may be provided by the dual structure that often appears in the obscure word. Its structure may take the form of parallel syntax, or of similar sounds in two segments. However, an obscure word may just as easily be a simple sentence with no special syntactical or sound parallelism.

The following obscure word is addressed to people who

foul a public road or path by defecating or urinating there:

li be to hamal, pere ta šmak.
The road is still open, but it will close.

This proverb emphasizes the principle of proper etiquette that requires one to go to a little-frequented place to elimi-nate. The asocial act of fouling a public place serves as the middle, ambivalent item—the infraction—in a set of social categories that contrast the negative qualities of closure with the positive qualities of openness. The dyadic structure of the obscure word—the first part asserting openness, the second part creating closure—leaves little doubt in the offender's mind that he himself is acting out the infraction by defecating in and thereby closing an open space.

This obscure word may be said by a member of either sex or of any age group to another member of any age group or sex. A pun is intended, providing the double entendre that makes the proverb funny and effective. The word *be* alone means "road" or "path." It combines with *ȼoʔ* ("excrement") to form *sbe ȼoʔ* ("the path of excrement" or "anus"). However, *be* alone can also mean anus. Therefore, the obscure word may be interpreted in two different ways, each of which serves to embarrass an offender who is not discreet about where he chooses to eliminate. The person to whom it is addressed probably remains uncertain as to which meaning is intended by the accuser. He might mean, "The road is still open, but your deposit in the pathway will close it and make it repulsive for future passersby." Or if the accused was caught in the act, the accuser might mean, "Your anus is still open (your bowels are still moving), but it will close (you will soon finish)." In each interpretation, the offender's behavior is likened to that of a child or an animal, who does not know any better. On another level, the accuser's message may be understood as malicious by the transgressor, while remaining extremely funny to the other listeners. This message derives from a play on the word *mak*, which means "to constipate" as well as "to close." The reading of the proverb line could thus be, "Your bowels are still open, but they will become constipated." Such a reading wishes not only shame but also physical illness on the transgressor. By extension, it calls down a negative supernatural sanction on the wrongdoer, for constipation, like most other Chamula illnesses, is thought to have supernatural causes.

The open-closed contrast has other spatial meanings. Openness of the path is associated with a state of order and good behavior, whereas closedness or impassability of the path has a negative, antisocial connotation. Beyond the obvious, literal meaning of the open-closed contrast, there are other qualities that Chamulas associate with "open" (*hamal*) and "closed" (*makal*). According to the mythological account of the human occupation of the land, there has been a slow movement from closed woods (*te'tik*) to open fields and house areas (*hamalaltik*). It follows from the myth texts that the general trend of human qualities across the course of time has been from less social beings in the past to more social beings in the present. Chamula associations, then, place an asocial act like fouling a path in the same class as woods and antiquity, which have the asocial qualities of isolation and absence of human culture. An ill-tempered or antisocial person is frequently described as *toh makal ta k'oponel*, which means that his "manner of speech is very indirect or closed." This kind of person contrasts with one whose way of speaking is frank or "open." The latter type is often described as *lek hamal ta k'oponel* or "plainly open in manner of speech." In general, obscure words constitute an arsenal of defense for the social order. Their weapons are little more than contrasting social categories. Most Chamula obscure words are intelligible in terms of a paradigm based on those categories. Thus, obscure words provide a kind of informal statement of social rules as well as a means of enforcement.

Riddles

Riddles (*hak'om k'op*) are the least important subgenre of frivolous language. Riddles are used in children's play and joking and also in joking by men of all ages. Adult women are said never to use riddles. However, it is difficult to see how children could learn them at the very early age they do if their mothers did not teach them. I suspect that riddles may be used by mothers in teaching their children to talk, but have never heard any such performance.

The words *hak'om k'op*, which literally mean "question," must be understood only in a particular context to mean riddle as a kind of frivolous language. Informants frequently use *makal k'op*, meaning "hidden word," as a synonym for riddle. This implies that the point of the genre is to find the hidden word. As such, riddles are considered to be a kind of game, as are the exchanges of truly frivolous talk. These two genres of frivolous language also overlap with the category of traditional games (*tahimol*).

There are two kinds of riddles. Although Chamulas do not recognize the difference as an important one, and they do not have separate names, the stylistic differences between the two types are salient. The first kind of riddle is stated as a terse, often rhymed question, usually concluding with the line *k'usi ʔun*, "What is it?". The riddle typically contains a large number of Spanish loan words, and may therefore be of Spanish origin. Furthermore, many Chamula riddles have Spanish equivalents that are still popular in the state of Chiapas.

The following example of the genre as it exists in Chamula seems to be a favorite. Different versions of it were supplied by several informants, from eighteen to sixty years old:

Riddle:
   hmeʔ kumagre haval,
   My comadre is face up,
       kumpagre nuhul.
       My compadre is face down.

   k'usi ʔun.
   What is it?

Answer:
   teša.
   A roof tile.

The implication is that the compadres in question are having sexual intercourse. Although everyone seems to know the correct response, the riddle nearly always provokes great laughter. The double entendre comes from the fact that clay roof tiles are commonly "sexed" with regard to position, the "females" being face up and the "males" face down (Fig. 4).

In this riddle not only the roofing technology implied but also the ritual kin terms (*compadre* and *comadre*) used are of Spanish origin. Tile roofs, in fact are found on only about a tenth of Chamula houses, the other roofs being thatched. The *compadrazgo* relationship, however, plays an extremely important role in the lives of all Chamulas, for it provides an extra, non-kin-based network of alliance relationships on which they can depend for loans, favors, and general assistance. Because compadrazgo frequently binds individuals who either have unequal social status (as between a Ladino and an Indian) or experience strained relations for other reasons (as between brothers-in-law), the tie is highly ritualized and requires mutual respect. The significance of this ritual kinship relationship is expressed in and underlined by the riddle. Just as roof tiles cost something to install but

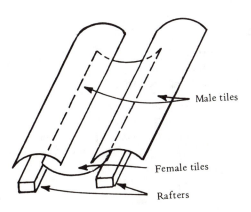

Figure 4. A Diagram of Clay Roof Tiles

protect one in time of need, so compadrazgo costs something
in terms of money and ritual obligations but provides help
in time of need. A degree of formality and respect is necessary
to maintain this relationship. Hence, one should never talk
publicly about the sexual activity of one's compadres. As in
other genres of frivolous language, riddles help to underline
norms by appearing to flaunt them.

The second type of riddle is asked as a casual question,
without special twists of sound or parallel syntax. This kind
of riddle, which seems more popular than the first, is used
in children's play groups and in men's drunken speech. It is
more subtle and causes greater laughter than the first, more
structured kind because its form does not immediately give
away the fact that it is a riddle. The person to whom the
riddle is asked must first realize that the question is being
asked in fun and then respond in the appropriate joking
manner. If he should miss the fact that he has been asked a
riddle and answers it as an ordinary question, he suffers
ridicule from the listeners.

The following example came from the conversation of two
men on the road from Chamula to San Cristóbal. An informant overheard the exchange and reconstructed it later with
no difficulty, for it was a well-known riddle. One of the men,
who had a cold and was forced to blow his nose frequently,
casually asked his friend:

Man 1:
    mi šana? k'usi li vinik sbie.
    Do you know what that man's name is?
        mi ?o šavil li vinik.
        Have you seen that man?

    k'alal ta šanave, ta šyal ta šmuy,
    When he walks, he goes down and up,
        ta šyal ta šmuy ta spas k'alal ta šanave.
        Down and up he goes when he is walking.

    mi ?o šavil ?un.
    Have you seen him?

Man 2:
    ?a vul ša ta ko?nton.
    Now I remember.

Man 1:
ʔa veno, mi šanaʔ bu nakal li vinik sbiʔe.
Well, do you know where he lives, that man?

Man 2:
ʔa mu hnaʔ ʔun bi.
No, I don't know, after all.

Man 1:
pere ʔoy hun vinik, pere mu snaʔ šlub tahmek.
But there is such a man, but he never gets tired.
skotol k'ak'al ta šanav tahmek.
Every day he walks a lot.

mi šanaʔ k'usi ʔun.
Do you know what he is?

Man 2:
hnaʔ
Yes, I know.

Man 1:
ʔa veno, pere bu nakal.
Ah, well then, where does he live?
šanaʔ un.
Do you know?

Man 2:
pere li vinik šavale nakal ta hniʔtik.
Well, the man you're talking about lives in our noses.
haʔ li hsimtike ta šyal ta šmuy ta spase.
It's our snot that goes down and up.

(They both laugh.)

The riddle about the mucus is funny in part because it deals
with a topic that has a definite etiquette associated with it.
To blow one's nose, by closing one nostril with a finger and
exhaling forcefully through the other, is proper anytime and
almost anywhere, but to let one's nose run is considered
extremely bad manners. For the mucus to drip on one's
clothing is even worse. For example, *simalal ʔanȼ* ("snotty
woman") is considered a very strong insult. To have dried
mucus on one's clothing is a sure sign of poor personal habits
and lack of standards. Thus, riddles, like the other genres of
frivolous language, are funny because they address topics and
situations that deviate from norms in everyday life. By

calling public attention to breaches in etiquette and normative behavior, they etch the norms all the clearer in the public
eye.

Time-Space Attributes

Throughout the subgenres of frivolous language, the
present social order, at the center of the universe, is both
assumed and informally defended. This defensive attitude,
enhanced by the humorous structure and subject matter,
unifies, for Chamulas, various kinds of verbal behavior whose
analogues in other cultures may have little in common.
Together these subgenres function as a kind of informal
charter for Chamula behavior. The charter is informal in the
sense that the settings for performance do not have ritual or
religious significance. The characteristic statement of a norm
in the subgenres is usually given in negative form. That is,
incorrect models for behavior are proposed, alluded to, or
acted out. The subgenres nevertheless form a "charter"
because they imply their normative opposite. The ambiguity
and ambivalence of the content of the subgenres, combined
with the complementary use of verbal play and multiple
meaning, which are also ambiguous, help to emphasize the
purity and desirability of good social behavior. For example,
to joke with one's compadre about his sexual activity is
improper. But to laugh at a hypothetical case of such
improper action is to say "This doesn't fit." Humor in
frivolous language, then, is an index of "bad fit" in social
categories. Humor is also active in that it elicits laughter,
which is a strong sanction against deviant behavior.

The time-space principle contributes to the working of
frivolous language as an informal charter. First, most behavior
settings for frivolous talk are well within the "safe" range of
the time-space continuum, that is, in familiar places in the
present. Second, most of the negative phenomena that they
humorously verbalize have a precedent in true ancient narrative, the narrative genre dealing with events of the first three
creations. Thus, frivolous talk dips into the reservoir of
information contained in other genres of pure words in order

to provide commonly-known, asocial examples. The referent items with distant time-space associations are nearly always introduced in order to place the correct behavior in sharp relief against them. Participants and listeners, in other words, must know about the coming of order in the past in order to maintain it informally in the present with appropriate precultural or asocial images.

An example of a lie that was very popular in Chamula illustrates the working of the time-space principle. The story is classified as a lie, incidentally, rather than a true recent narrative, because no one claimed to be sure that it had happened just as he told it.

Sometime in December 1968, the past presidente's wife threatened to leave him, complaining that he did not buy meat for his household. All that he bought was more land. He was angered by her criticism, for he knew that more land would guarantee them a better maize supply. One day they had this angry exchange:

Wife:
  č'abal k'usi šavič' talel.
  You bring home nothing.
    č'abal k'usi šaman talel.
    You buy nothing.
  č'abal hbek'et hti? ška?i.
  I have no meat, which I crave.

Husband:
  mi šak'an ?abek'et čati? ?ava?i, ti?an kat.
  If you crave meat, eat my penis.

No one knew for sure whether or not she had left him after that squelch, but the story had spread throughout several hamlets of Chamula by the time I left for the United States in January 1969. Nearly everyone agreed that the woman's demands were unreasonable, for her husband supplied her with abundant maize and beans. Furthermore, he provided her with ample status as the wife of a past presidente. These factors should have sufficed. Moreover, meat is a luxury, which most Chamula families have only for fiesta days, curing ceremonies, and other ritual meals. It was therefore improper for her to demand a regular supply of it. The humor of the lie is enhanced by the fact that meat also means "sexual relations." Thus, she could be understood to be asking for a more active sex life. However, it would also be outrageously improper for her actually to bite her husband's penis, as he "invited" her to do, for oral-genital contact is considered to be animal-like. Furthermore, certain predatory animals are know to have the custom of subsisting only on meat. The husband therefore likened his wife's appetites for meat and sex to those of predatory animals. Social distance played an important role in making the past presidente's squelch both humorous and effective. He likened the woman's appetites not only to beasts of the forest but to marginal human beings at the edge of the earth, whose behavioral associations are definitely not within the present moral universe.

(6) Traditional Games

> *Elder Child:*
> Where's my dog?
> I'm going to whistle for him.
>
> He's not here.
> Where can he be?
>
> *Younger child:*
> Here I am!
> Here I am!
>
> *Elder Child:*
> Shut up!
> *You* can't talk.
>
> —From a Chamula game

Traditional games (*tahimol*) include all those games that have definite rules. Improvised games that children play are not included, because Chamulas believe that such games change radically from performance to performance. Included are games which, in Chamula terms, "do not know how to change" (*mu sna? shel sbaik*). Significantly, both the verbal and nonverbal aspects of traditional games belong to the supercategory of recent words. Therefore, it would seem that Chamulas regard patterned, predictable action as analogous to or equivalent to traditional language. Since traditional games belong to recent words, they are also associated with the present social order. They attempt both to teach it and to maintain it informally.

There are two subtypes of traditional games. Children's traditional games (*tahimol sventa h?ololetik*) are generally those that are not wholly verbal. Younger children of from three to ten years old lack the knowledge of language necessary for playing verbal punning games. The genre of traditional games that is intended for adults (*tahimol sventa muk'ta kirsano*) consists almost exclusively of verbal humor or verbal games. Most humorous verbal behavior for adults overlaps with the category of frivolous language (Fig. 3).

The subgenre of frivolous language that ranks most important as an adult game is truly frivolous talk or verbal dueling. Curiously, although older children of from ten to twelve years in age play verbal games nearly as much as do adults, such games are considered to be more typical of adult entertainment than of children's entertainment. This distinction follows the reasoning that adults have greater skill in the use and manipulation of language than do children and adolescents. Generally there is an increase in the sophisticated use of language from children's games through adult games. Children's games emphasize verbatim repetition of words and phrases. In adult games, however, multiple meanings of a single word or phrase receive the emphasis. Language learning and socialization predominate in children's games; language use and manipulation, such as multiple referents in puns, prevail in adult verbal games.

Children's Games

Chamula children play strikingly few nonverbal games of skill. Wrestling and footracing occur often among little boys, but these are never staged in a formal way. There is a boys' game in which improvised vehicles—usually loose planks placed over two rounded logs—are ridden down a hill or slope. These are not raced, but each participant is given a turn and his ride is judged good or bad by the others; no one wins or loses. Small girls are said to compete to see who can make the most tortillas or small clay pots in a given time. Yet just as often, the activity in itself suffices, and there is no winner or loser. Neither boys nor girls engage in any sport or athletic activity unless they have been to school, where boys learn to play soccer and basketball, and both boys and girls learn Ladino games, marches in information, and drill instruction. Boys who have been to school also learn how to play marbles. Their rules are the same as the Ladino children's. These activities, however, are unfamiliar to the great majority of Chamula children, who never go to school.

Traditional games are well known to all children. Although apparently not numerous, they have wide popularity. Some of them are here described briefly, followed by the complete text of a performance showing the nature of the verbal content of the games. The text should also illustrate the unitary nature of verbal and nonverbal behavior; that is, their joint behavior as language.

Scratch-up-the-coin

Any number of boys may play the game of scratch-up-the-coin (*hoḏ'olahel ta tak'in*). Someone presents a coin, which he agrees beforehand will be spent among them all for candy or the like. To decide who will hide the coin, they count to ten in the order in which they happen to be standing, each child saying the consecutive number as his turn comes. The child who says "ten" is the one who gets to bury the coin. While the others hide their eyes, he buries it in the dirt, pasture grass, or forest floor. The hider then returns to the spot where the others are waiting and tells them to go hunting. The hider gives clues, while the hunters take sticks and machetes and dig around in likely places. The hider may give false clues and actually deliver the coin to the hunter whom he chooses. The one who finds the coin may either hide it again or be the one to buy some treat for all of the players.

Dog Knot

Two boys play the game of dog knot (*bok ḏ'i?*). One chases the other and, when he is caught, throws him to the ground. The chaser tries to get the other boy into the position for sexual mounting, like dogs. He then fastens himself to the other with his arms and simulates intercourse. The object is for the "female" to disengage himself from the attacker, who is now attached to him. He may kick, turn over, or use whatever method he wishes in order to get rid of the "male." Once the "male" has been physically disengaged, he grabs the tunic of the other from behind and holds on to it as the "female" tries to run away. When the "female" finally escapes, the boy playing her part becomes the male aggressor and begins the game once again. The rules are few, but strict. The "female" may not take off her tunic in order to escape the male's grasp. Human copulation positions are not permitted, because it is considered more difficult for the aggressor to get the "female" into the correct canine position. This game is a great favorite at fiestas for boys up to about twelve years old.

Peter the Lizard

Both girls and boys play the game Peter the Lizard (*petul ʔokoȼ*), but in sexually segregated groups. Children as old as thirteen or fourteen may play, although the most typical age is five to eight years. The usual setting is the woods. The searchers stay in one place and hide their eyes. Peter the Lizard, the one who is "it," goes into the woods to hide. He shouts *la ʔ me ʼ* ("Come on!") when he is hidden, and the searchers go out to find him. As they hunt him, they shout the rhymed verse:

buyot, buyot, buyot, petul ʔokoȼ.
Where are you? Where are you? Where are you, Peter
    Lizard?

Peter should answer with a whistle if they are off his track. If they are close, he should say nothing, so as not to give himself away. When they find Peter, he should attempt to run away. He is usually unsuccessful, and all the searchers pile on top of him to trap him. The one who finds him first gets to be Peter the Lizard for the next round.

Demon Game

Two boys usually play the game demon (*tahimol pukuh*). The most appropriate setting is the woods. One boy hides while the demon hides his eyes. Then the demon goes to find his victim. When he finds him, he blindfolds his victim with a rag and carries him on his back to a "cave," which is any arbitrary place, where he deposits his victim. The dual object is for the demon to lose the victim in the woods, and for the victim to escape at any stage of the game. Once the victim is deposited in the cave, the demon goes away and hides for a few minutes to give the victim a chance to get away and hide again. Then the whole thing is repeated. If the territory is familiar and the children are old enough, there is no danger of their getting lost. However, informants say that children occasionally do become lost while playing demon, thereby doubtless enforcing the Chamula belief in a demon that is supposed to steal people and leave them lost in the woods.

Flag Game

Both sexes may play the flag game (*tahimol banyera*), but usually in segregated groups. Their age ranges from five to about fifteen years. The most common setting for the game is the open sheep pastures that are often located near house compounds. I saw no more than about twelve players engaged in this game at a single performance, but Chamulas say that as many as twenty can play. The person who is *yahval banyera* ("owner of the flag") ties a rag or other piece of cloth loosely to the end of a stick or pole about ten feet long. He holds it and stands in the center of a circle (about fifteen feet in diameter) formed by the other players, who are called *kačuko ʔetik* ("Guatemalans"). He then inclines the pole to a height just over the players' raised hands and begins to swing the flag around the circle, jerking it up when someone seems about to reach it. When someone finally grabs it, he must jerk it off the role and run with it. The others pursue him until someone catches him and forcibly takes away the flag. The process is then repeated with the rescuer of the flag as the new "owner of the flag."

Weasel Game

The weasel game (*tahimol saʔben*) may be played by children of either sex but is usually in segregated groups. There are four parts, and four children are required. The older children usually play the parts of the "owner of the chicken" (*yahval ʔalak'*) and the "dog" (*ḋ'iʔ*). The younger children take the parts of the "chicken" (*ʔalak'*) and "weasel" (*saʔben*). The dog and man are perhaps played by the older children because they are more completely socialized and thus fit the more human roles. The man (usually the oldest child) and dog form a corral by joining hands, and the chicken gets inside it. The weasel runs around the corral trying to grab the chicken by the hands and pull him out to steal him away. The man and dog try to prevent this by raising and lowering their hands to protect the chicken. When the weasel finally manages to steal the chicken, they run away, and the man sends his dog to chase them. The dog, usually being an older child, manages to catch them and throw them to the ground, which ends the sequence. Although informants say that roles change in repeated sequences of the game, the only time that I saw it played, the players kept the same roles for all sequences.

Following is a dialogue taken from a performance of this game. It is characterized by the exact repetition of key phrases, words, and syntax, which is no doubt an advantage for language-learning. These stylistic traits are also present in the marginal genres. The oldest child has an important role in supervising and directing the activities of the others:

Owner (oldest child, directing one of the two younger children):
    veno, Ho?ot la me sa?benot ?un.
    Well, you are the weasel.

Dog (middle child):
    Ho?on la me ¢'i?un ?ek ?un.
    I'm the dog then.

Owner (to other youngest child):
    Ho?ot la me ?alak'ot, ?ek ?un.
    You're the chicken, then.

    va?un, ta hpastik hkoraltik ?un.
    Well, let's make the corral.

(He joins hands with the dog.)

veno, bučʼun ti ?alak'e ha? me ta š?oč ta yut koral ?un.
Well, whoever is the chicken should get inside the corral.
    bučʼun ti sa?bene ha? ta škom ta pat koral ne.
    Whoever is the weasel should stay outside the corral.
    bučʼun ti ¢'i?e Ho?on ta hči?in ?ek ne.
    Whoever is the dog will stay with me.

(To chicken)

k'alal mi tal s¢akot ti sa?bene, ta me ša?avan ?un.
When the weasel comes to grab you, you yell.

Chicken:
> ta me ši²oč ta koral ²un.
> I'll go into the corral.

(He enters.)

Owner:
> ²očan.
> Go on in.

(Owner and dog make a corral with their arms to protect the chicken.)

Chicken (making proper squawking noises):
> ²eke
> Squawk!
>> ²eke
>> Squawk!

(The weasel grabs it, catching the protectors off guard.)

Owner:
> bat ša ta čon ti kalak'tike.
> Our chicken has been stolen by the beast.
>> bat ša ta čon.
>> He's been stolen by the beast!

> bu ti čon.
> Where's the beast?
>> bu ti čon, mu sa²ben.
>> Where's the beast, the bad weasel?
>>> bu ti hȼ'i²tik.
>>> Where's our dog?

Chicken (struggling to free himself from the weasel):
> mu hna² buy.
> I don't know where.

Dog:
> li²une.
> Here I am.

Owner (to dog):
> ²an.
> Shut up.
>> mu šak'opoh ²ek ²un.
>> You aren't supposed to talk.

Chicken:
    liʔ šae.
    Here he is.
      liʔ šae.
      Here he is.

Owner:
    ʔik'o talel ti ¢'iʔe.
    Call the dog.

    (To dog)

    ʔusko
    Sic 'im!
      ʔusko.
      Sic 'im!

    mako me ta be.
    Block his path.
      mako me ta be.
      Block his path!

(Chicken escapes from weasel.)
    lok' ša.
    He got away!
      lok' ša.
      He got away!

    haʔ lasibtas ʔel, mu ¢'iʔe.
    Well, you frightened him (the weasel), you damned dog.
      haʔ la skolta ʔeč' ʔel.
      He let him get away.

    le šae.
    There he is!
      le šae.
      There he is!

    ʔusko.
    Sic 'im!
      ʔusko.
      Sic 'im!

    bu ti ¢'iʔ.
    Where's the dog?
      bu ti ¢'iʔ.
      Where's the dog?

Dog:
  li'e.
  Here.

Owner:
  ʔusko.
  Sic 'im!
    ʔusko.
    Sic 'im!

  mako me ta be.
  Block his path!
    mako me ta be.
    Block his path!

  te me tal.
  There he comes!
    te me tal.
    There he comes!

(Dog grabs weasel by the tail; that is, he grabs the weasel's tunic from behind. The chicken gets away when the weasel turns to free himself from the dog.)

Owner:
  ȼako me.
  Grab him!
    ȼako me.
    Grab him!

  mu me šakolta.
  Don't let him go!
    mu me šakolta.
    Don't let him go!

Dog:
  ʔay ʔay. lah ša stiʔun.
  Oh! Oh! He bit me!
    ʔay ʔay. lah ša stiʔun.
    Oh! Oh! He bit me!

(He releases the weasel, for the weasel literally bites him on the arm.)

Owner:
  k'uši bat.
  Where did he go?

(To dog)
ši šabat ʔek.
You go that way.
  ši čibat ʔeke.
  I'll go this way.
bu ti hȼ'iʔtik.
Where are our dogs?

Dog:
li ʔune.
Here I am.

Owner:
ʔan.
Shut up!
  k'u čaʔal čak'opoh ʔek ʔun.
  Why are you talking again?

Dog:
ʔaaa. pere yuʔun č'ay koʔnton.
Oh. I forgot.

Owner (chastising dog):
k'alal mi hkik'ote, mu ša me šatak'avʔun.
When I call you, don't answer me any more.

Dog:
veno. moʔoh ša.
Okay. I won't any more.

Owner:
liʔ ša li mu saʔbene
Here comes the weasel!

ʔusko
Sic 'im!
  ʔusko
  Sic 'im!

leʔe.
There!
  leʔe.
  There!

(Dog corners weasel.)
  mu me šakolta.
  Don't let him go!

mu me šakolta.
Don't let him go!

ʔusko.
Sic 'im!
  ʔusko.
  Sic 'im!

Dog (grabs weasel and speaks to him):
mala ʔun to ʔun.
Wait a minute for me.

ta la šahmah škaltik ʔun ti k'alal mi la htaʔot ta ¢akel ne.
We're going to play like I'm hitting you when I catch you
  and grab you.

Weasel (to dog):
ʔan, pere mu me ¢o¢uk šamahun ʔun.
Oh, but don't hit me hard.

Dog:
ʔan, moʔoh ʔun.
No, I won't.

*(He throws the weasel down and pins him to the ground,
biting him good-naturedly on the neck.)*

In addition to the repetition of words and phrases, another
characteristic of children's traditional games that stands out
clearly in this game is their effort to duplicate the categories
of cultural and noncultural behavior, their interaction, and
their conflict. The eldest child asserts that the children
playing the parts of the animals should not speak, which
emphasizes language as an important difference between
cultural and natural behavior. In the text of the weasel game,
the man, in fact, speaks the most; the dog says more than he
should, as noted by the owner; the chicken speaks some;
and the weasel hardly speaks at all. This situation reflects
the Chamula view of the life cycle as a metaphor of human
progress through the four creations. In the game, younger
children play the roles with the more distant time-space
associations; older children assume the roles with closer
time-space associations.

The primary spatial pattern that exists among the participants is a corral formed by a man and his dog. A chicken is

inside the corral and a weasel is outside. The purpose of
the game is for the man and his dog (a domestic animal) to
protect the chicken (also a domestic animal) from the weasel
(a predatory wild animal), who tries to get the chicken and
eat it. In the one performance of this game that I was able to
witness, the weasel caught the chicken and bit it. When the
dog tried to intervene in the chicken's favor, the weasel also
bit the dog. It was unclear whether the weasel succeeded
in killing the chicken. The dog finally caught the weasel, but
only after suffering a bite. Order—that is, the victory of a
domestic animal over a wild animal—prevailed, but only with
confusion and difficulty. Once the corral broke apart, the
delimitation of natural and cultural boundaries became less
certain, and security disappeared. Both chicken and dog
were bitten in the play setting. This was really an honest
representation of reality, an example of the unfortunate
difference between ideal and real behavior.

Children appear to learn through this game that biting and
preying on others are a part of the natural world and are
also, through the concept of animal soul companions, a part
of the social world. For instance, strong animal soul companions, such as jaguars and weasels, are carnivorous and are
associated with the woods and tropical lowlands. Both of
these places have distant time-space associations and are
potentially dangerous. The social spirit, however, should
redirect the predatory appetites of a person with a strong
animal soul companion to the altruistic defense of his weaker
fellows. Conversely, the asocial spirit allows the natural
predatory appetites of witches' animal soul companions to
behave with no restraint. Therefore, the weasel game may be
seen as an effort to teach social distance and the nature-
culture boundary—concepts that are necessary for understanding the universe.

Nearly all children's games have this quality of teaching
through imitation of behavior appropriate to different social
categories. Competition per se is of little importance. Skill
and achievement are also minimized. When there are winners,
as in the coin game, their success is complete only upon
redistribution of whatever is won as a prize. More often than

not, there are no winners. Successful performance of a role is usually considered of itself to make the game worthwhile. Standard Chamula values are taught through games. Some of the most important of these are respect for rank, separateness between human and nonhuman activities and beings, and the importance of equal distribution of goods.

Adult Games

In contrast with children's traditional games, in which both verbal content and physical action are of equal importance, the few adult traditional games that are recognized are strictly verbal. To my knowledge, neither Chamula men nor women engage in any traditional sports, nonpractical exhibitions of skill, or other activities that might be called games of physical action—with the possible exception of certain ritual games. Nor are there any games for both adults and children. Adults make and give to their children small toys that are miniatures of objects which the boys and girls will use as adults, yet I have never seen a parent actually play with a child using the toys. The parent of the same sex will show the child how to use the toys if he uses them incorrectly, but play settings involving adults and their children do not seem to exist.

There is some reason to speculate that lack of leisure time may be the best reason for lack of traditional adult games, beyond verbal games. Chamula men and women are ceaselessly busy. When they have leisure time, they are likely to spend it at one of the many annual fiestas in Chamula Ceremonial Center. In the daily round, men do not have large segments of leisure time. While walking along the path with friends, the time is perfect for informal joking and playing verbal punning games. Such a setting does not allow time for any other kind of game. Likewise, the innumerable occasions, formal and informal, on which men drink rum and chicha serve as perfect settings for verbal games, but not for other kinds of games. Women do not have much leisure time either. Ideally, when they are not involved in the daily water-carrying, wood-gathering, food-preparation, and child-care activities, they are processing raw wool or weaving woolen clothing. This routine provides ample time for verbal entertainment but very little time for activities that would distract them from performing household tasks. Women seem to prefer true recent narratives as verbal entertainment. Men also tell true recent narratives but generally prefer several genres of frivolous language as verbal entertainment, especially truly frivolous talk, buried speech, and lies.

The only men who play games other than verbal ones with any regularity are the political cargoholders and their assistants who have had considerable experience in the Ladino world. They occasionally have large amounts of leisure time, during which they must be present at the town hall but have nothing particular to do. This group of men includes very few officials over the age of forty. For amazing lengths of time they play a card game like the game of hearts. I did not learn the rules, but the Ladino secretary explained that the game is played as they had learned it from Ladinos on the coffee plantations. The group who plays this card game, however, includes only a fraction of one percent of the total male population of Chamula. In sum, although adult games exist as a separate genre in the Chamula taxonomy of pure words, in reality they overlap nearly completely with the subgenres of frivolous language.

Ritual Games

There is another kind of game that bears the generic label *tahimol* but which Chamulas are unable to include consistently anywhere in the taxonomy. It actually forms a conceptual bridge between recent words and ancient words. The genre, which occurs as a part of or an adjunct to religious ritual, is known as ritual games (*tahimol sventa k'inetik*). Since games in this genre occur in set fashion year after year and are performed only by certain ritual personnel, they have attributes that are typical of the domain of ancient words, the other supercategory of Chamula pure words. When pressed, Chamulas so classified them, while insisting that they also had attributes of traditional games. However,

Chamulas preferred to ignore them altogether in the taxonomy, for reasons that are still unclear. These games consist mostly of ritual actions and gestures. It follows that the limited amount of language which they contain resembles the style of the genre of ancient words called language for rendering holy. In fact, however, they are an intermediate genre, forming a point of transition between recent words and ancient words, while belonging officially to neither category.

The concept of *tahimol* ("play" or "game") is important to each fiesta within the annual cycle as well as to the cycle itself. Nearly all major fiestas have several performances by clowns (*šokavan*, literally "ropers"), who follow the fire bull charged with fireworks, "fighting" it as it runs around in a circle in the atrium of the church. Such bull fights are enjoyed tremendously by the spectators, who refer to them casually as a "kind of game" (*htos tahimol*). Yet the Chamulas' only explanation for them is simply, "That's the custom" (*stalel heč*). Although the game of fire bull is a customary action of the fiestas, it is apparently enjoyed strictly for its amusement value. No one has an outwardly reverent, respectful attitude toward this activity. Significantly, such games occur in a sacred space (the church atrium) but before the principal ritual personnel and ritual objects have appeared. The clowns typically perform several times on the morning of a fiesta, but while they do, the principal ritual focus remains inside the church. The clowns disappear before the noon procession of the saints. Furthermore, the clowns chase the bull in a clockwise direction around the cross in the atrium, the opposite direction to that in which the saints will march around the same sacred space. In this sense, the ritual game is an inversion of proper temporal and spatial orientations; it is an extreme statement of the childhood of mankind, before the coming of cosmic order. In a similar but not so extreme sense, children's traditional games are not-yet-perfect imitations of adult behavior. Their intent is positive, while they themselves are imperfect. It is possible, therefore, that ritual games are both "in" and "not in" the category of pure words, because they represent dramas of reversal and of the precultural conditions of mankind. Ordinary games teach by the imitation of proper behavior and by exposing and laughing at deviant behavior. Ritual games tend to represent complete reversals of and antecedents to cultural behavior.

Ritual games have a similar meaning in the Festival of Games (*k'in tahimoltik*). This major five-day fiesta, celebrated in February, corresponds generally to the pre-Lenten carnival time in the Catholic calendar. It was the best-attended fiesta in 1968. The fiesta is totally different in spirit from the other annual fiestas in that it has mixed secular and sacred significance. At one and the same time it provides the occasion for the annual cult worship of the sun and moon (Christ and the Virgin Mary) and for a remarkable series of ritual games. Included is an all-night torchlight procession, in which three groups (one from each of the barrios) bring bulls up to the highlands for a ritual sacrifice at dawn. They arrive at about the same time and parade playfully with the bulls around the Chamula plaza before the sacrifice. Structurally, this is not unlike the more common fire bull game. A week later, as an adjunct to the major ritual segments of the fiesta, a mock war is fought with horse manure, in which the two sides, Guatemala and Mexico, compete with each other three times, each side winning once, the third time being a draw.

Chamulas said that the spirit of these and the other games played at the Festival of Games was one of fun, that the purpose of the fiesta was for all to have a good time. Yet everyone knew that the most important of all Chamula deities, the sun and the moon, were also being honored at the fiesta. This seeming paradox between great fun and religious significance may be explained by the very nature of the sun and the moon, who were the precursors and givers of all order, and who therefore are most appropriately surrounded and even preceded ritually by ambiguous and negative symbols. Just as the Festival of Games occurs very early in the annual fiesta cycle, it also occurs in the dark of the moon and at the beginning of the annual solar and agricultural cycles. This is a period of short days, killing frosts, and agricultural dormancy. Likewise, games, which are frivolous activities of youth and abandon, are associated with the less socialized end of the ontogenetic cycle of human development. Just as games provide a means of social control for adults, the Festival of Games provides a ritual restatement of the dawn of normative order: the creation of the solar and lunar cycles, the beginning of festivals and agriculture, the integration of the three Chamula barrios as equal members of a federal unit, and the knowledge of good and evil. Just as deviant behavior occurs in the Festival of Games (including transvestism, horse manure battles, and perverse activities of monkey-demon characters), so it occurs in the sexual fantasies of truly frivolous talk, in the human misfortunes of true recent narrative, and in some of the children's games, such as dog knot and demons. Norms are made known by their breach as well as by their observance.

In some respects, the ambiguous position of ritual games among other games, and of the Festival of Games among other fiestas, is explained by the fact that they have a double task. First, in their informal aspect, they teach and inculcate values by both example and breach of norms, which is generally the function of the entire category of recent words in the oral tradition. Second, in their more formal aspect, they provide, in ritual settings, dramatic examples of pre-cultural behavior, which sharply contrast with the positive assertion of the values of the social order in ancient words. The basic characteristics of these two categories of pure words are actually extensions of the two fundamental moods that pervade Chamula social life and thought, its formal (order-giving) and informal (order-maintaining) aspects.

(7) True Ancient Narrative

When San Juan arrived with his sheep, they
 saw it all:
How he arrived,
How he began to prepare his home,
How he went to bring the building stones,
How the bell in the tree rang all by itself.

The ancestors saw it.
 And when they were old, they told their
  children how they had come to be.

That is why everyone knows how the very first
 people came to be;
 When at last the ancestors died, they had
  already told their children how things
  were long ago.
  —Salvador Guzmán Bakbolom, Text 137

True ancient narrative (*bač'i ʔantivo
k'op*) is a genre that relates the true events of the ancient
past. No exact period of occurrence distinguishes the events
of true recent narrative from those of true ancient narrative.
The time spans involved are relative ones. Generally, the
events of the Fourth Creation, the present era, are reported
in true recent narrative; the events of the First through the
Third Creations are reported in true ancient narrative. The
boundary between the two spans of time can be as recent as
the oldest living generation, or it can be as much as four-
hundred years ago, depending on individual opinions of the
informants. The importance difference between the present
era and the past three eras lies on a qualitative, not a quanti-
tative, level. Events of the first three creations could probably
not occur at the present time in Chamula, although they
could easily occur at the present time in distant places. The
only circumstance that would cause them to recur in Chamula
would be the failure of Chamulas to please the saints and
other deities. This failure could bring about punishment and
the possible destruction of the Fourth Creation. Such a
possibility stands as a constant threat. Generally, however,
the plots, circumstances, characters, and places of occurrence

of true ancient narrative are not typical of present Chamula life. These narratives are concerned with the creation and institutionalization of order on earth, particularly in Chamula. Generally, the First Creation narratives report the transition from precultural chaos to order. The Second and Third Creation narratives report events of less etiological significance than those of the First Creation, including the secondary works of major deities, feats of minor supernaturals, tales of anthropomorphic animals, and supernatural tests and punishments of human beings. True ancient narrative thus includes much of what is frequently glossed as myth, legend, and folktale. However, those European genres mean little in the Chamula taxonomy. All true ancient narratives are simply regarded as true accounts of the past.

Settings for Performance

True ancient narratives are by custom neither owned nor performed nor listened to by specific groups of people. Elderly people tend to tell such narratives more than younger people only because age is respected and older people in fact know more about the past. Therefore, they are asked the pertinent questions that stimulate the performance of the genre more often than are children and young adults. This does not mean that younger persons are prohibited by custom from telling such stories. They often do, although not as frequently as their elders.

The setting for telling such tales is just as flexible as are reconteur and audience. Formal settings are not required, with one important exception. The mood in which these tales are told, however, is a serious one. They contain critical background material and explanations for the existing social order. Their spirit is thus not frivolous. Just as the presence of candles, incense, pine needles, and a cross can make almost any place sacred, so certain subject matter, linguistic style, and manner of suggesting a topic can make any place a proper setting for the performance of true ancient narrative. Although a tale of this genre may be funny and cause uproarious laughter, it is not told just for amusement. In this respect it contrasts with many of the genres of frivolous language, which, although they ultimately serve as devices of social control, are often thought to be performed just for fun. No one in Chamula, however, ever says simply, "Tell me a story." A performance is nearly always preceded by an object, circumstance, or experience that needs elucidation with information from the past. Such a concrete stimulus suggests the relevant narrative for a specific performance of true ancient narrative. Moreover, it is the case with both narrative genres, ancient and recent, that the raconteurs do not worry about verbatim retelling of tales as they have heard them, so long as the kernel idea is retained. Nor is extra embellishment necessary. Proper narrative style, however, is considered necessary for a good performance.

Style

The narrative style used for telling true ancient narrative is generally more formal with regard to couplets and meta-phor than is that for true recent narrative. Nearly all of the genres of recent words emphasize repetition of key words, concepts, and syntax. Multiple meanings for single words are also important, as in punning. True ancient narrative uses the same devices in a more formal, elaborate fashion. Parallel structure and nonparallel metaphoric restatement remain, but their content now consists of religious symbols instead of, say, deviant behavior. Multifaceted symbols of ritual importance take the place of sexual and derisive puns. Multiple meaning continues, but its content changes and its density increases. True ancient narrative is characterized by several stylistic devices of its own, in addition to those common to the recent narrative genre.

The repetition of synonyms that have a similar sound is one important device used through all the genres of ancient words. It restates a thing or idea in another form which sounds like the first, as in the following example:

> ha? la ta sk'an ?oy sk'u?,
> (San Juan) wanted them to have clothing,

same-sound
synonyms
	{	ti yalab,
		His progeny,
		   ti snič'nab ?une.
		   His children.

Strings of stylized transitional clauses of about the same syllable length and terminal sound are another important device, which adds narrative elegance and prepares the listener for something important to follow. More practically, it is an excellent stalling device when the narrator is not entirely sure of what to say next. Parallel syntax, a device used in the marginal genres and in recent words, plays an even more important part in the style of true ancient narratives. It is related to the parallel metaphoric couplet. An example of both these devices follows:

?a li sčih li san huan
San Juan's sheep

stylized
transitional
clauses
	{	tana le ?une—
		Most certainly—
		  heč ?o šal ?un,
		  And therefore,
		    k'el?avil ?un—
		    Pay attention—

parallel
syntax
	{	?oy sak sk'u?,
		Provide white clothing,
		  ?oy ?ik' sk'u?.
		  Provide black clothing.

Finally, the device of metaphoric couplets, common to several other genres, occurs in all of the genres of ancient words. It is so common, in fact, that it can be taken for granted whenever Chamulas speak formally, in whatever genre, for whatever reason. There are two types of metaphoric couplet. The nonparallel metaphoric couplet, simply divided by a caesura, contains a statement and restatement of one idea. Parallel syntax and sound are not present. The semantic element is given once and then repeated, affirmed or answered in a phrase of approximately the same length.

These forms are not necessarily stable from one performance to the next. The second type, the parallel metaphoric couplet, is more typical of the other genres of ancient words than it is of true ancient narrative. It is "bound," where the nonparallel form is not, in that the two parts of the couplet usually remain together and recombine together as a unit. The first part implies and requires the second part. They resemble the fixed dyadic formulas that are used in many parts of the world, including the Ancient Maya. They are the stylistic building blocks of the other formal genres. The following example, which tells of the removal of the primeval oceans in the First Creation by the hand of *htotik*, the sun (Text 182), includes both forms of the metaphoric couplet:

lik la sbek' batel ti nab.
He began to sweep away the sea.
   k'alal la ti sbek' batel ti nab, ta huhot
   When he swept away the sea, the earth
šokon banamil.
   was empty in all directions.

nonparallel metaphoric couplet
{ puru ša la banamil kom ta ʔora.
  Now only the land remained, nothing more.
   pero puru la stenleh.
   Only the open plains, nothing more.

parallel metaphoric couplets
{ muʔyuk la viɟetik,
  No mountains,
   muʔyuk la kirsano,
   No people.

{ muʔyuk la ton,
  No stones,
   muʔyuk la teʔtik,
   No woods,

puru la baɟ'i banamil.
Only the earth itself.

A Ritual Setting

There is only one ritual setting of a narrative that the Chamulas classify as true ancient narrative. With this one exception, the physical settings for the performance of the genre are not prescribed. The exception to the usual context of this genre occurs at none other than the Festival of Games, already noted for its peculiar and ambiguous place in the annual fiesta cycle. Two weeks before and during this five-day festival, a life-term cargo official called the *ʔabito* (also known as *piškal*), meaning "crier," reads a paper in Spanish which announces the arrival of the Spaniards. He also announces the days on which the fiesta will be celebrated each year. This announcement, though officially "read," is actually recited from memory at various fixed places in Chamula Ceremonial Center. The "reading of the paper" has great symbolic significance, although very few listeners understand what the crier is saying because he does not speak or pronounce Spanish well and it is not widely understood in Chamula. The Spanish language is symbolically significant in that it is precultural, that is, it preceded Tzotzil. Even so, the message is important. Appropriately, it serves as the charter for the Festival of Games. Without it, informants said, the fiesta would not be proper and could not be celebrated. The groups who listen to the reading usually include the other Festival of Games personnel. They shout "Viva" (Spanish for "Long may he live!" or "Cheers!") at the end of each phrase uttered by the crier. On this occasion, true ancient narrative functions as an active part of the total ritual performance. Verbatim recitation is necessary each time it is performed. A portion of the text of the crier's speech follows:[1]

> *Crier:*
> viva ʔel mehiko.
> Vino de México.
> He came from Mexico City.
> > viva ʔel vatemala.
> > Vino de Guatemala.
> > He came from Guatemala.
> > > viva ʔel tušta.
> > > Vino de Tuxtla.
> > > He came from Tuxtla Gutiérrez.
> > > > viva li čapa.
> > > > Vino de Chiapa.
> > > > He came from Chiapa de Corzo.

viva li san kisto.
Vino de San Cristóbal.
He came from San Cristóbal.

Audience (shouting):
Viva.
¡Viva!
Long may he live!

Crier:
viva kon su vantera.
Vino con su bandera.
He came with his flag.
viva kon su tampora.
Vino con su tambor.
He came with his drum.
viva kon su korneto.
Vino con su corneta.
He came with his trumpet.

Audience:
Viva.
¡Viva!
Long may he live!

Crier:
se hve la monte,
Se fue al monte,
He went to the bushes,
aser su korkovya
A hacer su corcovia
To make love
kon su nana mariya.
Con su Nana María.
To his mistress Nana María.[2]

Audience:
Viva.
¡Viva!
Long may he live!

Crier:
lekreso se kome pamasakil,[3]
Regresó a comer dulce de calabaza,
He came back and ate candied squash,

kon su merkuča,[4]
Con su mercucha,
With his candy,

kon su morsia.[5]
Con su morcilla.
And his blood sausage.

Audience:
Viva.
¡Viva!
Long may he live!

Many topics mentioned in the proclamation have symbolic significance for the Festival of Games. There are characters who play the Spanish soldiers and a man who masquerades as Cortéz' mistress. The flags, drums, and trumpet are also important in certain ritual sequences of the fiesta. The narrative, then, is in some respects dramatized by the ritual events that accompany and follow the recitation.

A Text: "The Destruction of the First People"

In all other texts of true ancient narrative, the story and the performance are relevant to ritual behavior only as background material. The information in the narratives is assumed by all those who have an ordinary understanding of Chamula religious, cosmological, and historical concepts. The performance of these stories requires some stimulus or outright request for the information that they contain.

The following text illustrates a typical context of performance as well as typical features of content, form, and style. Titled "The Destruction of the First People" (Text 133), the narrative was told to my informant, Marian López Calixto, by his grandmother when she was visiting at his home several years earlier during the dry season. He recalled that the time was around noon, when everyone was complaining about the heat. The grandmother criticized them harshly, saying that long ago when the sun disappeared, it was a sign that destruction was close at hand. She insisted that people should live with heat and not complain, for the

heat of the sun was essential to life.[6] She then told the
following story about the destruction of the First Creation,
which made her point clearly.

>ʔoy hun kuento voʔnee tahmek.
>There is a story of long, long ago.
>>lah yalbun kaʔi ti hyayae.
>>My grandmother told it to me.

>haʔ la ti ʔantivoʔetike.
>It was in the time of the ancients.
>>ʔik'ubik la ta ʔosil voʔob la k'ak'al.
>>The earth darkened for five days.

>heč la ti htotike ta vinahele k'epel toʔoš la lek.
>It happened that the sun was still bright and clear.
>>sta la ti ʔolol k'ak'al ʔune, ʔik'ub la ʔun.
>>Then, at mid-day, it got dark.

>"ta ša me šihlahotik ʔun," ši la ti kirsanoʔetik ʔune.
>"We will surely die," said the people.[7]
>>"k'uši ša noʔoš šihbatotik li ʔune," ši la ti kirsanoʔetike.
>>"Only, how are we going to escape from here?" said the
>>people.

>vaʔun, ʔik'ub ti banamil ʔune.
>Well, the earth darkened.

>lah la svok'anik la ti sbinik ʔune.
>They broke their pots.
>>heč la ti sbinik ʔo la ʔep lah svok'anik ta ʔora.
>>In that way, they broke many of their pots right away.

>heč ti binetik k'alal la ʔik'ub ti ʔosile k'opoh la.
>And so, when the earth had darkened, those pots spoke.
>>ta ʔora tahmek ti binetike.
>>At once the pots (spoke).

>vaʔun, k'alal ti ʔik'ub ʔune, lok' la talel ti pukuhetikne.
>Well, when it darkened, the demons came forth (from the
>   broken pots).
>>tal la leʔon, tal la mokoč, tal la bolom.
>>The lion, the snake, the jaguar came forth.

>heč ti povre kirsanoʔetike lahik ta tiʔel ta pukuh ti
>Thus the poor people perished in the jaws of the
>   kirsanoʔetike.
>   demons.

š?avanetik ša la tahmek ti povre kirsano?etike.
How much the poor people shrieked then!

?i ?oy ta ?uni ?ololetik.
There were little children.
lok' ta šik'ik.
From them sprouted wings.

"ta me šačamik ?un, me?" ši la ti ?olole.
"You will surely die, mother," said one child.
heč la ti ?olole lok' la ta pana ta ?ora,
And so the child went outside at once,
?i k'atah ša la ta mut ti ?olole.
Whereupon the child changed into a bird.

ha? la kuč yu?un li ?ololetike.
The children survived in that way.
?a ti sme?ike ti stotike ti ?ololetike.
The mothers and fathers of the children died.

ha? mu?yuk la škuč yu?un.
They did not survive.
ha? la te čamik ta snaik ti kirsano?etike.
These people perished in their houses.

va?un, k'alal la sakub li ?osil ?une, mu ša la hunuk ti
Well, when dawn came upon the earth, there was no longer
kirsano?etike.
a single person left.
tuk ša la ti mutetike.
There were only birds.

"Ho?one ti hbi?e hešun," ši la ti mute.
"My name is 'jay,' " said one bird.
"Ho?one ti hbi?e karpintero?un."
"My name is 'woodpecker.' "

"ča? tos ?oy tos ti hbi?e.
"Actually I have two names."
?tuktuk ?un," ši la ti mutetike.
"I am the solitary one also," said the bird.

?oy hlom ti mut le ?une.
There is a kind of bird up there.
k'alal ta štonin ti ?uni mut, hlom ta te? ta šak' yuni tas
When the little bird is laying, it's in the wood itself that
ta k'atoh.
she makes her nest, in a rotten pine tree.

k'alal bu ša mol ti k'atohe, ha? ta šbat shom ti te?.
When the rotten pines are good and old, she goes to
    peck in the wood.

hal shom tahmek,
There she continues to peck it for a long time,
    huhu likel ta štal shom ti yuni nae.
    Every little while she comes to peck her little home.

k'alal mi sta shomel yu?un ti snae, ta šak' ti stone.
When she has finished the hole for her house, she lays her
    eggs.
    mu ?epuk ta šak' ti ston: ?uni ?oš beh no?oš.
    Not many eggs does she lay: only three eggs and no
        more.

heč ?a ?al heč la spas ti ?antivo?etike.
The reason is that the ancients did it that way.

?ik'eš ti kirsano?etike.
The people were transformed.
    k'ešik ?un.
    They changed.

kom lek ta ?ač' ti kirsano?etike.
The people were good once again.
    sakub lek ti banamile.
    The earth brightened.

lok' la talel ti htotike.
The sun came out.
    sakhaman ša la talel ti šohobale.
    Its rays came forth in soft white radiance.

heč ta ti htotik ta vinahele yal la talel ta banamil ta la spas
And so it was that Our Father in Heaven came down to
    yan ti kirsano?etike;
    earth to create men anew;
    mel¢ah ti kirsano?etike.
    To prepare mankind.

k'alal spas kirsano ti htotik la vinahele, puru la ?ač'el la
When Our Father in Heaven made the people, it was from
    spas ta ba?yel;
    clay that he first made them;
    la smel¢ah ti kirsano?e.
    From which he created the people.

č'abal la bu šbak' tahmek.
But they could not move very well at all.
　heče? la te va?al čak čumante?.
　Quite incorrectly, they stood there like stumps.

"k'usi ta škut," ši la ti htotik ta vinahelne.
"What shall I do?" said Our Father in Heaven.
　lah la stuki no?oš stok.
　And he destroyed them once again.

smel¢an la yan,
Our Father was going to create another kind,
　ti k'usi ša la švul ta shol ti htotike
　One that had just occurred to him.

lah la sk'asan ta skotol ti ?ač'ele.
He broke apart all of the clay.
　slilin la skotol tahmek ti ?ač'eletikne.
　He shook the clay all about.

lik la spas ta č'uč'ul ti ?ač'ele.
He commenced to pulverize the clay.
　?i smel¢an ?un.
　And he prepared the clay.

k'alal la ti mel¢ah yu?un ti htotike, lah la sk'opon.
When Our Father had created them, he spoke to them.
　lah la spikbe sk'ob.
　He pulsed their wrists.

k'alal lah la ya?i yu?un kušul ti ?ac'ele, yočel la ta sa?el
When he felt that the clay was alive, he began searching
　sve?el, ti k'utik momolal.
　for their food, which would be various kinds of grass.
　sta la ta sa?el.
　He found them.

lah la stihanbe ta ye ti momoletike, mu la sk'anik.
He touched the grasses to their mouths, but they did not
　like them.
　"k'usi la škak'be ?un ča?e" ši la ti htotik ?une.
　"What shall I give them, then?" said Our Father.

sa? la talel ?itah.
He went to search for greens.
　sk'anik hutuk, pere hutuk la tahmek.
　They liked them, but only a very little bit.

ʔisnop la lek ti htotike.
Our Father thought over the matter.
  "ta hbohkik la koʔe," ši la ti htotike.
  "Let's cut off my thigh," said Our Father.

ʔisboh la ti yoʔe.
And he cut off his thigh.
  lah la sta bu la lek tahmek ti sbek'tale ʔishos.
  He found the place where his body was the very best
      and scraped it off.

yak'be la ti ʔač'el spasoh ʔune.
And he gave it to the clay he had made.
  lek ša la šaʔik ti ʔač'ele.
  That tasted very good to the clay (people).

spohpoh ša la sbaʔik tahmek.
Then they fought trying to take it away from each other.
  "yuʔun haʔ ta sk'anik ti hbek'tal ʔun čaʔe," ši la ti
  "It must be that they like my body, then," said
      htotik ʔune."
      Our Father.

heč la ti ʔač'el ʔune k'opoh la likel.
So it was that the clay soon began to speak.
  pas la ta kirsano ʔun.
  It became human.

hun la ʔanȼ.
One (part) was a woman.
  hun la vinik.
  One (part) was a man.

"pasokik.
"Give it a try.
  k'uši šamelȼahik," ši la ti htotike.
  How will you multiply?" said Our Father.

"veno," ši ti vinik.
"Well, this way," said the man.
  lah ša spasik ščiʔuk ʔanȼ ʔune.
  He did something with the woman.

mu la snaʔik k'uši la ta pasel ti yolik.
They did not know how to make their offspring.
  hečeʔ la ta šnopnun la ta spasik.
  In vain they thought about what to do.

heč la ti ʔanȼ ʔeke mu la snaʔ ʔek.
And the woman did not know either.

ʔoy la te bahal hun pukuh ta čukinab.
There happened to be enclosed there in the jail a demon.

likel la lok' talel ta ʔora.
Quickly he came out.

"mi mu šanaʔ Hoʔote.
"Don't you know how to do it?

pastik ʔavil," ši la ti pukuhe.
Let's give you a lesson," said the demon.

pet sut la ʔeč'el ti ʔanȼ.
He carried the woman off in an embrace.

heč la ti vinike te la bat sk'el ʔek.
And it happened that the man went to see for himself.

"ši la pasele," ši ti pukuhe.
"This is the way it is done," said the demon.

"ʔaaa . . . vis ʔelanil ta pasel," ši ti vinike.
"Oh . . . *That's* the way it is done," said the man.

ʔi spas la ti vinik ʔek.
And the man did it too.

ščan la me ʔun.
He learned how.

haʔ yuʔun čopol lok' ti kirsanoʔetike;
And that is the reason that people turned out badly;[8]

ta sȼakik čih ʔi ti sȼak vuro.
That they fuck sheep and fuck burros.

toh čopol ta spasik.
They do much that is evil.

mu štun
It is not proper.

My informant believed that the events in the narrative took place at the end of the First Creation and the beginning of the Second Creation. This dating illustrates that a single narrative may report events of more than one creation, although the majority of temporal identifications place events of a single narrative in a single creation period. In either case the sequence of creations in the narratives is always unidirectional. The progression is orthogenetic; the direction is toward the present state of order. The three creations thus form the basic temporal backdrop to all the events of true ancient narratives. These events, in turn, make the present Fourth Creation intelligible and desirable by providing a reference to the chaotic past.

The text also presents a typical case of the juxtaposition of First and Second Creation time references with a place of occurrence, which could have been in the most distant reaches of the earth, wherever there were people. Its universality, he explained, followed from the fact that the different languages and peoples of the earth had not yet been differentiated at the time of the story. Therefore, the events could just as well have happened at the edge of the earth as in Chamula. This indefiniteness illustrates the principle of time-space unity in Chamula thought.

Not all of the possible narrative devices occur in the text, which suggests that idiosyncratic preferences of individual raconteurs are the rule rather than the exception. No informant ever told a story the same way twice. The narrative devices provide for a great variation in the texture of plots, that is, in their fine detail, while the plots themselves seldom change from informant to informant. There is a marked tendency for the degree of elaboration of narrative texture to vary from a low point in true recent narrative to a high point in true ancient narrative. This increase is particularly notable in the use of such devices as parallel syntax and metaphoric couplets.

The reasons for the increased formality of the style of true ancient narrative seem to be associated with the fact that ritual and other cosmological symbols comprise much of the subject matter of the genre. Since these symbols are by their nature imbued with multiple meanings and associations that refer back to the cycles of creation, it is aesthetically fitting that their linguistic environment should emphasize redundancy. The religious and logical role of Chamula symbols is "multivocal," to borrow a useful term from Victor Turner (1967: 48–52), meaning that they have many semantic referents. It follows that narrative references

to these symbols should be multivocal. For example, in
the "The Destruction of the First People," the sunrise and
recreation of man are treated with considerable stylistic
elegance and metaphoric repetition:

ʔik'eš ti kirsanoʔetike.
The people were transformed.
   k'ešik ʔun.
   They were changed.
kom lek ta ʔač' ti kirsanoʔetike.
The people were good once again.
   sakub lek ti banamile.
   The earth brightened.
lok' la talel ti htotike.
The Sun came out.
   sakhaman ša la talel ti šohobale.
   Its rays came forth in soft, white radiance.
heč la ti htotik ta vinahele yal la talel ta banamil ta la
And so it was that Our Father in Heaven (the sun) came
     spas yan ti kirsanoʔetike;
     down to earth to create men anew;
   melȼah ti kirsanoʔetike.
   To prepare mankind.

This passage restates symbolically the dawn of order itself
from chaos, with the very first rising of the sun to its apex
in the heavens. That event in Chamula cosmogony was of
such profound importance to the coming of order, life, and
cyclical time that human existence would be inconceivable
without it. Its symbolic significance makes intelligible the
stylistic exuberance in the report of the new dawn and the
re-creation of mankind.
   The frequent tendency to extreme redundancy of
message at points that the narrator judges to be of high
symbolic importance may be called metaphoric stacking. This
device functions as a kind of native criticism, by means of
which the narrator may indicate to his audience the parts he
considers most important. Metaphoric stacking in true
ancient narrative represents a form of continuity from the

simple redundancy of verbatim repetition found in the
marginal genres, games, and frivolous talk. Stylistic redundancy plays an even more important role in the other genres
of ancient words. It is therefore useful to consider metaphoric
stacking as an elementary form of ancient words. Parallel
syntax, stylistic complexity, and symbolic redundancy are
present in much though not all of true ancient narrative, but
these qualities literally pervade the other three genres of
ancient words. Whereas formal settings are only implied by
the mood of true ancient narrative, the other genres of
ancient words are actually used in formal settings as aspects
of ritual action.

Time-Space Attributes

   The cosmological referents of true ancient narrative may
be regarded as primary information axes of ancient words.
They provide "assumed" knowledge, which makes the rest of
ancient words intelligible to adult Chamulas. An example is
the following summary of a long narrative that took place in
the First Creation (Text 184):

   A long time ago, the Jews[9] decided that they were going
   to kill "Our Father" (the Sun). They caught him in a tree
   and tried to hang him, but he would not die. He escaped and
   went to hide in a sweat-bath house. They found him there,
   hit him and bit his head and threw rocks at it, but could not
   hurt him. They hurt their own mouths instead. They made a
   cross and hung him from it, then stuck him and cut him with
   knives and lances. He still would not die. They decided to
   try to burn him, again without success, for he came out of
   the fire younger than he was before. They decided that
   it would rejuvenate them also, so all the Jews jumped into
   the fire and died, leaving a metal cross behind, which is
   now the constellation the Jewish Cross (the Southern
   Cross). This is why they always burn the Judas on Holy
   Saturday.

   The time-space coordinates of the setting are of "equal
value"; that is, the story takes place anywhere on the earth

during the First Creation. The diffuseness of the time-space setting is a sign that the narrative may carry some etiological information, which it does. A constellation, a ritual custom, and a series of beliefs about the world of the sun are explained. The Jews, who ruled the earth before the coming of the sun, try unsuccessfully to bite and eat the sun, who is their rival for rule on the earth. This event is repeated whenever there is an eclipse of the sun. It happens when the Jews, who still lead their animal-like existence beyond the edge of the earth, occasionally muster the strength and numbers to try to eat the sun again. The sun and the Jews are archenemies, the one representing the essence of temporal and spatial order, the other the essence of chaos. Thus, it is logical that the constellation called the Jewish Cross should appear during the dry season early in the evening, from eight o'clock to midnight, for that is the time when the dark earth must wait longest for the reappearance of the sun in the morning. Moreover, thieves, murderers, and witches are believed to pray to this constellation instead of to the sun, "Our Father," because their evil deeds, which oppose the social order, also take place at night, a time when society is without the immediate presence of the order-giving sun. The ritual burning of the straw *huraš* (Judas or Jew) on Holy Saturday also inverts the entire symbolic milieu associated with the Jews. He is burned at the time he most fears, midday, when the sun is at its apogee; he is destroyed by the element he most fears, fire; and this occurs in the place he most fears, the Chamula Cermonial Center, the most sacred of spaces and the navel of the universe. So far from the moral universe are the Jews at present that they are believed to live in a special compartment that lies beneath the underworld. This place lies spatially outside the daily path of the sun through the underworld and is therefore in a position analogous to the temporal place of the Jews in the cycle of creation, that is, before the sun. This logical unity between similar values of space and time appears throughout the text.

The text is also replete with important ritual symbols. The head of the sun, which was so hard that the Jews hurt their mouths when trying to bite it, is also the sacred object of

the cult sponsored by the nichim and the pasión at the
Festival of Games in February. The symbolic representations
of the sun's head are metal flagpole tips, which are kept in a
special chest. During all festivals they are carried on poles
with cloth banners by the cargoholders' assistants. A ceremony focusing on the metal tips occurs during the Festival
of Games in February. The cross or tree is also central to
ritual symbolism, for the sun's death and other persecutions
are associated with it. A cross, or a cross substitute, usually
a pine branch, should be present in every ritual setting.

The circumstances that prompted the telling of the story
also had space-time associations. The informant who told
the narrative to me was working on the lowland coffee
plantations with some friends, when they saw some Guatemalans who had just arrived to work on the plantation also.
My informant's friend remarked that the Guatemalans, who
have garish, multicolored costumes, looked like Jews, and
then proceeded to tell the narrative. According to the scale
of relative social distance, Guatemala lies with the United
States on the very edge of the earth, where people still
preserve savage customs, like those of the Jews. Thus, not
only the content, redundant style, and logic of the narrative,
but also the circumstances of its performance, become
intelligible through the time-space principle.

Knowledge such as that reported in this true ancient
narrative provides the background information about order
that is essential for all adult Chamulas. Without this information, ritual action—and by extension, everyday secular
action—would have no meaning, no structure. With this
information, coded in complementary time-space values,
Chamulas look out at the world of the sun, past and present,
far and near, as an internally consistent system.

When they [Lacandones[1]] want to get married,
They do nothing more than touch each
other's genitals,
To see if they are men or women.

It is their manner of courtship.
They ask each other if they are men or
women.

And when they baptize their children,
They do it with a stick.

They have no compadres;
Alone they baptize their children.
Nor is there any church for baptism.

And if they don't like their children,
They don't even nurse them.

And if they die,
They don't even bury them,
But throw them into the ditches of stagnant
water.
—Marian López Calixto, Text 63

This genre generally includes all ritual speech that is not addressed directly to the supernaturals. The name of the genre, *k'op ta šak' rioš*, means, figuratively, "language for rendering holy." Although *rioš* is a loan word from the Spanish *dios*, meaning "god," the Tzotzil meaning is much more general than the Spanish. *Rioš* refers to a whole set of religious phenomena, including God (synonym of *htotik*, the sun); the individual saints and their images; religious acts, such as censing an altar or flag; religious gestures, such as crossing oneself; and perhaps more. Therefore, the noun and verb combination from which the name of the genre is derived has at least two relevant meanings. First, *ʔak' rioš* means "to render to God or to the deities." Second, it means "to perform religious acts." The best gloss, suggesting the many possible meanings, is thus, "language for rendering holy."

This genre is actively involved in the ritual process. The words spoken as language for rendering holy are supposed to

A Man Encounters San Juan
(See Text 127)

please the deities, although they are not addressed directly to them. This genre, as well as prayer and song, is actually performed in the ritual setting. Its setting implies the presence of metaphoric heat, for ritual language shares with other ritual symbols the qualities of increased heat, expressed in its case as multivocality and redundancy of message. Related to the heat metaphor is the fact that deities consume essences and humans consume substances. This is one of the reasons that ritual speech, music, candles, incense, tobacco, rum, fireworks, flowers, and leaves accompany most Chamula rituals. They emit heat, smoke, aroma, or sound, which serve as the gods' food. Men may participate in the religious experience by consuming, producing, or simply being in the presence of the gods' ritual substances. Formal language is one of these substances.

Although Chamula, like many societies, emphasizes the difference between ordinary and ritual acts, rituals are by no means rare; neither are they the exclusive domain of ritual officials. Most of the public fiestas (numbering more than thirty) require at least fifteen days of ritual preparation in addition to the time of the fiesta itself. Furthermore, most religious cargos have other obligations, in addition to public fiestas, which must be carried out at daily or twenty-day intervals, corresponding to the duration of the Ancient Maya month. Although much of this ritual activity is not public, the sky rockets and hand cannons that punctuate the private parts of the ritual sequences can be heard for miles around. Even in the most distant hamlets the ritual mood is never farther away than a neighbor's curing ceremony, a funeral here, or a new house-blessing ceremony there. One does not have to travel far in Chamula to see the sacred trappings of fresh pine boughs on a household altar or at a roadside shrine. The ritual mood may be present in the smallest business transaction or request for a favor. In sum, Chamulas are seldom out of sight and sound of the ritual setting.

Style and Form

With few exceptions, the basic stylistic unit of language for rendering holy is the parallel metaphoric couplet. There are hundreds of these formal dyadic phrases in the language, many of them used in prayer and song as well as in language for rendering holy. In the latter genre, style and syntax may vary slightly with setting, but in the majority of cases only the couplet combinations and single-word substitutions within the couplets will vary from setting to setting. The dyadic style remains the same. This is particularly true of the ritual formulas used by the several kinds of cargoholders. Each of the eight mayordomos, for example, says about the same ritual formulas as his counterparts, for their tasks are much alike. Nevertheless, the saints and other deities whom each invokes are slightly different, as is the time at which they are invoked in the ritual year and the order in which they are invoked. This is reflected in slight differences in the ritual formulas. In like fashion, most drinking ceremonies are similar in structure and relevant ritual formulas from one setting to the next. Only single-word substitutions are made. Similarly, ritual formulas of petition and gratitude do not vary significantly from one setting to another. The names of participants simply fit into ready-made slots in the formulas. The slight variations from performance to performance that make fixed sequences relevant to different settings do not count as a significant change for the Chamulas.

There are six subgenres of language for rendering holy. The criterial attributes that distinguish the categories are not uniform; neither are the attributes always linguistic. For example, three life crisis situations are the significant criteria for distinguishing three genres: ritual language for marriage (*sventa nupunel*), ritual language for baptism (*sventa šič' Ho? h'olol*), and ritual language for burial (*sventa muklumal*). No linguistic significance is attached to the distinction between these genres of language for rendering holy, for most of the ritual speech patterns and styles that occur in one also occur in the others. Yet two other subgenres in this category of ritual speech contain considerable internal variation in both setting and linguistic characteristics. These are ritual language for laymen (*sventa kirsano*) and ritual language for cargoholders and shamans (*sventa h'abteletik šči?uk h'ilol*). Each of these categories includes a wide range of verbal behavior, which might suggest further subdivisions to accommodate the observable differences, except that they would not conform to the Chamula view of the taxonomic situation. Only one of the six genres of language for rendering holy has both linguistic and contextual discreteness. This genre is the Chamula invocation that accompanies the gesture of crossing oneself, called ritual language for measuring the face (*sventa bisobsatik*), after the Catholic custom.

Thus, Chamula categories of language for rendering holy are distinguished from one another by nonuniform, sometimes nonlinguistic criteria. Some are distinct from the others because they are associated with different life crises; others are distinct because of the lay or religious affiliation of the officiant; one alone is distinguished by both linguistic and contextual criteria. As a result, it is difficult to treat the Chamula taxonomy as a scheme of variation according to consistent criteria. In fact, the joint relevance of its several criteria amounts to an honest expression of the complexity of the ritual mood in Chamula.

Oral Tradition As Specialized Knowledge

Little attention has so far been given to the process of teaching and inculcating the forms, content, and style of the various genres. For all genres of recent words and for true ancient narrative, special training is not necessary at all. These genres are learned by the ordinary processes of socialization and language acquisition. Everyone, ideally, has equal access to the information. In contrast, some of the genres of language for rendering holy, prayer, and song are traditionally learned, performed, and taught by specialists.

Chamulas learn such specialized knowledge in various ways. In the case of drum and flute players (*kantoletik*) and the crier at the Festival of Games, their jobs are for life and are hereditary. Thus, the matter of learning is a relatively slow but simple process of transmission of knowledge from father to son. Prospective cargoholders may learn some of the ritual formulas and prayers of the office to which they aspire by listening in as minor assistants at cargo functions. Some cargo positions (particularly the pasión and nichim) tend to be filled by men in successive generations from a limited number of families. In those cases, knowledge is passed informally from father to son or uncle to nephew within the kin group. Much more frequently, a new cargoholder must present gifts of liquor and food to a past cargoholder, requesting that he serve as ritual tutor or adviser for the novice's coming year in office. The ritual adviser, called *yahvotik*, has numerous sessions with the new cargoholder before he takes office and stays by his side during the major ritual proceedings for his entire year in office. Many times I have seen both cargoholder and adviser chanting and saying the same lines, the adviser correcting the novice when necessary. The term in office actually serves as a cargoholder's apprenticeship, after which he too can act as an adviser if he has performed his cargo well.

Shamans have a somewhat different position, in that their knowledge is supposedly acquired by revelation. Because their knowledge of ritual formulas and prayers is believed to be an individual matter, no institutionalized tutorship exists for them. In practice, however, aspiring shamans (those who have had the three required revelatory dreams) attempt to listen to many curing sessions in addition to those in which they and their families are personally involved. Learning is greatly facilitated in the frequent cases when a son decides to follow the shaman's career of his own father. In these cases, the boy can accompany his father as an assistant on curing missions and thereby learns the correct ritual formulas. Shamans have also been said to sell their ritual knowledge and prayers for a price, but I do not know of any specific case of such a transaction.

Aspiring musicians usually persuade a friend or relative to teach them the basic principles of harp and guitar. They begin their careers as specialists by playing at local affairs, such as funerals. Then they may be invited to other ritual affairs at the hamlet level. Later, they may ask to join a recognized harp and guitar group as a substitute (*k'ešol*) for a member of the group who has passed out or simply gone to sleep during a long performance. Only after a long, often informal apprenticeship does an aspiring musician get the opportunity to play for the prestigious major cargo rituals. This advancement to junior musician (*ʔič'inal mastaro*) gives him the opportunity to pursue several more years of apprenticeship in order to learn the words to the songs for particular cargo rituals, after which he may become a senior musician (*bankilal mastaro*). In sum, there is no single way by which one acquires the knowledge of specialized genres of ancient words.

Ritual Language for Measuring the Face

Some knowledge of ritual language is expected of every adult Chamula. The invocation said while crossing oneself or "measuring the face" is such a genre of ritual language. It is known by all Chamulas over twelve years of age and ranks as the most basic piece of religious language that Chamulas use regularly. Doubtless of Spanish Catholic origin, it precedes all prayers but is not itself a prayer. It simply acknowledges deities and confirms one's loyalty to them, and is not used to speak directly to the deities. By virtue of this quality, it is a part of language for rendering holy rather than of prayer. Chamulas should cross themselves before and after saying any prayers; when passing in front of any religious shrine, however small; upon entering and leaving any church or chapel, particularly the church in Chamula Ceremonial Center; and before beginning any major ritual sequence. Chamulas should also cross themselves at the portal shrines upon entering the sacred valley of the ceremonial center (Map 2). These entry portals, located in small mountain passes, are called *bisobsatik*, named for the same gesture that gives its name to the genre of measuring the face.

Chamulas cross themselves with the right hand. The hand is held with the thumb upright and the index finger bent across it and behind it; the other three fingers are held upright. A spoken invocation corresponds to the positions of the hand. By far the most common (*bankilal* or "senior" form) of the three variant forms of the invocation is: (1) *rioš* (God), (2) *totil* (the Father), (3) *rioš* (God), (4) *nič'onil* (the

Son), (5) *rioš* (God), (6) *spiritu santo* (the Holy Spirit),
(7) *kahval, amen* (My Lord, amen). The hand is moved from
the forehead between the eyes at (1) to the right temple (2),
the left temple (3), the right side of the chest just below the
shoulder (4), the left side of the chest (5), the center of the
chest but somewhat lower on the body (6), and finally, the
chin (7). Each part of the invocation is spoken as the hand
is moved. This is the all-purpose gesture, suitable for crossing
oneself whenever and wherever necessary. The invocation
and its accompanying gestures can be scanned in formal
couplet structures: 1–2 / 3–4 / 5–6 / 7.

Another form (*ʔidinal* or "junior" form) of measuring the
face is used for invoking minor saints. It involves thirteen
positions and a slightly different hand position. The least
important variant, also used for invoking lesser saints, is
called the Little Salvador (*bik'it šalik*) form. Named for
a minor representation of the Sun-Christ deity, it has five
positions. The general pattern of the corresponding gestures
of all three invocations—from up to down—is related to the
time-space principles of the Chamulas, which illustrates an
important trait of language for rendering holy, namely, that
language, cosmos and ritual action always work together.
They are inseparable and share the same logical and organizational principles.

Ritual Language for Life Crises

The three subcategories of ritual language for the three
main crises of life—baptism, marriage, and burial—are distinguished from each other only by setting. Similar forms of
language for rendering holy are used at each of these rituals,
although the content of the formulas varies. In general, the
forms of speech are said in a prescribed manner in the ritual
setting. They are intended to please the deities but are not
themselves said to the deities. The three ritual settings of life
crises utilize song and prayer as well as language for rendering
holy, and these three genres of ancient words frequently
occur together in the same ritual sequence. Because the data
on language for rendering holy are more complete for

weddings and burials than for baptisms, examples are taken from only those two settings.[2]

Marriage

In order to arrange a marriage, friends and relatives of the would-be groom go as petitioners on as many as eight nighttime expeditions to the house of the girl whom the boy wishes to purchase and take as his bride. Their purpose is to persuade the father of the would-be bride to let his daughter become the wife of the petitioners' candidate. The father may receive them or send them away. When he agrees to talk to them, usually on the third or fourth visit, serious negotiations begin about brideprice and other gifts that must be exchanged.

The following exchange takes place at the door of the girl's house when the petitioning party arrives around midnight. The head delegate, who is often the boy's father, speaks first:

Petitioner:
> tataya?o, mi nakalot.
> In-laws, do you live here?

Father of Girl:
> nakalun. k'usi mantal.
> I live here. What do you want?

Petitioner:
> mu?yuk lital hk'oponot,
> Only that I have come to talk to you,
>> mu lekil k'oponeluk;
>> And my talk is not pleasant;

> yu?un lital hk'oponot yu?un ?amoton,
> For I have come to talk to you about your gift,
>> yu?un ?avabolta?el,
>> About your offspring,

> ti lah yak'bot,
> Given to you,
>> ti la sk'elanbote,
>> Conceded to you,

> ti sme? vinahel,
> By the Mother of Heaven,

ti sme? lorya,
By the Mother of Glory,

ti mu me ?atukuk ?atotik,
That you may not father her alone,
    ti mu me ?atukuk ?ame?in.
    That you may not mother her alone.

ti la? me hkomon totintik;
Come, let us both be as fathers to her;
    ti la? me hkomon me?intik;
    Come, let us both be as mothers to her;

ti motone,
The gift,
    ta ?avabolta?ele,
    Your offspring,

ti lah yak'bote,
Given to you,
    ti la sk'elanbote,
    Conceded to you,

ti sme? vinahele,
By the Mother of Heaven,
    ti sme? lorya.
    By the Mother of Glory.

(At this point the father may either receive the petitioners or send them away to come back another time with more gifts.)

Burial

A similar parallel structure occurs in the mourning lament that follows. In this case the words are spoken throughout the three-day mourning and burial period by the wife of the deceased. The mourner wails the lines as she kneels beside her husband's corpse:

ti ?ay, kahval.
Oh, my Lord!
    hesus.
    Jesus!

to¢an, salvarol.
Rise up, Savior.
    to¢an, manvel. ti ?ay.
    Rise up, Emmanuel. Oh.

k'u noʔoš čaʔal ʔeč bat ti hmalal.
Why, oh why, did my husband depart like that?
  lah ša ʔakomesun šči ʔuk koltik ʔune.
  Now you have left me with our children.

ʔay, kahval.
Oh, my Lord!
  ʔay, hesus.
  Oh, Jesus!

bat ša ti hnup ʔune.
Now my husband is gone.
  bat ša ti hčiʔil ʔune.
  Now my companion is gone.

kahval.
My Lord!
  hesus.
  Jesus!

mi ta to štal ti ʔok'ob ʔune.
Is there still a chance he will come back tomorrow?
  mi ta to štal ti čaʔeh ʔune.
  Is there still a chance he will come back the day after
    tomorrow.

kahval.
My Lord!
  hesus.
  Jesus!

The phrases of the lament can be easily transposed so that the proper relationship to the deceased is clear from the speech of the mourner. The same lament follows, only slightly changed for the parents of the deceased, who speak together:

ʔay, labat ša ʔun, kol.
Oh, you have now departed, my son.
  labat ša ʔun, hničʼon.
  You have now departed, my child.

lakomesun ša ʔun.
Now you have left me.[3]

Hoʔot baʔyel labat ʔun.
You were the first to go.

Hoʔot baʔyel lak'ot ʔun.
You were the first to arrive.[4]

mi yuʔun časutalel ti tanaʔe.
Could it be that you will return soon?
    mi yuʔun časutalel ti ʔok'obe, kol. ti ʔay.
    Could it be that you will return tomorrow, my son. Oh!

kahval.
My Lord!
    hesus.
    Jesus!

kom ša me ta ʔanič'nab ʔune.
Your children survive you.
    kom ša me ta ʔavahnil ʔune.
    Your wife survives you.

ʔay, kol.
Oh, my son.
    nič'on.
    Flesh of my flesh.

labat ša ʔun.
Now you have gone away.
    lak'ot ša ʔun.
    Now you have arrived.

Later, on the night before the burial (the second night),
the wife of the deceased must "give a blessing" (*šak' rioš*) to
the deceased while kneeling at his feet. It is essentially
the same as the lament, because the basic style and syntax
of the formulas can accommodate slight changes in content.
The words are said three times by the spouse of the deceased
amid weeping, once at twelve midnight, again about 2:00
A.M., and finally at 4:00 A.M. A round of drinks is served
after each utterance:

labat ša me ʔun hnup.
Now you have departed, my husband.
    labat ša me ʔun hčiʔil.
    Now you have departed, my companion.

ʔay, kahval.
Oh, my Lord!

ʔay, hesus.
Oh, Jesus!

mi ta to šasutalel ti ʔok'ob ʔune.
Could it be that you will still return tomorrow?
　mi ta to šasutalel ti čaʔeh ʔune.
　Could it be that you still return the day after tomorrow?

lah ša lakomesun ʔun.
Now you have abandoned me.

ʔay, kahval.
Oh, my Lord!
　ʔay hesus.
　Oh, Jesus!

k'u čaʔal ti mu koʔoluk šihbatik ʔune.
Why couldn't we have departed together?
　k'u čaʔal ti mu koʔoluk šihk'ot ʔune.
　Why couldn't we have arrived together?

ʔay, hnupʔo.
Oh, my husband!
　ʔay, hčiʔilʔo.
　Oh, my companion!

kahval.
My Lord!
　hesus.
　Jesus!

Nearly all Chamulas insist that language for rendering holy which pertains to life crisis rituals should be common knowledge for all adults. People should learn the relevant formulas and couplets so that only limited hesitation and instruction are necessary when it comes time to use them in context. This, however, is far from the actual case. For example, in the funeral from which the above excerpts were taken, the wife had to be coaxed and helped by her father-in-law to say the proper words.

Ritual Language for Laymen

The overlap between ritual language for laymen and that for life crises lies in their similarity of both setting and style.

The difference lies in the fact that the genre for laymen is even more generalized as common knowledge. Not only should every adult know ritual speech for laymen, but nearly all do.

Requests, Presentations, and Expressions of Gratitude
Some of the most common forms belonging to this category are polite formulas for requests, gift presentations (which usually precede a request), and expressions of gratitude. This kind of speech is commonly called simply *lekil k'op* or "nice talk," for it pleases men and deities alike. Like most other forms of language for rendering holy, it is fixed in style, syntax, and rhythm, but allows for slight variations in setting by means of "open slots" in the rote sequences, where words can be substituted to make it specifically appropriate to each situation.

An example comes from part of a drinking ceremony after a baptism, when the parents, the child, and the godparents have just left the church, where the child was baptized by the priest. The ritual at the church being completed and the child named (thus no longer being a *maš* or "monkey" for lack of a name), the parents and godparents now have a tie of ritual kinship (compadrazgo or "co-parenthood") to each other. They have become "co-parents" of the child and ideally should cooperate in caring for it. More important, the relationship is one of confidence and solidarity. One can count on his *kumpagre* and *kumagre* (Tzotzil for Spanish *compadre* and *comadre*) for help, advice, and loans. The sealing of such a relationship is therefore a happy time. The following language for rendering holy precedes a drinking ritual in the atrium of the church in Chamula Ceremonial Center. The participants are seated on the concrete walk that goes around the inside of the atrium and have finished the prescribed baptismal meal of tortillas and hard-boiled eggs. The father of the child begins a very polite statement, which precedes the giving of a bottle of rum in gratitude to his new kumpagre and kumagre:

Father:
teke ča²e, kumpagre, hme² kumagre,
Well, then, compadre, comadre,

laʔ kučʼtik hutebuk.
Come, let us drink a little bit.

kolaval ʔabolahik yuʔun ti hničʼone.
Thank you for doing the favor for my child.

biʔin ʔo sbekʼtal.
His body is named forever.
   biʔin ʔo stakipal.
   His flesh is named forever.

laʔ, kučʼtik hutebuk.
Come, let us drink a little bit.

Godfather:
šuʔuk, kumpagre.
Very well, compadre.
   kolaval.
   Thank you.

(He accepts two liter-sized bottles of rum offered by the father and places them in front of him.)

Godfather:
teke, čaʔe kumpagre. kolaval tahmek.
Well then, compadre. Thank you very much.
   kolaval tahmek, hmeʔ kumagre.
   Thank you very much, comadre.

Father and Mother (together):
baȼʼi huteb tahmek, kumpagre, hmeʔ kumagre.
It is but a very small amount, compadre, comadre.

(They proceed with the drinking ceremony.)

Drinking Ceremonies
The drinking ceremony itself uses a separate set of formulas, which are related to the words of ritual gratitude, thanks, presentation, and petition. The drinking ceremony occurs in nearly all of the countless public and private ritual settings in Chamula. Symbolically, the drinking ritual achieves at least four objectives. It emphasizes the principle of equality, for each participant receives an equal amount. It emphasizes the principle of rank, for equal portions are served according to rank order, with high-prestige cargo positions, age, and

masculinity generally taking precedence over low-prestige cargo positions, youth, and femininity, although there are many exceptions. It literally produces and also symbolizes the heat that is considered desirable for human interaction with deities and with each other. Finally, it symbolizes solidarity among the participants, for the liquor has been given and received by members of a group that has a common objective or common interest.

Few business, personal, or supernatural transactions of any importance take place without some kind of formal exchange, and this usually implies the presence of an alcoholic beverage or one of its accepted substitutes, like Pepsi Cola, Fanta (orange soda pop), or Coca Cola. The ceremony involves simply the distribution and consumption of a set amount of liquor. A child or other young person present is appointed drink-server. His task is to see that each participant receives an equal amount of liquor and also to see that the given amount of liquor stretches to allow equal portions to all. On each round, each participant should toast every other participant in rank order. As he says the toast to his superiors, he ideally bows to them and receives release from them. They release him by touching his bowed head with their right hand. He should then, theoretically, shake hands with equals, as he says the toast. He concludes by toasting his inferiors in the rank order, but without bow or handshake. In practice, however, the toasts alone are usually said to all, which leaves the appropriate gestures to be "understood" but not performed. Thus, in the drinking ceremony, language carries a special burden of nonlinguistic information.

In the toast itself, all persons are addressed by appropriate consanguineal or affinal kin terms if the occasion is not a cargo affair. If it is a cargo affair, titles appropriate to the cargo position are used to address participants. Given names are seldom used. Following is a skeleton scheme of the drinking ceremony, with substitutions and variants indicated:

Receiver (taking the shot glass from the drink-server and addressing all present in rank order);

ta me h¢ak
I am going to take it,

    (or)

ta me škuč'
I am going to drink it,

    (or)

ta me škič'
I am going to receive it,

bankil ("older brother") or appropriate consanguineal or affinal term of address, or cargoholder's title.

Person toasted (to giver of toast; replying in the verb frame in which he was toasted):

¢ako me
Take it,

    (or)

ʔuč' o me
Drink it,

    (or)

ʔič' o me
Receive it,

ki¢'in ("younger brother") or appropriate term of address for person toasting, or cargoholder's title.

(The Receiver drinks, preferably in a single swallow.)

Receiver (returning the glass to the drink-server):
kolaval, bankil. liʔ me hbis.
Thank you, older brother
   (or appropriate term of
    address). Here is my glass.

Drink-provider:
huteb poš.
It's only a little liquor,

    (or)

ba¢'i huteb poš.
It's only a very little liquor,

ki¢'in ("younger brother") or appropriate term of address for person who has thanked him.

Although the drinking ceremony is classified by Chamulas as ritual speech appropriate for laymen, it occurs as well in cargo affairs and other ritual contexts. The designation means simply that it is a form of language for rendering holy that is universally known and used among adult Chamulas.

Other Polite Formulas

Although usually used to accompany some ritual transaction, language for rendering holy may also be used outside
the formal ritual setting if stereotyped and formal conversation is required. An example comes from the funeral and
mourning period. On the occasion of the performance of the
following text, the wife of the deceased was embarrassed to
say the appropriate ritual words, for fear she would not say
them correctly. Her father-in-law encouraged her. This
exchange, made in the politest of terms, illustrates a kind of
language for rendering holy that does not require simultaneous
ritual action. The formal mood suffices as an appropriate
setting:

Father-in-law:
    yos, kahval, hesus, kišlel,
    God, My Lord, Jesus, younger sister,

    mi mu ša?abolah hbel,
    Won't you please speak one word,
        ča?beluk,
        Two words,

    yu?un ti hlahele,
    For the one gone,
        yu?un ti htubele;
        For the one snuffed out;[5]

    yu?un sta ti ?o?lol ?ak'obal.
    For it is nearly midnight.

    heč ?o šal mi mu ša?abolah, šakuč,
    Therefore won't you please, won't you bear it,
        šaɗ'ik ta vokol, kišlel.
        Won't you endure the task, younger sister?

Daughter-in-law:
    ?ay, kahval, hesus, bankil, mu šaval heč.
    Oh, My Lord, Jesus, older brother, don't say that.

    mu k'usi hna?.
    I don't know anything at all.
        ha? no?oš hna? yuč'el li poš.
        I only know how to drink liquor.

pero li ʔak' rioš, mu hnaʔ.
But the blessing, I don't know.
   saʔo yan.
   Look for someone else.

Father-in-law:
pero mu šaval heč, kišlel.
But don't say that, younger sister.

ʔabolahan,
Please,
   ʔavokoluk
   Won't you do the favor?

ti bal ti hbele,
Of assuring the one word,
   ti čaʔbele,
   The two words,

lahyak'bot,
For the one given to you,
   la sk'elanbot ti htotike,
   For the one conceded to you by Our Father,

yuʔun ti hlahele,
For the one gone,
   yuʔun ti htubele,
   For the one snuffed out,

bal šaʔi ti hbele ti čaʔbele,
To assure that he hears one word, two words,
   sventa yo sbisol sat.
   That he may be blessed.

teke, laʔ kuč'tik hutebuk, kišlel.
Well then, come. Let us drink a little bit, younger sister.

(She finally agrees to say the blessing, and they drink together.)

Ritual Language for Cargoholders and Shamans

The settings of cargo and curing ceremonies are so numerous and varied that it is possible to offer a survey of only the principal forms and settings. The kinds of language for rendering holy used by cargoholders and shamans involve a specialized knowledge that must be learned in specified ways. Because the ritual speech is performed by specialists, Chamulas expect little variation to occur from one performance to the next. It is not, they maintain, subject to the failings of laymen's "cold" memory. This opinion, however, represents the ideal for which each actual performance is no more than an approximation. As with the other kinds of language for rendering holy, this genre is neither spoken directly to the supernaturals nor sung. It shares with all of the genres of ancient words an abundance of religious symbols with multiple meanings. Frequently the parallel syntax and metaphoric couplets serve as means of suggesting the multiple referents of ritual symbols.

Cargoholders at Festivals

One of the best-known examples of the genre occurs two weeks before the Festival of Games in February. It has the function of a ritual announcement. The three outgoing pasiones, the officials in charge of the fiesta, go to key hamlets in their barrios on Sunday afternoon two weeks before the festival begins. There the "monkey assistants"[6] dance and the "fireworks-shooters" fire hand cannons and rockets. The purpose of the announcement is both to give information about the fiesta and to recruit firewood-gatherers for the coming weekend. The pasión himself shouts the following message to whoever may have been attracted by the noise. Recruits who have been contacted previously must also appear to hear the pasión's speech:

> ʔabolahan yuʔun siʔ
> Please, for the sake of his firewood,
> > yuʔun sk'ok',
> > For the sake of his fire,
>
> ti yahvalel vinahel,
> Of the Owner of Heaven,
> > ti yahvalel lorya,
> > Of the Owner of Glory,
>
> ti buč'u stohotike,
> He who pays for our guilt,
> > ti buč'u smanotike,

He who buys us out of difficulties,
ti buč'u la hyak' hč'uleltik,
He who gave us our souls,
    ti buč'u la hyak' kanimatik,
    He who gave us our spirit,
ha? si?.
It is his firewood.
    ha? sk'ok' ti htotike.
    It is his fire of our Father (the sun).

?avokoluk tahmek,
Please, I beg you,
    ti k'alal vašakib k'ak'ale,
    Eight days from now,
čahmalakutik ta te?tik,
We shall await you in the forest,
    te šava?i ta te?tik,
    You shall hear where to find us in the forest,
te š?ok' korneta,
There the horn will be crying,
    te ta st'omesik yolon k'ok',
    There they will be firing sky rockets;
ta ?ošib ?ora ?ik'luman,
At three o'clock in the morning,
    ?avokoluk tahmek.
    Please, I beg you.

Eight days later, following the wood-gathering session, all
of the pasión's assistants and wood-gatherers go to the pasión's
house for the noon meal. After three rounds of liquor have
been served to them, several dishes of food are served,
including one of cabbage soup with chile and another of
beans. While the wood-gatherers are eating, the pasión's
four monkey assistants and the monkey assistants of other
fiesta officials get together to thank the pasión for the meal.
This highly stylized expression of gratitude, which is actually
chanted, is considered to be language for rendering holy. The
group of monkeys chant it while shaking gourd rattles and
marking the rhythm with stationary dance steps. It is not
considered a song, however, but rather a kind of language for
rendering holy.

Chanted:
> ʔasite veʔlil,
> Greasy food,
>> ʔasite komer,
>> Greasy food,
>
> ʔasite ʔitah,
> Greasy cabbage,
>> ʔasite napuš.
>> Greasy turnips.

Sung:
> la la ti la lai.
>> la la ti la lai.

(The above sequence is repeated until the end of the cabbage soup course, which the chant describes. When the bean course is distributed, the second part of the chant begins.)

Chanted:
> ʔasite čenek',
> Greasy beans,
>> ʔasite prihol,
>> Greasy beans,
>
> ʔasite veʔlil,
> Greasy food,
>> ʔasite comer.
>> Greasy food.

Sung:
> la la ti la lai.
>> la la ti la lai.

This sequence, too, is repeated indefinitely, until the bean course is finished, when another round of liquor is offered.

This is a useful text to explore for time-space coding. The Festival of Games, with which the text is associated, is atypical of Chamula festivals. It is long (five days as opposed to the regular three days) and has many attributes—linguistic, spatial, and temporal—that are unique in the fiesta cycle. The fiesta itself occurs very early in the annual cycle. Appropriately, the fiesta is a cult to the sun and moon, who were the givers of order. The monkey characters, associated with the Jews, play an especially prominent part in the fiesta, for they represent the antithesis of order, which must be ritually stated to make way for the coming of order. Many narratives refer to the terrible monkeys of the First Creation. Others tell of the first people, who ate their children at puberty and were changed into monkeys by the Sun-Creator. These characters, the sun and the monkeys, are principal figures at the Festival of Games because that fiesta in many ways recapitulates the first principles of order.

The meal served after the wood-gathering expedition and before the official beginning of the fiesta at the home of the pasión who sponsored the work party is in fact a ritual feast. In addition to the main "hot" dish of beef tripe soup, the helpers receive coffee, beans, cabbage soup, and tortillas, as well as rum and tobacco. There are significant exceptions to this consumption of many "hot" substances. The pasión himself fasts, eating only a tortilla and drinking some rum. The monkeys drink no rum at all, consuming instead their own supply of chile broth, which they carry in horn containers. They eat the rest of the ritual meal, however. Both omissions symbolically separate the representatives of disorder (the monkeys) and order (pasiónes) from each other as well as from the rest of the personnel.

During the meal the monkeys stand before the bench where the pasión is seated and chant their words of gratitude for the meal, emphasizing the greasy tripe soup. This chant is "precultural" in a symbolic sense, for Spanish words are self-consciously used by monkeys: *comer*, "to eat;" *aceite*, "oil" or "grease"; and *frijol*, "bean." It reflects the Chamula belief that Spanish was the general language all over the earth before Tzotzil ("the true language"), just as monkeys preceded "good" people. Furthermore, greasy food is associated with Ladinos as well as with the first ancestors, who boiled up their fat babies as stewing meat. The consumption of the frankly greasy meal at the wood-gathering ceremony and the fact that the monkeys seem happy about the grease and chant partially in Spanish make sense in terms of the time-space principle. So does the time and place of the wood-gathering expedition itself, which occurs in the woods and begins before dawn. The woods, the darkness, the grease, the monkeys, the Ladinos, the Spanish language, and even the time of the entire activity, before the fiesta, are all symbols that are hostile to life and order. The fact that the monkeys use rattles and chant the language for rendering holy instead of singing the common song with harp and guitar accompaniment also makes the event intelligible as a kind of inverted ritual prelude to the order-giving cult to the sun which follows in the festival.

All Chamulas, when asked why the monkeys chant the greasy food lines, simply explained that it was the custom. The meaning of the monkeys' lines is felt by them rather than being understood intellectually. Part of what is implicit to them is knowledge of the First Creation barbarities and about the categories of social distance. These are matters assumed a priori by Chamula participants and observers. The time-space principle which expresses itself in the organization and content of this and other genres of oral tradition is a useful approximation of information that the Chamulas assume.

Ritual Language for Cargoholders in Other Settings

Another type of ritual speech for cargoholders occurs in the annual ritual of induction into the cargo system. This affair begins every year on December 30 with the formal blessing of the incoming cargoholders. The ceremony is called the receiving of blessings for incoming cargoholders (*šič' rioš ʔač' hʔopisial*). It takes place after the appointees have agreed to accept their respective cargos in a previous ceremony called the delivery of credentials (*tenel vun*), which takes place in mid-November. By the time of the induction ceremony, each new cargoholder has ideally recovered from the shock of being named to the position. He realizes that he must sacrifice a year of gainful labor and spend thousands of pesos (probably borrowed) for the public well-being throughout the coming year. The blessing which he receives is thus well-deserved.[7]

In the following example, the outgoing first alcalde for

Barrio San Juan and his assistants have just arrived, after a
long early morning walk, at the house of the first alcalde's
replacement for the following year. The assistants announce
their arrival by setting off hand cannons and skyrockets. The
inductee, however, does not come out of his house but
simply stands in the open door, listening to those who give
the blessing (*hʔak'rioš̌etik*). They line up in the patio parallel
to the front of the house. The outgoing official, who stands
in the middle of the group, leads the blessing:

mi teyot htot.
Are you there, Father?
    mi teyot hmeʔ.
    Are you there, Mother?

č'ul bankilal kurus,
Holy senior cross,
    č'ul bankilal vašton,
    Holy senior staff,

ʔul ta bahel ʔabek'tal,
May your body emerge,
    ʔul ta bahel ʔatakipal,
    May your flesh emerge,

čak k'u čaʔal ʔuninal rioš,
Like unto the young god,
    čak k'u čaʔal ʔuninal hesus,
    Like unto the young Jesus,[8]

heč vok';
As he burst forth;
    heč ʔayan;
    As he was born;

ta ʔabek'tal,
So with your body,
    ta ʔatakipale,
    So with your flesh,

heč noplih ʔo,
So it was considered,
    heč t'uhlih ʔo,
    So it was chosen,

ta ʔabek'tal,
Your body,
   ta ʔatakipal,
   Your flesh,

ta ʔarma rioš,
At the armory of God,
   ta ʔarma hesukristo.
   At the armory of Jesus Christ.[9]

ta hel tos,
At the changing of tasks,
   ta hel mok,
   At the crossing of the wall,

ti stomele,
At the oath-taking,
   ti sbičel,
   At the assumption,

ti č'ul bankilal kurus,
Of the holy senior cross,
   ti č'ul bankilal vašton,
   Of the holy senior staff,

ti sčabi bel yolon yok,
That which is cared for at the feet,
   ti sčabi bel yolon sk'ob,
   That which is watched over beneath the hands,

ti muk'ul san juan,
Of great San Juan,
   ti muk'ul patron.
   Of the Great Patron.

ti hbeh ša me viȼ,
There upon the mountain,
   ti hbeh ša me sȼeleh.
   There upon the hill.

htatik ta ʔak'oponel,
We seek your sacred words,
   htatik ta ʔatiʔinel,
   We seek your blessed speech,

ti mu me lekil ʔabteluk,
Even though the effort be worthless,
   ti mu me lekil patanuk,
   Even though the tribute be in vain,

ti taʔival na me,
At the frosty house,
   ti taʔival k'ulebal me.
   At the frosty place of wealth.[10]

ti haʔ me ¢o¢ naʔbil,
May his knowledge be strong,
   ti haʔ me ¢o¢ k'elbil,
   May his vigilance be constant,
      ti haʔ me ¢o¢ k'esbil,
      May he be strong before the cause of shame.[11]

ti sak sbek'tale,
May his body be clean,
   ti sak stakipale,
   May his flesh be pure,

ti bahbil yoke,
His feet dedicated,
   ti bahbil sk'obe,
   His hands devoted,

ti k'u škutik ʔo,
In whatever we must say,
   ti k'u hpastik ʔo,
   In whatever we must do,

ti haʔ me sčabibel yolon yok,
For that which is cared for at the feet,
   ti haʔ me sčabibel yolon sk'ob,
   For that which is watched over beneath the hands,

ti muk'ul san huane,
Of the Great San Juan,
   ti muk'ul patrone.
   Of the Great Patron.

ti mu nan ʔepuk hlubes hbatik,
So that we may not get tired,
   ti mu nan ʔepuk hčames hbatik,
   So that we may not get sick,

mu ša me htabetik ʔo syalebal yok,
So that we will not falter at the feet,
   mu ša me htabetik ʔo syalebal sk'ob,
   So that we will not blunder beneath the hands,

ti baʔyel htotike,
Of our first Father,

ti ba'yel hme'tike;
Of our first Mother;

ti buč'u ba'yel 'eč'em 'o yoke,
Whose feet were the first to pass by,
    ti buč'u ba'yel 'eč'em 'o sk'obe,
    Whose hands were the first to create,

heč me ti vinahelal Ho',
As the heavenly rain,
    heč me ti vinahelal krasya'e.
    As the celestial grace.

ti mu me htukuk hmakitik,
May we not impede it even a little bit,
    ti mu me htukuk hke'ovtatik.
    May we not cast even a shadow upon it.

ti 'ak' 'o to me smaki,
And although they threaten it,
    ti 'ak' 'o to me ske'ovta,
    Although they cast aspersion upon it,

ti ba'yel htotike,
That of the first Father,
    ti ba'yel hme'tike.
    That of the first Mother,

ti k'uyepal lamal pak'al ta yolon kuruse,
However much the flowers lie discarded at the foot of the
        cross,
    ti k'uyepal lamal pak'al ta yolon pašyone,
    However much the flowers lie scattered at the foot of
        the Passion,

ti sak tinane,
Clean and pure they shall be replaced,
    ti sak buȼ'ane.
    Clean and pure they shall be kissed,

'oy ta yašinal 'ak',
There they shall be beneath the protective vine.
    'oy ta yašinal te'.
    There they shall be beneath protective plants.

s'ok',
They shall cry,
    s'avan,
    They shall exclaim,

ta yolon kurus,
Beneath the Cross,
  ta yolon pašyon,
  Beneath the Passion,

yaya tot,
Of the Reverend Fathers,
  yaya me ?.
  Of the Reverend Mothers.

mu nan ?epuk hlubes hbatik,
May we not become tired,
  mu nan ?epuk hčames hbatik,
  May we not become ill,

yaluk nan talel sk'ak'al,
That their heat shall descend,
  yaluk nan talel sk'išnal,
  That their warmth shall fall upon us,

ti vinahelal Ho?e,
The heavenly rain,
  ti vinahelal krasyae,
  The celestial grace,

yayatot,
Of the Reverend Father,
  hkaša?il.
  Of the Blessed Mother.

After the blessing is completed, the incoming alcalde offers several bottles of liquor in gratitude. They are drunk with ritual propriety in front of the patio cross, which has been freshly decked with pine boughs in preparation for the blessing. Then the incoming official offers a meal of beans, tortillas, and coffee to the blessing party. After appropriate expressions of gratitude, they depart. Some of the party will return the following morning to escort the new official to the Chamula Ceremonial Center for the taking of the oath of office.

Shamans' Use of Ritual Language
One other major setting of ritual language is the domain of curing and shamanism. Unlike certain nearby communities, such as Zinacantan, Chamula has no organization of shamans

on the local or municipio level. Shamanism is a specialty
for individual practitioners. The shamans of some hamlets
cooperate in celebrating waterhole-cleaning ceremonies at
the fiesta of Santa Cruz in early May. Others cooperate with
religious and political officials to pray for rain in time of
drought. However, there is no regular ritual expression of
the shamans' collective responsibility for the well-being of
the whole municipio. The individual quality of shamanistic
practice produces a corresponding lack of completely
standardized ritual formulas. Individual shamans are said to
adhere to curing formulas that have been shown by personal
revelation and experience to be effective for specific illnesses.
However, the formal statements of presentation, gratitude,
and request for the shaman are similar to those for the layman. Although shamans' ritual language is idiosyncratic in
some respects, it is classified by Chamulas with cargoholder's
speech, because its setting, form, and style are mostly
invariant. Only slight variations in content occur from one
shaman's ritual speech to the next shaman's speech for the
same purpose. The data on ritual language associated with
shamanism are unfortunately not full enough to select a
single text as typical.

Because of the wide domain of verbal behavior covered by
language for rendering holy, it is an omnipresent factor on
the Chamula scene. Each and every Chamula adult knows
and uses some formulas belonging to the genre. As shown by
the examples, highly loaded symbolic statements are reinforced by the rhythm and the various repetitive devices used
to express them. It seems that multiple meanings of ritual
symbols are encoded in the mesh of symmetry, parallelism,
and metaphoric stacking. A few key words arranged formally,
as in a series of metaphoric couplets, convey more information than a simple prose exposition of a concept. The greater
the symbolic significance of a social transaction, the more
highly condensed and redundant is the language used to
conduct it. Also, the more invariant that transaction, the
more invariant and stylized are the formulas of the condensed language. These tendencies find even more extreme

expression in the two remaining genres of ancient words, prayer and song.

(9) Prayer

The men were only sitting there;
  The hoe, the axe, and the machete were
    working alone.

The Earth Gods saw that the men did not want
    to work,
  So they went to tell Our Father in Heaven:

"It's better that you make them work.
  Otherwise, they will not pray to you,

If they are not tired, they will not pray to
    you," said the Earth Gods.
  "Very well. May they be made to work,"
    said Our Father in Heaven.

So the people went to work.
  That is why, when they begin to work, the
    people now pray to Our Father:

"My Lord, Jesus,
  What will you offer me?
  What will you concede to me?"
  So the people say when they begin to work.
    —Mateo Méndez Tzotzek, Text 106

Resal ("prayer") is a loan word from the
Spanish *rezar*, "to pray," or *rezo*, "prayer." The word for
prayer in Tzotzil means simply "talk directed to the deities."
The verb "to pray (to)" in Chamula (*k'opon*, transitive;
k'opoh, intransitive) is the same as "to talk (to)." The direct
communication with supernaturals requires in all cases a
highly stylized mode of speech. Metaphoric couplets and
parallel syntax thus enter into nearly every verbal transaction
between men and supernaturals, including the prayers of
both laymen and ritual specialists. However, shamans and
cargoholders know many more prayers as well as longer
prayers than the average layman. Specialists also allow themselves less variation than laymen in the content of their
prayers from one performance to the next. Chamulas explain
this difference by the fact that deities demand uniformity
from those who specialize in communication with them.

The genre of prayer includes a large number of subcategories: for laymen, for the dead, for cargoholders, for shamans, for the priest, and for evil people. The performer is the
distinguishing attribute in all cases but one, prayers for the
dead, which are defined by the recipient of the prayer rather
than by the performer. These categories are further subdivided according to where and by whom they are performed.
For example, there are two settings for shamans' prayers: at
the patient's (or the shaman's) home and at the church in
Chamula ceremonial center. These are the two principal foci
of curing activity in Chamula. In the case of prayers for evil
people, the subcategories are divided according to the four
kinds of evil individuals who pray for help in their endeavors:
Protestants, witches, murderers, and thieves. The class of cargoholders' prayers could be subdivided into as many subcategories as there are officials, fiestas, and deities. Similarly,
laymen's prayers are subdivided into as many subclasses as
there are individual ritual settings. The prayers for the dead
are subdivided according to the two occasions when Chamulas deal with the dead: at funerals and at the Feast of the
Dead on November 1, when the dead return to earth. Despite
these differentiations within each genre, nearly all prayers
are alike in structure, style, and rhythm. Only the priests'
prayers—which are now in Spanish rather than Latin—and
the evil persons' prayers—which are supposedly said back-
wards with certain reversals and antisocial substitutions—are
structurally different.[1] In sum, the genre of prayer reveals
a set of nonuniform criteria for intracategory distinctions,
not unlike the situation noted for subgenre distinctions in
language for rendering holy.

Settings for Performance

All prayer settings are also ritual settings, and most ritual
settings include some or all of the various elementary ritual
objects: crosses; pine needles or branches; resin incense;
tobacco, usually in cigarettes, sometimes in powdered form;
sugar cane rum or another beverage, usually alcoholic; and
candles. Even settings for evil peoples' prayers involve these

symbols, although they use symbols in perverse ways, such as turning the candles upside down and extinguishing them with black fuel oil. Proper behavior requires that candles, which are life symbols, be kept upright and that the officiant "feed" the flame of the candles with rum liquor.

The place of offering prayers is also significant to Chamulas. Evil people pray at night in caves and are believed to perform rituals while naked. The feeling against such asocial behavior makes it imperative to find an alibi if one is found praying outside at night in an unconventional place; otherwise an accusation of witchcraft would almost certainly be forthcoming. Daytime settings present greater flexibility and safety for prayer. Ideally the place of performance is constant for cargoholders' prayer, but laymen's prayers may be said almost anywhere that the need arises. Ordinarily, laymen pray at the church in Chamula Ceremonial Center, at roadside shrines, or in their homes. However, if a man on the road was seized with fear that the soul of a witch had just passed by him in the form of an animal, he could pray to San Juan for help immediately. He would only have to plant three pine sprigs or other sacred plants and begin to pray. Although I was told that a "reverent attitude" is also a sufficient setting for lay prayers, all the prayer settings that I saw involved one or more ritual objects.

Prayers for Laymen

All adult Chamulas should have some knowledge of the various prayers for laymen (*resal sventa kirsano*). They should know the prayers necessary for individual petitions for help and protection from deities. They should know a certain number of lay prayers for life crisis rituals and for the patient's part in curing rituals. In many cases a single prayer serves several purposes. In other cases, slight alterations make a single memorized prayer useful for many contexts. Because of the couplet structure of Chamula prayers, such substitutions are easy to make. Although individual couplets remain intact, they can recombine with other couplets to produce the right prayer for specified settings. Many prayers have only one passage that states the purpose of context of the prayer. Such a passage can be repeated and addressed to as many saints or other deities as necessary. This flexibility greatly extends the potential length of prayers. It also explains the mechanism by which lay prayers may vary considerably from person to person, even though their component parts (the individual couplets) are constant.

The deities addressed in prayer vary from one person to the next because all deities and saints do not protect all people uniformly at all times. Only *htotik* (the sun, "Our Father," and Jesus), *hme?tik* (the moon, "Our Mother," and the Virgin Mary), San Juan (the patron saint of Chamula), the earth gods, and *htotik hermanya* (San Jerónimo, who protects people's animal souls) are relevant to every person in Chamula. They form the nucleus of deities whose favor is needed by all. Other saints and deities help individuals according to special revelations and arrangements. The occupation of the person who prays is one criterion for choosing which supernaturals are essential to his well-being. According to this belief, which is probably of mixed Spanish Catholic and aboriginal origin, certain saints protect travelers; others, carpenters; still others, potters, owners of sheep and chickens, or musicians. The nature of the request in a prayer also determines which deities are addressed. For instance, if a man wishes to pray for the safety of his chickens from coyotes, he would probably address San Antonio, patron saint of barnyard fowl, and San Jerónimo, patron saint of animal soul companions. San Jerónimo's assistance would be needed because he is in a position to punish the animal soul companions (coyotes) of persons who kill chickens.

The following example of lay prayer comes from a series of salutation prayers (*nupel*) which laymen should offer to the saints in the church during and after major fiestas. These salutations should be accompanied by an offering of candles to one's favorite saints. The size, color, and number of candles depend on one's financial situation and on the nature of the request. The offering is made by melting a bit of wax and sticking the candles to a board or to the bare ground in front of the saint's image. Ideally, the entire family should participate in these fiesta salutations, but the head of the household, usually the eldest male, should lead the prayer. His wife and older children may say the prayer with him. In this particular text, Manvel has just lighted one twenty-centavo white candle for San Juan, whose fiesta has been celebrated. He and his family kneel on both knees and cross themselves, saying the accompanying ritual speech for measuring the face:

> baȼ'i rioš,
> Very God,
>> totil,
>> The Father,
>
> baȼ'i rioš,
> Very God,
>> nič'onil,
>> The Son,
>
> baȼ'i rioš,
> Very God,
>> spritu santo,
>> The Holy Spirit,
>
> Hesus.
> Jesus.
>
> lital to yolon ʔavok,
> I have come before your feet,
>> lital to yolon ʔak'ob,
>> I have come before your hands,
>
> šči ʔuk hnup,
> With my wife,
>> šči ʔuk hči ʔil,
>> With my companion,
>
> šči ʔuk kol,
> With my children,
>> šči ʔuk hnič'on.
>> With my offspring.
>
> hbeh yoh kantila,
> But a feeble candle,
>> lah yoh ničim.
>> But a withered flower.
>
> muk'ta san huan,
> Great San Juan,

muk'ta patron,
Great Patron,

lital ta yolon ʔavok,
I have come before your feet,
   lital ta yolon ʔak'ob,
   I have come before your hands,

san huan,
San Juan,
   patron.
   Patron.

tal ta ʔak'inale,
The time of your fiesta has come,
   tal ta ʔalekilalel,
   The time of your goodness has come,
      tal ta ʔavuȼilal;
      The time of your greatness has come;

ʔeč' ʔo ta ʔak'inal,
The time of your fiesta has passed,
   ʔeč' ʔo ta ʔalekilalel,
   The time of your goodness has passed,

k'alal to me hunab ʔosil,
Unto the whole earth,
   k'alal to me hunab banamil,
   Unto the whole of the land,

ta ʔak'inal,
Your festival,
   ta ʔalekilale,
   Your goodness,
      ta ʔavuȼilal,
      Your greatness,

muk'ta san huan,
Great San Juan,
   muk'ta patron.
   Great Patron.

mu to me šahipun,
May you not throw me aside,
   mu to me šatenun.
   May you not cast me away.

k'elun to me,
Watch over me,

ʔilun to me.
Care for me.

¢'ikbun to me hmul,
Be patient with my failings,
    ¢'ikbun to me hkoloʔ,
    Forgive my evil,

san huan,
San Juan,
    patron.
    Patron.

k'elun to me,
Watch over me,
    ʔilun to me,
    Care for me,

ti šmale,
At the setting of the sun,
    ti sakube,
    At the whitening of the dawn,

san huan,
San Juan,
    patron.
    Patron.

mu hnaʔ ta ʔak'oponel,
I do not know how to pray to you,
    mu hnaʔ ta ʔanupel,
    I do not know how to greet you,

pere ʔošib perton hbek'tal,
But give my body three pardons,
    pere ʔošib perton htakipal.
    But give my flesh three forgivenesses.

mu hnaʔ ta ʔak'oponel,
I do not know how to pray to you,
    mu hnaʔ ta ʔanupele.
    I do not know how to greet you.

hbelyo heč,
What I have said is wretched,
    hbelyo mečuk,
    What I have spoken is unworthy,

ta ʔak'oponele,
As a prayer to you,

ta ʔanupele.
As a greeting to you.

hesus sirikočyo,
Jesus, have mercy,
    kahval.
    My Lord.

baȼ'i rioš,
Very God,
    totil,
    The Father,

baȼ'i rioš,
Very God,
    nič'onil,
    The Son,

baȼ'i rioš,
Very God,
    spritu santo,
    The Holy Spirit,

hesus.
Jesus.

After finishing this prayer, the family party moves on to greet other saints in the church, probably to recite the same kind of prayer. In this prayer, the triple repetition of syntax and triple metaphoric restatement appear occasionally, though not as often as the couplet. This is by no means an exception to the rule of parallel structure in ritual speech, but rather a more emphatic statement of it. It is a heightened form of metaphoric stacking, which reflects the symbolic importance of the message.

Prayers for the Dead

Structurally and stylistically, prayers for the dead (*resal sventa h ʔanima*) are similar to the prayers for laymen. Indeed, they are said by laymen, and are generally known and used by all adults. Their classification as a separate genre came about because their context is unique. People use prayers for the dead to enlist the help of the deities in establishing communication with dead relatives. This happens on only two occasions: at funerals and at the annual Festival of the Dead, from October 30 through November 1. The dead are strange beings, for they are neither human nor animal nor divine. They belong in an intermediate category, which is the reason that people need a special medium for communication with them. This also explains why language for rendering holy, or formal ritual language, cannot be used alone to deal with the dead.

In the following fragmentary prayer for the dead, the setting is the early morning of November 1, when the dead are supposed to return to earth. At two o'clock that morning, each household prepares an elaborate meal for both the dead and the living. A table lavishly decorated with pine boughs and orange marigolds is set for several of the household's ancestors.[2] To receive a place at the table for the dead usually implies that the ancestor so honored gave or sold to living members of the household significant pieces of property, usually land. After generous portions of cabbage soup, meat, and other delicacies have been served to the dead and the candles have been lighted, the head of the household and his wife begin to call the souls of the dead. They call on souls of other relatives in addition to those for whom food is provided. Their calling requires the help of the deities. Kneeling before the table, which is in the position of the household altar, the husband and wife burst into startlingly dramatic sobs and pray amid tears, their bodies swaying back and forth in seeming anguish:

> misirikočyo, kahval,
> Have pity on me, my Lord,
>> misirikočyo, hesus,
>> Have pity on me, Jesus,
>
> toȼan, salvarol,
> Rise up, Savior,
>> toȼan, manvel,
>> Rise up, Emmanuel.
>
> hoybih talel ta ʔaničim bae,
> Turn your flowery countenance toward me,
>> hoybih talel ta ʔaničim sate.
>> Turn your flowery face toward me.

mi škol ʔo talel sč'ulel.
Have their souls departed toward us?
    mi škol ʔo talel yanima.
    Have their spirits commenced to return?

ti hvok'ebe,
Those of our forebears,
    ti kayanebe.
    Those of our ancestors?

ʔay, kahval,
Oh, my Lord!
    ʔay, hesus.
    Oh, Jesus!

koltabun me talel sč'ulel ʔun,
Release their souls and send them to us,
    koltabun me talel yanima ʔun,
    Release their spirits and send them to us,

ti hvok'ebe,
Those of our forebears,
    ti kayanebe,
    Those of our ancestors,

ti hmuk'tot,
Of our grandfathers,
    ti hyayaʔe.
    Of our grandmothers.

ʔay, tot.
Oh, Father!
    ʔay, yaya.
    Oh, Grandmother!
        ʔay, muk'tot.
        Oh, Grandfather!

ti laʔ me k'elo ti hnatikune,
Come and see our house,
    ti laʔ me ʔilo ti hk'ulebtikune.
    Come and look at the humble place of our wealth.

ti naʔo me talel ti hnatikune,
Find your way to come to our house,
    ti naʔo me talel ti hk'ulebtikune.
    Find your way to come to the humble place of our
        wealth.

ʔay, tot.
Oh, Father!
    ʔay, meʔ.
    Oh, Mother!

naʔo me talel ti hnatikune,
Find your way to our house,
    naʔo me talel ti hk'ulebtikune.
    Find your way to the humble place of our wealth.

ti laʔ me ȼako ti hčeš ʔitah ʔaloʔ ʔune,
Come, take and eat a bit of cabbage,
    ti laʔ me ȼako ti hčeš napuš ʔaloʔ ʔune.
    Come, take and eat a bit of turnip green.

k'ano me talel ti ʔošib perton ʔune,
Oh, beg that the three pardons be given,
    k'ano me talel ti ʔišib lesina ʔune.
    Oh, beg that the three forgivenesses be granted.

ʔay, kahval.
Oh, my Lord!
    ʔay, hesus.
    Oh, Jesus!

mi školtalel sč'ulel ti htotʔune.
Has the soul of our father departed?
    mi školtalel sč'ulel ti hmeʔune.
    Has the soul of our mother departed?

ʔay, kahval.
Oh, my Lord!
    ʔay, hesus.
    Oh, Jesus!

mu to me šavik' ti hč'ulel ʔune,
But do not yet call our souls,
    mu to me šavik' ti kanimae.
    But do not yet call our spirits.

ʔok' ʔavanan to me ta yolon kurus,
Cry and make a loud noise beneath the Cross,
    ʔok' ʔavanan to me ta yolon pašyon.
    Cry and make a loud noise beneath the passion.

bal to me šavaʔi ti hčeš ʔitah ʔaloʔe,
Come, eat and savor your cabbage,
    bal to me šavaʔi ti hčeš napuš ʔaloʔe.
    Come, eat and savor your turnip greens.

bal to me šava?i ti hbeh ?akantila,
Come and savor the essence of your candles,
    bal to me šava?i ti hbeh ?aničim.
    Come and savor the essence of your flowers.

kahval,
My Lord,
    hesus.
    Jesus.

kolta bun me talel sč'ulel ti htote,
Release and send us the soul of our father,
    kolta bun me talel sč'ulel ti hme?e.
    Release and send us the spirit of our mother.

to¢an, salvarol,
Rise up, Savior,
    to¢an, manvel.
    Rise up, Emmanuel.

la? me k'elo ti hnatik ?une,
Come and see our house,
    la? me k'elo ti hk'ulebtik ?une.
    Come and see the humble place of our wealth.

tot,
Father,
    me?e.
    Mother.

After the prayer, liquor is served to both living and dead participants. Then the living eat their food, while the souls of the dead come in and skim the essence from their food. The prayer is repeated at various times throughout the day the Festival of the Dead.

Prayers for Cargoholders

Cargoholders are more bound than lay people to say their prayers (*resal sventa h?abteletik*) and other ritual formulas in the correct manner. This ideal is encouraged by the ritual advisers who tutor new cargoholders and accompany them in their many duties. Since the new cargoholder learns the one correct version from his adviser, he is expected to use that version and pass it on when he serves as tutor to someone else in the future.

The new cargoholder must learn his prayers with exceeding care. They are so structured that substitutions, variations, and expansions can and do occur at various places. For instance, one phrase in a prayer implies not only a certain second phrase for the completion of a couplet, but also several more couplets for the completion of a sequence. The sequences of couplets can be duplicated or dropped completely, as the situation dictates. Such variation often occurs in a single cargoholder's prayers from one fiesta to the next. The reason for this variation is that different saints require greater or lesser attention from each cargoholder at each fiesta. Therefore, it is not contradictory for Chamulas to say that prayers for cargoholders do not change when in fact it would seem to the outside observer that they do. The point is that the alternatives for acceptable variation are built into the canons of style.

The following example comes from the annual change-of-office ceremony for the most prestigious mayordomo cargo, that of San Juan. The three-day ritual takes place between December 22 and 24. The incoming mayordomo's entourage of assistants comes to his house in his hamlet at dawn on December 22. After a morning of drinking liquor and partaking of a ritual meal, the whole party begins the procession to Chamula Ceremonial Center amid singing, hand cannon blasts, and skyrocket explosions. All the assistants carry ritual objects from the mayordomo's household in bundles on their backs. They literally move him to his new house and new role. At about two o'clock in the afternoon, they arrive at the incoming mayordomo's house in the center, which he has previously made arrangements to rent. When they arrive at the new house, they go to the patio cross, which the mayordomo's flower gatherers have previously decorated with pine boughs and other plants. An assistant places a lighted censer before the patio shrine, and the whole party together, led by the ritual adviser and the incoming

mayordomo, begins to pray for the success of their coming
year of service to San Juan, the patron saint of Chamula.
They begin by crossing themselves and making the proper
salutations:

misirikočyo, kahval.
Have mercy, my Lord.

muk'ul san huan,
Great San Juan,
   muk'ul patron.
   Great Patron.

k'u yepal čital ta yolon ?avok,
How much I come before your feet,
   k'u yepal čital ta yolon ?ak'ob,
   How much I come before your hands,

šči?uk hnup,
With my spouse,
   šči?uk hči?il,
   With my companion,

šči?uk ?avob,
With your guitar,
   šči?uk ?asot,
   With your gourd rattle,

šči?uk ?avah,
With your servant,
   mastaro,
   The musician,

šči?uk ?avah,
With your servant,
   ?ulovil,
   The gruel-maker,

šči?uk ?avah,
With your servant,
   ¢ayovil,
   The cook,

šči?uk ?atuk',
With your shot guns,
   šči?uk ?akanyon.
   With your canons.

ta ¢obol ma ʔavalab,
Your children are gathered together,
　　ta ¢obol ma ʔanič'nab,
　　Your offspring are gathered together,

ta ʔayilele,
For you to see,
　　ta ʔak'elele.
　　For you to witness.

muk'ul san huan,
Great San Juan,
　　muk'ul patron.
　　Great Patron.

ta ša me šaʔoč ta kok,
Now you are to be delivered at my feet,
　　ta ša me šaʔoč ta hk'ob.
　　Now you are to be entrusted to my hands.

Hoʔon ša me ʔavač' mosovun,
Now I am your new servant,
　　Hoʔon ša me ʔavač' kiʔara ʔun.
　　Now I am your new attendant.

čahtotin ʔo,
I shall be as father to you,
　　čahmeʔin ʔo.
　　I shall be as mother to you.

ti hun ʔavil,
For one year,
　　ti hun k'ak'al,
　　The same as for each day,

muk'ul san huan,
Great San Juan,
　　muk'ul patron.
　　Great Patron.

štun ʔo hbeh pom,
There is incense for you,
　　štun ʔo hbeh č'aʔil.
　　There is smoke for you.

čahpet,
I shall embrace you,
　　čahkuč,
　　I shall carry you,

ti hun ʔavile,
For one year,
　ti hun k'ak'ale.
　The same as for each day.

kahval,
My Lord,
　hesus.
　Jesus.

ta ȼobol ma ʔavalab,
Your children are gathered together,
　ta ȼobol ma ʔaničʼnab,
　Your offspring are gathered together,

ta ʔavilele,
For you to see,
　ta ʔak'elele.
　For you to witness.

ti mu me šuʔ ta hun yahval,
One alone cannot assume your care,
　ti mu me šuʔ ta hun svinkilel.
　A man alone cannot do your will.

ti ʔaʔto me lek.
What a good thing it is!
　ti ʔaʔto me ʔuȼ.
　What a joy it is!

ta ȼobol ʔavalab,
That your children are gathered together,
　ta ȼobol ʔaničʼnab,
　That your offspring are gathered together,

ti vaʔalan me ʔun,
To stand up for you,
　ti tak'lan me ʔun.
　To stand firmly for you.

ti mu me k'usi hnupankutik,
May nothing befall us,
　ti mu me k'usi hyaʔinkutik,
　May nothing harm us,

ta sakhamanuk me ʔaničim ba,
May your flowery countenance shine in white radiance,

ta sakhamanuk me ʔaničim sat,
May your flowery face shine in soft brilliance,
ti k'elunkutik me,
That you may watch over us,
   ti ʔilunkutik me,
   That you may care for us,
šči ʔuk ʔavah mastaro,
And your musicians,
   šči ʔuk ʔavah ʔantunyero,
   And your canoneers,
      šči ʔuk ʔavah ¢ayovil.
      And your cook.
ti mu me k'usi hnupankutik,
May nothing befall us,
   ti mu me k'usi hyaʔinkutik,
   May nothing harm us,
muk'ul san huan,
Great San Juan,
   muk'ul patron.
   Great Patron.
ta ša me šaʔoč ta kok ʔun,
Now you are to be delivered at my feet,
   ta ša me šaʔoč ta hk'ob ʔun,
   Now you are to be entrusted to my hands,
šči ʔuk hnup,
And those of my spouse,
   šči ʔuk hči ʔil,
   My companion;
šči ʔuk htot,
And those of my father,
   šči ʔuk hme ʔ;
   And my mother;
šči ʔuk ʔavalab,
And those of your children,
   šči ʔuk ʔanič'nab,
   And your offspring,
ti Hoʔot me ʔak'elel,
For you to witness,
   ti Hoʔot me ʔavilel,
   For you to see,

ti hun ʔavil,
For one year,
   ti hun k'ak'al,
   As for each day,

muk'ul san huan,
Great San Juan,
   muk'ul patron.
   Great Patron.

hsaʔ banamil,
I search over the earth,
   hsaʔ vinahel,
   I search over the heavens,

vašton vinik,
Man of the care of authority,
   vašton hkašlan,
   Ladino of the staff,

yahvalel vinahele,
Patron of Heaven,
   yahvalel lorya,
   Owner of Glory,

htot san mačyo, kahval,
Our Father Saint Matthew, our Lord,
   htot san mačyo, hesus,
   Our Father Saint Matthew, Jesus,

smeʔ vinahel,
Mother of Heaven,
   smeʔ lorya,
   Mother of Glory,

skurusil htot,
Father of the Cross,
   spašyonal htot,
   Father of the Passion,

k'uyepal ta šaʔoč ta kok.
How is it that you come before my feet?
   k'uyepal ta šaʔoč ta hk'ob.
   How is it that you commend yourself to my hands?

ti muk'ul san huane,
Great San Juan,
   ti muk'ul patrone,
   Great Patron,

ti hun ʔavile,
For one year,
　ti hun k'ak'ale.
　As for each day.

They all cross themselves, thereby taking temporary leave of the deities. The incoming mayordomo remains at the altar for more prayer while canoneers shoot fireworks to mark their arrival in the Chamula Ceremonial Center. The women and assistants begin placing the goods in and around the house for the next two days of ritual, in which the new mayordomo will formally assume the burden of serving San Juan for one year.

This text has interesting time-space coding. The high redundancy and dense metaphoric stacking indicate that spiritual heat and the ritual mood are intense. Thus, the repetitive dyadic style is much more than a mnemonic device, being itself a reflection of the cyclical cosmic order that is always implicit and sometimes explicit in the ritual setting. Just as redundancy was necessary in the several creations to bring man to his present state of order, it is likewise necessary in symbolic restatements of the conditions of that order. The need for redundancy applies to ritual action and symbolism as well as to the language used to execute the ritual and to talk about it. Thus, it seems plausible that the two- to four-part parallel structure in prayer recapitulates in style the polysegmental temporal and spatial realities of its content. In this way, stylistic redundancy becomes an aspect of the time-space principle.

These stylistic and symbolic dimensions can be observed jointly in the italicized passage of the preceding prayer. The passage begins with the couplet, "Now I am your new servant; /Now I am your new attendant." This is said in impassioned singsong tones, the speakers facing the pine-laden shrine, incense burners pouring out aromatic smoke to the open sky, harps and guitars sounding, skyrockets and cannon bursting in the air. The ritual setting breaks the spatial and temporal barrier between men and gods. The past becomes present; the dwelling place of the gods becomes the same as the sacred space in which the officials carry out their tasks. The incense mentioned in the prayer, like the formal language used to deliver the prayer, is one of the media, one of the essences, which unite the space of men and the space of gods and make them one for the ritual setting.

In the prayer the incoming cargoholder also promises to carry the burden of the saint, which he will literally do when he carries the litter of the saint in processions in the sacred space of the church atrium. This concept of carrying the burden of time and deity for a yearly cycle is not unlike the "year-bearer" concept of Maya antiquity (see Bricker, 1966). The cargoholder metaphorically promises to accept the burden of cyclical time ("I shall embrace you;/I shall carry you"), a task that he will share with the deity for his year in office, "as for each day." The incense, which the mayordomo must burn each day, will not only tie the servant to his sacred patron but also serve as food for San Juan and impart holiness to his servant. The cargoholder, through his identification with the maintenance of cosmic order, carries the presence of virtuous men into the most distant reaches of time and space. As he announces in the prayer with all humility, he will serve as "father" and "mother" to San Juan. He thereby ties himself metaphorically to the first two creations, to the lineages of the gods, and to the sacred if threatening space at the edge of the universe.

Prayers for Shamans

Prayers for shamans (*resal sventa h'ilol*) are less strict than prayers for cargoholders with regard to variations from one performance to the next. The reason is that shamans know their prayers by revelation, usually through dreams, which makes them subject to some reinterpretation and revision at the shaman's discretion.[3] However, revision and change in shamans' prayers usually involve merely a reshuffling of couplet sequences that are known to all shamans. The verbal aspect of a shaman's performance is crucial to his reputation. A good shaman not only makes correct diagnoses but also knows how to pray, how much and to whom to pray, and with what paraphernalia, in order to cure each patient's ailment.

Chamula illnesses usually have physical manifestations, but not always. The reason for ambiguity in this matter is that all Chamula illnesses are believed to be caused by one or a combination of a vast number of afflictions of the soul. Each person has three souls or spirits. One dwells on the tip of the tongue and is associated with his candle of fate in the sky. The other two souls (a junior form and a senior form) are shared by one's animal soul companion. The junior animal lives in Tzontevitz Mountain in a corral that is cared for by the junior form of San Jerónimo. The senior animal lives in a corral in the sky and is watched over by the sun deity and the senior form of San Jerónimo.[4] Any misfortune that happens to these souls will in the near future make the person with whom they are associated either ill or vulnerable to illness. By pulsing the wrist to obtain the message of the blood, and by the ability to "see" (*ʔil*, "to see," is the root of *hʔilol*, "shaman" or "seer"), the shaman determines what has happened to the soul, how serious it is, and whose fault it is. Common illnesses involve partial loss of the soul, sale of the soul to the earth god, release of the soul animal from its corral, or beating of the soul animal by another, stronger animal. Sometimes these misfortunes are the victim's own fault, but more often they are caused by the powerful, aggressive soul of a witch who either works for himself or hires out to the victim's enemy. The nature of the illness and its cause determine the content of the curing ceremony. The prayer and the shaman's symbols (certain kinds and quantities of plants, candles, liquor, and other substances) are designed to restore the proper condition to the soul. When the soul regains its health, the illness passes.

The following prayer for shamans was offered in a ceremony for an adolescent boy who was suffering from several kinds of *mahbenal*, an illness caused by the beating of a person's animal soul companion by a larger animal, probably the soul companion of a witch. Pulsing had taken place on the previous day, shortly after the boy's father called the shaman. The symptoms and pulsing revealed that the boy was

in a very bad condition. He had coughed blood and suffered
from a nosebleed all of the previous night. The diagnosis was
that he had both "red punishment" and "green punishment."
The shaman told the father what kinds, colors, and quantity
of candles to buy as well as the kinds of plants and herbs to
bring for the ceremony. The shaman pulsed the boy again
on the morning of the ceremony and declared that his
condition had worsened and that it would require a longer
prayer to achieve the cure. Although the addition would cost
more in cash payment to the curer than he had previously
announced, the father told him to proceed. After the initial
preparations, which included the placing of dozens of candles
in rows by color and size in front of the house cross, the
shaman began. He lighted the candles, sprinkled a jigger of
rum over them, and began to pray. He first blew over the
opening of a tiny hollow gourd to "call" the soul of the
patient back to its owner. The text of the prayer is here
greatly abbreviated, for the praying itself lasted over an hour:

> uh . . . uh . . .
> Uh . . . uh . . .
> *(Shaman blows over the opening of a gourd while offering
> it in each of the four directions.)*[5]
> nompare rioš totik,
> In the name of God the Father,
>> nompare rioš nič'onil,
>> In the name of God the Son,
>
> hesuk ʔune,
> Jesus,
>> kahval.
>> My Lord.
> to¢an, šalik,
> Rise up, Savior,
>> to¢an, manvel, kahval.
>> Rise up, Emmanuel, my Lord.
> bat ta ʔaničim ba ʔune,
> Your flowery countenance has turned away,
>> bat ta ʔaničim sat ʔune, kahval.
>> Your flowery face has looked askance, my Lord.

čahta ti ta ʔalel ʔune,
I seek you in this petition,
 čahta ti ta lok'esel ʔune, kahval,
 I seek you in this cure, my Lord,

yuʔun li stohol ʔavok ʔune,
For the payment[6] lies at your feet,
 yuʔun li stohol ʔak'ob,
 For the payment lies before your hands,

tana ne kahval,
Oh yes, my Lord
 tana.
 Oh yes.

bu naka šavak' ʔun,
It is a matter of what you alone give,
 bu naka šakelanʔun, kahval.
 It is a matter of what you alone present, my Lord.
lavak'be ti šc'ulel ʔune;
You gave him his soul;
 lavak'be ti yanima ʔune, kahval, tana.
 You gave him his spirit, oh yes, my Lord.

baȼ'i yolonuk ta ʔavokik ʔun,
He is truly before your feet,
 yolonuk ta ʔak'obikik ʔun, kahval.
 He is before your hands, my Lord.

ȼoyanbikun ti ta ʔapatik ʔune,
May we commend him to follow behind you,
 ȼoyanbikun ti ta ʔašokonik ʔune, kahval.
 May we commend him to be at your side, my Lord.

baȼ'i laʔ to sk'el ʔasatik ʔune.
Truly, come, let your face shine upon us!
 laʔ to sk'el ʔavelovik ʔune.
 Come, watch over us!

toȼan, šalik,
Rise up, Savior,
 toȼan, manvel, kahval.
 Rise up, Emmanuel, my Lord

haʔuk tana ʔune, kahval.
Whatever may be your will, my Lord,
 haʔuk tana ʔune, hkašlan.
 Whatever may be your will, Ladino.

k'uyepal ti ku?un šivulel tana.
So much is my burden!
    li hvuleb šivulel tana.
    And here I bring my burden!

li yav ?anukulik ?une,
To the place of your leather rope,
    li yav ?ač'ohonik ?une,
    To the place of your cord,[7]
        li yav ?amahbenik, tana, kahval.
        To the place of your punishment, oh yes, my Lord.

ha?uk tana ?une, kahval,
Whatever may be your will, my Lord,
    ha?uk tana ne, hkašlan.
    Whatever may be your will, Ladino.

ti ?ošlahun čolun ša me talel,
The thirteen rows have been supplied,
    ti ?ošlahun melun ša me talel.
    The thirteen lines have been made.[8]

ti yaš ni?anun ša me talel,
The green sprigs of pine have been supplied,
    ti yaš ¢'ahanun ša me talel.
    The green boughs of pine have been placed.

ti č'ul roša?un ša me talel,
The sacred rose has been brought,
    ti č'ul man¢aniyo?un ša me talel,
    The sacred manzanilla has been brought,
        ti č'ul ničimun ša me talel.
        The sacred plants have been placed.

?a li kič'oh tal ?une,
We have brought them,
    ?a li kapoh tal ?une, kahval,
    We have blended them together, my Lord,

yu?un švul hyamtik ?o,
So that it will be eased,
    yu?un švul hyočtik ?o,
    So that it will be loosened,

li mu šanvil mahbenale,
The awful punishment[9] of the traveler,
    li mu nupetbe mahbenal,
    The awful punishment that he encountered,

li mu yašal mahbenal,
The awful green punishment,
   li mu ȼahal mahbenal, tana kahval . . .
   The awful red punishment, oh yes, my Lord . . .

(Shaman repeats part of the above and invokes a long series of saints.)

kušes²o talel ²uninal bak,
Bring health back to his little bones,
   kušes²o talel ti ²uninal č'uš.
   Bring vigor back into his little muscles.

la² ²etuk ša me batel ²un, kahval,
Come, remove it and take it away, my Lord,
   ²ič' ²abel lok'el tana ²un,
   Command it to come out,

mu šanvil mahbenal,
The awful punishment of the traveler,
   mu nupetbe mahbenal,
   The awful punishment that he encountered,

mu č'ulelal mahbenal,
The awful punishment of his soul,
   mu č'ulelal ši²el tana ²un, kahval.
   The awful fright of his soul, my Lord.

²ič' ²abel lok'el ²un,
Take it away,
   ²ič' ²avaleb lok'el ²un,
   Command it to depart,

tana ²un, kahval,
Oh yes, my Lord,
   hesus.
   Jesus.

(Shaman blows on the gourd again, once in each of the four directions.)

uh . . . uh . . .
Uh . . . uh . . .

nompre rioš,
In the name of God,
   kahval,
   My Lord,

heč yepal yo keʔun,
So my mouth rests,
   heč yepal yo htiʔ ʔun.
   I shall say no more.

(After the prayer, all participants drink liquor and then eat cabbage soup, beans, and tortillas, which concludes the ceremony.)

The text indicates the typical rhythmic difference between prayers and language for rendering holy. Here the rhythmic intervals are determined by the placement of the word *kahval* ("my Lord"). Each phrase rises and falls in pitch and intensity of tone between the points at which "my Lord" is spoken. The variation in pitch and tone within these couplet "verses" is so great that it almost seems as though the shamans sing their prayers. This intoned quality characterizes nearly all subgenres of prayer. In prayers for shamans this song-like or chanted quality is heightened because each couplet or triplet receives a complete curve of pitch variation, which makes the sound more melodic than chant-like. Of all the genres of ancient words, only prayer and song address the deities directly, which may explain why they use delivery styles that are so distinctly removed from ordinary speech. They might be called the "linguistic essence," to borrow a metaphor from other Chamula ritual substances. These genres might be said to represent an extreme expression of the Chamula equation: the greater the symbolic significance of a social transaction, the more highly stylized, invariant, and symbolically condensed is the language used to conduct the transaction.

(10) Song

When Our Father put on a fiesta long ago, he
prepared rum liquor.
It was from the juice of flowers that he
made it.

San Juan had maize and sugarcane beer as a
drink.
He made it very sweet for them to drink.

Then they tasted their drinks;
They exchanged a measure-full of their
drinks . . .

"Ah! I feel like we ought to be singing!" said
San Juan.
"Ah! That's a wonderful idea!" said Our
Father in Heaven.
—Manuel López Calixto, Text 141

Chamulas do not classify as "song"
(*k'ehoh*) any music that does not have a religious context.
Most songs can also be performed in secular contexts, but
informants insist that all songs are ultimately destined to
please the deities. That is why they are addressed to the
deities. Ladino music is not "song," even though Ladino
records are sometimes played on battery-operated phono-
graphs during religious fiestas. In fact, a hired Ladino band
often plays in the kiosk of the church during fiestas. Regardless of its fiesta setting, such music is dismissed by Chamulas
as *musika* (from the Spanish *música*, meaning "music").
This category lies literally in another world as far as their
taxonomy is concerned. Although it is proper background
noise for fiestas, it does not approach the domain of song.
The instruments used to play it are not Chamula instruments,
and the language of the lyrics is Spanish, not *baḏ'i k'op*, the
"true language."
Song to Chamulas means any religious musical piece that
can be sung. It should always be addressed directly to supernaturals. The singer, however, need not be human. For
instance, the flute is said to "sing" or "cry" in a drum and
flute combination. In other words, it is not necessary for a

person to perform the physical act of singing in order for
a piece to be considered song. At funerals, for example,
harp and guitar play constantly, but no one sings. The reason,
Chamulas say, is that no one is happy. Nevertheless, Chamulas
maintain that if people wanted to sing, they could do so; it is
simply not the custom. They explain that the harp "sings"
in the case of funerals. Thus, the possibility of singing by any
of several agents seems to characterize all "song," which
implies that words are either performed or implicitly contained in the performance. The musical totality (words and
music) is called song. The music or rhythm alone is called
son. *Son* is not a distinct genre of song, but an aspect of it.
For example, an inexperienced harpist might ask his superior:
"What *son* does the 'Third Song of San Juan' have?" A
similar question could be asked of a flute or drum player.

Chamulas recognize two major kinds of song. The distinctive feature of each is the deity to whom it is addressed: the
patron of souls or the saints. The first genre seems to include
only one song and some variants, always played on harp
and guitar or on a button accordion, the three main Chamula
instruments. This song is perhaps the most popular of all
Chamula songs. It is sometimes used in association with curing
ceremonies. Songs of the second genre, for the saints, are
subdivided according to the instruments on which they are
played. The first subgroup is songs for musicians who play
harp and guitar (*sventa mastaro*). Those instruments and the
songs performed on them are associated with most cargo and
life crisis rituals, and with some curing rituals. To most
Chamulas, it is without significance that the instruments,
melodies, and harmonies of this group are of sixteenth- and
seventeenth-century European origin (Harrison and Harrison,
1968).

The second subgroup of songs for the saints includes songs
for drum and flute musicians (*sventa kantol*). Unlike the
string musicians, who must be recruited to assist each cargoholder for his term of office, drum and flute musicians have
life positions, which are passed on in the male line. They do
not appear at all cargo affairs and must be formally invited
by the appropriate cargoholders. In addition to the drum

and reed flute, these musicians or their assistants play the horn (*korneta* or *ʔok'es*). They also play a clay ocarina and a hollow wooden stick on Good Friday. Although the role of all of these instruments is not entirely clear to me, they belong together as a group.[2] Musicians place all of the wind and percussion instruments before the string instruments in "order of creation." This judgment coincides with the Western view of their history, since most of the nonstring instruments and their songs are of pre-Columbian origin. The drum and flute musicians play their instruments during the climax segments of major public ritual. Such songs have no words. They "sing" by themselves.

Settings for Performance

A Chamula narrative (Text 141) tells of the origins of song. It appeared after the Creator and San Juan had first tasted liquor and found it pleasant. They decided that people, too, should drink liquor, dance, sing, and be happy. These activities would "warm their hearts" and provide the right setting for them to speak to the gods. Song, therefore, is crucially important to the ritual setting because it provides aspects of "metaphoric heat" that are desirable for communication with the supernaturals. Song contributes heat and happiness, which are qualities valued by men and gods alike. It is the distilled heat of language.

Although ritual provides the primary setting of Chamula songs, their performance is by no means restricted to formal ritual sequences. Wandering guitarists at fiestas, who are usually adolescent boys, seem to play and sing the saints' songs and the soul songs for amusement. These performers, usually playing the guitar or accordion, are not associated with any cargoholder or ritual group. Such casual playing and singing also take place at Chamula homes during the leisure time at noon and in the evening. Chamula men also take guitars to the coffee plantations and sing the religious songs informally in the evening in workers' quarters. Harps are also used for informal singing and playing sessions, but not as much as guitars, because they are more difficult to transport.

Whether informal or formal, the playing of instruments is strictly a male activity. In general singing is also a male activity, although wives of cargoholders are expected to sing at certain ritual affairs. I never saw women or girls singing publicly in informal contexts.

Within the formal ritual context, a harp-and-guitar musician (*mastaro*, from the Spanish *maestro*, meaning "teacher" or "musical director") is technically the servant of the sponsoring cargoholder. However, these musicians frequently assume a more directive role in the ritual proceedings. The intoxication of ritual personnel usually explains this passing of authority to the musicians. The ritual personnel are supposed to know when to request specific songs in the ritual sequence. The task of the musicians (usually two guitarists and two harpists) is to follow the lead of the cargoholder or ritual adviser when either remembers to start a song. He usually does so by setting the rhythm with a gourd rattle and singing the first line *a cappella*. The harp and guitar begin the accompaniment following his lead. Musicians may sing along with the cargoholder and his assistants. Good musicians should, however, be prepared for the frequent occasions on which neither cargoholder nor ritual adviser is sober or attentive enough to begin the correct song at the correct time. In that event, the senior musician (the "first harpist") must know all of the songs associated with the ritual sequence. He must also know the correct order in which the songs are sung, as well as all of the words. Ultimately, the musicians may have to function autonomously in any cargo affair. They are, therefore, critically important as ritual "prompters," who see to it that rituals proceed even though the officials themselves may be incapacitated.

Style

Composed entirely of formal metaphoric couplets, the verbal content of the harp and guitar songs for the saints amounts to a narrative of the progress of a ritual. Each ritual sequence usually involves the salutation of deities by the cargoholders. This action is duly narrated by couplets of praise and supplication in the corresponding song. Follow-

ing the proper number of invocations of deities, often
accompanied by just as many songs, a major piece of ritual
action usually follows in the sequence. This too is narrated
by the appropriate song. An example is the ritual sequence
called the "Clothes-washing of San Juan." The principal
motif of the accompanying song lyric runs: "We are washing
San Juan's clothes." As redundancy is greater in song lyrics
than in any other genre of pure words, it is not uncommon
for such a lyric as this one to be sung a hundred times in a
single morning of ritual washing of the saint's clothing.

The music is also extremely redundant and in this respect
complements the lyrics. Chamula musicians reported that
in all there are only six *sonetik* ("melodies"). These musical
lines can be used to accompany the hundreds of songs in
the Chamula tradition.

The songs for drum and flute musicians (*sventa kantol*)
have a similarly redundant narrative role in ritual. Although
songs for these instruments have no words, they seem to
signal the location of important foci of ritual activity amid
the chaos that seems to accompany public ceremonials. As
ritual personnel repeat the important parts of their actions at
different places, the drum and flute, as well as the fireworks,
announce the new location. There is a similar role for drum
and flute music in Zinacantan (Haviland, 1967: 108).

Song thus restates in its own medium the essence of the
ritual proceedings it accompanies. It carries the same information as ritual action, prayers, and language for rendering
holy, but in condensed form. The monotonous repetition
of lines that describe significant parts of the ritual illustrates
the unity of redundancy, on the one hand, and symbolic
condensation, on the other. Information that is sung is
critical and must therefore be repeated many times.

Songs for the Patron of Souls

The genre of songs for the patron of souls (*k'ehoh sventa
yahval hč'uleletik*) is associated with one definite melody.
This melody is related to the chaconne and saraband forms,
which were probably introduced by Dominican missionaries

in the sixteenth century (Harrison and Harrison, 1968). The words, however, refer to pre-Columbian concepts about animal-soul companions. I heard only one text sung to the melody, although I was assured by Chamulas that there are others. Chamulas refer to this song as "Song of the Jaguar Animal" (*bolomčon*). Curiously, it does not have any specific ritual context. Frequently it is sung at certain curing ceremonies and used as filler for cargo rituals when no songs for the saints are required. It is also performed by wandering musicians at the Festival of Games. Most Chamulas claimed that the form was borrowed from Zinacantan, but this belief does not seem to diminish the importance of the genre to Chamulas.

The following text of this song was performed as filler during an alférez ceremony in the atrium of the Chamula church. By "filler" is meant that the song maintained the ritual mood but did not accompany any particular ritual action. In fact, the alférez himself was absent during the performance. Ritual drinking of rum followed the performance. Both harpist and guitarist played and sang. Some of the alférez's assistants also sang the "Song of the Jaguar Animal":

bolomčon ta vinahel,
Jaguar Animal in heaven,
    bolomčon ta banamil.
    Jaguar Animal on earth.

yahvalel ta vinahel,
Patron of heaven,
    yahvalel ta banamil.
    Patron of earth.

koškoš ʔavakan, bolomčon,
Your legs are lame, Jaguar Animal,
    natik ʔavakan, bolomčon.
    Your legs are long, Jaguar Animal.

tintin ʔavisim, bolomčon,
Your whiskers are spiny, Jaguar Animal,
    natik ʔavisim, bolomčon.
    Your whiskers are long, Jaguar Animal.

likan, tot,
Get up, father,
    likan, meʔ.
    Get up, mother.

vaʔalan, tot,
Stand up, father,
    vaʔalan, meʔ.
    Stand up, mother.

toȼan, tot,
Rise up, father,
    toȼan, meʔ.
    Rise up, mother.

(This sequence is repeated four times.)

The relevance of this song to its particular setting was somewhat unclear. The performers reported that it was not an obligatory performance. It is possible, however, that the song was a commentary on the importance of their ritual tasks. The jaguar is the most powerful of all the soul companion animals and is therefore believed to be the soul companion of powerful men, such as cargoholders and famous shamans. The "earth" and "heaven" in the text refer to the two dwelling places (corrals) of animal soul companions. The text implies no cult of the jaguar, although its pre-Columbian antecendent might have carried such a meaning. It expresses a matter of common knowledge: the jaguar is strong and commands respect from his animal inferiors. The same relationship holds for the animal's human counterparts. It is possible that the performers sang this song at this time because it indirectly expressed their respect for the alférez whom they were serving. It might also have expressed a certain pride in the significance of their own ritual tasks. Either of these possible interpretations depends on the message redundancy or metaphoric stacking that characterizes the song text. The considerable importance of the jaguar in Chamula beliefs about the soul and the cosmos is emphasized through the "stacking" of information about the great cat of the lowland jungles.

Songs for the Saints

The category of songs for the saints (*k'ehoh sventa htotiketike*) includes a very large corpus of harp and guitar songs that are used to accompany nearly all cargo and life crisis rituals and some shamanistic rituals. Like the songs for the patron of souls, the melodies, instruments, and harmonies of saints' songs were no doubt introduced by the Spaniards Their verbal content, however, is patterned on the familiar Maya metaphoric couplets. When asked about songs in general, Chamulas usually commented on songs for the saints first. The reason is that hardly a day passes without some cargoholder sponsoring a public or private ritual in the ceremonial center. On fiesta days, dozens of cargoholders sponsor such religious ceremonials. Each official at the proceedings has harpists and guitarists to accompany his ritual activities. The cargoholder uses a small gourd rattle to accompany his own singing and to mark the proper rhythm for the musicians. More important, the rattle serves as a signal to begin and end the songs. When the official shouts "Musicians," they cease playing. Then they rest or begin another song. The musicians should be able to handle their responsibilities alone in case the cargoholder is busy or incapacitated.

Most ritual sequences involve songs that invoke deities at the same time that they narrate the ritual action taking place. Each major ritual sequence has from two to twelve songs associated with it. They ordinarily should be sung in a specific order, yet drunkenness and commotion sometimes make it hard to achieve this ideal. A typical sequence of four songs is sung at the Festival of San Juan. The setting is a six-hour ceremony of praise, which the mayordomo for San Juan must perform in front of the image of the saint in Chamula church on the morning of the day of his fiesta (June 24). The performance precedes the noon climax of the fiesta, when fourteen saints' images are carried in procession around the atrium of the church. Preparation for this event begins at about five o'clock in the morning, when the mayordomos for all the saints go to the church in full fiesta costume with their respective groups of ritual assistants. After prayers, the censing of the shrines of the various saints (whom they have previously dressed in special fiesta attire), and the drinking of several rounds of liquor, they begin to sing and dance before their saints. All mayordomos engage in this activity with the help of their assistants. The following lyric is the first and principal song of a set of four sung by the mayordomo for San Juan. The text is reproduced with full redundancy, just as it is performed at the fiesta:[3]

    sk'ak'alil la ʔak'inale,
It is the day of your fiesta,
    sk'ak'alil la ʔapašku ʔale.
    It is the day of your passion.

muk'ulil san huane,
Great San Juan,
    muk'ulil patrone.
    Great Patron.

k'uyepal čihšanavotik ʔo ta hlikel bi,
How soon we are to be walking!
    k'uyepal čihšanavotik ʔo ta htabel bi.
    How soon we are to be commencing the procession!

sk'ak'alil ʔaničim ba,
It is the day of your flowery countenance,
    sk'ak'alil ʔaničim sat.
    It is the day of your flowery face.

la la li la lai la ʔo (*nonsense syllables*)
    la la li la lai la a.

la la li la lai la a.
    la la li la lai la ʔo.

muk'ulil san huan ʔo,
Great San Juan,
    muk'ulil patron ʔo,
    Great Patron,

sk'ak'alil ʔaničim ba,
It is the day of your flowery countenance,
    sk'ak'alil ʔaničim sat.
    It is the day of your flowery face.

sk'ak'alil ʔak'inale,
It is the day of your fiesta,
   sk'ak'alil ʔapaškuʔale.
   It is the day of your passion.

k'uyepal čihšanavotik ʔo bi,
How much we shall be walking,
   k'uyepal čihbeʔinotik ʔo bi,
   How much we shall be traveling,

la la li la lai la a.
   la la li la lai la a

la la li la lai la a.
   la la li la lai la ʔo.

muk'ulil san huan ʔo,
Great San Juan,
   muk'ulil patron ʔo,
   Great Patron,

sk'ak'alil ʔaničim ba,
It is the day of your flowery countenance,
   sk'ak'alil ʔaničim sat.
   It is the day of your flowery face.

sk'ak'alil ʔak'inale,
It is the day of your festival,
   sk'ak'alil ʔapaškuʔale.
   It is the day of your passion.

la la li la lai la a.
   la la li la lai la a.

la la li la lai la a.
   la la li la lai la ʔo.

(San Juan is also known as vaštonal vinik *or "man of the staff of authority," as suggested in the following couplets.)*

k'uyepal čihšanavotik,
How much we shall be walking!
   k'uyepal čihbeʔinotik ʔo.
   How much we shall be traveling!

vaštonal vinik ʔo,
Man of the cane of authority,
   vaštonal kašlan ʔo,
   Ladino of the sacred staff,
     vaštonal hesus ʔo,
     Jesus of the sacred staff,

sk'ak'alil ʔak'inale,
It is the day of your fiesta,
  sk'ak'alil ʔapaškuʔale.
  It is the day of your passion.

la la li la lai la ʔo.
  la la li la lai la a.

la la li la lai la a.
  la la li la lai la ʔo.

sk'ak'alil ʔapaškuʔale,
It is the day of your passion,
  sk'ak'alil ʔak'inale,
  It is the day of your fiesta,
    sk'ak'alil ʔaničim ba,
    It is the day of your flowery countenance,

vaštonal vinik ʔo,
Man of the cane of authority,
  vaštonal hkašlan ʔo.
  Ladino of the sacred staff.

la la li la lai la a.
  la la li la lai la ʔo.

la la li la lai la a.
  la la li la lai la ʔo.

k'uyepal čihšanav ʔo bi,
How much I shall be walking!
  k'uyepal čihbeʔin ʔo bi.
  How much I shall be traveling!

sk'ak'alil ʔaničim ba,
It is the day of your flowery countenance,
  sk'ak'alil ʔaničim sat,
  It is the day of your flowery face,
    sk'ak'alil ʔak'inale,
    It is the day of your fiesta,

vaštonal vinik ʔo,
Man of the cane of authority,
  vaštonal kašlan ʔo.
  Ladino of the sacred staff.

la la li la lai la a.
  la la li la lai la a.

la la li la lai la a.
   la la li la lai la ʔo.
sk'ak'alil ʔaničim ba,
It is the day of your flowery countenance,
   sk'ak'alil ʔaničim sat.
   It is the day of your flowery face.

*(The mayordomo shakes his rattle, shouts "Musicians,"
and the song concludes.)*

The nonsense syllables occur at regular intervals throughout the text. They are sung to the same musical line as the
words and are typical of actual performances of songs. Also
typical is the abrupt ending. The songs are structured so
that they may be extended and repeated indefinitely, as the
timing of the ritual requires. The same quality makes it
possible to bring the songs to a close with no more than a
final restatement of one of the key couplets, as in the
example.

In general, song represents an extreme expression of the
stylistic patterns that exist throughout Chamula oral tradition. Repetition and metaphoric stacking, for example,
begin to manifest themselves in emotional speech and in the
genres of recent words, reach a vigorous level of expression
in most of the genres of ancient words, and attain a still
higher degree of frequency in song. Furthermore, songs are
constructed for indefinite repetition, which is a necessary
attribute, according to Chamulas, because song is the deities'
favorite sound from people. Its verbal "essence," therefore,
must be supplied generously. The complementary medium
of music facilitates repetition because, according to Chamulas,
people do not tire of singing as they do of praying. Repetition also emphasizes the significance of the religious symbols,
which are invariably present in song.

Time-Space Attributes

Song contains extreme expressions of nonlinguistic time-
space associations which vary along a continuum reaching

from ordinary speech through ancient words. An example comes from a fragment of song for the entering-of-office ritual for a cargoholder called Mayordomo Santo. This song is performed during the preparation of the sweet maize gruel that is to be given by the mayordomo as part of a ritual meal on December 23, the second day of the ceremonies. The gruel is prepared in giant ceramic pots and served hot. It symbolizes the heavenly rain of San Juan and the sun, which comes down to earth as the warm rays of heat from the sky. Drinking the substance imparts heat and an aspect of divinity to the consumer. The mayordomo and his ritual adviser sing the following song to the accompaniment of rattles, which they play, and of harp and guitar, which their musicians play, as the gruel is being prepared. It has both a four-part parallel structure and complex metaphoric stacking.

> ta ša me šyal ta Hoʔ,
> Now it is surely descending as rain,
>> la ʔačʼul šohobale bi.
>> Your blessed radiance.
>
> ta ša me šyal ta Hoʔ,
> Now it is surely descending as rain,
>> la ʔačʼul nakʼobale bi, mukʼul patron.
>> Your blessed shadow, Great patron.
>
> la la li la lai la ʔo
>> la la li la lai la a
>
> la li la la lai la ʔo
>> la la li la lai la a
>
> ta ša me šyal ta Hoʔ,
> Now it is surely descending as rain,
>> la ʔačʼul kompirale bi.
>> Your blessed ritual meal.
>
> ta ša me šyal ta Hoʔ,
> Now it is surely descending as rain,
>> la ʔačʼul korason bi, mukʼul patron.
>> Your blessed heart, Great patron.
>
> la la li la lai la ʔo
>> la la li la lai la a

la la li la lai la ʔo
　la la li la lai la a

The gruel is expressed metaphorically in five different
ways: as rain, radiance, shadow, ritual meal, and heart—all
of San Juan, who is the sun's kinsman. The metaphors share
the quality of heat and heavenly origin (heat is heavenly rain;
regular rain comes from caves in the mountains). The
metaphors also establish a tie between the ritual setting and
the limits of the cosmos. The symbol of rain also links the
event to the establishment of the cyclical ordering of time
in the beginning, for the people of the First Creation (those
who ate their children as stewing meat) were destroyed by a
rain of boiling water sent by the sun-creator. Better people
were created to replace them.

The mayordomo, as a Chamula, is a descendant of those
better people. Furthermore, he participates in his cargo role
as a maintainer of order. He expresses this function, among
many other ways, by serving a ritual meal of sweet maize
gruel. It is relevant that the sun-creator originally cut the
first ear of maize from his own groin to provide the staple
food for his children. Furthermore, human semen, the life-
giving symbol par excellence, is called "gruel" (ʔul) in men's
speech.[4] Not only are semen and gruel similar in appearance,
but they are also believed to have a similar anatomical origin.
It can therefore be seen that the hot rain from heaven and
all of its extensions symbolize the life-force itself. The song
expresses metaphorically the idea that the mayordomo is
embarking on a reaffirmation of order, a concept which is so
general that time, space, reproduction, and sustenance are
all implied at once, and are not easily separated.

(11) Language, Cosmos, and Social Order

> The hummingbirds have their time of singing;
> They begin to cry when the maize is in
> flower.
>
> For only two months do they sing;
> When the ears of maize are tender, their
> voices are still.
>
> It is only when the maize is in flower;
> So Our Father the Sun wanted it to be.
>
> But, how long ago it was he made it that way
> we do not know for certain.
> Don't you see that it all began when Our
> Father in Heaven was still walking
> upon the earth?
> —Manuel López Calixto, Text 149

An abstract principle—the cohesion of complementary values of space and time—gives conceptual unity to the extremely varied domain of traditional verbal behavior that Chamulas classify as *k'op*. Moreover, the same principle operates as a fundamental organizational concept in Chamula thinking, symbolism, religion, and cosmology. This unity stems from the fact that oral tradition, like any expressive domain, is a "social fact," which shares organizational principles with the society in which it lives. It is by nature not simply a reflection or commentary on social life, but is actively involved in maintaining the integrity and internal consistency of social life. Time and space form a single primordial structural reality for Chamulas, and oral tradition is part of this reality. It offers analytical axes for making intelligible a wide range of phenomena that relate to oral tradition, without ignoring ethnographic minutiae.

Through a model, it is possible to summarize and extend the time-space perspective of Chamula verbal behavior. The model need not necessarily explain or even predict, although it may do so. Its purpose is simply to describe and hopefully to make intelligible a large and varied corpus of data. A good model is one which, under a given set of conditions and within a given domain, makes intelligible the most information and ignores the least.

The Oral Tradition As a System of Information

The Chamula taxonomy itself provides the basic categories of the descriptive model, which is concerned with both language for people whose hearts are heated and pure words as they are presently used in the spatial limits of Chamula. These two categories are special kinds of *k'op* ("language"), which has multiple meanings in addition to its meaning as "traditional verbal behavior." The word means not only "language" but also "argument," "subject," or "word." In all of these meanings, the exchange of information is involved. Furthermore, two of the meanings—"language" and "traditional verbal behavior"—imply certain patterns of invariance. In language itself, words and strict rules for combining them can generate infinite numbers of sentences. Traditional verbal behavior is even more invariant than language itself, for it involves patterns which, by Chamula definition, "do not know how to change" (*mu sna? shel sbaik*). Their traditional genres that "do not know how to change" also deal with assumptions and rules which themselves should not vary beyond given alternatives.

Oral tradition is thus primarily concerned with norms and with limits of permitted variation within them. In this sense, oral tradition is a relatively invariant language that provides information which helps people to deal with the relatively invariant aspects of the social system. Socialization of the young, social control, ritual process, and humor all assume invariant patterns of action, language, and thought. Together, these patterns reflect the very structure of the Chamula cosmos and make up a collective Chamula value judgment of what matters in their society and what must be taught, preserved, defended, and maintained, formally and informally, if the community is to survive. Because the whole domain of verbal behavior is patterned after the very structure of the Chamula universe—the world of the sun—it follows that no genre is primary or secondary with regard to information.

Each genre assumes, and makes sense in terms of, information contained in all other genres. In this way the system is learned and used. Therefore, one must understand the whole in order to appreciate fully the role and structure of the parts.

A Model of Chamula Oral Tradition

It is possible to construct a model that describes some of the patterns of variation and association within the whole domain of language (Fig. 5). Chamula may be represented at the center of an octagonal diagram, which is to be read either outward from or inward toward the center. In any one of the eight sections, at any point between the center and the outer line of the diagram, a line can be traced around the other sections at points equidistant from the center. The line so described will show points of association among the eight dimensions. The diagram attempts to show aspects of cosmology and world view that appear to be intimately and systematically related to Chamula genres of verbal behavior. The outermost segment of the diagram suggests aspects of symbolic inversion which may be used against the moral order by the antisocial forces of the universe. The model restates the argument that a metalanguage of time and space binds together the normative, the credible, and the desirable in linguistic behavior as the same categories of time and space hold the moral universe together. This relationship is hardly surprising, for language is viewed by Chamulas as a distinctively human trait, which occurs in its perfect form only in the Chamula dialect of Tzotzil (*baȼ'i k'op*, the "true language"). It would rather come as a surprise if the organization of linguistic information about the universe did not show a significant relationship to the structure of the universe itself.

Time and Space Variables in Narratives

For a concrete illustration of the suggested association of time and space categories (Sections A and B, Fig. 5), one may look to the two narrative genres (Section D). Represent-

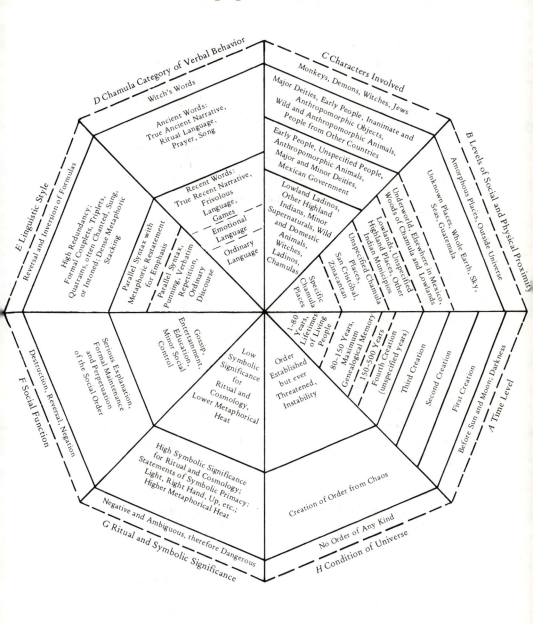

Figure 5. A Model of Chamula Oral Tradition and Cosmology

ing both recent words and ancient words, they illustrate
some of the patterns that characterize all of the individual
genres. Chamulas constantly insist that behavior outgrown
by Chamulas after the First, Second, and Third Creations
still survives at the edges of their spatial universe, which
suggests that time and space are aspects of the same cosmological reality, just as they were in the beginning when the
sun-creator initiated the First Creation and all later temporal
categories with his first spatial orbit around the universe. In
consequence, the information contained in the narratives
should demonstrate the same time-space unity.

The validity of this statement is shown by a comparison
of the temporal and spatial variables of 184 texts of true
recent narrative and true ancient narrative. On a simple
graph, values for the time at which each narrative took place
may be plotted with values for the most distant place name
mentioned in the same text (Fig. 6). These specific temporal
and spatial data as well as genre label were elicited for each
text. The time axis begins with the present and goes progressively back to the First Creation. The space axis begins with
Chamula and has categories of space increasingly unlike
Chamula and socially distant. The resulting graph shows
absolute and median distributions of all 184 texts with regard
to time and place of occurrence. Both distributions show that
increasing temporal removal from the present coincides with
increasing social distance. In general, events of true recent
narrative take place within the known universe of the average
Chamula and during the Fourth (present) Creation. Events
of true ancient narrative usually occur in unknown and very
distant reaches of space and during the First, Second, and
Third Creations.

There are interesting exceptions to these tendencies. The
texts that form the small cluster in the lower right corner
of the graph do not follow the general distribution. Informants believed that the events in those narratives occurred
close to home but long ago. These exceptional narratives
deal with explanations of sacred place names. The texts
report that the sacred places were nearly always affected or

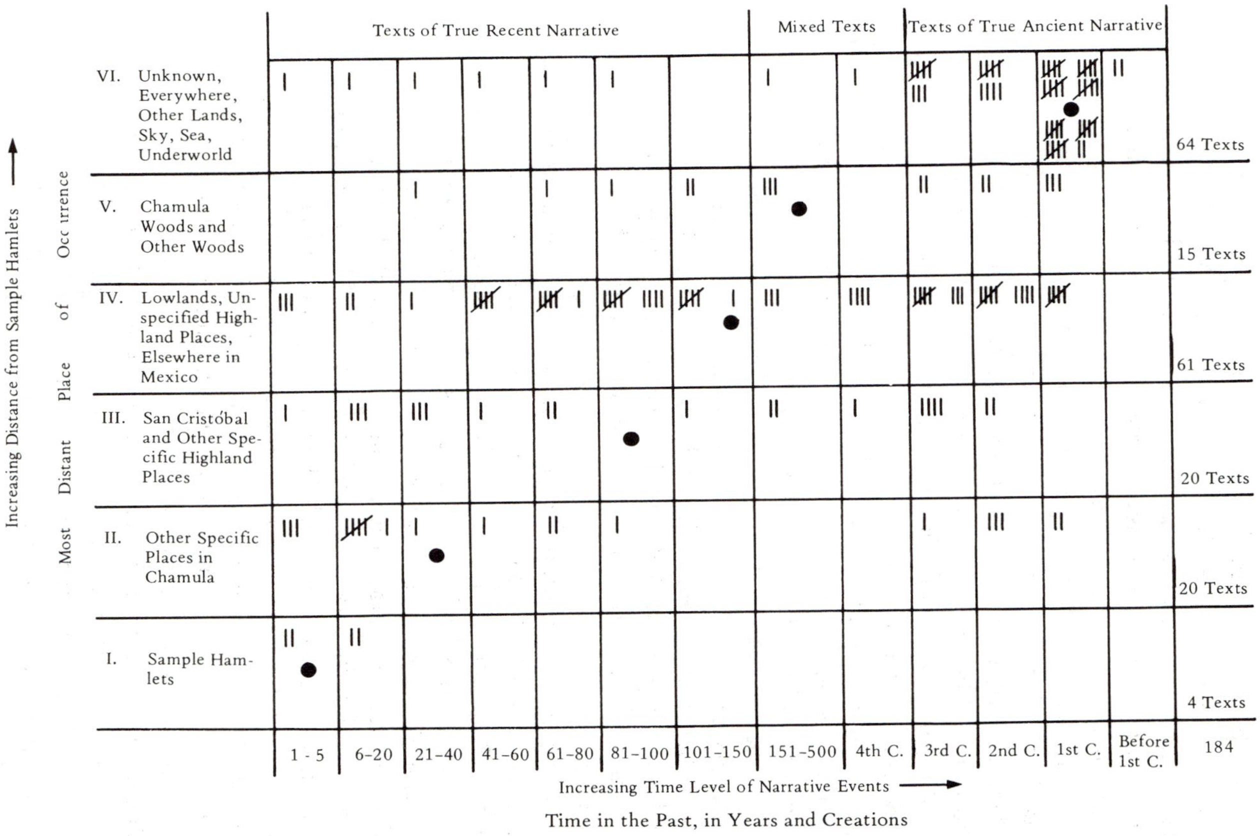

Texts of True Ancient Narrative

Mixed Texts

Texts of True Recent Narrative

			64 Texts
			15 Texts
			61 Texts
			20 Texts
			20 Texts
			4 Texts
			184

VI. Unknown, Everywhere, Other Lands, Sky, Sea, Underworld

V. Chamula Woods and Other Woods

IV. Lowlands, Unspecified Highland Places, Elsewhere in Mexico

III. San Cristóbal and Other Specific Highland Places

II. Other Specific Places in Chamula

I. Sample Hamlets

Columns: 1–5 | 6–20 | 21–40 | 41–60 | 61–80 | 81–100 | 101–150 | 151–500 | 4th C. | 3rd C. | 2nd C. | 1st C. | Before 1st C.

Increasing Time Level of Narrative Events →

Time in the Past, in Years and Creations

Most Distant ← Place of Occurrence

Increasing Distance from Sample Hamlets ←

Figure 6. Time and Space Variation in Narrative Genres, Showing Medians (●) and Absolute Distributions

formed by deities, who themselves were omnipresent in the universe long ago. Therefore, they were at one and the same time associated with a specific event in ancient Chamula and in the whole universe. Also, the place names in the narratives were then and are still places of ritual activity. The ritual act transcends space through communication with deities. As Victor Turner observed, ritual is "in and out of time" (1968: 5). Similarly, ritual has spatial implications which are both in and beyond the place of its celebration. The diffuseness of the ritual symbols causes them to transcend their particular context or place.

The other exceptions lie in the upper left corner of the graph. The texts that treat the few events which took place recently and far away report acts of extremely asocial behavior and natural disaster. Typical narratives of this category are recent accounts of witchcraft (for witches' souls are believed to be unusually mobile) and of tragedies like the volcanic eruption of 1903, which was so devastating that Chamulas believe that people all over the earth suffered from it.

The general pattern is for shockingly asocial and strange events, as well as for sacred events, to be placed at a comfortable distance from home, and for more normal events to be placed closer to home. Time and space work together as logical helpmates in the presentation of credible events. The distribution of character dyads in a small sample from the larger corpus illustrates how narrative content behaves within the time-space continuum.[1] The sets of dyads showing character interaction are listed in order of time level to which the texts belong. They offer a candid picture of the Chamula world view. In general, the characters with the most ancient time associations in narratives are those who also appear with the greatest frequency in ritual settings. Those with the most recent time associations make up the known social universe of Chamulas. The characters who participate in narratives that take place between ancient and modern times comprise an ambiguous and dangerous domain, with which modern Chamulas deal only at a distance, and preferably not at all.

Time	*Character dyads*
1–5 years ago	Chamula–Chamula; Chamula–Ladino.
6–20 years ago	Chamula–Chamulas; Chamula–wild animal.
21–40 years ago	Ladino–Ladino; Chamula–Tenejapaneco witch; Chamula–other Indian shaman.
41–60 years ago	Chamula–demon; Ladino–minor deity; major deity–Indian and Ladino.
61–100 years ago	Chamula–wild animal; Chamula–Ladino; Chamula–Chamula shaman; Chamula–domestic animal.
101–500 years ago	Chamula–Chamula; Chamula–demon; Chamula–Ladino; unidentified man–unidentified man; unidentified man–wild animal; unidentified man–sea monster; unidentified man–unidentified man; unidentified man–unknown fate.
Fourth Creation	Chamula–Ladino; Ladino–major deity; Ladino–Ladino; unidentified man–anthropomorphic animal; anthropomorphic animal–wild animal; unidentified man–unidentified man.
Third Creation	anthropomorphic animal–early Chamula; anthropomorphic animal–anthropomorphic animal; anthropomorphic animal–unidentified woman; early Ladino–anthropomorphic animal; Ladino–Ladino.
Second Creation	major deity–wild animal; inanimate object–wild animal; Jew–major deity; major deity–inanimate object.
First Creation	major deity–inanimate objects; major deity–major deity; major deity–wild animal.

The time-space continuum behaves with striking consistency as a principle in many facets of Chamula thinking. Moreover, this principle has implications for the whole of Chamula language, not just for the narrative genres. The marginal genres and the supercategory of recent words, which also includes frivolous talk and games, behave with regard to space and time in a way similar to true recent narrative. All of these genres have rather homely, ordinary contexts of performance with no significant ritual associations. They assume the social order. In contrast, the supercategory of ancient words, including prayer, song, and ritual speech, as well as narratives, behaves like true ancient narrative with respect to time and space. Diffuseness of spatial implication, invocation of deities, and the practice of ritual acts all have associations with antiquity. They formally state and maintain the social order.

Ancient words are not, however, in any sense primary. The genres of ancient words have no greater analytical potential for understanding Chamulas in their universe than do the other genres. The same time-space principle is discernible in the social categories of all genres. The only variable from one genre to the other is the content and associations of the complementary time-space coding. The relationship between time and space variables in any one text or performance usually remains remarkably constant. For example, biting and food consumption are concepts that are highly relevant to Chamula interpretations of social versus asocial behavior. Yet it would be foolish to turn exclusively to true ancient narratives for an investigation of why Chamulas think that people radically unlike themselves bite one another and render lard from Indians. Children learn these concepts through regular language. For example, a Chamula mother might say to her young son, "Don't run away to Tuxtla or they'll cook you up into lard." Children also learn these concepts through games and frivolous talk before they have ever heard the narratives about the beastly behavior of the people of the First Creation, who ate their babies when they were fat and juicy. However, when children do hear comments on biting behavior and social distance in the genres of ancient words, they can make sense of them because they have been using the same fundamental concepts to order their experience all along. Thus, no genre is primary or secondary with regard to information. Any part should ideally make sense in terms of any other part.

Style and Cosmos

Complementing the time-space associations throughout Chamula verbal behavior is the way people speak. Verbal expression moves in a clear continuum from lesser to greater stylistic formality, invariance, redundancy, and metaphoric heat as it moves from ordinary discourse to ancient words. The complexity of semantic reference also changes from one-word-one-referent relationships in ordinary discourse, through punning and verbal play with multiple ambiguous referents in the marginal genres and recent words, to multi-vocal ritual and religious symbolism in ancient words. In every case the style of a genre of language has metaphoric value of its own, enabling a speaker to establish the mood and symbolic significance of his utterance by the way he speaks. The continuum of style is an approximation of the language-learning process itself. Children begin their mastery of language by learning to repeat single words correctly and to relate them to the correct referents. Greater linguistic sophistication is required for using metaphoric restatement, parallel syntax, punning, and other forms of linguistic play. Mastery of formal dyadic couplets and other parallel structures, with the hundreds of alternative ways they can be combined, as well as of metaphoric stacking, is an even more sophisticated technique, which Chamulas achieve only in the "mature heat" of adulthood. Many forms are known only by specialists.

Thus, the life cycle, language learning, stylistic complexity of language genre, context of performance, and metaphoric heat are all intimately related to the time-space principle. This principle characterizes the whole of language and not simply the formal genres. A piece of gossip in true recent narrative does not require great stylistic embellishment

and redundancy because its message is not crucial to the
formal maintenance of order. It probably deals only with a
breach in the present social order. It corrects informally.
In contrast, redundancy and formal dyadic style are required
in order to give the proper emphasis to words that refer to
ritual symbols, those objects and concepts which are highly
imbued with multiple meanings. The diffuseness of the
semantic referents of ritual symbols seems to require verbal
representations that are analogous to the concepts themselves. For example, the sun is omnipotent and omnipresent.
These features make intelligible the dozens of metaphors,
sometimes stated consecutively and in dyadic structures,
which are used in talking about and to him. The sun deity's
multiple aspects and the cycles of time that he represents
suggest a kind of cyclically patterned style of speech as
appropriate for referring to him. Like meets like.

Change in the Oral Tradition

It might be argued that the systematic organization which
is claimed for Chamula oral tradition ignores individual and
group manipulation of the tradition for their own interests.
This would be a fair criticism, except that the scope of this
study does not permit treatment of individual variations in
rendering the same traditional information. Factors of change
and flexibility in oral traditions have already been investigated
very well by others, especially Raymond Firth (1961),
Edmund Leach (1965), and Jan Vansina (1965), and there
is no reason to doubt that oral traditions provide models
for change and variation as well as for stability. Moreover,
the inadequacies that have been observed in static, functional
approaches to oral tradition may, in part, be an aspect, of a
false dilemma. Anthropologists and folklorists have tended
to give an inordinate amount of research time to narratives
of origin and explanation, which, relative to other genres in a
single tradition, tend by their nature to be conservative,
and not enough time to ordinary gossip, recent history, and
other less formal genres. The latter genres thrive on multiple
interpretations and meanings. In any oral tradition, there

will doubtless be genres that are more and less amenable to
manipulation and multiple interpretation. These differences
will probably be discovered by means of a thorough rather
than a selective investigation of an oral tradition.

A more fruitful problem than the identification of change
in an oral tradition is the matter of how people change it.
What precisely do they manipulate in their traditions in
order to accommodate new situations and new interests?
Pre-existing patterns usually provide the raw material for
any cultural change. In Chamula, it appears that the same
time-space principle which orders the existing content of
the tradition also regulates changes in it and accretions to it.

An example may be drawn from true recent narrative. In
the last few decades a new folk hero, Don Erasto Urbina,
has appeared in the genre. Urbina was a Ladino, as are certain forms of the earth gods and the Chamula images of the
saints. He rose from obscurity in the 1930s to a kind of
apotheosis in Chamula tradition after his death in 1962. But
one generation removed from an Indian background, and
therefore knowledgeable about Indian languages and customs,
Urbina became one of the greatest protectors of Indians in
recent highland Chiapas history. In 1934, at the beginning
of the Indigenista Movement in Mexico,[2] the Departamento
de Acción Social, Cultural y Protección Indígena was created,
and in 1936 Urbina took over the office of this agency in
San Cristóbal. He used it very creatively, achieving protection
for Indians to the extent of guaranteeing their safety on the
sidewalks of San Cristóbal, which hitherto had been off-limits
to them; Indians had previously been required to walk in the
streets. Urbina enforced in every way possible the law in the
1917 Constitution called the Ley de 6 de enero, which
guaranteed the freedoms and rights of indentured servants
and peons. In 1936 he founded the Sindicato de Trabajadores
Indígenas, which raised a furor among landholding elements
in Chiapas by acting as a contracting agency for highland
Indian labor in the lowland coffee plantations and trying to
provide the best possible conditions for the Indians—usually
against the landholders' interests. The Sindicato also gave
Indians a place to sleep in San Cristóbal whenever they had

reason to stay overnight. Before this, Indians who were not attached to Ladino households had no place to sleep except in the gutters and market stalls. Urbina became mayor of San Cristóbal in the 1950s, in which capacity he helped the Indians to take advantage of municipal services that had not been available to them. Toward the end of his life he became owner of a hardware store, where the Indians' credit was always good, and they paid reasonable prices. He had innumerable friends and compadres among Ladinos and Indians alike. His death in 1962 caused great sadness in the Indian community.

Urbina so impressed the Chamulas with his goodness that he has entered tradition as a folk hero of the Mexican Revolution (Texts 33 and 135), a conflict in which he never actually took any active part. Since Urbina was a Ladino, it might seem peculiar at first that he emerged as a hero. After all, Chamulas generally remember the Mexican Revolution as a fight between equally evil Ladino forces. Yet in one tale (Text 33), he is credited with solving the entire conflict; in the other (Text 135), he is credited with a kind of mystical partnership with San Cristóbal in saving the San Cristóbal church from destruction by the Carrancistas[3] during the Revolution. The time-space associations are extraordinary. Spatial associations (the sky, Mexico City, the sacred shrine of Ladino San Cristóbal) are at a level that would usually be associated with the more distant past. Furthermore, Urbina is mentioned as a latter-day colleague of San Cristóbal, in a text whose main events refer back to the First Creation. Urbina has clearly been given some of the godlike qualities of temporal removal. The time-space associations of the war itself are also relatively distant in a negative sense, for Chamulas view the conflict as a universal upheaval. However, the authority of the distant past seems to be necessary in order to give Urbina a credible, hallowed place in the oral tradition. Curiously, it was not possible to collect many texts about Urbina's actual decisions in favor of the Indians in the field of municipal administration, an area in which he actively helped them (Texts 30, 40, and 46). And even in those few "historical" texts, the occurrence is pushed back in time in a pattern similar to that for Urbina's alleged revolutionary exploits.

It is thus clear that the tradition tends to accommodate new information according to the same principles that give credibility and stability to existing information. These principles again seem to require spatio-temporal variables of similar value. Urbina's behavior, as a Ladino of Indian background, was in some respects like that of the saints and has been dealt with accordingly. Although much more research on this process will be necessary to affirm or reject the hypothesis of accretion and change by spatio-temporal accommodation, the data hold promise for interesting work in that direction.

(12) A Perspective on the Study of
Oral Tradition

Every construction or fabrication has the
cosmogony as a paradigmatic model.
—Mircea Eliade, *The Sacred and the Profane*

It was because men were grouped and thought
of themselves in the form of groups that in their
ideas they grouped other things.
—Emile Durkheim and Marcel Mauss,
Primitive Classification

The way in which Chamulas think about
themselves and their world is illuminated through traditional
language and related expressive media. From this corpus,
it appears that the whole of Chamula oral tradition serves
as a system of normative information about man in the
universe of the sun, the primordial giver of order. The complementary attributes of time and space—set at the time of
the sun deity's first ascent into the sky—provide the categories
of the credible, the good, and the desirable, as well as the
negative categories. The time-space principle governing the
internal organization, style, and content of Chamula oral
tradition serves also as a key to understanding the logic of
other domains, such as their world view and ritual. The sense
and form of these aspects of Chamula life appear to be
articulated by the same principle of complementary values
that prevails in the domain of oral tradition.

The joint presence of complementary and same-value
attributes may be another way of explaining how ethics are
synonymous with aesthetics. Although this idea has been
present in Western thought for a long time, from Plato
through Ludwig Wittgenstein and Claude Lévi-Strauss, there
is no reason to believe that the notion is particularly ethno-

A Man and His Burden
(See Text 27)

centric. Few societies view rule-governed social behavior—
ethics—as either homogeneous or continuous on earth.
Rather, the rules of a particular society provide the norm
for that society. From this point of view, all else is judged
on a decreasing scale of values to the extent that others'
customs differ from its own. Also, people are consistently
aware that even within the moral universe of a particular
society, rule-governed behavior does not always prevail as
it should. It is neither homogeneous nor continuous. This
discrepancy explains the need for sacred ritual symbols,
which express quintessential custom, the essential unity of
social existence (V. Turner, 1968: 269–283). Ritual harkens
back to the first cosmogonic moment in time and space,
thus making a temporal bridge that connects the past and
the present, near and far, and fills the asocial void, within
the society as without, with an ideal model of order. In the
case of Chamula, this ritual stage is logically indistinguishable
from the language, action, and thought used to create it.
Ethics join aesthetics in the ritual setting just as they do in
the prosaic setting of roadside gossip. In both events, rule

maintenance functions as an impetus to the verbal performance and its associated action. The same applies to games,
jokes, and proverbs. A metalanguage of time and space
makes them all intelligible as statements about the same
reality, the moral world of *htotik*, the sun, in which Chamulas
live.

Chamula oral tradition is not merely a body of supporting
information in the cultural context, but is both explicitly
and implicitly involved in the everyday life and ritual life
of 40,000 nonliterate Chamula Indians. It is as relevant
throughout the life cycle of all laymen as it is throughout
the careers of shamans and cargoholders. Chamula oral
tradition is not only associated with norms but is also actively
involved in teaching, maintaining, and reinterpreting them.
It provides an implicit conceptual scheme for ordering information that may not itself be stated in the oral tradition.
It also serves to order past and new experiences in credible,
intelligible ways. In this respect, oral tradition is more
effective even than language, for it selects and keeps for
greater or lesser lengths of time meaningful segments of
experience. Language may do the same thing, yet because
of its infinite capacity for expansion, its unconscious patterning, and its transience, it is not so amenable for use as a
conscious system of cultural reference as is the oral tradition.

For these reasons, oral tradition deserves to be treated as
a totality. Its day in the isolated appendices of anthropological monographs is hopefully doomed. Both conceptually,
from the Chamula point of view, and analytically, from my
point of view, it has a discreteness, being a separate system
of information that is concerned with ideal models of
behavior and interaction. The significance of oral tradition
compares to the primacy of social and economic organization
and kinship in the study of society. In sum, oral tradition
has enormous importance as a logically catalogued reservoir
of information in Chamula society. Furthermore, it is in
the totality of folk categories of verbal behavior—*k'op*—that
structural resonance with other Chamula symbolic domains
is most clearly discernible. Some general implications follow.

If the consideration of Chamula oral tradition were restricted to what is called myth, folktale, legend, folk music, or pun, it would provide no more than a distorted view of the collective representations of the community. These Western genres are not significant, as such, in Chamula. Furthermore, even if they were significant to Chamulas, these few "standard genres" would account for no more than a fraction of the vast amount of information contained in the many classes of Chamula verbal behavior. Taken alone, individual Chamula genres are mere fragments of the totality of specialized verbal competence that must be mastered by a successful adult. This fact has important implications for the study of other aspects of the society. For example, to attempt to understand Chamula religion and cosmology by exploring true ancient narrative alone would produce distortions similar to those that might result from discussing a kinship system without discussing the terms for generations below "ego" or the terms for affines. In kinship studies, anthropologists make every effort to emphasize the culture-specific meanings of kin terms within a whole system. One should do the same for verbal behavior. This perspective would introduce some much-needed caution into the cross-cultural comparative method that is frequently found in folklore studies.

A holistic consideration of oral tradition also reveals critical ways in which patterns of ideal behavior are acquired and maintained throughout the cultural fabric, from court procedure to play, from games to ritual, from joking to prayer, from linguistic style to world view. The comprehensive view of ideal behavior afforded by this perspective should therefore provide an interesting dimension to the study of such domains as law, ritual, and social organization. Whenever the study of these topics has used oral traditional materials, it has frequently relied on formal genres, such as myth and ritual speech. The point is that social rules relevant to such studies are probably to be found encoded in less cryptic fashion in the more informal genres.

Even in the anthropological study of religion, the holistic view of oral tradition might show that some poorly considered questions have been asked of traditional genres.

Social anthropologists have tended to concentrate on narrative and ritual genres, which has often led to tired discussions of myth and ritual. These genres have been assigned false primacy in the analysis of meaning in religious concepts. The fact is that religious concepts are encoded throughout the oral tradition. For example, Chamula children are taught the less formal genres long before they learn the special qualities of the formal genres. True ancient narratives make sense only because they relate the same kinds of category relationships that the children have already heard and learned to use much earlier in genres such as games and frivolous language. Even the linguistic formulas that have become canonized as ritual language are closely related to the emotion-imbued repetitive speech patterns which occur in the informal genres and even in the marginal genres. In like manner, that which is sacred is grasped as well by the child who divides candy equally among his friends at play as by the cargoholder who presents equal portions of rum to his ritual assistants. The sacred is an ideal statement; its ideal categories lace society at all levels. The total view of oral tradition bears out this point.

Recent considerations of myth may beg the question of explanation by assuming that "mythic thought" has a logic of its own and therefore belongs to a different order of translatability, comprehension, and meaning that do the infrastructures that make up the rest of the cultural content.[1] The Chamula data, however, indicate that true ancient narrative (which some might gloss as "myth") has no special logical discreteness over any other genres. All of the genres respond analytically as different aspects of the same primordial time-space principle, which has different style and content associations at various levels.

Moreover, there is sometimes a lack of precision in the use of the word "myth." It might be that, if native genre names were available for many of the societies whose myths are frequently found in cross-cultural sources, the investigator would find himself embarrassed to be dealing with speculative gossip, jokes, or secular narrative. These could not honestly be treated as "myths" in a cross-cultural study. Nor could they in any sense be said to have a privileged logic until one knew how their respective societies felt about them. Surely, therefore, folk taxonomies combined with close textual analysis based on social categories and cosmology of particular societies will lead to a deeper understanding of oral tradition than will intuition and global comparison. Folk exegesis of narratives in their proper contexts will surely reveal more about their meaning than will intuition alone. Structural analysis can only gain from a consideration of native categories of meaning. A "myth" is often not a myth.

The holistic perspective also provides a useful context in which to observe how children acquire adult verbal competence. The Chamula data indicate that children learn their oral tradition as a stylistic and generic continuum. Prayer, for example, is a sophisticated form which is learned as a separate category relatively late in childhood. Yet it presupposes certain religious information and the ability to use formal dyadic structures and other forms of redundancy. Children learn these things much earlier in their linguistic play with games and frivolous language. To ignore the whole in studying any of the separate genres would be to ignore a very significant dimension of Chamula communication, namely, that oral tradition behaves as a system of interpenetrating styles and information.

To conclude on a more general, speculative note, it may be that the systematic collection and analysis of whole oral traditions will show that no men, literate or nonliterate, can be completely ahistorical or objective in their conception of the past. Ideas of history for Chamulas, as for most people, seem to be derived from their subjective evaluation of contemporary social and spatial categories of the universe. Just as evolutionary thinking in nineteenth century Europe appeared on the rising tide of knowledge about the spatial extent and diversity of lands and of species of life on earth, so the modern Chamula's view of the past is conditioned by his conception of the spatial extent and diversity of beings in the present. It is an effective system, in which even my wife and I were included as sometime-supernaturals and sometime-demons, for we had come from the edges of the earth.

Accordingly, Chamulas considered us to be their primitive contemporaries and asked the eternal question, "Do people bite in your country?"

Appendix Bibliography Notes Index

(Appendix) Narrative Text Abstracts

Following are brief abstracts of 184
narrative texts, both true recent narratives and true ancient
narratives. In no way does the narrative style of the abstracts
attempt to represent the style of the texts. The titles were
arbitrarily assigned, since Chamulas do not recognize set
titles for the narratives. The data in the headnote to each
text were elicited by questionnaire and by unstructured
interview. When such information was explicitly stated in
the narrative itself, the questions were asked anyway, in
order to confirm or clarify the data in the texts. Following
the title of most texts are cross-references to other texts
in which similar motifs and textual variants occur. Frequently
the cross-references refer to another narrative that is virtually
the same. Just as often, they refer only to a major motif
sequence, not to the narrative as a whole.

The abstracts are followed by brief references to relevant
published and unpublished material. In most cases these
references are to similar tales and motifs. Generally, the
annotations offer comparative data from three types of
source: Maya and Nahuatl ethnohistoric documents, other
Meso-American collections, and standard European and
American indices. There are hundreds of motifs and dozens

of tale types, particularly those dealing with the saints, which are of obvious Spanish origin; just as many tales can be traced to pre-Columbian Maya sources. However, the syncretistic nature of the texts is such that the Spanish or aboriginal identity of the motifs is not recognized in any way by Chamulas. To them, the narratives represent a true account of the past, in which Spaniards and Catholic saints interact as coevals with earth gods and sun and moon deities. The two traditions have merged to such an extent that I do not feel that there is much to be gained, at the level of sociological interpretation, from identification of provenience of motifs and tale types. However, the annotations may be of interest for comparative purposes.

A source of published comparative material for the Chiapas highlands is Vogt (1969: 307–366, 625–642). Most of the Zinacanteco texts included in Vogt are from Robert Laughlin's large collection (1960), which is available in the Harvard Chiapas Project File. See also Laughlin (1962) and Blaffer (1972), which are based on the Zinacanteco narrative tradition. Fragmentary sources of oral tradition for the Chiapas highlands are Holland (1963) and Guiteras-Holmes (1961). The most complete sources on the oral tradition of the Maya area are the ethnohistorical documents: for the Quiché, the *Popol Vuh* (Goetz and Morley, 1950); for the Cakchiquel, *The Annals of the Cakchiquel* (Recinos and Goetz, 1953); and for the Yucatec Maya, *The Book of Chilam Balam of Chumayel* (Roys, 1967). General surveys of the contemporary and ancient Maya oral tradition appear in Thompson (1965, 1967, and 1970). Thompson (1967) also provides a bibliography on Maya oral tradition. Edmonson (1967) covers the whole of Meso-American Indian narrative tradition, with a strong bibliography on Maya sources. See also Mendelson (1967). There are thus abundant, if mostly fragmentary, sources for comparative purposes, although there are as yet no major modern published collections of Maya material.

True Recent Narrative

   1. The Coyote Pack (cf. Texts 17, 41, 84, 94, 96, 101, 142)

Informant: Marian López Calixto
Time Level: 1–5 years ago
Most Distant Space Category: Zinacantan

One day when a man with his dog was taking care of his sheep, the dog disappeared into the woods. A coyote had killed him. The man became angry and built a fire by the coyote's hiding place. The coyote did not die and decided to kill the man's sheep for spite. When the sheep were dead and the old man (a Zinacanteco) was asking Our Father what to do about the loss, a coyote (who was actually a Huixteco witch) came and spoke to him. The man killed the coyote, but the next day the dead coyote had turned into many live coyotes that were threatening all the neighbors' flocks of sheep. The neighbors got together to go and kill them in the woods, but the coyotes fled from the hunters. Later the neighbors repaired their sheep sheds, hoping that the coyotes would not return. Some said that the coyotes were found dead in the forest, but no one is sure that these were actually the coyotes that they had been hunting.

2. Bad Omens (cf. Text 149)
Informant: Marian López Calixto
Time Level: 1–5 years ago
Most Distant Space Category: Seas, heavens, underworld

A man, because of witchcraft executed against him, was about to die. He was so near death, in fact, that his soul had already departed for the underworld and his grave had been dug. Yet the souls of crickets and of his own dead children, already in the underworld, encouraged the soul of the sick man to go to heaven to find out by what sign he was meant to die. The fact was that he had seen an owl and a night hummingbird, which he thought were signs that he would die. Our Father said that he was not scheduled to die, so his soul returned to earth and the man got better. The signs that he saw, however, are generally valid, and the man had reason to worry. Owls and night hummingbirds are bad omens. (E.C. Parsons, 1936: 362; Sahagún, 1957: V, 161–163)

3. The Killing of a Soul Animal (cf. Texts 19, 35)
Informant: Marian López Calixto

Time Level: 1–5 years ago
Most Distant Space Category: Sample Chamula hamlets
There was a woman who scolded a weasel, not knowing that it was actually her own soul animal. The weasel was angry and decided to eat the woman's baby chicks and eggs that had not yet hatched. The woman saw the weasel go to the chicken's nest and ran it off, chasing it to its cave. She dug it out and clubbed it to death and then burned it up with fuel oil. She died three days later, for it had been her own soul animal. (La Farge and Byers, 1931: 134)

4. The Cabildo Dispute (cf. Text 5)
Informant: Salvador Guzmán Bakbolom
Time Level: 1–5 years ago
Most Distant Space Category: Elsewhere in Mexico
The officials of Chamula decided to repair the town hall, for it leaked and the secretary said that his papers were getting ruined. They decided to collect thirty pesos per man at the New Year. Some wanted to go talk to government officials in Tuxtla to see if they would help. It is said that the officials gave them a million and a half pesos, but that they did not tell anyone about it, the officials pocketing the money for themselves. Of course, the gossip got out, and the people of Parajes Pistik, Baš?ek'en, and Hol¢emen organized to do something about it, sending a delegation to Mexico City to see what had really happened. The presidente of Mexico said that he had indeed sent the money. After the old cabildo had been torn down, the presidente and officials received a telegram telling them to go to San Cristóbal. Manuel Castellanos told them that they were suspected of embezzlement. They denied it. On the way home, they were ambushed by the people from Pistik, but no one was killed. When they got to Chamula, they organized a defense against the rebels, spending the night waiting in the presidente's house and finally chasing the rebels away, killing one man in the process. The presidente stayed in office, but he had to return the tax money which had been collected.

5. The Cabildo Uprising (cf. Text 4).
Informant: Manual López Calixto

Time Level: 1–5 years ago
Most Distant Space Category: Elsewhere in Mexico

The elders and the presidente agreed to assess each head
of a household in Chamula thirty pesos for the construction
of a new municipal building in Chamula Ceremonial Center.
Widows were to contribute only fifteen pesos. Some people
opposed this high tax and sent a representative to Mexico
City to see whether the national officials would contribute
or had already contributed to the construction of the cabildo.
The presidente had not wanted to accept Ladino money
because he did not want Ladino intervention in the internal
affairs of Chamula. Those who were opposed to the tax went
to Mexico City and persuaded officials there to give money
to Chamula for the building. The people of Chamula found
out about this and opposed the tax levied by the presidente,
thinking that he was going to keep the federal funds for
himself. After they nearly drove the presidente out at gunpoint, a federal official came to talk to the people and told
them that even with the federal contribution of 100,000
pesos, some local funds would be needed. This news calmed
the people down, and the trouble was over for the time
being.

6. Incest
Informant: Marian López Calixto
Time Level: 1–5 years ago
Most Distant Space Category: Sample Chamula hamlets

There was a widow with three children who went to see a
divorced man. He had divorced his first wife because she
was too old and ugly. His ex-wife was the elder sister of the
widow who came to see him. They decided to get married
anyway, but with her there were problems too, for she often
had sexual relations with her sixteen-year-old son. At about
the same time the son married a local whore, to whom both
he and his stepfather had access, for they all lived in the same
house. Owing to these and other problems (the old man was
sterile), he turned all of these people out of his house. He
found still another woman, who was already pregnant by
another man. He began living with her so that he might claim

the child. Meanwhile, his former "family" had turned into a band of thieves, who lived in a cave nearby. They were forced to flee to Hot Country and sold their land and belongings in Chamula. The woman went to the coffee plantations as a whore; she is still there today. Her son returned to Chamula and became a bum, now known as the "coyote man," for he lives in a cave and eats only what he can steal or beg from respectable people.

7. The Disappearance of Salvador Sethol
Informant: Salvador Guzmán Bakbolom
Time Level: 1–5 years ago
Most Distant Space Category: Hot Country
Salvador Sethol was a scribe for one of the political officials in Chamula. He also had a job in San Cristóbal. Once he asked his employer for time off and went to Tuxtla to accept a bribe of four hundred pesos from federal officials in exchange for information about hidden sugarcane liquor stills in Chamula. He gave some of the bribe money to friends and stupidly told several people about his good fortune. Political officials in Chamula found out about his arrangement with the federal liquor inspection authorities (who had not yet come to Chamula). The people who had stills were advised to hide all evidence of their activity. A group of liquor manufacturers were authorized by the presidente to do away with the traitor, and as far as he was concerned, his disappearance would be work of the demon. The vigilante committee took him away to the bushes one night at midnight and killed him and threw him in a deep cavern. His father tried to find him, but no one knew anything. He had simply disappeared. It was no one's fault but his own.

8. Another Church for Chamula
Informant: Salvador Guzmán Bakbolom
Time Level: 1–5 years ago
Most Distant Space Category: Chamula hamlets contiguous to sample hamlets
Some time ago the Ladino priest of Chamula wanted to build a chapel near the road on which trucks go to Larrainzar

and Chenalhó. He thought it would be a good place for a church. The problem was that there were not enough people to contribute the money necessary to build it. Therefore, when partly finished, it was abandoned. The idea for the church had come from a talking saint who lived in a man's humble dwelling at the foot of a nearby mountain. The saint had begun to talk, saying that he had been at that house for a long time but that no one ever came to pray to him. He asked the owner to find a better, more accessible location. The owner went to speak with the priest, saying that his saint had talked and wanted a mass every day. The priest got the construction started at the place where the man wanted it. People from Chamula, Mitontic, Larrainzar, and Chenalhó began to offer candles there during the construction, but now they have all given up hope that the church will ever be finished.

9. The Hope of Eternal Life (cf. Texts 12, 30)
Informant: Salvador Guzmán Bakbolom
Time Level: 1–5 years ago
Most Distant Space Category: Chamula hamlets contiguous
to sample hamlets

A brother and his three sisters became Protestants and thought that, because they would thus have eternal life, they could rob and kill and do just as they pleased without any real fear of punishment. While they were asleep one night, the neighbors got together and burned down their house. Three of them were murdered on the spot as they ran out of the burning house. One woman escaped and ran naked to San Cristóbal at three in the morning to get the Protestant pastor to come and help her. He was the one who had told them that there was only one god and that their Chamula gods were foolish. The true god was everywhere, he said. The pastor went to report the events to the presidente, who sent investigators. The murderers had fled and the house was a pile of ashes. Not until the following fiesta of San Mateo did they catch one of the murderers, who came to the fiesta with his family. They arrested him and took him to the San Cristóbal jail.

10. The Trial of a Witch (cf. Texts 17, 19, 21, 29)
Informant: Salvador Guzmán Bakbolom
Time Level: 1–5 years ago
Most Distant Space Category: Chamula hamlets contiguous
to sample hamlets

A witch went to a cave to pray with three friends. Some
people saw them and followed them. They placed their
candles at the mouth of the cave, threw fuel oil and liquor
on them, and prayed over them. The people who had watched
were very frightened, for they thought that the witch had
"given them sickness." They went to the presidente, who
told the witch to come to the center the next morning. She
said that she had gone to the cave, but only to call the soul
of her grandson who had fallen down there the day before.
The presidente did not punish her but ordered her to do all
her "curing" in the future at less asocial times and places
than at midnight in a cave. The witch said that the story was
all a lie but that people would now ignore and throw sticks
at her, thinking she was a witch. And they did, although the
presidente had promised her protection.

11. Too Little Land (cf. Texts 27, 45, 55)
Informant: Manuel López Calixto
Time Level: 5–20 years ago
Most Distant Space Category: Hot Country

Many years ago there was a famine. People had only a few
tortillas and sugar water to eat. There was very little corn
and the people were starving. Today, to assure a corn supply,
Chamulas raise corn in Hot Country and wherever else they
can find land. The problem in Chamula itself is limited land,
which is why the famine came to pass. With land and rain,
all will grow well. People, particularly Chamulas, will not
starve again.

12. The Converted Shamans (cf. Texts 9, 30)
Informant: Marian López Calixto
Time Level: 5–20 years ago
Most Distant Space Category: Highland places not con-
tiguous to Chamula

A witch wanted to convert an apprentice shaman to evil

arts, but the shaman defeated the witch by urinating on his candle. Several shamans of the same persuasion (desiring to kill witches) got together and converted to Protestantism. They renounced their native healing customs, formed a cult, and won converts; they burned roadside cross-shrines, saying that the native symbols were not in fact gods. God was everywhere and did not allow those who believed in him to die. In their services they took off their clothes, danced naked on the altar, and had intercourse in the meeting place. Our Father was not happy to see all this awful behavior, but it happened in only one place, Chanal. These people were very bad.

13. The Guardian of the Milpas (cf. Text 149)
Informant: Marian López Calixto
Time Level: 5–20 years ago
Most Distant Space Category: Hot Country
A man once killed a lizard in his milpa and, as a result, became a pauper. He discussed the matter with a friend, and the friend told him that the reason for his poverty was that he had killed either a lizard, an iguana or a cat. He admitted that he had killed a lizard. This was his downfall. His milpa failed, and eventually he went to beg in San Cristóbal. The fact is that the lizard is the guardian of the milpa.

14. The Charcoal Cruncher
Informant: Marian López Calixto
Time Limit: 5–20 years ago
Most Distant Space Category: Specified Chamula hamlet
A man was married to a woman whose father had seemed a little too anxious to give her away. When they were sleeping together on the first night, the girl's head detached itself and went wandering about. The man told his father-in-law about the problem and together they went to look for her. They found her head tied to a stump with her own hair. Her father asked her what was happening. She said that she had only gone out to find charcoal to crunch and that she had caught her hair on the stump and could not return by daybreak. The husband was angry and asked his father-in-law for his money back. He gave it to him. The husband knew why his father-in-

law had been so eager to get rid of his daughter, for she was a charcoal cruncher.

15. The Buzzard (cf. Text 118)
Informant: Marian López Calixto
Time Level: 5–20 years ago
Most Distant Space Category: Specified Chamula hamlet other than sample hamlets.

A lazy man was in his milpa. A buzzard came along, and the man decided that he would like to fly about and lead a leisurely life like a buzzard. He proposed to the buzzard that they change clothes. When they changed, the man flew away like a buzzard. Then, when the buzzard went to the man's home that night, dressed in the man's clothing, he was asked by his wife why he had feathers on his feet and legs. She was told of the exchange and was frightened and disgusted by it. The next morning she saw the buzzard perched on the side of a pot. She tossed boiling water on him and burned his neck. That is why buzzards have red, featherless necks. (Laughlin, 1960: Tales 42, 48; Guiteras-Holmes, 1961: 204)

16. The Deer Turns into a Snake (cf. Texts 57, 60, 73, 90, 132, 133, 173)
Informant: Salvador Guzmán Bakbolom
Time Level: 5–20 years ago
Most Distant Space Category: Chamula hamlets contiguous to sample hamlets

A man had seen some deer on a mountain near Paraje Ranchu. He told his friends about it, and they decided to go together to hunt the deer. When they got to the place where the deer were supposed to be, they found only a coiled snake. They jumped back when the snake tried to strike at them. Frightened, they went leaping down the mountain trail and gave up the hunt.

17. The Successful Witch (cf. Texts 1, 10, 17, 19, 21, 29, 41, 84, 94, 96, 106, 142)
Informant: Marian López Calixto
Time Level: 5–20 years ago

Most Distant Space Category: Highland places not contiguous to Chamula

There was a rich man whom a witch hated because he (the witch) was poor and envied the rich man's resources. The witch decided to try to injure the rich man. He went to a cave and prayed to the earth gods. The earth gods released a herd of a thousand coyotes, which went to attack the rich man in his house. He tried to kill some of them, but they eventually killed him. The same witch, in the form of a goat, attacked another man. The goat charged the house and entered it.

18. The Lazy Woman
Informant: Marian López Calixto
Time Level: 5–20 years ago
Most Distant Space Category: Specified Chamula hamlet other than sample hamlets.

A man had a very lazy wife who did not want to do anything. Her mother-in-law made maize gruel, but the girl refused to drink any. All but the girl went to take a sweat bath. When they were gone, the girl drank a lot of very hot maize gruel, and screamed because it was so hot. When the family arrived to see what had happened, the girl could not talk. All she could say was nonsense syllables. She had lost her mind and finally died. She was laid out in the house for three days and was taken to be buried on the fourth day. Her husband was sad for a year. (S. Thompson, 1961: Tale Type 1373)

19. The Witch Who Went To See the Sun (cf. Texts 3, 10, 17, 21, 29, 35)
Informant: Marian López Calixto
Time Level: 5–20 years ago
Most Distant Space Category: Seas, heavens, underworld

There was a witch in a Chamula hamlet whose soul went to heaven to see the sun. The sun was very beautiful. The witch spread roses on the sun's path. When the witch came back to earth, he was sick for three days, but he had seen a great deal. He reported it to some of his friends. When the sun comes up in the morning, he is very small, but he gets

bigger as the day goes on. When the days are short, the sun
goes in a truck so he can go faster; when the days are long,
the sun rides a burro. When the sun sets in the evening,
he goes into the ocean in a wide-mouthed gourd.

20. Sickness at the Coffee Plantation
Informant: Marian López Calixto
Time Level: 5–20 years ago
Most Distant Space Category: Hot Country
The informant's older brother and his father went to the
coffee plantation to work. His brother got a tumor on his
foot. The father found a curer there, who treated his son's
foot. Then the father took him home and called a local curer
to see him. The curer said that he was very sick but was not
going to die. He did finally get better, but now Marian's
father refuses to go back to the finca to work.

21. An Attack on a Witch (cf. Texts 10, 17, 19, 29)
Informant: Salvador Guzmán Bakbolom
Time Level: 5–20 years ago
Most Distant Space Category: Sample Chamula hamlets
There was an old man who got sick and called a shaman in
to help him. The shaman told the man that a witch had
"struck" him and his illness was grave indeed. The first
shaman failed to help him, so he called in his two sons-in-law
and asked them and his daughters to help him kill his enemy
with the aid of a new shaman. The shamans informed him
which witch had hurt him. In order to deceive the witch, one
son-in-law took a bottle of rum and gave it to the witch,
after convincing him to come to heal his son, who he said,
was sick. Just as the witch took the bottle, both sons-in-law
of the victim attacked the witch with machetes. He escaped
badly cut, but they killed his wife. The witch informed the
authorities, and all were arrested, including the shaman and
the original victim. The original patient soon died, and so did
his wife. The shaman was released. The witch is still alive
but has scars on his face. The murderers fled with their wives.

22. The Price of Polygamy
Informant: Salvador Guzmán Bakbolom

Time Level: 5–20 years ago
Most Distant Space Category: Sample Chamula hamlets

There was a married Chamula man who fell in love with the younger sister of his wife. He told his wife that he planned to marry her sister "so that she (the wife) would have someone to help her around the house." The wife was angry, but agreed to live with her sister if he could support them both. The couple went to seal the deal with a drink. The wife passed out and the husband sang. Then he went to see his brother-in-law, who was the guardian of the younger sister, and gave him two liters of rum before announcing his business. He said that he wanted to marry his wife's younger sister because his wife was tired of making tortillas, and besides, she was pregnant and needed someone to help her. With this, the brother-in-law, in a drunken rage, shot him with his rifle. The man died in his chair. Then the murderer went to bed with his wife. The murdered man's wife came to look for her husband and found him dead. Then her brother, still drunk, attacked her. She ran away. The man cut up his dead brother-in-law with an axe. They caught him and put him in jail. The murdered man received an autopsy and burial and his heart and brain were examined for the cause of death. He deserved punishment for wanting to take his sister-in-law as a second wife.

23. Death Comes to the German (cf. Texts 25, 60, 65, 71, 76, 80, 90, 105, 112, 132, 145, 150, 173, 174)
Informant: Salvador Guzmán Bakbolom
Time Level: 5–20 years ago
Most Distant Space Category: Specified Chamula hamlet other than sample hamlets

A German went to talk with his fellow foreigners at the radio tower on top of Tzontevitz Mountain. They told him that there was a lot of money buried in the mountain, so they organized a dig, complete with engineers, who showed them just where to dig. They found Chamula workers for the project with the pretext that they were digging gravel for the road. All went well until the second day, when snakes began to appear in and around the site. Cows also began to appear around the site. This happened every day. All of this suggested that the earth god in the mountain was angry with them and was giving them open hints to get out. Then the German encouraged the Chamula workers by offering them a share of the money they would find, thereby admitting that the gravel had been a pretext. They agreed to this and also agreed to keep quiet about it. One day, amid more snakes and cows, they heard a festival within the mountain. They heard drums trumpets, rockets, and music, as well as the singing of monkey assistants and the sound of running water. A brother of one of the workers, who was a shaman, agreed to come and calm the earth god for two-hundred pesos. A Thursday rite was set and carried out. For a while, they thought the trouble was over. They rested for three days, and on the third day after work had started again (a Wednesday), some assassins killed the German and his friends with machetes and left them where the tools were stored. The workers found them later that morning along with their dogs and horses, which had also been killed, and ran away, afraid that they would be accused. No one touched the bodies, and the coyotes and buzzards ate them up. The workers found out that some people from Tzontevitz had heard the shaman's ritual on behalf of the German. Those people realized that if in fact the German found money in the mountain, they would get none of it and would remain poor. Also, the earth god needed the money, they said, to produce rain and to provide for the general well-being of the maize, beans, potatoes, and squash. Therefore, the people from Tzontevitz felt that they had to kill the German.

24. The Defender of Owl Rock
Informant: Salvador López Sethol
Time Level: 5–20 years ago
Most Distant Space Category: Chamula hamlets contiguous to sample hamlets
When the road to Larrainzar was being constructed, the engineers were going to break a certain rock that had served as a landmark for many years. It is called Owl Rock. The road was to pass through the place where Owl Rock was located. Owl Rock talked to the engineer and told him that

violation of the rock would create havoc, for Owl Rock was
the guardian of a sacred mountain and all the animals
therein. Because the engineer had a very strong animal soul,
he was convinced not to break the rock. As a reward, the
engineer received a job in the mountain for three days, at the
end of which time he became rich. But not all have had such
good luck in dealing with Owl Rock. Three men have died
there.

> *25. The Earth God's Daughter (cf. Texts 23, 25, 60, 65, 71,
> 76, 80, 90, 105, 112, 132, 145, 150, 173, 174)*
> *Informant: Marian López Calixto*
> *Time Level: 21–40 years ago*
> *Most Distant Space Category: Chamula and other highland
> woods*

A woman went to the milpa to get three ears of maize.
Her husband came home and was furious that she had
gathered so much, but the fact was that the three ears had
magically multiplied. He was so angry, without reason, that
he struck her in the nose. The woman cleaned her bloody
nose with an ear of maize, and that is how red maize came
into being. When he struck her, a thunderbolt struck nearby
and rain began. The father of the woman was an earth god
and had come to rescue his daughter. The woman left her
two children with a magical food-producing pot. The father
was not supposed to see it, but he found it and ate from it
and then broke it, leaving the children without a source of
food. The woman returned and gave them red maize to eat.
She also gave them white maize (from her tears). In the
meantime, the man went to reclaim his wife at the house of
the earth god. The god would not return her to her husband.
He drove him away and the husband died of grief. Later,
the woman gave red maize to all who had been her friends.
(Goetz and Morley, 1950: 125; S. Thompson, 1961: Tale
Type 565; Guiteras-Holmes, 1961: 192, 218; Laughlin, 1960:
Tales 72, 78; E.C. Parsons, 1936: 339; Hansen, 1957: Tale
Type 569)

> *26. The Spirit of the Forest (*pak'inte?*) (cf. Text 108)*
> *Informant: Manuel López Calixto*
> *Time Level: 21–40 years ago*

Most Distant Space Category: Specified Chamula hamlet other than sample hamlets

A Chamula man met the spirit of the forest on the edge of the road one night. The spirit of the forest lured the man into the woods and caused him to get lost. To defend himself from the creature, the man was clever enough to take off his clothing and put it on inside out. The spirit of the forest was deceived into thinking that they were two of a kind, for they now looked alike. The man gave the spirit of the forest three cigarettes and their friendship was sealed; she showed the man the way back to the road. One can always deceive the spirit of the forest by wearing one's clothing inside out. One should be very careful, though, for she (or he) looks like a person. She will do no actual damage but will certainly lose one in the woods if one does not take the proper precautions.

27. The Great Famine (cf. Text 11)
Informant: Marian López Calixto
Time Level: 21–40 years ago
Most Distant Space Category: Elsewhere in Mexico

There was a famine. When the people carried maize, they washed their backs and then drank the water so they would feel full. They were very hungry and cried a lot. They all looked for fern heads to eat. Some people still remembered where maize was hidden; those who did not, died. They sucked on anything they could find, even old banana and orange peels. No one walked around. It was very hot during the day and there were heavy frosts at night. Even the Ladinos were hungry and dying. Not everyone died of hunger, but many did. It was a punishment sent by Our Father because people had not taken enough care of their maize, a part of his body. Now they take very good care of it.

28. The Marble Trick
Informant: Manuel López Calixto
Time Level: 21–40 years ago
Most Distant Space Category: San Cristóbal

A Ladina asked a Ladino if he would lend her two marbles. The man innocently said that he did not have any marbles

because he did not need them; the woman said that she
did need them. Finally he caught on that what she wanted
was "marbles to play with," that is, testicles. Then they went
to "play at marbles," that is, to make love. The man blamed
it all on the woman and her tricks.

29. Tenejapaneco Witchcraft
Informant: Marian López Calixto
Time Level: 21–40 years ago
Most Distant Space Category: Indian municipios contiguous
to Chamula

There are still witches in Tenejapa today. Once a Chamula
man and woman went to Tenejapa to sell wool clothing and
had a quarrel with a Tenejapaneco over the price of a piece
of cloth. He wanted it for less than they were willing to take.
The Tenejapaneco was so angry that he bewitched them, and
on their way home they found a pot full of worms and bats
and smoke. These jumped into the woman's carrying net and
in that way were transported to contaminate their home and
property. Their animals died; sheep, chickens, dogs, and
horses, all were afflicted with worms and bat bites. The witch
had put chile in the pot also, so that bites of various sorts
would get all of their animals. The man and woman died;
then the witch sent a plague of locusts to Chamula. The
Chamulas went to get a witch from Venustiano Carranza to
avenge the evil of the other witch. He cut off the witchcraft
of the Tenejapanecos. The survivors were very grateful.
(Barlow and Ramírez, 1962: 55–61; Cicco and Horcasitas,
1962: 75–76; Anderson, 1957: 313–316; E.C. Parsons, 1936:
324–328; Miller, 1956: 81; Johnson and Johnson, 1939:
218–221; S. Thompson, 1955–1958: Motifs A2003, C322;
J.E.S. Thompson, 1930: 128–129; Hansen, 1957: Tale
Type 836F)

30. The Burning of the Saints (cf. Texts 9, 12, 37, 40)
Informant: Mateo Méndez Tzotzek
Time Level: 21–40 years ago
Most Distant Space Category: The whole earth

The Protestants once burned the saints in the church in
Chamula. They said that they were not gods but carved

pieces of wood. They could not really talk. There was only one god, and he was not Our Father. They said that Our Father was like a demon, and that the only true god was in a cave somewhere. They burned the saints and closed the church in Chamula Ceremonial Center. Before this happened, some good Chamulas had replaced the true saints in the church with old ones of no significance. These were the ones that the Protestants burned. San Juan and San Mateo and the others had been rescued and stored in a safe place when they came to burn the saints and close the church. Don Erasto Urbina later helped to solve the problem, for even the Ladino churches of San Cristóbal had been closed by the Protestants. Through Urbina's intervention, the churches from Chamula to Tuxtla were at last reopened. All was resolved, thanks to Don Erasto. Now the people could have fiestas once again.

31. Building the Road to Tuxtla
Informant: Mateo Méndez Tzotzek
Time Level: 21–40 years ago
Most Distant Space Category: Highland places not contiguous to Chamula

When they built the car road to Tuxtla, many people died, Ladinos and Indians alike. Dynamite was used, and many people died because they did not really understand it and there was a lack of co-ordination. The Indians, who liked the yellow cord used for the fuse, sometimes grabbed it at the wrong time. One time, lightning unexpectedly hit the charge. By the Bell Cave many died because the earth god who lived in the cave did not want the road to pass by his door. The engineer went to talk to the earth god and finally persuaded the people that if they did not want at least half of their number to stay forever with the earth god, they would have to put the road through Nachih (a paraje of Zinacantan). This would avoid the route by Bell Cave which the earth god opposed. The earth god nevertheless deceived the driver of one bus and took everyone in the bus into the mountain to become his servants.

32. Sodomy
Informant: Manuel López Calixto

Time Level: 41–60 years ago
Most Distant Space Category: Chamula hamlet other than sample hamlets.

An unmarried Chamula man found a sheep feeding along the road to San Cristóbal and had intercourse with it. Another man saw him and told the Chamula officials at the town hall about it. Mayordomos were sent to arrest the offender. They brought him to the town hall, fined him, and put him in jail for the night. He then fled to the coffee plantations, for he had shamed his father so much that the latter would no longer allow his son to live at home.

33. Don Erasto Urbina and the Revolution (cf. Texts 30, 40, 46, 135)
Informant: Marian López Calixto
Time Level: 41–60 years ago
Most Distant Space Category: Mexico City

Long ago there was a war between the Chamulas and the Ladinos on the one side and the Carrancistas and the Mexican government on the other. A Ladino who wished to rescue his fellows from bondage and servitude went to Mexico City to present his case to the highest authority. The authorities would not listen to him and sent him to work in the fields. He recruited the Carrancistas, who at first said they would defend the Indians in Chiapas, but they plundered Mexico City and then went to take over San Cristóbal. They had betrayed the Ladino who brought them. During the occupation of the town they made the Indians their servants. They went to Chamula, stealing animals and food and raping the women. Another Ladino went to Mexico City and arranged to have an airplane go to San Cristóbal to frighten the Carrancistas with a rain of ash and fire. They ran away to their homes. It was the Ladino Erasto Urbina who went to Mexico to bring the airplane. That solved things and the war ended. Only the animal souls of the Carrancistas remain today; they are the hard-tailed rats.

34. The Little Old Baby (cf. Texts 30, 37)
Informant: Marian López Calixto
Time Level: 41–60 years ago

Most Distant Space Category: Hot Country

There was a strange child born to a woman. She felt no pain in childbirth, and when she looked at her son, she saw that he was already a bearded old man. The child spoke immediately and asked what kind of sickness they would prefer—chicken pox, famine, volcanic ash, or itch; they could have their choice. They told their neighbors about it, and soon the epidemic began. It was a fever (referring to the influenza epidemic of 1918). Many people died. On another occasion a man was walking along the road at night and decided to urinate. There by the side of the road he found the Mother of Sickness. She had drums, guitars, and an accordion and predicted that the masks were coming, that sickness was coming. She had monkey assistants and flags and was having a celebration. Then she turned into a dog, and the man woke up near a cave. He had suffered a severe blow on his head. He told his story and soon the sickness came. Soon so many people had died that there was no one to bury them. They rotted and the dogs ate them. Those still alive ran away, naked for fear the sickness was on their clothing. The epidemic was terrible.

35. The Perils of an Animal Soul (cf. Texts 3, 19)
Informant: Salvador Guzmán Bakbolom
Time Level: 41–60 years ago
Most Distant Space Category: Hot Country

The godfather of the informant had a jaguar as his animal soul. Once (in a dream) his soul leapt down from a tree and bit a person. He killed the person and took his heart and tongue to his fellow jaguars. He had the custom of doing this every night, for his fellow jaguars were cowardly. The people who traveled frequently on the road decided to kill the jaguar. They shot him once, and he grabbed the bullet in his paw. He realized that he would have to try to escape and went bounding off into the woods. At this point the informant's godfather awoke and was terribly sick. The skin peeled off his hands and he could not eat. This skin condition and the illness had been caused by the bullets, which had struck his animal soul. He announced that he had to suffer in order to defend the weaker animal souls. His soul was on the third

level; coyote and fox were on the second level; opossum,
weasel, and skunk were on the first. Since he was a strong
shaman, he was a jaguar; average shamans were coyotes and
foxes; weak people were opossums, weasels, and skunks.
(La Farge and Byers, 1931: 134)

36. Pajarito's Rebellion
Informant: Mateo Méndez Tzotzek
Time Level: 41–60 years ago
Most Distant Space Category: Hot Country
The Chamula presidente, under the influence of a rebel
named Pajarito, issued an order for all Chamulas to get
together to learn a new cult. The best members of the new
cult were named "captain," "judge," and "attorney," and
these became recruiters for more converts. Those who did
not want to convert were executed. Many died in this way.
Then the tide changed and the members of the new cult
began to lose battles. It looked as though Pajarito's people
were losing. Some fled to what is now Rincón Chamula. One
(a captain) fled to San Cristóbal and to the church of San
Nicolás, where he hid until San Cristóbal officials helped
anti-Pajarito elements to find and execute him at the graveyard. Before they shot him, he asked to be buried face down,
for this would enable him to arise after three days. This did
not happen, even though they had buried him as he asked.
With the captain dead, peace began to return, and the Ladino
population moved back to Chenalhó, San Andrés, Tenejapa,
and Zinacantan (they had left when the trouble started).
The remainder of Pajarito's men (those who had not already
fled to Rincón Chamula) went to Tuxtla en masse in order to
reclaim the cane of San Juan, which the Ladinos had stolen
long ago. The forces in Tuxtla decided to trick the rebels by
offering them free food at Jompana. The women could
provide it and then flee, whereupon the Tuxtla forces would
massacre Pajarito's forces. It happened in this way, and all
of Pajarito's men were killed. The rod of San Juan remained
in Tuxtla and even today continues to give Ladinos great
wealth, while Indians remain as poor as ever. The missing
rod of San Juan is the Mother of Money.

37. The Wrath of the Saints (cf. Texts 30, 34)
Informant: Mateo Méndez Tzotzek
Time Level: 41–60 years ago
Most Distant Space Category: The whole earth
When the plague came, it was because the Carrancistas were burning the saints in the churches. Some saints did not want to burn and ascended to heaven in balls of fire. Others were burned and these were the ones who, with Our Father, sent the plague. It was not the Chamulas' fault, but many died in the plague anyway. Many did not even get properly buried, for there was no one strong enough to do it; the gods ate them. After the plague had passed, there came a famine and more people died, even the Ladinos and the Carrancistas themselves. People were dying everywhere, in their houses, in the paths, in the woods.

38. The Mexican Revolution (cf. Texts 33, 40, 46, 68, 136)
Informant: Mateo Méndez Tzotzek
Time Level: 41–60 years ago
Most Distant Space Category: Elsewhere in Mexico
Of the soldiers of long ago, the first to come was Pineda. He and his troops lived in San Cristóbal for a year. Then came Carranza, who fought with Pineda because he wanted to rule San Cristóbal. Pineda lost and left. The Carrancistas were in power for two years. They were awful to the Indians and Ladinos alike. They made the women stay and be raped while they sent the men to look for food for their horses. They stole food, livestock, everything from the Chamulas. Then the Pinedistas came back and fought them in two hamlets. The Carrancistas fled, and the Pinedistas returned to power. Then the Obregonistas came with an airplane and drove out the Pinedistas. They were good people and treated everyone well. They brought metal money instead of the paper money that had been used before.

39. The Little Red Man (cf. Texts 44, 47, 58, 75, 81, 89, 95, 110, 128, 133, 137, 156, 159, 166, 177, 179, 184)
Informant: Manuel López Calixto
Time Level: 41–60 years ago
Most Distant Space Category: Indian municipios contiguous to Chamula

A man was walking on the road to San Cristóbal, telling of his meeting with the devil one night. The man asked the devil what his name was, and the devil said, "Little Red Man." The man said that that was his name also. The devil asked where the little red man was, and the man pulled out his penis, which had red skin. The devil then thought he was a friend and did not harm him. The man defended himself with his penis—also with his cane, which was black like the devil's. All this happened when the man was a maize beer merchant, going alone to Amatenango where he bought maize beer and carried it back to sell in Chamula. Everything was much cheaper then.

40. Don Erasto Urbina Helps the Chamulas (cf. Texts 30, 33, 46, 68, 135)
Informant: Manuel López Calixto
Time Level: 61–80 years ago
Most Distant Space Category: Chamula hamlets contiguous to sample hamlets

In the past, cargo officials did not know how to read and write. Neither did they know Spanish. Even the escribanos, who did know Spanish, were few in number. But the escribanos got together and thought that it would be better if some reform took place, for when the cargo officials tried to solve court disputes, they only got drunk. This was unfair to the people who came to court. Don Erasto Urbina came to help solve the problem. He suggested that officials be required to have some elementary education, that they be young, and that they know Spanish. The people agreed and the custom changed. This is why there are schools in Chamula, in order to educate the cargo officials.

41. How Coyotes Came to Chamula (cf. Texts 1, 17, 84, 94, 96, 101, 142)
Informant: Salvador Guzmán Bakbolom
Time Level: 61–80 years ago
Most Distant Space Category: Hot Country

Some Chamulas were walking home from Hot Country after unsuccessfully trying to get work on the coffee plantations. They were very hungry and went hunting in a place recommended by a Ladino. They found deer, rabbits, and armadillos there and killed them. When they began to eat them, they also began to grow tails and turn into animals themselves. They turned into coyotes and stayed there near Motosintla. Two other Chamula men found some puppies on the road home from the coffee plantation. These were coyote pups from the people who had been converted. Back in Chamula, the coyote puppies ate well and grew up and then ran away into the woods. That is why there are coyotes in Chamula today.

42. The Man Who Talked to Jaguars
Informant: Salvador Guzmán Bakbolom
Time Level: 61–80 years ago
Most Distant Space Category: Chamula or other highland woods
There was a man who had the custom of going to the woods to talk to the jaguars. They understood each other's speech. He decided not to go one day, and the jaguar came to find out why he had not come. He scratched on the roof of the man's house and made terrible noises. The man was scared and tried to make his house jaguar-proof. One night he was sleeping soundly and, he thought, securely. The jaguars tore a hole in the wall and ate him. They were angry that the man had not lived up to his agreement to talk to them in the forest.

43. When the Bishop Came to Chamula
Informant: Manuel López Calixto
Time Level: 61–80 years ago
Most Distant Space Category: Chamula hamlets contiguous to sample hamlets
The bishop came long ago to leave the speech for the Festival of Games in February. Now the passions, who are in charge of this festival, go to the crier with rum every year before the fiesta so that he will make his speech.

44. A Narrow Escape (cf. Texts 39, 58, 75, 81, 89, 95, 110, 128, 133, 137, 156, 159, 166, 177, 179, 184)
Informant: Manuel López Calixto
Time Level: 61–80 years ago

Most Distant Space Category: Hot Country

Three men were walking along a road at night. One man stayed behind and the others did not wait for him. When he was alone, he felt that a demon was near. He ran back at once, losing his sandal. He hid under a rotting fallen pine tree. The demon was looking for him, and he could feel him walking on top of the tree. The demon could not find the man, who stayed under the tree until morning, having lost nothing more than one sandal. He was not hurt.

45. The Golden Days of Yesteryear (cf. Texts 11, 53, 55)
Informant: Salvador Guzmán Bakbolom
Time Level: 61–80 years ago
Most Distant Space Category: Unspecified Chamula hamlet

Before the reforms, the officials of Chamula did not want as presidente anyone who could read and who knew Spanish; if he could not do these things, he would make judgments based on how much people gave him, and this was then divided up among all the officials. If the presidente could read and knew Spanish, he would have more power over the rest of the officials; that is why they sought the oldest and most senile man for the job. Little by little the number of cargo positions increased, and then they started to make younger, more educated people presidente. This was when fiestas were simpler, the saints' cults less developed, and people still wore shirts of wool. Their rain capes were made of palm leaves. They could grow many vegetables that they cannot grow now. It does not rain as much today as it did before. Our Father is punishing people for being so wasteful. Houses used to be tied together with vines, for nails were very expensive. Now, people are more educated and they know about more things. There are many more sicknesses today. That is why there are more curers today. Work has changed as well. People used to make sandals in hamlet Peteh, which they do not now. Now people would rather go to work on the coffee plantations than take care of milpas, for they can earn more money there. Some people just go to the fincas forever. Now people buy more luxury items, such as gas lights and corn grinders.

46. The Carrancistas (cf. Texts 33, 38, 40, 68, 135)
Informant: Manuel López Calixto
Time Level: 61–80 years ago
Most Distant Space Category: Elsewhere in Mexico
When the Carrancistas were in San Cristóbal, the people could not go to the market without harassment. The soldiers made the Chamula men go look for food for their horses and raped that women before the would let the Indians cross the bridge and go to the market. They had to wait hidden in the forest until the soldiers went in to lunch, when they could cross the bridge into town; by then it was three o'clock in the afternoon and there was little market activity. Then Don Erasto Urbina went to Mexico and brought back other soldiers, who drove out the "raccoon solders," as the Carrancistas were called, because of the masks they wore. Don Erasto stayed in power and did what he could to raise the Indians' standard of living.

47. The Backwards-Wailing Man (valopat''ok') *(cf. Texts 39, 44, 58, 75, 81, 89, 95, 110, 128, 133, 137, 156, 159, 166, 177, 179, 184)*
Informant: Marian López Calixto
Time Level: 61–80 years ago
Most Distant Space Category: Hot Country
A man was walking in the forest and heard the cry of a demon, the backwards-wailing man. He answered its cry and soon came face to face with it. It had a horrible, hairy double body and swang from vines in the trees. He shot it one time with his shotgun and hit the creature in the hand, but one lick was enough to make the wound better. Then the demon bit the man and started to eat him. His friend ran home to tell the awful news to the man's friends and relatives. The man's mother got two hundred soldiers to go with her to rescue her son. Some fled and others were killed by the backwards-wailing man. It grabbed them with its long hair and ate with both mouths, defecating as it ate.

48. The Penalty for Adultery
Informant: Salvador López Sethol
Time Level: 61–80 years ago

Most Distant Space Category: Indian municipios contiguous to Chamula

A man was unsuccessful in hunting deer and returned home to find his wife having intercourse with another man. When the adulterous man was urinating through a crack in the house, the husband cut off his penis and carried it with him on the hunt. He was now successful and brought back both deer and the man's penis, roasted to look like the deer. In the meantime, the wife had buried her dead lover beneath the bed. Upon returning, the man gave his wife the penis to eat, and she consumed it unaware. She became very thirsty and drank a great deal of water, then burst and died. She was buried with her lover. The avenged husband remarried to a good woman and had continued success in deer hunting. If, however, this wife were unfaithful, he would no longer have luck at hunting. (Guiteras-Holmes, 1961: 261; Laughlin, 1960: Tales 26, 86; J.E.S. Thompson, 1930: 120–123)

49. Never Trust a Woman
Informant: Salvador López Sethol
Time Level: 61–80 years ago
Most Distant Space Category: Hot Country

A man returning from Hot Country met a beautiful woman on the road who was not his wife. She seduced him. On the way home afterwards, he found that he had no penis, only a vagina. He went to a shaman, who told him to find a white cow, mount her, have intercourse with her, and then his penis would return. This he did, and finally the white cow turned into a woman. He was cured. Another man turned into a woman and was never cured. He died of shame before his wife, who grabbed for his penis and found only a vagina. Still another man left his lover to go home to his wife. Halfway home he realized that he had no penis. Rather than suffer shame before his wife, he returned to his lover who had bewitched him and taken away his penis. When he finally agreed to stay with her, she lowered his penis down from the roof of the hut. So he lost his vagina and stayed with his lover.

50. The Eruption (cf. Text 62)
Informant: Mateo Méndez Tzotzek
Time Level: 61–80 years ago
Most Distant Space Category: The whole earth

When the eruption occurred, it meant that Our Father was angry and was sending it as a punishment to his children. He did not like the way that they shouted and killed each other and had too much excrement from overeating. The full destruction did not come to pass, however, because the people had prayed to Our Father and given him candles and flowers so that he would not be angry with them. Therefore, Our Father had tied up the Mother of Earthquakes with metal chains so that she could not move her tail much (she had a human face and a fish tail, as in the mermaid sculpture of her on the corner of the Hotel Santa Clara in San Cristóbal). She was forced to be quiet in her mountain home. But Our Father did send volcanic ash as a lesser punishment. There was a roar of the earth gods, just like thunder, and the ash rose out of the mountain like clouds and came down as rain and hail, in small and large pieces. The sky was black and the sun invisible and people could not see their way on the paths. Sheep and cattle, horses and rabbits, died because of the ash that they ate with the grass. The ash polluted the water supply and caused the meat in the market in San Cristóbal to rot. On the second day the sky was clear and everyone was happy.

51. The War of 1867–1869
Informant: Mateo Méndez Tzotzek
Time Level: 61–80 years ago
Most Distant Space Category: San Cristóbal

The Chamulas had a war with the soldiers from San Cristóbal. The Chamulas were led by Díaz Cuxcat. Earlier the Chamulas had celebrated fiestas in every paraje, especially one that had its own saint. The Chamulas there went to the river with guitars and fireworks and the saint. When the priest found out that they had a saint, he wanted to see it. The Chamulas, hearing of this, went to close the road. They killed the priest and his horse. The soldiers came to get him and to punish the Chamulas. They waited for the Chamulas,

eating lunch while they waited. The Chamulas surprised
them, whereupon they fled, leaving guns and food behind.
When they came back, the Chamulas found out and waited
with their wives, who planned to "cool" the guns by showing
their "cold" bare bottoms. When the soldiers came, the
women bent over and pulled up their skirts, but it did not
work and they died there. The soldiers won and many
Chamulas died.

*52. The Woods Monster (*poč'lom*)*
Informant: Marian López Calixto
Time Level: 81–100 years ago
*Most Distant Space Category: Chamula hamlets contiguous
to sample hamlets*

A man had to sleep in the woods one night when he was
traveling late. A woods monster cried out and scared him, and
he ran home, even though it was dark. The woods monster
came to cry at his house. Then he cried at all four corners of
the house. Frightened, the man prayed to Our Father for
advice. Our Father told him to wash his shotgun in garlic
and tobacco water and to pack its charge with underarm hair.
Then he should go out naked to shoot the woods monster.
This he did while the woods monster was praying and dancing
by the patio cross. He killed it and cut it up with a machete
and the next morning found a female pig with the same
wound, which showed that a witch who lived nearby had
come in the form of a woods monster to do him harm. In the
meantime, two friends of the woods monster had gone to
drink the blood of a sick person who lived nearby. No one
succeeded in killing them.

53. The Golden Past (cf. Texts 45, 55)
Informant: Manuel López Calixto
Time Level: 81–100 years ago
Most Distant Space Category: Hot Country

Long ago everything was much cheaper. Clothing and
cloth were less expensive, even though there were no trucks
to bring them; they came by oxcart from Hot Country.
The oxen worked so long and hard that they made leather
shoes for them. The Ladinos rode about in horsedrawn carts,

and horses were everywhere. This was the case when the parks in San Cristóbal still had large trees. Those were the days when things were cheap and wages were low also. The workers on the coffee plantations earned only fifty centavos a day, and even that was a lot. Although goods are more expensive today, wages are higher than in the old days.

54. The Rabbit's Hat (cf. Texts 54, 72, 77, 94, 96, 105, 142, 176)
Informant: Salvador Guzmán Bakbolom
Time Level: 81–100 years ago
Most Distant Space Category: Hot Country
A rabbit had a hat and a deer did not. The rabbit lent his hat to the deer, saying that he could not walk well with it, for he was very little. The deer said that he could, for he was big and the people could not catch him. When the rabbit arrived home, he told his father that he had lost his hat in the woods. The father did not believe him and sent him to look for it. He tried to find the deer, but could not and had to go home to tell his father. The father became very angry and pulled hard on the rabbit's ears. That is why rabbits have long ears. (Guiteras-Holmes, 1961: 186; Laughlin, 1960: Tale 90; Foster, 1945: 220; Redfield, 1935: 36; Hansen, 1957: Tale Type 74X)

55. Why Chamulas Now Go to the Coffee Plantations (cf. Texts 11, 27, 45, 53, 68)
Informant: Manuel López Calixto
Time Level: 81–100 years ago
Most Distant Space Category: Hot Country
A long time ago the land was very good; everything grew well. Every year in the Maya month of Great Whiteness (March–April) it began to rain, and the milpas grew very fast. The people did not have to go to the coffee plantations as laborers. They only worked occasionally as porters on the oxroad to Tuxtla. They also had many more sheep in those days. They provided lots of wool for clothing and lots of fertilizer for the fields. Little by little, Chamulas grew poorer. The rains began to come later and the ground became poorer and less able to produce good crops. Drought came to be a

regular thing, and coyotes were so hungry that they would come to eat the withering crops. And so the people became poor. They began to divide their lands among their sons and started working in Hot Country to earn money to buy food. That is why so many people in Peteh hamlet are now day laborers in the fincas.

56. The War of Santa Rosa
Informant: Marian López Calixto
Time Level: 81–100 years ago
Most Distant Space Category: Unspecified Chamula hamlet

It was when the people began to pray that Chamula officials thought the soldiers would come to break up their new religious organization. The presidente sent out an order for everyone to come into Chamula Ceremonial Center with their machetes, canes, the sticks of their looms, knives, guns, etc. The teacher's wife thought that she was Santa Rosa, the mother of god, and everyone started to pray to her. She told them that they had to pray so that they would not die. They organized into four defensive groups to protect themselves from government forces who opposed the religious movement. They practiced military maneuvers in Chamula Ceremonial Center. These activities were so frenzied and disorganized that many were killed. Those who fled from the movement and refused to participate were sent to be executed by guillotine. Other prisoners were beheaded on a stump behind the cabildo, and the water in the nearby lake was red with blood. Thus, it was a lie that their religious movement was an order of Our Father, for they killed each other as much as they armed themselves to resist the eventual intervention of the federal troops. The soldiers finally came and defeated the Chamulas, who had turned the whole religion into a reason for killing their fellow Chamulas for whatever reason.

57. Iguanas (cf. Texts 16, 60, 73, 90, 132, 133, 173)
Informant: Manuel López Calixto
Time Level: 81–100 years ago
Most Distant Space Category: Hot Country

Long ago the iguana had a snake as its mother; the iguana

was borne by a snake who gave birth to one of each, a snake and an iguana. That is why his head and tail are just like those of snakes. Now, if an iguana tries to escape into a hole or cave, one should not try to dig it out with a green stick, for it may turn into a snake. They are good to eat, but dangerous to hunt, for they may turn into snakes.

58. The Power of Innocence (cf. Texts 39, 44, 47, 75, 81, 89, 95, 110, 128, 133, 137, 156, 159, 166, 177, 179, 184)
Informant: Salvador López Sethol
Time Level: 81–100 years ago
Most Distant Space Category: Unspecified Chamula hamlet
An innocent man (a Chamula) was pursued by his neighbors because they were jealous of his wealth and ability to work productively. He escaped them by enormous jumps, which immediately identified him with the demon. In the fight that followed, the innocent man killed his attackers with a machete; their weapons would not kill him because he was innocent. The wives of the murdered men went for consolation and justice to the presidente of the municipio. He sent them away crying, for, he said, justice had been done to their husbands for trying to kill an innocent man.

59. A Defense Against a Jaguar
Informant: Salvador López Sethol
Time Level: 81–100 years ago
Most Distant Space Category: Unspecified Chamula hamlet
A messenger set out late at night on an errand from the Ladino secretary (of Chamula) to the secretary of another municipio. He carried powdered tobacco, which had the ability to warn him if danger were approaching. A jaguar tried to attack and eat him, but his tobacco turned into fire and then into a strong man who killed the jaguar. At this point, the messenger turned into a jaguar himself and arrived in that form at his destination. He received the message and returned to Chamula, where he was embarrassed to be seen at the municipal headquarters. He delivered the message through another man and went to the church to pray for his own recovery. In the morning the secretary was dead. His animal soul had been killed when the tobacco killed the

jaguar. The messenger went to the church to ask pardon for killing the secretary. (Laughlin, 1960: Tale 131; La Farge and Byers, 1931: 134)

> *60. The Snake Pit (cf. Texts 16, 23, 25, 57, 60, 65, 71, 73, 76, 80, 90, 105, 112, 132, 133, 145, 150, 173, 174)*
> *Informant: Salvador Guzmán Bakbolom*
> *Time Level: 81–100 years ago*
> *Most Distant Space Category: Chamula woods*

An old man who was working in his milpa with his helpers told them that by a mountain in Larraínzar there were cattle running loose which seemed to have no owner. The men went with lariats and other equipment to catch them and bring them home. When they appeared near the corral where the cattle were supposed to be, all they found were coiled up snakes. Even the posts of the corral were covered with snakes. The cattle were there, all right, but the earth god had sent the snakes to defend them, for they belonged to him. The men were frightened and hurried home.

> *61. The Abduction*
> *Informant: Salvador Guzmán Bakbolom'*
> *Time Level: 81–100 years ago*
> *Most Distant Space Category: Unspecified Chamula hamlet*

There was a man who was looking for a wife. He found just the right girl, but she would not agree to marry him and neither would her father agree to it. Then the man made a bull-roarer and painted his face with grease and carbon black from the bottom of a tortilla griddle. He put on a hat and a red neckerchief and then went at night to the girl's house. She came out to urinate, and he grabbed her and carried her away. She thought he was a demon. He carried her to his house and took her virginity violently, but then told her not to be afraid for he would return her to her home the next night. When the man was attacking her once again, he perspired so much that the charcoal paint on his face began to run off and the sweat fell on the girl's face and awakened her. She saw that it was the boy whose petition her father had turned down. She decided that she liked what he had to offer so much that she agreed to marry him. They asked her

father about brideprice, but he was furious and knocked
the boy down. They escaped, eloping into the woods.

62. The Volcanic Ash Fall (cf. Text 50)
Informant: Salvador Guzmán Bakbolom
Time Level: 81–100 years ago
Most Distant Space Category: The whole earth
When the ash fell, the ground was white and the horses and
sheep could not eat. The atmosphere was gray, as in a storm
during the cold, dry season. People could not see the path-
ways or the sun, and they were afraid. It seemed to them
that the ash came from the sky, but the truth was that a
mountain had exploded. It had sounded like thunder when
it erupted, and the people expected rain. But when the ash
began to fall, many thought that the end of the world had
come and they would never see another day. People cried in
dispair for the three days that the ash remained on the
ground. Many sheep were lost.

63. The Lacandones
Informant: Marian López Calixto
Time Level: 81–100 years ago
Most Distant Space Category: Elsewhere in Mexico
The Lacandón Indians are ugly, and one can tell their sex
only by lifting their robes. They have jaguars for cats and
lions for dogs, and they still use bows and arrows. They cook
rocks instead of eggs. They do not practice baptism, but do
practice infanticide if they do not want their children.

64. The Speechless Dog (cf. Texts 87, 91, 104)
Informant: Manuel López Calixto
Time Level: 101–150 years ago
Most Distant Space Category: Indian municipios con-
tiguous to Chamula
A Chamula man went walking with his dog. He met a girl
on the road and they talked of getting married. They agreed
that they would like to get married. When the man got
home, the dog told the man's parents what had happened.
The man scolded the dog for talking. The next day the dog
could not talk. Our Father had taken away his voice and

left him with only a bark, as he now has, for he thought it improper that dogs should talk. (Guiteras-Holmes, 1961: 261)

> *65. The Earth God's Grandchildren (cf. Texts 23, 25, 71, 76, 80, 85, 90, 105, 112, 145, 150, 173)*
> *Informant: Salvador Guzmán Bakbolom*
> *Time Level: 101–150 years ago*
> *Most Distant Space Category: Hot Country*

There was a lazy man who would not work in his milpa. He had only two plots of milpa. His wife went to each of the four corners of his milpa and gathered four ears of corn. These increased magically to many ears. This made her husband so angry that he struck her with one of the ears, and the blood that came out turned the white corn red, thereby creating red corn. She was hurt and went home to her father, an earth god, leaving behind a magical pot that would produce tortillas for her two children and telling them not to tell their father about it. But they did, and he tried to make it produce food for him. When it would not, he broke it. The mother replaced the pot a second time and the same thing happened. The mother and her father became angry with the children and sent them into the woods to find food. They turned into squirrels and have remained in the woods ever since. (Laughlin, 1960: Tales 72, 78; Goetz and Morley, 1950: 125; E.C. Parsons, 1936: 339; Guiteras-Holmes, 1961: 192, 218; Hansen, 1957: Tale Type 569)

> *66. The Perils of the Road (cf. Text 69)*
> *Informant: Manuel López Calixto*
> *Time Level: 101–150 years ago*
> *Most Distant Space Category: Hot Country*

In the old days, there were many threats to travelers. Since it took eleven days to go from Chamula to the coffee plantations by foot, they had to spend many days a year traveling to and from Hot Country. They put salt out to protect themselves from jaguars. The lions would come to lick the salt and, being grateful, would defend those who had put it out and keep the jaguars away. This is why they surrounded themselves with salt in the old days—to win the affection of the lions. The old days were hard and dangerous. They were even afraid to roast meat for fear that the jaguars would smell it. Salt was their only protection.

67. The Mother of Winds
Informant: Marian López Calixto
Time Level: 101–150 years ago
Most Distant Space Category: Chamula or other highland woods

Long ago the Mother of Winds lived. She had a very ugly face and neck; her neck was double, like a twin. When the strong, cold north winds came, it was because of her. One night she went out, as if she were flying. When she came back, her head was very swollen and she said that it hurt and went to bed. When asked what was wrong, she said that she had traveled over all lands and that the trees and rocks got in her way and that she hit them with her head. She was sick for three days. She was deaf and could not hear people speak. It is no longer like that, for the people killed her.

68. Padre Miguel Helps the Chamulas (cf. Texts 33, 38, 40, 46, 135)
Informant: Salvador Guzmán Bakbolom
Time Level: 101–150 years ago
Most Distant Space Category: Mexico City

There was a war over the tribute and lack of freedom from which the people suffered. They were completely tied to the Ladino landlords. All that they wanted in favors and goods came from them, and the people could go nowhere else. They had to cheat them to get food and drink. Miguel (a priest?) realized that all the people were suffering and determined to fight to help them. He went recruiting help from far and wide. The presidentes of some of the villages said that he was drunk and crazy and sent him to hard labor when he talked of freeing the people from their chains. He caused three mountains to crumble in order to prove his point, and finally the people began enlisting to his cause. These, the Carrancistas, entered and sacked Mexico City, thus liberating it. They did the same in Tuxtla, San Cristóbal, and Chamula. In their efforts they tortured and killed the landlords, thus freeing the people. However, the same Carrancistas were bad to the Chamulas. They robbed food and animals and raped the women. They were stronger and forced most of the Chamulas to fight on their side. They were in control of San Cristóbal for one year, and then they left. They killed Padre Miguel. Even after his death, however, his causes lived on and were won. The people were liberated and freed from their chains and work contracts. That is why they have a fiesta for Padre Miguel each year on September 16.

69. Saved by a Mirror (cf. Text 66)
Informant: Manuel López Calixto
Time Level: 101–150 years ago
Most Distant Space Category: Hot Country
Long ago, one could not walk along the road because there were so many jaguars. They howled when they came down to the road and scared the people. One time when a man was being chased, it occurred to him to take out his mirror. When the jaguar saw his own gaping mouth, he stopped from fright and ran away. He thought that there was another jaguar there. The road in those days was awful, passing through pure wilderness. Now the roads pass through open country and there are trucks that go to Hot Country, so there is no reason to be afraid. Before there were trucks, people had to bring their corn up from Hot Country on horseback and it cost much more to buy it. The reason that so many Chamulas now work in Hot Country is that it is so much easier and safer to get there and back. (S. Thompson, 1961: Tale Type 1168)

70. The Deceived Fiancé
Informant: Salvador López Sethol
Time Level: 101–150 years ago
Most Distant Space Category: Unspecified Chamula hamlet
A man seeking a wife and a princess seeking a husband met in the woods and agreed to be married as soon as she could get rid of her ugly fiancé, who was about to marry her. Since the first one to take her virginity was bound to marry her, the first man stained his white trousers with rabbit

blood and appeared at the wedding of the princess and the man whom she hated, claiming that he had had the first sexual access to her. The king saw the ugly fiancé's clean trousers and agreed to kill him and let the princess marry the one she really loved. The ugly pretender died, tied to the hooves of four mules.

71. Encounter with an Earth God (cf. Texts 23, 25, 65, 71, 76, 80, 90, 105, 132, 139, 145, 150, 173, 174)

Informant: Marian López Calixto
Time Level: 101–150 years ago
Most Distant Space Category: Chamula or other highland woods

A man went to the mountains to look for deer. He met a Ladino (an earth god), who said that there were no deer there, it was too close to his house, and the man had better leave. The man hid until he saw the deer pass by, loaded like burros. They carried bags of gunpowder that the earth god put in a nearby lake. The deer went off to eat, while the earth god tried out his cannons and shotguns, loaded with some of the gunpowder. The man started home to tell his wife about it, when an old man came by with a good hunting dog. As they went into the woods, the man stopped and relieved himself. The earth god came and asked him why he was defecating there. The men hurried home, frightened by the encounter with the earth god.

72. The Rabbit Who Watched the Milpa (cf. Texts 54, 77, 94, 96, 142, 176)

Informant: Salvador Guzmán Bakbolom
Time Level: 101–150 years ago
Most Distant Space Category: Unspecified Chamula hamlet

Once a man caught a rabbit eating in his milpa. The rabbit denied that he had been eating the maize and said that the only thing he had eaten was grass. The man believed him and asked him to do the favor of watching the milpa to see who in fact was eating the maize. A squirrel came to eat maize, and the rabbit told him that if he did not leave, he would tell the owner of the milpa about it. The squirrel refused to stop

eating maize, so the rabbit told the owner. The owner came
with his shotgun and killed the squirrel.

*73. The Snake Woman (cf. Texts 16, 57, 60, 90, 132, 133,
173)*
Informant: Marian López Calixto
Time Level: 151–500 years ago
*Most Distant Space Category: Indian municipios con-
tiguous to Chamula*

A man who did not have a wife met a lovely young woman
at the river. She seduced him and they went off to make love
at the man's house. He was just getting ready to make love
and his penis was erect when he heard a rattling noise. The
woman had turned into a rattlesnake. Afraid, he killed the
snake with his machete and buried it. The next day when he
went to see the grave, he found a live woman with a snake's
head lying there. This creature he also killed and buried.
Later, when he was preparing the ground for his milpa, he
struck the spot of the tomb with his hoe. Many snakes
emerged from the ground and one of them bit him. The
man died. (Mason, 1963: 205)

74. The Man and the Whale
Informant: Marian López Calixto
Time Level: 151–500 years ago
Most Distant Space Category: Hot Country

A man was bathing by a river in Hot Country and a sea
monster (whale) swallowed him. He was inside, still alive,
for a week. Then he took his knife and tried to cut himself
out. He was successful in escaping by gagging the whale with
knife cuts on his insides. This happened when the whale was
dozing on a beach. The man emerged, badly injured, and his
friends took him home to his wife. He grew thinner and
turned to flesh and bones. He finally died. (S. Thompson,
1961: Tale Type 1889; Laughlin, 1960: Tale 97; Redfield
and Villa Rojas, 1934: 336; Hansen, 1957: Tale Type 333A)

*75. The Heroes of Bell Cave (cf. Texts 39, 44, 47, 58, 81,
89, 95, 110, 128, 133, 137, 156, 159, 166, 177, 179, 184)*

Informant: Salvador Guzmán Bakbolom
Time Level: 151–500 years ago
Most Distant Space Category: Hot Country

There were two old Chamula men who frequently traveled the trail to Tuxtla in the old days, selling sandals and leather. By Bell Cave lived a terrible demon who made the road virtually impassable to all but the most courageous, for the demon killed and ate nearly all travelers. They determined to kill this demon. When he appeared, they traced a cross on the ground with their clubs. This forced the demon to jab his sword into the ground and not into them. Right on the spot of the cross they clubbed him to death, and his sword was useless to him. They cut off his head and cut out his heart, on which they put salt. These they took to show to the officials in Tuxtla as proof that the demon was slain and that the road was now open. Passing through Chiapa de Corzo, they received great acclaim from the townspeople. Then the governor of the state saw their proof of the slaying of the demon and was overjoyed. He gave each of them a twenty-peso reward. They had some drinks, and Tuxtla had a festival in their honor. The road to San Cristóbal was at last open.

76. The Defenders of Chamula (cf. Texts 23, 25, 60, 65, 71, 76, 80, 90, 105, 112, 132, 145, 150, 173, 174)
Informant: Salvador López Sethol
Time Level: 151–500 years ago
Most Distant Space Category: Chamula woods

There was a war. Some powerful soldiers survived and lived in a cave near Chamula. The group's leader was the younger brother of San Juan. A relative of the informant had talked to this leader, who was like an earth god. In talking to the leader, the man risked a great deal, for earth gods are difficult to deal with. Because he succeeded in talking to the leader of the soldiers, he became a very powerful man, physically and spiritually. He found that in the event of difficulty, the soldiers would come to the aid of Chamula. This man became a very powerful shaman.

77. The Magical Rabbit (cf. Texts 54, 72, 94, 96, 105, 142, 176)

Informant: Salvador Guzmán Bakbolom
Time Level: 151–500 years ago
Most Distant Space Category: Chamula woods
A man worked all day cutting down the forest and clearing a plot for his milpa. A rabbit came each night and caused the clearing to grow up again. He commanded the plants to grow up by magical words. Two times this happened, and each time the man caught the rabbit in the act, commanding the trees to grow up again. The man threw a stone at the rabbit's head and killed him. The man went home happy that he had solved the problem. (Goetz and Morley, 1950: 132, 133; J.E.S. Thompson, 1930: 134–135; Guiteras-Holmes, 1961: 185; Foster, 1945: 235; Mason, 1963: 206)

78. A Trip to the Underworld (cf. Texts 92, 120)
Informant: Salvador Guzmán Bakbolom
Time Level: 151–500 years ago
Most Distant Space Category: Seas, heavens, underworld
A man's wife died and he decided to go and see her in the underworld. He walked eight days to get there and had to cross a lake with the help of a black dog. When he got there, he talked with the earthbearer, with San Pedro and San Lorenzo (the patrons of the underworld), and asked their permission to see his wife. When he found her, she said that it would be better if he were to go home, for it was not yet time for him to be there. He finally spent the night there, but did not sleep with his wife; he talked to her and then went to look at her, but saw only a pile of bones. He was very scared and decided to go home. He went home the same way he had come and told his relatives about it. He died three days later from the scare in the underworld. (Guiteras-Holmes, 1961: 258–260; Laughlin, 1960: Tales 9, 19, 33; Madsen, 1960: 215; Mason, 1963: 208; Slocum, 1965: 25–37)

79. The Drought
Informant: Marian López Calixto
Time Level: 151–500 years ago
Most Distant Space Category: Hot Country
For abstract, see Ch. 4.

80. Help from the Earth Gods (cf. Texts 23, 25, 60, 65,

71, 76, 90, 105, 112, 132, 145, 150, 173, 174)
Informant: Salvador Guzmán Bakbolom
Time Level: 151–500 years ago
Most Distant Space Category: Chamula woods
There was a poor man who decided to go to a cave to ask
the earth gods for money and food, for he did not have a
cent to buy maize or clothing. He was going to fast for
thirteen days by the cave, he told his neighbors, and if
buzzards came, they would know he was dead and could
come to bury him. He fasted the thirteen days. He then met
a Ladino at the door of the cave, who told him to sit down
and wait for the earth god to talk to him. Knowing that if
he should sit down he would magically remain stuck there
forever, he remained standing until the earth god granted him
an audience. He told him that he was poor and that he
needed maize to eat. The earth god gave him an old hoe and
sent him home, warning him not to look back. He obeyed.
When the man got home, he put the hoe in a box with his
incense. During the night he heard a noise and got up to find
the box full of money with a coiled snake on top of it. He
put the snake in another box, and before morning the second
box was full of money. The man became rich, for his boxes
never ceased to produce money. He bought horses and land
and built a new house. (E.C. Parsons, 1936: 335)

81. The Deception of the Devil (cf. Texts 39, 44, 47, 58,
75, 89, 95, 110, 128, 133, 137, 156, 159, 166, 179, 184)
Informant: Juan Méndez Tzotzek
Time Level: 151–500 years ago
Most Distant Space Category: Highland places not con-
tiguous to Chamula
A man met a devil on the road and asked him for money.
The devil said that he would give it to the man, provided he
agreed to join him after a hundred years and accompany
him forever. The devil gave a lot of money to the man, who
was so happy that he went to San Cristóbal to spend it. He
met a compadre and told him the story. The compadre said
that he had the money for only one hundred days, not years.
On the hundredth day the man and his wife went to gather

wood. The wife cut herself with the axe and the man carried her home, to find the devil waiting there. He said that the devil could not take him away at that time, for his wife was badly hurt and he could not leave her. The devil said that he would cure her, and he made a poultice of tallow to put on the cut. He asked her to walk, to see if it was better. She did, but came back saying that it was still all runny and awful. He tried to cure her again, but a liquid kept running out of the cut. He finally gave up and told the man to stay there with his poor wife, who was almost sure to die. The devil went away, but it turned out that the "cut" was her vagina and that the woman had simply been urinating on the devil.

82. The Origin of Domestic Animals
Informant: Marian López Calixto
Time Level: Fourth Creation
Most Distant Space Category: Elsewhere in Mexico

A long time ago, there were no domestic animals. People killed and ate their brothers-in-law. When they ran out of them, they took off their clothing and cooked it, but they did not like it. They decided to go hunting in the mountains. They found some deer and killed all they could. They took them home and cooked them. Then they went to hunt rabbits and killed as many of them as they could. They cut off both animals' feet and buried them in a corral, in the hopes that they would reproduce. When they came to look again, they found the corral full of sheep. They killed them and buried a foot also. The next time, it was full of cows. They killed one of them and buried a foot. When they got home, they cooked their food. When they let the cows loose, they did not run away but grazed quietly in the grass. The sheep and horses multiplied and they no longer killed them. They killed cows when they wanted meat. The learned to ride horses. When they rode to the mountains, they found monkeys; one wrapped his tail around a man's neck and carried him to his cave, the horse running back to the man's house. The man died when the monkeys had anal intercourse with him, then they hanged him from a tree. They ate the excrement from the man and hung his clothes from the tree. His friends came to look for him and came across the monkeys, who chased them. The men killed the monkeys with a stick and ate them. They made pants of the skins. (M. Siegal, 1943: 123; La Farge, 1947: 51)

83. Why It Rains in June
Informant: Marian López Calixto
Time Level: Fourth Creation
Most Distant Space Category: Unknown
During the rainy season a woman cooked some food and ate part of it, leaving the rest for the morning meal. When she woke up, it was gone. She went to the garden to find a cabbage and heard someone talking, telling her to give him food, but she saw no one. Then she put the cabbage on to cook while she was off taking care of her sheep. When she came back, the cabbage was gone. The wailing one (a demon) started to cry because he was so hungry; that is why it rains so much during the month of June.

84. The Coyote Wins (cf. Texts 1, 17, 41, 94, 96, 101, 142)
Informant: Marian López Calixto
Time Level: Fourth Creation
Most Distant Space Category: Unspecified Chamula hamlet
A coyote was killing a man's sheep. The man took his rifle to the corral but fell asleep while waiting. The coyote came, killed all of the sheep, and hung the guts and skins on the man's neck. He woke up and screamed for his friends, but the coyote got away.

85. The Origin of Flying Squirrels (cf. Texts 65, 136)
Informant: Marian López Calixto
Time Level: Fourth Creation
Most Distant Space Category: Hot Country
Long ago the squirrel had no husband. There was a vampire bat who had no wife. The vampire bat came searching for the squirrel with a letter of authorization from somewhere (Our Father). The squirrel took the letter, looked at it and ate it. The vampire bat chased the squirrel all around the branches

of the tree and finally seduced her. That was what the letter authorized. The offspring of this union were flying squirrels. That is how they came into existence. The three animals now exist separately: squirrels, flying squirrels, and vampire bats.

86. From Silver to Gunpowder
Informant: Marian López Calixto
Time Level: Fourth Creation
Most Distant Space Category: San Cristóbal

There was a Chamula man who took wood to sell to the Ladinos when they were still operating a silver mine in Paraje Minaš. The Ladinos gave him gifts of silver, so he knew that the mine was rich. He pretended one day to lose his tumpline. This gave him a chance to see where the Ladinos entered the hill to get the silver. When he saw, he threw stones at the Ladinos and struck them on the head. When they were knocked out, the man went to the mine and took out a load of silver. He took it home and when he was about to show it to his wife, it turned to gunpowder. He went back for more, but just as he was about to enter the mine, a huge lightning bolt struck it and destroyed it. He was so scared that he ran all the way to San Cristóbal.

87. Why Dogs Cannot Talk (cf. Texts 64, 91, 104)
Informant: Salvador López Sethol
Time Level: Fourth Creation
Most Distant Space Category: Unspecified Chamula hamlet

When dogs could talk long ago, they told lies. They informed their masters about the unfaithfulness of their wives, whom the men would kill, quite unjustly, for they had sometimes not been unfaithful. Our Father became angry and put the dogs' anuses where their mouths had been and vice versa. So dogs no longer can talk but only have bad breath. Now married men and women are freer to associated with each other, for they are no longer so afraid of an accusation of adultery and death. (Anderson, 1957: 313–316; Guiteras-Holmes, 1961: 261; J.E.S. Thompson, 1970: 332; Foster, 1945: 236)

True Ancient Narrative

88. The Worm Boy
Informant: Marian López Calixto
Time Level: Third Creation
Most Distant Space Category: Highland places not contiguous to Chamula

There was a family of early Indians. They had a son, Pašik, who was in fact a worm. He could choose the form he wished. He went to give his father a message and then turned into a worm. His mother came to call both of them and, in so doing, stepped on her son. Since she had killed him, she became ill and died. That is why bad women have a worm as their animal soul companion.

89. A Kidnapping by a Demon (cf. Texts 39, 44, 47, 58, 75, 81, 95, 110, 128, 133, 137, 156, 159, 166, 177, 179, 184)
Informant: Marian López Calixto
Time Level: Third Creation
Most Distant Space Category: Chamula woods

A woman went out early in the morning to wash the maize for the day and disappeared. She reappeared one night in the front yard. She could not speak and was ill. They put some tobacco and garlic water on her face and put her to bed. The man smelled her hand and knew that a demon had probably stolen her away. That night the demon scratched on the house and the woman talked in her sleep. The man sweated a great deal while worrying about his wife. The next day she came to and talked. She had been taken to the demons' cave and was raped by all of the demons. They had eaten only salted meat. Their heat was from a pine cone fire. The chief demon raped her and begat a child, which was born in three weeks. One day she tricked the child into taking her on a flight (for she could not fly as the demons did). Since the baby demon was just learning to fly, the woman succeeded in making him crash into a tree branch near her home. He fell, and she escaped and went home. The baby demon was eaten by his father in his wrath at losing his wife. The woman finally died. Her family's diagnosis of her con-

dition had been correct. The demon had carried her away.
(Madsen, 1960: 134–135)

> *90. The Magical Machete (cf. Texts 16, 23, 25, 57, 60, 65,*
> *71, 73, 76, 80, 90, 105, 112, 132, 133, 145, 150, 173,*
> *174)*
> *Informant: Marian López Calixto*
> *Time Level: Third Creation*
> *Most Distant Space Category: Hot Country*

A man in Hot Country found a snake, almost dead, by the
road. The snake asked the man to carry him to his home, the
house of an earth god. The man knocked on the door. While
talking to the earth god, he put one foot inside the door.
Another snake came and bit him on the heel. He bled a lot
and fell to the ground. The blood was used to cure the sick
snake. The man's friends came to look for him, and the earth
god said that he was there taking care of his chickens. His
friends wanted to take him home, but the earth god said no
and offered them a machete instead, which they took to the
dead man's wife. She did not want it and they took it back
to the earth god, who told them to keep it. They prayed to
it and put it in the chicken house; the chickens grew and
reproduced well, for it was a magical machete.

> *91. The Dog Who Ate His Master (cf. Texts 64, 87, 104)*
> *Informant: Marian López Calixto*
> *Time Level: Third Creation*
> *Most Distant Space Category: Country other than Mexico*

There was a man who went hunting with his spear. He had
a dog who went along with him. He threw his spear at a
squirrel whom he had seen stealing maize in his milpa. The
squirrel that he killed was his own soul animal. Therefore,
the man died. His dog took his hat and trotted home to tell
the man's wife. Both went to the site of the man's misfortune.
The dog dug up the body of the squirrel that had been the
man's animal soul and tried to feed it worms, grubs, and
acorns, hoping to revive it and, therefore, his master. But it
was no use; both were dead. When the woman was not looking, the dog dug up and ate the bones of his master and of
the squirrel, his master's animal soul. The woman never

found out, for the dog's mouth was sealed and his deed hidden; he could no longer talk. (Guiteras-Holmes, 1961: 261; La Farge and Byers, 1931: 134)

92. The Food of the Dead (cf. Texts 78, 120)
Informant: Manuel López Calixto
Time Level: Third Creation
Most Distant Space Category: The whole earth

Many years ago a man's wife died, leaving him with two sons. All cried and were very sad. The man asked his mother to take care of the children for a while and he went to the graveyard. He cried by a grave and then saw his wife by the edge of a lake. He crawled into the grave and found himself in the underworld. He found his wife and started to talk to the woman. She was unhappy that he had left her children and said that he should go home, but he spent the night there in the underworld. She asked him to watch the beans, but told him not to blow on them. He did, and they turned into flies and flew away. She cooked more and they went to bed. When he embraced her, she turned into a pile of bones. He was very frightened. At dawn, she was herself again, but he decided to go home. When he got home, he went to his mother's house and told her all about it. He died three days later, since only his body had returned to earth. He had only come back to tell about the food of the dead. (Laughlin, 1960: Tales 9, 19, 33; Guiteras-Holmes, 1961: 258–260; E.C. Parsons, 1936: 362; Foster, 1945: 202; Madsen, 1960: 215; Mason, 1963: 208; Slocum, 1965: 25–37)

93. The Bear Child
Informant: Marian López Calixto
Time Level: Third Creation
Most Distant Space Category: Hot Country

There was a woman who had a son who talked a lot. One night he was talking and the woman told him to calm down, but he went on talking. The woman refused to answer, but neither could she sleep. Their house was in the hills, and a bear heard the talking and came to the house, looking for food. He carried off the woman to his home in a cave and shut the door. She was now his wife. He brought her raw

meat and tortillas, but she would not eat the meat. The bear
was very sad, for she only ate the tortillas. The bear ate
the meat and went to bring her more tortillas. While he was
gone, the woman escaped. When she arrived home, she told
her relatives that a bear was going to eat her. They told her to
hide, but the bear was hidden already in her house and
grabbed her and carried her back to his cave, where she
stayed for an entire year. Slowly she learned to eat raw meat.
The bear wanted to make love and did, and they had a son.
The woman was happy there and did not want to leave. When
the child was two years old, they left him in a field because
he had bitten his mother while nursing. A man came by and
carried the baby home; he then bit the man, who decided
that he must be the child of a monster. He decided to kill
him. The bear came to look for his son but could not find
him. He found the house and killed everyone in it. The bear
just arrived home when he died; the men came and found him
and his wife, whom they killed. They burned both of them
because the woman had started to eat their children as well
as her own. Only ashes remained. (Foster, 1945: 211; Boas,
1912: 75; Mason, 1936: 208; Mason and Espinosa, 1924:
249, 252, 254, 256)

> *94. The Rabbit Who Outwitted the Coyote (cf. Texts 1,*
> *17, 41, 54, 72, 77, 84, 96, 101, 105, 142, 176)*
> *Informant: Marian López Calixto*
> *Time Level: Third Creation*
> *Most Distant Space Category: Elsewhere in Mexico*

There was a coyote who played his guitar. A rabbit was
attracted by the noise. The coyote was afraid at first, for the
rabbit wore a man's hat. The rabbit invited him to talk, but
the coyote told him to be quiet, that he would eat him. The
rabbit invited the coyote to play his guitar so that he could
dance. The coyote agreed, and during the dance the rabbit
farted and it sounded like human speech. The coyote looked
the other way for the approaching people. The rabbit got
away and the coyote, embarrassed, chased him to the bank of
a river. Then the rabbit suggested that the coyote have some
cheese. Pointing to the cheese at the bottom of the river
(the moon's reflection), the rabbit suggested that the coyote

drink up the water to get the cheese. The coyote then drank the water and could not move when the rabbit escaped. Later, the coyote plugged up the rabbit's hole with resin, and the rabbit got caught fighting his way through the sticky stuff. The coyote at last caught him and had him in the pot for cooking. He went to get his relatives to share the feast, and when they returned, the rabbit had escaped. (S. Thompson, 1961: Tale Type 34; Laughlin, 1960: Tales 49, 90; Foster, 1945: 219; Boas, 1912: 237–238; Mechling, 1912: 202; Mason, 1963: 204; Recinos, 1918: 473; Hansen, 1957: Tale Type 34)

> *95. The Origin of the Sexes (cf. Texts 39, 44, 47, 58, 75, 81, 89, 110, 128, 133, 137, 156, 159, 166, 169, 177, 179, 182, 184)*
> *Informant: Marian López Calixto*
> *Time Level: Third Creation*
> *Most Distant Space Category: Unknown*

Long ago the people had no mouths, only bodies, legs and arms, and eye sockets in their faces. They could not stand, and when they moved, it was on all fours. When they ate, they would stick out their intestines to absorb food. They were naked and slept in the trees. There was a man with an axe who fixed these people. He cut out the form of the testicles and penis from the undifferentiated body. He found another of the early people and felt around and found no testicles that could be released, so he simply cut a slit in her pelvic area. She became a woman. Then he cut mouths in the peoples' faces and they spoke. When he was cutting the woman's genitalia, his axe slipped, making a larger cut than he had expected, which is why the vagina is so large. Then he showed them how to have intercourse, and from that time to this we have been bad, for the man was Judas. (Recinos and Goetz, 1953: 46–47; J.E.S. Thompson, 1970: 332; Guiteras-Holmes, 1961: 157, 187)

> *96. The Tar Baby (cf. Texts 1, 17, 41, 54, 72, 77, 84, 94, 101, 105, 142, 176)*
> *Informant: Salvador López Sethol*
> *Time Level: Third Creation*

Most Distant Space Category: Unspecified Chamula hamlet

A man was losing his milpa to some creature that ate from it every night. He made a resin doll to trap the culprit. The real thief, a rabbit, was caught in the resin, but he convinced the coyote to take his place with the promise that he would win a lovely bride from the owner. The owner of the milpa accused the coyote, for he was stuck in the resin. The owner burned the coyote's anus and released him to find the real culprit, the rabbit. The coyote invited the rabbit to a fiesta. There was none—only a punishment, the burning of the rabbit's anus. The two of them went to the river to cool their anuses, but the coyote could not swim and drowned. The milpa owner pulled the rabbit's ears for letting the coyote drown. (S. Thompson, 1961: Tale Type 175; Laughlin, 1960: Tales 21, 49, 90; J.E.S. Thompson, 1930: 134–135; Foster, 1945: 218, 220; Boas, 1912: 204–205, 235; Mechling, 1912: 200–201; Recinos, 1918: 472–473; Mason and Espinosa, 1912: 164–165; Hansen, 1957: Tale Types 74K, 175)

97. Why Ladinos Have No Shame (cf. Text 109)
Informant: Mateo Méndez Tzotzek
Time Level: Third Creation
Most Distant Space Category: San Cristóbal

Long ago the Ladinos had a dog for a father. There were no houses, and a dog and a Ladina had intercourse, the woman helping the dog. She waited on her hands and knees. They did it many times, and the woman became pregnant. When her son was born, he was the first Ladino. Slowly they multiplied. That is why Ladinos have no shame, why they embrace and make love by the side of the road, just like dogs. Ladinos are not afraid because they are powerful and can hit Indians. Indians do not have a dog for a father and are afraid and do have shame. (Guiteras-Holmes, 1961: 157, 194)

98. The Princess and the Pauper
Informant: Salvador López Sethol
Time Level: Third Creation
Most Distant Space Category: Seas, heavens, underworld

Juan found work across the ocean with a strange man who turned out to be a king. He asked three men how to get to the home of the king and finally reached the shore of the ocean, where he hid and helped one of the king's three daughters (the youngest) find her clothing after she and her sisters had bathed. As a reward, the princess turned into a dove and took Juan to the place of his employment with her father, the king. The king assigned him four tasks: to get three fish from a hole in the earth, to get three loads of firewood, to get three mules to carry the wood, and to bring it to the king's house. For all of these tasks he was allowed only limited time. Should he fail to do any one of them, he would be killed. The grateful princess helped him each time, but once they caught the mules, they escaped to Chamula, fleeing again across the sea. The king and his queen pursued them, but failed to find them, for they turned into various parts of the landscape as they were overtaken. First, the mule changed to a church, the princess to the Virgin of Guadalupe, and the boy to the bell-ringer; second, the boy changed into a gardener; and third, the boy changed into an alligator. When the queen realized that she was being duped, it was too late. They arrived at the boy's house and built separate houses. The princess assigned tasks to her servants to see if they would make better husbands than Juan. They failed, for one servant washed pots but put one of them on as a hat; another washed his hands in a metal pan but hung it around his neck; finally, another ate a meal with the princess but got a fishbone in his throat and nearly died. Having proved that the other men were fools, she married Juan. (S. Thompson, 1961: Tale Type 313; J.E.S. Thompson, 1930: 167–172; Reid, 1935: 110–112)

99. Hiccoughs Will Not Kill You
Informant: Marian López Calixto
Time Level: Third Creation
Most Distant Space Category: Hot Country
   A man was just about dead. He was suffering from hiccoughs. His soul saw that he was about dead. People thought he was dead and buried him. A year passed and they went to take care of the grave on All Saints' Day. His wife was very sad and wailed long over his grave. That night he appeared

at the house, risen from the dead. He was thin, but not decomposed. The fact was that he had never been dead and had not gone to the underworld. They put a liter of blood in him (from the clinic doctor) and then he lived for five more years. They buried him again when he died, but his grandsons dug him up to see him. They broke off a finger and it had no blood. The ancestors were very strange and very bad indeed.

100. Love Survives Death
Informant: Marian López Calixto
Time Level: Third Creation
Most Distant Space Category: Unknown

A woman died, her soul going to heaven instead of to the underworld, and her husband was very sad. He watched over her and tried to have intercourse with her body, but finally buried her. After four years, he collected and washed her bones, storing them in a big pot and hoping that they would return to life. A bird came and asked him if he wanted to see his wife. He went to heaven to see her and stayed there. His relatives found and burned his wife's bones. (Laughlin, 1960: Tales 9, 19, 33; Guiteras-Holmes, 1961: 258–260; E.C. Parsons, 1936: 362; Madsen, 1960: 215; Mason, 1963: 208; Slocum, 1965: 25–37)

101. The Deceitful Coyote (cf. Texts 1, 17, 41, 84, 94, 96, 142)
Informant: Marian López Calixto
Time Level: Third Creation
Most Distant Space Category: Zinacantan

There was a boy who was taking care of his grandmother's sheep. A coyote came and asked him for some sheep. The boy thought about it and gave him four sheep. He pretended that the coyote had stolen them and this is what he told his grandmother. She took her dogs and went to talk to the coyote. She asked him why he had stolen her sheep. He said that he had not stolen them but that her grandson had given them to him. Finally the boy admitted that he had lied, and the grandmother punished him by tying him to a stump, thrashing him with a whip, and then leaving him tied there all night without food. Then the coyote helped him by bringing him a raw chicken to eat. The coyote helped him eat it by feeding it to him with his paw, but it made the boy nauseated. Then he fed him raw sheep meat. When the boy was taken home and fed by his parents the next morning, he was not hungry and acted strange. He felt sick and went outside to sleep.

102. Roses Are Better Than Money
Informant: Salvador Guzmán Bakbolom
Time Level: Third Creation
Most Distant Space Category: San Cristóbal
The Chamulas spread money on the ground, hoping that Our Father would walk on it. The Ladinos did the same with rose petals. He walked on the roses, which turned to money when the Ladinos collected them afterward. That is why Ladinos are so rich, since Our Father wanted them to be. That way they could give jobs to Indians and pay them.

103. The Ladder to Heaven
Informant: Juan Méndez Tzotzek
Time Level: Third Creation
Most Distant Space Category: Elsewhere in Mexico
A long time ago, the Ladinos were the first to whom Our Father gave souls. They were formed first, and everyone spoke Spanish. When there were many people, they decided to build a ladder to heaven to see Our Father. Everyone cooperated because everyone could speak the same language. Our Father did not like this and changed their one language to many so that they could not communicate. This is the reason that the Indians speak Tzotzil, for they were the children of the second man who was created. Since the Ladinos were the children of the first man, everyone has to learn Spanish. With the change in language, different ethnic groups formed. The Ladinos mistreated the Indians, but when Our Father found out, there was a war, which was resolved by Miguel Hidalgo. The Spaniards were driven back to Spain. (La Farge, 1947: 64)

104. The Deceitful Dog (cf. Texts, 64, 87, 91)
Informant: Marian López Calixto

Time Level: Third Creation
Most Distant Space Category: Hot Country

A man's wife died and he was very sad. He went to clear roots from his milpa and got caught beneath a tree. His burro pulled him out. When he arrived home, he was very hungry. Then he went to look in the tortilla gourd and found fresh tortillas there. While he was eating them, wondering who had made them, he noticed dog hairs on them. It turned out that his wife, who was up in a cloud, had made them, but the dog said that he had done it. The man heard something in the cloud and went outside. He saw a woman up there but did not recognize her as his wife and was very scared, so he shot her. Many bones fell to the ground. As she died, his wife asked why he had shot her, for she had only been taking care of him. He opened the dog's mouth and rubbed it in the ground as punishment for lying. (Foster, 1945: 211)

105. How the Rabbit Got His Ears (cf. Texts 23, 25, 60, 65, 71, 72, 76, 80, 90, 96, 112, 132, 142, 145, 150, 174, 176)
Informant: Mateo Méndez Tzotzek
Time Level: Third Creation
Most Distant Space Category: Chamula woods

When Our Father was still living on earth with his mother, he went to clear a plot for his milpa. The next day he found that the trees which he had cut the previous day were standing again. This happened for three days, and on the fourth he decided to find out who was playing this prank. The culprits turned out to be a rabbit and a deer, who ordered the forest magically to grow up again. Helping them were two kinds of wasps and a bee, but they did not talk. Our Father pulled their ears and cut off the tail of both the rabbit and the deer, thereby giving them their present form. Then, with his fingernail, Our Father nearly severed the middle of the bodies of the two kinds of wasp and the bee. That is why their bodies are nearly divided into distinct sections; it was their punishment for helping the deer and rabbit. The animals did not want Our Father to invade the forest and to make his milpa there. He also named these animals so that their cleverness would be known by people. He was so disgusted that he gave them to the earth god to take care of, for he really wanted to do away with them. However, the earth god agreed to be their patron forever and took them to his cave. The earth god refused to accept the wasps and the bee; they would remain animals of the earth and would have no patron. The fate of deer and rabbit is watched over by the earth gods, but anything can happen to insects. (Guiteras-Holmes, 1961: 185; Goetz and Morley, 1950: 132–133; Valladares, 1957: 239–241; Slocum, 1965: 1–3; J.E.S. Thompson, 1930: 134–135; Foster, 1945: 235; Mason, 1963: 206)

106. The Third People (cf. Text 168)
Informant: Mateo Méndez Tzotzek
Time Level: Third Creation
Most Distant Space Category: Unspecified Chamula hamlet
The third people were made of clay, but were more successful than the previous creations of Our Father. They knew how to have festivals, dance, and work. Our Father tried to feed them pine cones, acorns, and grass, but they refused these foods. He took off a piece of his flesh and gave it to them. This was maize. The people took it and were happy. That inspired them to take the image of Our Father in a procession around the church atrium, and they did nearly everything correctly in the festival that they had for him. Then Our Father called on Judas to teach them to procreate, which he did. Our Father gave people hoes, machetes, and axes with which to work, but the tools worked by themselves and the people rested. Then the earth gods told Our Father that if he allowed the people's tools to work alone, they would not get tired and therefore would not pray to Our Father. In order to protect himself and his cult, he ordered the people to work themselves, and that is why people are devout and pray to Our Father for good fortune and good harvests. (Laughlin, 1960: Tale 54; Guiteras-Holmes, 1961: 157, 187; Recinos and Goetz, 1953: 46–47; Roys, 1967: 117; J.E.S. Thompson, 1930: 150; 1970: 332; E.C. Parsons, 1936: 349; Foster, 1945: 236; Madsen, 1960: 126; Cline, 1944: 108, 110; Hansen, 1957: Tale Type 798; La Farge, 1947: 51)

107. A Penis Measuring Contest (cf. Texts 130, 181)
Informant: Marian López Calixto
Time Level: Third Creation
Most Distant Space Category: Chamula hamlets contiguous
to sample hamlets
Some early people were talking and decided to find out
which one had the largest penis. They climbed up on a rock
(which was still soft) to measure them, but found that they
had been changed into vaginas and that they were now
women.

108. An Encounter with the Spirit of the Forest (pak'inte?)
(cf. Text 26)
Informant: Marian López Calixto
Time Level: Third Creation
Most Distant Space Category: Unknown
A man was walking in the fields, whistling and looking for
a wife. He heard an answer to his whistle and went to see
what it was. It was his mother, who said that she had lost her
sheep and would like him to help her find them. The
mother was really the spirit of the forest in disguise, who
led him on and on in the fog until he was tired out and lost.
She told him to come and make love to her; he tried, but she
turned into a tree, scaring him. He took off his clothes and
finally remembered how to get home. He arrived home and
told his mother what had happened.

109. The Origin of Ladinos (cf. Texts 54, 97, 116, 131,
164, 165, 175)
Informant: Marian López Calixto
Time Level: Second and Third Creations
Most Distant Space Category: Unknown
After the big flood, which was sent by Our Father to
punish the early people for eating their children, there was
only one mestiza left, for she had sat out the flood on a
hilltop with her dog. The little dog played a lot and excited
the woman, so she pushed him under her skirts. The dog
did not respond—he just sat there and looked—so she pushed
his penis into her vagina. Then the dog got an erection, but
his penis was not long enough, so the woman pulled it. That

is why a dog's penis now has an "apple." The woman became pregnant, and her son was the first Ladino. Our Father decided to make another people as well, in the hope that they would turn out better; that is when he made the Indians. At first they could not talk, only laugh, but when he brought them maize (part of his body), they began to move and talk. Our Father kept coming to see what they were doing and went to heaven to watch them from afar. Two Ladinos and two Indians were left on earth; slowly they multiplied. Our Father left the command that they should not eat their children. (J.E.S. Thompson, 1930: 119–140, 166; 1970: 332; Roys, 1967: 99; Recinos and Goetz, 1953: 46–47; Tozzer, 1907: 153–154; Laughlin, 1960: Tales 7, 24, 55; Redfield and Villa Rojas, 1934: 330–331; Guiteras-Holmes, 1961: 157, 187, 194; Madsen, 1960: 15–16, 125)

110. A Tenejapaneco and His Compadre (cf. Texts 39, 47, 58, 75, 81, 89, 95, 128, 133, 137, 156, 159, 166, 179, 184)
Informant: Marian López Calixto
Time Level: Second Creation
Most Distant Space Category: The whole earth
There was a Tenejapa man who was hunting in the woods with a friend. The Tenejapaneco met a demon, who said that the man would be given the power to fly if he would agree to accompany him (the demon). The man agreed, and they killed a deer to take to the demon's home for a feast. The two treated each other as compadres. The man was frightened at the feast and asked to be taken home. They went to Tenejapa and cooked the meat at the man's home. He put lots of chile in the broth, and when the demon drank his broth, he sneezed. At that moment the man whacked him on the head with a club. They buried him. The demon's wife came looking for him, but she could not find him and brought her relatives to hunt him. The Tenejapaneco had fled to the lake with his family to escape from the demons. They flew to the lake, found him, killed him, and took him home to skin and eat.

111. The Origin of the Stomach-Ache Bird

Informant: Marian López Calixto
Time Level: Second Creation
Most Distant Space Category: Hot Country

A woman was making love with her brother-in-law when her husband came home. When she was caught, the husband killed his younger brother. Then the younger brother and the woman turned into birds. The husband was furious and pursued them into the woods. He found them together in a tree, but they flew away when he tried to shoot them with his bow and arrow. He went home and told his mother that his wife—now a bird—had said, "My stomach hurts." That is how the stomach-ache bird came into being.

112. The Earth God's Daughter (cf. Texts 23, 25, 60, 65, 71, 76, 80, 90, 105, 132, 145, 150, 173, 174)
Informant: Manuel López Calixto
Time Level: Second Creation
Most Distant Space Category: Highland places not contiguous to Chamula

A man went to check his traps long ago and found a huge snake in the trap. He wanted to kill it, but when it asked him to take it home, he agreed. It turned out to be one of the earth god's children. As a reward, the earth god gave the man a beautiful white-skinned daughter for his wife. She made tortillas, producing many from very little dough. When she went to get corn, she harvested only two ears; the same with beans—only two pods. The man scolded her for getting so little and hit her in the nose, which began to bleed. She wiped the blood with an ear of corn, thereby making red corn. The earth god came to rescue his daughter. She left her two sons a magical pot that produced food, asking them not to tell their father about it. They disobeyed, and the father found out and broke the pot. She came again and carried her sons away. With that, a great thunderstorm came, for she was the daughter of the earth god who makes rain. (S. Thompson, 1961: Tale Type 565; Guiteras-Holmes, 1961: 192, 218; E.C. Parsons, 1936: 339; Hansen, 1957: Tale Type 569)

113. A Woman and Her Radish
Informant: Marian López Calixto

Time Level: Second Creation
Most Distant Space Category: Hot Country

Long ago when men were scarce, a woman became desperately anxious to be made love to. Her husband had many wives, and it was not yet her turn. She found a long white radish and masturbated with it. The man heard her in the night and discovered the next day what she had been doing. He would not tolerate this, so he put chile on the radish to cure her of the habit. That night she began to masturbate and the chile did its work. The woman died amid hollers and screams.

114. Our Father's Older Brother (cf. Texts 140, 167)
Informant: Salvador Guzmán Bakbolom
Time Level: Second Creation
Most Distant Space Category: Chamula woods

The moon had two sons who were good friends and workers. One day they found a tree with honey at the top and they decided to get it. The older brother of Our Father climbed up and was supposed to toss it to Our Father, who remained on the ground. Instead of tossing down the honey, the older brother first chewed the pieces of beeswax and then threw them down. Our Father became angry and turned a root of the tree into a gopher by hitting it with a piece of reed. The gopher gnawed the roots and the tree fell, killing the older brother. Our Father went home and told his mother that his older brother was dead. The moon began to cry, for she was concerned about who would do the work. She accused Our Father of being irresponsible and too playful. He agreed to bring back to life his older brother by placing three tortillas on his nose. This turned him into a pig. His nose was like a hoe so that he could eat worms and dirt instead of honey. Although his mother was shocked at the prank, she had no choice but to accept it. This was the origin of pigs and the reason that they are named Marian. (Goetz and Morley, 1950: 127–128; J.E.S. Thompson, 1930: 128; Guiteras-Holmes, 1961: 183–185; M. Siegal, 1943: 123–124; Slocum, 1965: 7–18; La Farge, 1947: 52–53)

115. San Juan's Wanderings (cf. Texts 119, 121, 126, 127, 162, 171)

Informant: Salvador Guzmán Bakbolom
Time Level: Second Creation
Most Distant Space Category: Hot Country

San Juan was looking for a house site long ago. The first one he found was in Hot Country, near Sitalá. The trouble there was that the ants bit his sheep. He would have to move on. He found another site in Chamula. It was no good either, for there was no water. San Juan's younger brother suggested that he look further for a place to build his house, for his sheep only slept and would not eat. In vain had he made the rock foundations for his house (a church). Then he found the present site of San Juan Church in Chamula and liked it. The lake was larger then and he made a mountain collapse, thereby filling up a part of the lake. It was then just right. In building the church, Our Father helped San Juan, but he had some difficulty in herding the stones into their places. They moved alone but unwillingly. One of these remained. It would not budge one inch further and stayed beside the road. When the other stones arrived at the house site, a bell chimed all by itself. When San Juan placed the high stones, they clung in place of their own accord, even though they were heavy. San Juan had at last found his home and moved in.

116. The Origin of Raccoons (cf. Texts 109, 131, 147, 164, 165, 175)
Informant: Manuel López Calixto
Time Level: Second Creation
Most Distant Space Category: Elsewhere in Mexico

Raccoons were once people. There was a flood, and the people fled to caves to avoid it. They were happy because they had escaped the rain. They ate bulbs and plants so that they would not starve. The flood passed and they survived, but soon a man, who was Our Father, came to ask them how they had survived the flood and what they had eaten. They told him, and he said that it was fine and sent them away. Already they were walking on all fours like raccoons. Our Father said that grass and bulbs would be their food, for they had disobeyed his orders by not perishing during the flood. However, the raccoon still remembers that he was once a person, for he likes hard maize and tender ears of new maize. That is why he digs in the milpa soon after planting and steals the new maize in August and September; he was once a person. (J.E.S. Thompson, 1930: 166, 119–140; 1970: 332; Guiteras-Holmes, 1961: 187; Tozzer, 1907: 153–154; Laughlin, 1960: Tales 7, 24; Redfield and Villa Rojas, 1934: 330–331; Foster, 1945: 236; Madsen, 1960: 15–16, 125; La Farge, 1947: 54–56)

117. The Witch from Zinacantan
Informant: Marian López Calixto
Time Level: Second Creation
Most Distant Space Category: Zinacantan

There was a bad Zinacanteca woman who had the custom of going to the graveyard on walks. She would look around to be sure that no one was there and then would command her flesh to come off. She would run around in a circle three times and touch the part of her body that she wished to disappear. Soon she would fly away, leaving her flesh in a mound. A man saw her flying one day and told his friends. They went to put salt on her abandoned flesh so that when she returned to it, she would die. She returned and commanded her flesh to reappear, but the salt had acted and the flesh remained in a pile. A man came out and said, "Look at her cunt." She was ashamed and soon began to die. Then they killed her and burned her body and buried the remains. They did not know who the woman was until people noted that a woman was missing. Her parents went to the graveyard and identified the remains of her body and clothes. They had to accept that their daughter had been a witch. (Laughlin, 1960: Tales 12, 47, 73, 182; Guiteras-Holmes, 1961: 316; E.C. Parsons, 1936: 364; Foster, 1945, 205–206; Brinton, 1883: 250)

118. Why the Buzzard Has a Red Neck (cf. Text 15)
Informant: Manuel López Calixto
Time Level: Second Creation
Most Distant Space Category: Hot Country

Long ago the buzzard was a person. The people of that time were lazy and envied the buzzard's carefree existence.

One man offered to change clothes with the buzzard and
the buzzard agreed; the man flew away. The buzzard, in the
man's clothing, went to the man's house. When his wife
saw feathers on his knee, she was suspicious and the buzzard
explained. The next morning the wife's true husband, in
buzzard's clothing, flew down to see his wife and she did not
recognize him. He wanted cooked corn, for he still had
human tastes. His wife did not recognize him and threw
boiling water on him, scalding his neck. That is why the
buzzard has a red neck. (Laughlin, 1960: Tales 42, 48;
Guiteras-Holmes, 1961: 204)

> *119. The Eagle and the Crane*
> *Informant: Marian López Calixto*
> *Time Level: Second Creation*
> *Most Distant Space Category: Hot Country*

One day a buzzard was wandering around and came to a
river where he saw an eagle, and he thought that the eagle's
head was very beautiful. He asked how he had made his head
look so nice, and the eagle told him to wash his head in the
river to clean it and then comb it so that he could find a
woman. The buzzard got in the river and washed and combed
his head, but his feathers fell out and his head was cold. As
he was shaking in the water, a "white woman" came by; she
was very tall and had long legs. They talked about his ugly
head, and eventually he asked her to marry him. She hesi-
tated, but finally said yes. He took her home. She was
hungry and wanted fish. He was not used to fishing and got
so excited when he saw one that he fell into the river and
drowned. She became worried and went to find him and
died after she found him dead. She was a crane. (Foster,
1945: 212-213)

> *120. A Wife Who Became a Sow (cf. Texts 78, 92)*
> *Informant: Marian López Calixto*
> *Time Level: Second Creation*
> *Most Distant Space Category: Seas, heavens, underworld*

A man had a very wonderful wife who died. His son also
died. The man cried all the time. He bought many candles
and went to see his wife, entering the underworld through a

cave, getting permission from San Pedro on the way. He found his wife getting ready to take a bath. She told him to watch the beans, but not to blow on them. He forgot and blew on them when they boiled; they all flew away, having turned into flies. They went to bed, but when he touched his wife, she turned into a sow. The man was very scared and fled home. Soon after he got there, he died; his mother died of grief soon afterward. (Guiteras-Holmes, 1961: 258–260; Laughlin, 1960: Tales 9, 19, 33; E.C. Parsons, 1936: 362; Madsen, 1960: 215; Mason, 1963: 208; Slocum, 1965: 25–37)

121. The Jobs of the Saints (cf. Texts 115, 126, 127, 129, 171)
Informant: Manuel López Calixto
Time Level: Second Creation
Most Distant Space Category: Unknown
When Our Father ascended to heaven, the saints asked where they were going to stay. Our Father said that he was going to stay in heaven. He told San Juan that he was going to stay on earth with his sons (people). San Lorenzo was going to stay on earth also, at the side of San Juan, because both had sheep. That is why Chamula and Zinacantan are in Cold Country and share the same boundary. Before, San Juan and San Lorenzo helped each other at work. That is why the Chamulas and the Zinacantecos get along well together. San Lorenzo only sowed milpa. That is why Zinacantecos do not go so much to the coffee plantations and why the Chamulas work for them in Hot Country. This was all planned by the saints so that everyone could earn a living. San Juan persuaded San Sebastián to watch his sheep, so he stayed in Cold Country also.

122. Butterflies
Informant: Marian López Calixto
Time Level: Second Creation
Most Distant Space Category: Seas, heavens, underworld
Our Father had many extra pieces of paper; he cut them into little pieces and scattered them over all the world, thereby creating butterflies. If there are a lot of butterflies,

it is because there will probably be a famine. First come the brown ones, in August; in September come the green ones. When the butterflies were made, Our Father gave them a soul. Every September the brown ones go away and the green ones come back in September. They too leave, and the brown ones come back in the following August. They do not all get to come back, for many die, just as there are many people who will die.

123. The Talking Grass
Informant: Manuel López Calixto
Time Level: Second Creation
Most Distant Space Category: Elsewhere in Mexico
Long ago, the people heard voices in their milpas but did not know where they came from. The voices were those of the grasses of the milpa who were protesting the pain that they suffered in being weeded and cut from the milpas. Our Father talked to the grass and also to the people. He told the people not to worry, that he had already arranged with the grasses to protest no longer, for the people would not kill them altogether, although they did have to defend his body (maize) from the weeds. Therefore, grass no longer protests.

124. Moss Mountain
Informant: Manuel López Calixto
Time Level: Second Creation
Most Distant Space Category: Sacred landmark in Chamula
Moss Mountain (Tzontevitz) is so called because the trees on it have white moss on them. People go there to pray for rain; they take candles, guitars, and skyrockets. When the mountain has received their offering, the rain starts to fall. There is a fiesta on Moss Mountain every day of Santa Cruz (in early May) at the crosses on the top of the mountain.

125. San José the Carpenter
Informant: Manuel López Calixto
Time Level: Second Creation
Most Distant Space Category: Unknown
San José taught people the carpenter's trade. He made the

chairs and tables for the saints when they walked on earth. He walked the earth with his godson, Our Father, and taught people all the tricks of the carpenter's trade.

126. The Seated Rock (cf. Texts 115, 121, 127, 129, 171)
Informant: Manuel López Calixto
Time Level: Second Creation
Most Distant Space Category: Hamlets contiguous to sample hamlets

When San Juan was making his house (the church) in Chamula, he rounded up the rocks and brought them in as if they were livestock. However, when they stopped to rest, there were some rocks that would not move on. They just stayed there seated; hence the name Seated Rock. The other rocks did not even need to be lifted into place, for they jumped into place themselves. Then San Juan asked San Sebastián, who was watching his sheep, how they were. He said, "Fine," except that one of them had died. San Juan took the skin to cover himself while working. That is why they use belts and pants of leather at the Fesitval of Games. He rolled more rocks to the Chamula Ceremonial Center, but after resting, one just stayed there by the side of the road. It is called Grinding Stone and is still there.

127. San Juan's Tree (cf. Texts 115, 121, 126, 129, 171)
Informant: Marian López Calixto
Time Level: Second Creation
Most Distant Space Category: Unknown

A man went with axe in hand to find San Juan. He found an orchid in a high treetop and cut two axe blows in the tree, but decided to leave it and go on to find San Juan. By a cave covered with moss, the man heard the voice of San Juan, but could not see him. He asked San Juan for a sheep, for he needed clothing. The man had a deerskin in his net bag, as well as a bit of salt. These two things San Juan changed to a sheep and magically tied it there to the pull strings of the man's net. The man was very grateful to San Juan and went away after thanking him. He looked back and all he could see of San Juan was a moss-covered rock. On his way home he cut down the tree that he had begun to cut earlier, for he

wanted to cut a drum from the trunk. It happened to be San
Juan's tree, which shaded his sheep. Therefore, San Juan
magically put the tree upright. The next day the man came
and cut it down again. San Juan told him to leave it and never
come back. With this, Our Father whipped the man and left
marks over most of his body. These blue marks are the veins
of our bodies. They are symbolized in the blue stitching of
the leather leggings of the monkey assistants during the
Festival of Games (Guiteras-Holmes, 1961: 185; Foster,
1945: 235; Mason, 1963: 206)

> *128. The War with Guatemala (cf. Texts 39, 44, 47, 58, 75,
> 81, 89, 95, 110, 133, 137, 156, 159, 166, 177, 179, 184)*
> *Informant: Salvador López Sethol*
> *Time Level: Second Creation*
> *Most Distant Space Category: Seas, heavens, underworld*

A demon had been carrying Chamulas off to Guatemala as
food for the Guatemalans. This he did through a series of
underground passageways that connect the two places. Three
brave Chamulas (one with a soul of fire, one with the soul of
a wasp, and one with the soul of a whirlwind) killed the
demon and took his head to Guatemala, where the burned
head was presented to the presidente of Guatemala (also a
demon). He recognized his son's burned head, became angry,
and imprisoned the three men. They escaped from prison
three times and finally agreed to be burned to death. They
emerged from the ashes as three red roosters and then turned
back into men, throwing ash at the assembled Guatemalans,
killing them all. The chief alone remained alive. They made a
treaty with him, promising to revive his people from death if
the Guatemalans promised to stop carrying off Chamulas to
eat. They signed a treaty, which now lies in the capital city
of Guatemala. The three men, each named Juan López Nona,
returned to Chamula and live as gods at the edge of the
earth, protecting Chamulas from war and other threats. In
the event of war, they will return to defend the Chamulas.

> *129. San Juan Comes to Chamula (cf. Texts 115, 121, 127,
> 161, 171)*
> *Informant: Mateo Méndez Tzotzek*

Time Level: Second Creation
Most Distant Space Category: Hot Country

Long ago, San Juan realized that he had to leave Sitalá because his sheep did not want to eat there. He had already started his house there, and he left the foundations and a bell. He went searching along the road to Simojovel. He was going to make his house there, but saw that there was no open land and that his sheep would not be able to eat, so he left his younger brother there. Then he went to a hamlet near San Andrés, and started to make his house there, but his sheep did not like it there either. He had to move on. There was a lake at the "earth's navel" and his sheep liked it there. That is where Chamula Ceremonial Center is now. He caused a hill to tumble down, filling in most of the lake. He sent men to quarries to get the rocks for his house, but the rocks did not want to move. He got other rocks and herded them into place, and his house was made. When he finished his house, he had a fiesta; that is why there is always a fiesta on June 24.

130. The Penis Measuring Stone (cf. Texts 107, 181)
Informant: Salvador Guzmán Bakbolom
Time Level: Second Creation
Most Distant Space Category: Chamula hamlet contiguous to sample hamlets

Long ago, there were two men who were just the same in size and height. The wondered if their penises were the same also. Each was modest and unwilling to compete, but they finally agreed to give it a try. There was a rock with a good surface for measuring, so they climbed up to the top of the rock to sit down and measure their penises. This would determine who could better please his wife. Finally they measured their penises and found them to be exactly the same size and length. They laughed about this. Even now the imprints of their penises and testicles are to be found at the Penis Measuring Stone.

131. The Origin of Monkeys (cf. Texts 109, 116, 136, 147, 164, 165, 175)
Informant: Mateo Méndez Tzotzek

Time Level: Second Creation
Most Distant Space Category: Unspecified Chamula hamlet
Our Father carved the second people from wood. When
they were finished, they began to talk. Our Father gave the
man a mouth bow, a one-string instrument, but he did not
know how to play it. Our Father broke his hands and feet
and made new ones, and they started to dance a little. Our
Father made a house, and they began to increase slowly and to
turn into people. They did not know how to do anything,
even talk, so Our Father killed them in a flood; only one man
and woman survived in a box that floated. A buzzard came
and ate on top of the box, and then the waters began to
recede. The earth had fallen in and the water flowed away
through sinkholes. Now there were hills, caves, and valleys.
The demons and snakes appeared. Then Our Father came back
to his home, and the man and the woman came there also.
He asked them if they wanted to stay with him and they said
no, because he had almost killed them. So he put tails on
them and they became monkeys. That was the end of the
second people. (Guiteras-Holmes, 1961: 157, 187; Recinos
and Goetz, 1953: 46–47; Goetz and Morley, 1950: 88–89,
92; Redfield and Villa Rojas, 1934: 330–331; J.E.S. Thompson, 1930: 119–140, 166; 1970: 332; Tozzer, 1907: 153–
154; Madsen, 1960: 15–16, 125)

> *132. The Origin of Reptiles (cf. Texts 16, 23, 25, 57, 60,*
> *65, 71, 76, 80, 90, 105, 112, 132, 133, 145, 150, 173,*
> *174)*
> *Informant: Mateo Méndez Tzotzek*
> *Time Level: Second Creation*
> *Most Distant Space Category: The whole earth*
At the end of the Second Creation, when the earth was
flooded by Our Father, the reptiles emerged: the sheepsnake,
the rattlesnake, and the whale [sic]. In the flood all was
destroyed except the reptiles, for the earth god came to take
care of them. He took them to his house (a cave) and maintained and fed them. When he fed them, they turned to
chickens, and later they would turn back into snakes and go
to their caves. That is why they are called the "chickens"
of the earth gods.

133. The First People (cf. Texts 16, 39, 44, 47, 57, 58,
60, 73, 75, 81, 89, 90, 95, 110, 132, 133, 137, 156, 159,
166, 169, 173, 177, 179, 182, 184)
Informant: Marian López Calixto
Time Level: First through Third Creations
Most Distant Space Category: The whole earth

A long time ago the sun disappeared for five days and the
people thought they were going to die. They broke their pots
so their souls could escape. When it was dark, out came the
demons, lions, snakes, jaguars; many people died and were
eaten by demons. The children grew wings and became birds.
When it became light again, there were no people—only birds.
Then Our Father came to make a different people out of
clay. When the people of clay were alive, he gave them a piece
of his body as food. They liked it. He told them to make love,
to make children, but they did not know how, so he let the
demon out of prison to teach them. This is why people turned
out badly and why they sometimes have intercourse with
sheep and donkeys, for the demon taught them to make love.
(Recinos and Goetz, 1953: 46–47; Goetz and Morley, 1950:
86; Roys, 1967: 117; J.E.S. Thompson, 1930: 150; 1970:
332; E.C. Parsons, 1936: 349; Laughlin, 1960: Tale 54;
Guiteras-Holmes, 1961: 152, 157, 187; Foster, 1945: 236;
Madsen, 1960: 126; Cline, 1944: 108–110; La Farge, 1947:
52; Hansen, 1957: Tale Type 798)

134. The Origin of Fish (cf. Text 177)
Informant: Manuel López Calixto
Time Level: First Creation
Most Distant Space Category: Seas, heavens, underworld

When people long ago were chipping at the cross of Our
Father, some of the wood chips jumped into the lake and
became fish. The larges pieces became large fish; the small
ones, small fish. They are now distributed over the entire
earth. Our Father left them from the time when he died on
the cross. This is why the pasiones eat fish on Ash Wednesday
(Fish Wednesday) of the Festival of Games. On Good Friday,
people also eat fish, which came from Our Father's cross.
A priest came from Mexico City long ago to give this order.
This is the reason fish are so expensive around the Festival

of Games and Lent. The custom is observed everywhere.

135. San Cristóbal the Traveler (cf. Texts 30, 33, 40, 46)
Informant: Manuel López Calixto
Time Level: First Creation
Most Distant Space Category: Elsewhere in Mexico

Long ago San Cristóbal was very poor. He was a carrier of goods. He came to the side of a lake to rest. While he was gone for a moment looking for a cane, a man came to the place where his load lay by the lake. The man was Our Father. He asked San Cristóbal for a ride across the lake on his shoulders. While they were going across, Our Father baptized San Cristóbal for being so kind to him. Thus, he became a god. Somehow a picture was made of them when the two were crossing the lake. This picture made San Cristóbal famous. A mere traveling salesman, he became famous and revered by the Ladinos. Don Erasto Urbina was his latterday helper, by whose order the San Cristóbal Church on the mountain was completed and protected from the Carrancistas when they came during the war.

136. The Origin of Squirrels and Monkeys (cf. Texts 65, 85, 131, 175)
Informant: Manuel López Calixto
Time Level: First Creation
Most Distant Space Category: The whole earth

The first people were turned into squirrels and monkeys at the time of the flood. When the flood came, the first people fled to the mountains. They lived beneath a tree, for they had no houses. Since they had no corn to eat, they ate acorns. They also ate other wild fruits and plants, and mushrooms. They thought that they would survive the flood at the top of the mountain. Our Father came to ask them how they had survived the flood and what they had eaten. They said that they had eaten wild fruits and plants. With this, Our Father turned them into squirrels and monkeys. They could no longer talk and walked on all fours. These animals had no shame, which is the way they remain today—going naked, exhibiting themselves, and eating improper food. It is their

own fault for eating wild plants and trying to escape the
flood when they were people long ago. The monkey is
smarter, for he lives only in the jungle, far away. The squirrel
is not so smart, for he lives everywhere, thereby exposing
himself to greater danger. (Goetz and Morley, 1950: 92, 128;
Laughlin, 1960: Tales 7, 24; J.E.S. Thompson, 1930: 19-40,
166; 1970: 332; Guiteras-Holmes, 1961: 157, 187; Tozzer,
1907: 153-154; Redfield and Villa Rojas, 1934: 330-331;
Foster, 1945: 236; Madsen, 1960: 15-16; La Farge, 1947:
54-56)

137. Adam and Eve (cf. Texts 39, 44, 47, 58, 75, 81, 89,
95, 110, 128, 133, 156, 159, 166, 169, 177, 182, 184)
Informant: Salvador Guzmán Bakbolom
Time Level: First Creation
Most Distant Space Category: The whole earth
Adam and Eve were gods, for they were the first people.
They had no houses and slept beneath the trees. The land
was flat and without form. They made their children of clay.
They talked. Yet Our Father was not happy, for the earth
was undifferentiated. He sent an earthquake, which caused
the earth to fall in and made relief in the landscape. Even
with this he was not happy, for the first people could not
sing, dance, sleep, or eat. Neither was there day or night.
People then learned to live and make love and there was day
and night. The demons taught them how to make love, and
soon the children of the first people were born. The demons
then tricked Our Father into drinking a foul beverage. They
gave him liquor and urine, which made him so happy that he
wanted his children to drink them too. Thus, he taught them
to drink and have festivals. Then he gave them maize and
other vegetables to eat. San Juan came soon after and gave
them wool for their clothing. All this they remembered and
passed on to their children. (Goetz and Morley, 1950: 86;
Recinos and Goetz, 1953: 46-47; Laughlin, 1960: Tale 54;
Roys, 1967: 117; Guiteras-Holmes, 1961: 157, 187; J.E.S.
Thompson, 1930: 119-140, 150; E.C. Parsons, 1936: 349;
Foster, 1945: 236; Madsen, 1960: 126; Cline, 1944: 108,
110; La Farge, 1947: 52; Hansen, 1957, Tale Type 798)

138. The Uses of Horses and Cows
Informant: Manuel López Calixto
Time Level: First Creation
Most Distant Space Category: The whole earth

Long ago, when things were still being organized, the horse and the cow asked Our Father for their tasks. The horse asked for his bridle and saddle and for grass to eat. The cow asked for nearly every kind of plant to eat, including maize. This is why cows break into the milpas and also why they are human food. They were given to the early people by Our Father to care for and to use. Mules were also given to Chamulas; their presence explains the name Chamula ("two mules"). There is another breed of small horse used by the Chanaleros which has an evil temper, just as their masters have. The patron saint and protector of horses is San Antonio.

139. San Miguel and His Instruments
Informant: Manuel López Calixto
Time Level: First Creation
Most Distant Space Category: The whole earth

San Miguel is the protector and patron of musicians and their instruments, the harp and guitar. Long ago, all the saints carried these instruments with them as they walked over the earth. San José was the carpenter who made the instruments. He taught the first people how to make them. San Miguel taught people how to play them. He was Our Father's musician long ago when the gods had fiestas. The same customs and instruments have come down to us today.

140. The Origin of Pigs and Gophers (cf. Texts 114, 167)
Informant: Manuel López Calixto
Time Level: First Creation
Most Distant Space Category: The whole earth

Our Father went with his older brother to look for honey. The older brother climbed up into a tree to get the honey comb. They decided that he would get the honey and toss it down to Our Father, who was waiting at the foot of the tree. The older brother tossed down only beeswax already chewed up, with no honey left. This made Our Father very angry, and he stuffed the wax into the foot of the tree. It turned into a gopher, which began to gnaw at the roots of the tree. It fell down and pinned the older brother under it. Our Father went home and asked for three small tortillas with two holes in each. He took them and put them on his older brother's nose. Then the older brother turned into a pig. Our Father showed him to his mother, who disapproved but could do nothing. That is why there are pigs and gophers today. (Goetz and Morley, 1950: 127–128; J.E.S. Thompson, 1930: 128; Guiteras-Holmes, 1961: 183–185; M. Siegal, 1943: 123–124; Slocum, 1965: 7–18; La Farge, 1947: 52–53)

141. The Origin of Alcoholic Beverages
Informant: Manuel López Calixto
Time Level: First Creation
Most Distant Space Category: The whole earth
Long ago the gods had their own drinks. Our Father had sugarcane liquor, and San Juan had sugarcane and maize beer. Our Father made his drink with the juice of flowers. They had a drinking party and exchanged drinks. When they were a little drunk, they began to sing. The first drink was sugarcane liquor; the second was maize beer. The first is better for celebrating fiestas. That is why everyone all over the earth knows it and uses it. Our Father and San Juan taught us.

142. The Adventures of Our Father
Informant: Marian López Calixto
Time Level: First Creation
Most Distant Space Category: The whole earth
A man (Our Father) was out walking and came to the house of a coyote-woman, whom he asked for lodging. While he was sleeping, the woman touched and bit his head, trying to kill him. Instead of dying, he resisted and simply planted some animals in her teeth to give her a toothache. He suggested that she take a sweatbath as a cure. When she and her husband went into the bathhouse, Our Father turned it into a mouthless cave. They burned to death and Our Father was happy. He went on down the road and rescued a man from a jaguar that wanted to eat him. He told the

jaguar to eat him instead. He called the jaguars over and made a ring of stones. Then he lay down in the middle of the circle and told them to sit on the stones and wait for the signal to eat him. They could not get up from the stones. While they were stuck there, Our Father killed them with his cane. Only two survived. Our Father told them to go and stay forever in the forest and not to bother people. Our Father went on his way and decided to build his house (a church). One of his workmen was late for work. Our Father went to find out why and saw that the man was home with his wife eating his children. Our Father punished him later by turning him into an alligator when he fell from the wall of Our Father's house. The alligator fled into the water nearby. Our Father was happy and went on working with his younger brother. The brother decided that he did not want to work on the church and went to the underworld to support the earth. His name is Miguel. (Laughlin, 1960: Tales 2, 55; Guiteras-Holmes, 1961: 182, 183)

143. Our Father's Blood
Informant: Manuel López Calixto
Time Level: First Creation
Most Distant Space Category: The whole earth

One should not steal chile, for it was once the blood of Our Father. When the demons were killing him long ago, they buried a knife in his foot. The blood that came out of his wound as they chased him turned to chile. Each drop turned to a chile plant. This is why there is chile almost everywhere. From the large drops of blood came the large-fruited chiles; from the small drops, the small-fruited chiles. Of all these, the Indians like the "dove's beak" chile best because it is the hottest. This is the chile that the monkey assistants eat during the Festival of Games. They take it then so that they will not tire of running. Because chile is so important, one must not steal it. If anyone does, his milpas will turn yellow and he will become poor. Our Father will punish him.

144. Why the Moon Has Only One Eye (cf. Texts 158, 161, 166, 177)
Informant: Marian López Calixto

Time Level: First Creation
Most Distant Space Category: Unknown

Long ago the moon was a person and lived on earth with
her children. Our Father was her most difficult child. The
moon, Our Father (Salvador), and his older brother (Marian)
took a sweatbath. Our Father was supposed to pour water
gently onto the red-hot stones, but instead, he tossed the
water carelessly so that it hit the moon in the face before
she had lain down properly. The steam and hot water burned
her eyes and blinded one of them. Our Father was glad, for
this helped in creating day and night. The moon would have
less heat and less light from her face, thereby being more
appropriate for night than was he with his own radiant heat.
With this accident, they began their wanderings, which made
day and night and prepared the earth for human habitation.

*145. The Origin of Rivers (cf. Texts 23, 25, 60, 65, 71, 76,
80, 90, 105, 112, 132, 150, 173)*
Informant: Manuel López Calixto
Time Level: First Creation
Most Distant Space Category: The whole earth

In the beginning, there were no channels for the rivers—
they covered the earth and the early people drowned. Our
Father was unhappy that the earth was covered by a lake
and decided to do something about it. He asked the earth
gods to make the river channels, which they did. The lake
became smaller. Our Father also said that he was going
to evaporate the seas as he rose and set so that they would
not cover the earth. River waters now evaporate when they
reach the oceans. (J.E.S. Thompson, 1930: 119–140, 166;
1970: 332; Guiteras-Holmes, 1961: 187; Tozzer, 1907: 153–
154; Redfield and Villa Rojas, 1934: 330–331; Madsen,
1960: 15–16, 125)

146. The Origin of Potatoes (cf. Text 177)
Informant: Manuel López Calixto
Time Level: First Creation
Most Distant Space Category: The whole earth

A long time ago, potatoes were the milk from the Virgin's
breasts. She sprinkled the milk on the earth, and it grew

leaves and roots and then turned to potatoes. She taught people how to eat them. Then her son, Our Father, gave part of his body as maize for food for the people. (Recinos and Goetz, 1953: 46–47)

147. The Origin of Soil (cf. Texts 109, 116, 131, 164, 165, 167)
Informant: Manuel López Calixto
Time Level: First Creation
Most Distant Space Category: The whole earth

Long ago there was no earth, only large rocks. One could not plant anything. Our Father did not like this and threw hot water on the earth to break up the rocks to gravel. When the hot water fell, it killed the first people, for it was also a punishment for them. Where there were forests and big caves, the rocks were not broken up. In open country, they turned to gravel immediately. That is why people can work today in open country. (Goetz and Morley, 1950: 90; Holland, 1963, 71–72; Laughlin, 1960: Tale 96)

148. Baptism
Informant: Manuel López Calixto
Time Level: First Creation
Most Distant Space Category: Unknown

In the past, people celebrated the Festival of San Juan Bautista beside a water tank so that he could baptize people there. San Juan killed and cooked a sheep as a free meal for those who came to his fiesta. This is why the outgoing alféreces of San Juan kill a bull each year. San Juan baptized the fruits of the trees as well as people. Even though it is the priest who actually performs the ceremony today, he does it in the name of San Juan.

149. Our Father's Tobacco Gourd (cf. Texts 2, 13)
Informant: Manuel López Calixto
Time Level: First Creation
Most Distant Space Category: The whole earth

Long ago the hummingbird was the tobacco gourd of Our Father. For that reason, one should not kill hummingbirds. If anyone does, the bird will punish him. The large hummingbird was Our Father's large tobacco gourd. The small hummingbird was his small tobacco gourd. When the humming bird sings as the maize comes into tassel, he is blessing the milpa and the young ears of maize. Thus, the hummingbird came to be an important sign of the time of flowering maize. To kill him would bring misfortune to the milpa.

150. Our Father Talks to the Earth Gods
Informant: Manuel López Calixto
Time Level: First Creation
Most Distant Space Category: The whole earth
When Our Father still walked the earth, he talked to the earth gods. He told them that they could not make it rain without talking to him first, so that he could punish the people if they did not "want" the rain enough (if they had not prayed enough). When there are thunderheads, the earth gods are talking to Our Father. Whether rain falls or not depends on him.

151. The Praying Crickets
Informant: Manuel López Calixto
Time Level: First Creation
Most Distant Space Category: The whole earth
When crickets sing, they are really praying. Our Father left it that way because people do not know the prayers; the crickets help them pray. That is why there are crickets all over the earth.

152. The Creation of the Heavens
Informant: Mateo Méndez Tzotzek
Time Level: First Creation
Most Distant Space Category: The whole earth
Our Father still lived on earth when he created the heavens and the stars. The sun comes out every day, but it is God the Father whom we see every day rather than the Savior, who lives in the Third Layer of Heaven. God the Father lives in the First Layer. The stars are in the Second Layer. At the tail of the constellation Scorpio is the path of ice; from there come the hail, water, and frost. If Scorpio's heart is red, it is going to be clear; if not, it will rain.

153. Why People No Longer Cook Their Children (cf. Texts 175, 183)
Informant: Manuel López Calixto
Time Level: First Creation
Most Distant Space Category: The whole earth

The early people ate their children when they had grown to be fat and juicy, cooking them in hot water. They pulled out their intestines as if they were pigs; after that they called them pigs instead of children. Our Father did not like this, and the people all died of a fever. Then Our Father created another people, who were good and did not do such awful things. The mothers nursed their children, embracing them. Our Father was happier now that his children knew how to eat corn, beans, and meat rather than their children.

154. The Secrets of Fire
Informant: Manuel López Calixto
Time Level: First Creation
Most Distant Space Category: The whole earth

The fire tells that we are going to be sick when the flame is blue or green. When it is red, we are going to fight with someone. When the fire begins to crackle and sputter, it is about to tell us something. The fire keeps everyone on earth alive; if it were not for fire, we would all die of hunger, for we would not be able to cook our food. Nor would we be able to warm ourselves. Even the Ladinos need fire. The early people made fire by rubbing two stones together and lighting dry pine needles, then putting pitch pine on the fire until it was well started. They found the rocks in caves; they were eventually stolen by the Ladinos who then made matches from them.

155. Albinos
Informant: Manuel López Calixto
Time Level: First Creation
Most Distant Space Category: Specified Chamula hamlet other than sample hamlets

Two men went to hunt rabbits at night, one a normal Indian, the other an albino. The albino could see the road very well and saw rabbits when the normal man could not. He could even shoot them at night. The albino could also see grasshoppers and other insects. The normal man tried to hide from the albino, but he found him right away, even though it was very dark. The albino caught insects at night and put them in the man's clothes, making him very angry. All albinos can see very well at night. It would be nice if everyone could see at night, but there are only a few albinos.

> *156. The First People Learn to Eat and Reproduce (cf.*
> *Texts 39, 44, 47, 58, 75, 81, 89, 95, 104, 110, 128, 133,*
> *137, 159, 166, 169, 177, 182)*
> *Informant: Manuel López Calixto*
> *Time Level: First Creation*
> *Most Distant Space Category: Unknown*

When people were first created, Our Father went to find food for them. First he gave them cabbage and they ate a little. The same happened with turnips. Then he gave them a bit of his groin, which they liked very much. That was their food. That is why people eat so much maize and why they should take care of it. Then Our Father told them to take a walk. They found a tree and sat down to rest. A man came and sat down beside them and asked if they knew how to make love. They said no, and the man said that he would teach them. He made love to the man's wife. The man was very scared, for he saw that it was the demon. Then he made love to his wife. That is why there are perverted people (sodomists), for the sexual act was learned from the devil. (Recinos and Goetz, 1953: 46–47; J.E.S. Thompson, 1970: 332; Guiteras-Holmes, 1961: 157, 187)

> *157. Pandora's Reeds (cf. Text 174)*
> *Informant: Manuel López Calixto*
> *Time Level: First Creation*
> *Most Distant Space Category: The whole earth*

Once there was a bad woman who took two reeds on a visit to a neighbor's house. She wanted to throw them away and asked her friend if there was a garbage pile. She gave the reeds to her friend to throw away, telling her not to take the tops off them. When the friend got to the garbage dump, she could not resist opening them, and out came fleas and lice, which got in her clothing and which she brought to the house. They spread all over. When her husband came home, he was very angry, but there was nothing he could do. That is why there are now fleas and lice everywhere. (Anderson, 1957: 313–316; Barlow and Ramírez, 1962: 55–61; Cicco and Horcasitas, 1962: 75–76; Johnson and Johnson, 1939: 217–226; Miller, 1956: 71–95; E.C. Parsons, 1936: 324–328; S. Thompson, 1955–1958: Motifs A2003, C322; Madsen, 1960: 131–132; Boas, 1912: 206; Hansen, 1957: Tale Type 836F)

158. The Origin of Beans (cf. Texts 144, 161, 166, 177)
Informant: Manuel López Calixto
Time Level: First Creation
Most Distant Space Category: The whole earth
Red beans were part of the necklace of the moon long ago. When she walked by, she dropped her necklace and it turned into beans, which sprouted right away. When her necklace broke, all the different kinds of beans came from it. She was going to put it back together until she saw that the beans had sprouted; then she did not want to collect them and she left them there. The string from her necklace turned into green beans.

159. Manzanilla Saves Our Father (cf. Texts 39, 44, 47, 58, 75, 81, 89, 95, 110, 128, 133, 137, 156, 166, 177, 179, 184)
Informant: Manuel López Calixto
Time Level: First Creation
Most Distant Space Category: The whole earth
Long ago, when the demon was trying to kill Our Father, he got a manzanilla spine in his face. He could not see and had to stop to take it out. In the meantime, Our Father disappeared. The demon started to follow his tracks, but they were now full of manzanilla plants. His feet got full of thorns and again he had to stop to take them out, forgetting all about chasing Our Father. That is why there is manzanilla, for it helped Our Father to escape from the demon.

160. The Food of the Gods

Informant: Manuel López Calixto
Time Level: First Creation
Most Distant Space Category: Seas, heavens, underworld
A long time ago, white candles were made of the tallow of
a sea animal. They are very important for the whole world
because they are the food of Our Father. Now candles are
made of paraffin and painted all colors, so people can select
the ones they want. Striped candles are for our souls. They
have their counterparts in heaven. Those of us who have long
candles will live to be old. Green candles are for prayers to
Our Father. Tallow candles are the food of Our Father.
Incense trees grow only in Hot Country. Our Father passed
through there planting them, for it is the favorite food of the
saints. That is why incense and candles are used by the ritual
officials and people who want to give a gift to Our Father.

161. The Sun and the Moon (cf. Texts 73, 158, 166, 177)
Informant: Manuel López Calixto
Time Level: First Creation
Most Distant Space Category: Unknown
The moon went up to heaven after the sun. The sun had
died, and his mother, the moon, cried a lot. He passed
through the underworld and, on the third day, was in the
heavens. When the moon saw his face there, she was happy
and went to see him. He told her that she was going to
"walk" at night, he in the day. When we die, we go to the
underworld, as Our Father did, but it was long ago when he
went to heaven. Sometimes the moon is dark; then we should
not sow milpa, for it will not sprout properly if we do. We
should bend the cornstalks when the moon is full so that it
will mature properly and not rot. When the moon is full, it
is a good time to cut house beams so that the worms will
not eat them; the wood is also stronger then, for the roots
absorb strength. (Guiteras-Holmes, 1961: 153)

162. Our Father's Fingernails
Informant: Manuel López Calixto
Time Level: First Creation
Most Distant Space Category: The whole earth

Fava beans were originally Our Father's fingernails. As he walked over the earth, he cut his nails and the trimmings turned into favas. There are two kinds of favas: the red favas are from the nails that came off with meat attached; the white ones did not have meat. There are favas everywhere because Our Father wandered over the whole earth before he went to heaven.

163. Sowing the Seeds of Creation
Informant: Marian López Calixto
Time Level: First Creation
Most Distant Space Category: Unknown

Long ago, Our Father had a lot of maize. From it, many things were made. Santo Tomás helped him in this project. They threw down some grains of maize, and milpas and people and other saints sprang up. The earth, sky, and seas were brought into view. San Juan, San Lorenzo, Santa Juana, and Santa Rosa came with the strewing of maize. From other grains came sheep and doves. The dove was disagreeable and ate many grains of maize, which were to have become baby human beings. Our Father struck the dove and punished it by sending it to live in the woods. This is the wild gray dove. The tame white one stayed with him and was good. The grains of maize eaten by the dove were the souls of the children to be born. They were awful; they could not learn to walk, had ugly faces, and could not eat. Neither did they have any arms. They were a failure, and Our Father decided to destroy them with a flood. San Isidro, Santo Tomás, and San Pablo stayed on earth to herd the bad people into the seas and lakes to the north and south. A man and his relatives hid in a cave, and the white dove told Our Father that they had survived the flood. They soon died, and Santo Tomás found a cowhide from an old rotten cow and turned it into a buzzard to eat all the rotten flesh on the earth. The dove went to the sky to advise the saints, who returned to recreate things. San Salvador created flowers. San José asked who would create the rest. Our Father himself created trees, flowers, grass, and the heavens. That is how the earth began. (Guiteras-Holmes, 1961: 157, 184; Laughlin, 1960: Tales 7, 24; Redfield and

Villa Rojas, 1934: 330–331; Recinos and Goetz, 1953: 46;
J.E.S. Thompson, 1970: 332; Tozzer, 1907: 153–154;
Madsen, 1960: 15–16, 125)

> *164. The Hot Water Flood (cf. Texts 109, 116, 131, 147, 165, 175)*
> *Informant: Mateo Méndez Tzotzek*
> *Time Level: First Creation*
> *Most Distant Space Category: Seas, heavens, underworld*

The first people had no houses and lived beneath the trees.
They had no maize or tortillas and ate only grass and wild
fruits. They could not speak or have festivals. There were no
saints and no church, only Our Father in heaven and on
earth. There were only sea and woods. Here Our Father lived
with his mother, but the people did not know it, for he
looked like them. That is why they made no fiestas. He
became angry and destroyed them in a hot water flood
because they could not speak. They all died. (Recinos and
Goetz, 1953: 46; Laughlin, 1960: Tale 96; Roys, 1967: 99;
Holland, 1963: 71–72)

> *165. A Better World (cf. Texts 109, 116, 131, 147, 164, 175)*
> *Informant: Marian López Calixto*
> *Time Level: First Creation*
> *Most Distant Space Category: The whole earth*

In the First Creation, the people were destroyed by a rain
of boiling water. They fled to caves. Others were caught while
sowing their milpas, tending their sheep, or doing other
things, for there was no warning. It rained boiling water for
three days and all people perished. One of the problems of
the First Creation was that San José, who made the physical
universe, had failed. There ought to have been more relief,
more rocks and boulders, but San José had made it all flat.
Our Father was disgusted with him for this oversight and,
after the hot water rain, took matters into his own hands and
made the Second Creation with more mountains and relief.
San José was embarrassed, but they agreed to work together
to recreate life in the Second Creation. (Holland, 1963: 71–
72; Laughlin, 1960: Tale 96)

166. Our Father Ascends to Heaven (cf. Texts 39, 44, 47, 58, 75, 81, 89, 95, 110, 128, 133, 137, 144, 156, 158, 159, 161, 177, 179, 184)
Informant: Salvador López Sethol
Time Level: First Creation
Most Distant Space Category: The whole earth
The Jews pursued the moon because they knew that the future sun was in her womb. The sun escaped from his mother's womb and fled. The Jews were afraid of him, for he was going to give sun and light that would kill them. They trapped him in a cave, and he sent a mouse messenger to the moon so that she would know where he was hiding. The Jews flushed him from the cave and trapped him in a lake. Our Father sent a fish messenger to the moon, reporting his whereabouts. The Jews flushed him from the lake and trapped him in a river. He sent another fish with a message to his mother. Then they trapped him in a hollow tree. A woodpecker freed him. God advised him by letter that he should surrender and die. This he did, and he sent the Jews for a big tree from which his cross would be made. The Jews were incompetent, and the tree fell and killed some of them. Our Father had to fell the tree himself. He then ordered the Jews to nail him to the cross. This they did, but overnight the body disappeared. All the Jews found were a rooster and a book. It was said that Our Father had gone to the sky to give heat and light. The Jews were frightened. Our Father went to the underworld for two days, appearing on the third day at six in the morning on the eastern horizon. The Jews were crying by ten, for death was near. At twelve noon they died, and the earth had full heat and light. God instructed Our Father that he was his father and sent him back down to earth on the fourth day to ask his mother to join him as the moon. He told her that she was to leave him gruel on the sixth step of the sky (the eastern horizon) each morning, to give him energy to heat the world by day. She was to light the earth at night. She agreed when she learned that God had planted his heart in her womb to conceive Our Father. Her earthly form remains today as the hen.
(M. Siegal, 1943: 125; Holland, 1963: 76)

167. Man's Uncle (cf. Texts 114, 140)
Informant: Salvador López Sethol
Time Level: First Creation
Most Distant Space Category: Hot Country
Our Father and his older brother found a bee hive with
honey in it. Our Father could not climb the tree, but his
older brother agreed to do so and to toss down the honey to
Our Father. The older brother tossed him only balls of
chewed comb. He got angry and created gophers from the
wax, so they would gnaw the tree down and kill the older
brother. Our Father placed a calabash on his older brother's
head and went to bring three small tortillas with two holes
in them from his mother, the moon. When he put the tortillas
on his older brother's nose, he turned into a herd of pigs.
Our Father kept two of them, male and female, which
became tame pigs. The others became wild pigs. Therefore,
the pig is man's uncle, since he is the elder brother of Our
Father. (Goetz and Morley, 1950: 127–128; J.E.S. Thompson, 1930: 128; Guiteras-Holmes, 1961: 183–185; M. Siegal,
1943: 123–124; Slocum, 1965: 7–18; La Farge, 1947: 52–53)

168. Why Chamulas Are Hard Workers
Informant: Salvador López Sethol
Time Level: First Creation
Most Distant Space Category: Unknown
Long ago, Our Father worked as a woodsman. He made
his implements (axe, hoe, and machete) of wood. He whipped
them with a lash and they worked alone. When Our Father
went to heaven, he wanted to leave his implements with his
children, the Chamulas. However, a demon spoke to him and
convinced him to leave the self-working tools to the Ladinos.
This is the reason that Chamulas have to work so much
harder than other people, for they must apply their own
energies in order to use their implements. (J.E.S. Thompson,
1970: 346)

169. The Beginning of Procreation (cf. Texts 95, 133, 137,
156, 182)
Informant: Salvador López Sethol
Time Level: First Creation

Most Distant Space Category: Country other than Mexico
When the first people (two of them) came to earth, they
had no clothing, no houses, no food. They went about naked,
slept in caves, and needed no food. Our Father came to help
them. He offered them branches and fruit, but they did not
want them. He removed his armpit, which became a maize
plant; people did like this. Then they learned to make milpas,
houses, ceramics, clothing, and to cook food. They acquired
turkeys and pigs. They learned to work with implements
with Our Father. They were happy, but had no children.
Our Father sent a messenger to teach them to have children.
They had tried with clay and then with sticks, but these
offspring could neither speak nor walk. Our Father decided
that his messenger should help them. He asked if the husband
were gone, and then told the woman to lie down and lift her
legs. His penis would not enter, so he opened her vagina with
an axe. Then he made love to her. The husband came home
after he had left. She instructed him how to make babies,
and their first child was born in nine days. Later it took nine
months. The husband was angry about how she had learned
to have sexual intercourse and forbade her ever to do it
again with another man. That was how the world was populated. (Guiteras-Holmes, 1961: 157, 187; Laughlin, 1960:
Tale 54; Recinos and Goetz, 1953: 46–47; E.C. Parsons,
1936: 349; J.E.S. Thompson, 1930: 150; 1970: 332; Foster,
1945: 236; Madsen, 1960: 126; Cline, 1944: 108–110; La
Farge, 1947: 52; Hansen, 1957: Tale Type 798)

170. Our Father's Footstool
Informant: Manuel López Calixto
Time Level: First Creation
Most Distant Space Category: The whole earth
The armadillo was the footstool of Our Father long ago.
When he rested, Our Father sat on him. When he sat on him,
little armadillos came out of the ground all around. He gave
souls to all useful animals, so that they could be eaten.

*171. The Teachings of San Juan (cf. Texts 115, 121, 126,
127, 129)*
Informant: Salvador López Sethol

Time Level: First Creation
Most Distant Space Category: Seas, heavens, underworld

San Juan came from the edge of the sky to make his home in the church in Chamula Ceremonial Center. He instructed the Chamulas to make his home. They did this and then San Juan went to the edge of the sky to live as a god. He instructed the Chamulas about making their clothing; then he gave them sheep, which Our Father had not given them in the First Creation. He instructed them to spin and to weave wool. The women first made their own attire, then that of their husbands. Then they learned to make the clothing of the other pueblos, which was the beginning of Chamula trade in woolen garments with other Indian peoples.

172. The Rabbit's Ears (cf. Texts 1, 17, 41, 54, 72, 77, 84, 94, 96, 101, 105, 176)
Informant: Salvador López Sethol
Time Level: First Creation
Most Distant Space Category: Chamula woods

Our Father was a woodsman. Once he found that the timber and brush he had cut the night before had grown up again overnight. This had happened several times, so he made a resin doll to catch the culprit. He placed it in the cleared ground. Next morning the coyote was stuck there. He told Our Father that a rabbit was the real culprit. Our Father freed him to go and bring the rabbit to him for justice. The coyote convinced the rabbit to go, but then the rabbit said that he knew where there was some good cheese. It was at the bottom of a clear lake (the reflection of the moon), so to get it, the coyote had to drink all of the water, at the rabbit's suggestion. The rabbit pretended to drink also, but did not. Soon the coyote was bloated, then burst and died. Our Father found the dead coyote and accused the rabbit, but he denied having killed the coyote or having made the forest grow up again. Finally he admitted that he had indeed done it. Our Father whipped him and pulled his ears, making them long, and then the rabbit ran away. (S. Thompson, 1961: Tale Type 34; Guiteras-Holmes, 1961: 185, 186; Laughlin, 1960: Tales 21, 49, 90; Goetz and Morley, 1950: 132–133; J.E.S. Thompson, 1930: 134–135; Foster, 1945:

218–220, 235; Boas, 1912; 204–206, 235, 237–238; Mechling,
1912: 200–202; Mason, 1963: 204, 206; Recinos, 1918: 472–
473; Mason and Espinosa, 1921: 164–165; Redfield, 1935:
36; Hansen, 1957: Tale Types 34, 74X, 175)

173. The Origin of Squirrels (cf. Texts 16, 23, 25, 57, 60,
65, 71, 73, 76, 80, 90, 105, 112, 132, 133, 145, 150, 174)
Informant: Salvador López Sethol
Time Level: First Creation
Most Distant Space Category: Chamula woods
A man killed a snake while walking in the forest. It was
the son of an earth god. A kind man helped the snake and
took it home on a mule. As a reward, the father of the snake
(an important earth god) gave the man one of his daughters
for a wife. The girl refused to have sexual intercourse with
the man and turned into a snake. The man was angry and
went to complain to her father. He corrected his daughter,
and she finally received the man sexually. He then became
lazy and gave up ordinary work. He went to the girl's father
for rainmaking lessons, but blundered and made too much
rain. Then the earth god gave him maize and bean seeds so he
could work like an ordinary man. His wife was an efficient
helper with the crops, but he scolded and struck her. She
went to her father, leaving her children a magical tortilla pot.
They showed it to their father, who broke it. The mother
replaced it, but it was again broken. The children went to
their grandfather's home, but were always hungry so that he
ran them into the woods, where they turned into squirrels.
(S. Thompson, 1961: Tale Type 565; Guiteras-Holmes,
1961: 192, 218; Laughlin, 1960: Tale 78; Hansen, 1957:
Tale Type 569)

174. Where Fleas Came From (cf. Texts 23, 25, 60, 65,
71, 76, 80, 90, 105, 112, 132, 145, 157, 173, 174)
Informant: Salvador López Sethol
Time Level: First Creation
Most Distant Space Category: Country other than Mexico
An earth god and his wife had fleas and lice in their home
and solicited a couple of poor early humans to come and
empty them by sackfuls into the river. The humans received

a small fee for their help and an interdiction not to look at what they were carrying. They yielded to temptation and looked into the sacks. The fleas and lice crawled onto them, and this was the way those pests came to man. The man became rich and successful, for the earth god paid him well for bringing fleas and lice to humans. (Anderson, 1957: 313–316; Barlow and Ramírez, 1962: 55–61; Cicco and Horcasitas, 1962: 75–76; Johnson and Johnson, 1939: 217–226; Miller, 1956: 81; E.C. Parsons, 1936: 324–328; S. Thompson, 1955: Motifs A2003, C322; Hansen, 1957: Tale Type 836F)

> *175. The Destruction of the First People (cf. Texts 109, 116, 131, 136, 147, 164, 165, 183)*
> *Informant: Salvador López Sethol*
> *Time Level: First Creation*
> *Most Distant Space Category: Hot Country*

The first people ate half their children when they were at the age of puberty. As punishment for this, Our Father sent a flood. Part of the people died, but others escaped in small boats. In their boats they ate burned maize, not tortillas. When the flood subsided after three days and they floated back to earth, Our Father came and found them eating burned maize. He was angry at their stupidity and said that he would no longer give them tortillas. They were turned into monkeys so that they might hunt their food in the forest. (Guiteras-Holmes, 1961: 157; Laughlin, 1960: Tales 2, 24, 55; Goetz and Morley, 1950: 128; Redfield and Villa Rojas, 1934: 330–331; J.E.S. Thompson, 1930: 19–40, 166; 1970: 332; Tozzer, 1907: 153–154; Foster, 1945: 236; Madsen, 1960: 15–16, 125; La Farge, 1947: 54–56)

> *176. The Rabbit and the Resin Doll (cf. Texts 54, 72, 77, 94, 96, 101, 105, 142)*
> *Informant: Marian López Calixto*
> *Time Level: First Creation*
> *Most Distant Space Category: The whole earth*

Our Father was clearing the brush for his milpa and discovered that a rabbit had magically caused the brush to reappear every night. The third time he put pieces of resin

at the four corners of his milpa to catch the rabbit. The
resin was shaped like a person. The rabbit got caught after
having an argument with the resin doll. Our Father came
and punished the rabbit, pulling his ears until they were long.
The rabbit fled into the woods. Then Our Father sowed
beans, squash, and maize. He made us from clay. Our arms
did not move nor did we want to eat the grass Our Father
offered us. We wanted to eat Our Father's body, and that
was the origin of maize. It was his body, which he gave to us.
(S. Thompson, 1961: Tale Type 175; Guiteras-Holmes, 1961:
157, 185, 187; Laughlin, 1960: Tales 21, 54; Goetz and
Morley, 1950: 134–135; J.E.S. Thompson, 1930: 150;
E.C. Parsons, 1936: 349; Foster, 1945: 218, 235, 236;
Madsen, 1960: 126; Boas, 1912: 204–205, 235; Mechling,
1912: 200–201; Mason, 1963: 206; Recinos, 1918: 472–473;
Cline, 1944: 108–110; Mason and Espinosa, 1921: 164–165;
La Farge, 1947: 51; Hansen, 1957: Tale Types 175, 789)

> *177. The Life of Our Father (cf. Texts 39, 44, 47, 58, 75,*
> *81, 89, 95, 110, 128, 133, 134, 137, 144, 146, 156, 158,*
> *159, 161, 166, 179, 184)*
> *Informant: Mateo Méndez Tzotzek*
> *Time Level: First Creation*
> *Most Distant Space Category: The whole earth*

The moon was pregnant, but she did not know why. She
went to look for a dry stick and gave it first to Nuestro
Señor de Nazarena, but it did not send out buds. Then she
gave it to San José, and since it sprouted as soon as he
grasped it, she knew that he had to be the father. When her
son was born, he had a halo. The Jews did not like it and
went to kill the mother and child. She fled to hide in the
milpa, nursing the baby; some milk spilled and became
potatoes. The mother wandered over the earth with her
child, the Jews always pursuing her. The child grew and
decided that they should go back to the place where he was
born. The Jews killed and buried him. On the third day, he
left the grave and went to heaven. They saw that he still had
his halo and decided to go to heaven to get him. They began
to make a ladder, but the angels destroyed it just as they
were about to reach heaven. Some of them died. On the

third day, Our Father came back to earth. The Jews wanted
to kill him again, but he told them to make him a cross. He
supervised the work and threw the wood shavings into the
river, where they became fish. They took the cross to the
Chamula church, but Our Father said that they had to wait
until the seventh Friday to kill him, which they did. As soon
as he was dead, the angels took prisoner all the Jews and
burned them. (E.C. Parsons, 1936: 352; Mason, 1963: 206)

178. The Hanging Man
Informant: Marian López Calixto
Time Level: First Creation
Most Distant Space Category: Chamula woods
A man did not know how to build his house, for it was
long ago and no one knew how. First he dug a hole in the
earth for his house, but he was cold and shivered all of the
night. Then he found a cave high on a rock ledge and decided
that it would be the best place for him to live. Our Father
made him leave just after he had moved in. The man refused
to leave according to Our Father's orders. With that, Our
Father turned him upside down and placed him feet up,
hanging from the roof, where he remains today. That is how
Hanging Man (a hamlet) got its name.

179. Adam and Eve (cf. Texts 39, 44, 47, 58, 75, 81, 89,
95, 110, 128, 133, 137, 156, 159, 166, 177, 184)
Informant: Marian López Calixto
Time Level: First Creation
Most Distant Space Category: Unspecified Chamula hamlet
A Jew escaped from prison and gave Eve an apple. Christ
found out and became angry, throwing the Jew back into
jail. The Jew persuaded his friends that they should kill
Christ, which they did with lances and knives. They then
tied him to the cross, but a rooster crowed, scaring the Jews
so that they fell and were killed. Another god (Rasarena)
came and lifted the cross into position. After half an hour,
Christ came back to life and tied a rope around one of the
dead Jews and hoisted him up on the church. This is the
origin of the Judas-burning custom at Easter. (Holland,
1963: 76)

180. The Baptism of San Pedro
Informant: Marian López Calixto
Time Level: First Creation
Most Distant Space Category: Unknown

San Juan met a man on the way to the River Jordan. When asked his name, the man said that he did not have one, but that Salvador called him Peter. San Juan invited him to go to the river with him and told him to stand in the water. He baptized him, giving him the name Pedro. He gave him the keys to the door of the underworld. Pedro went to heaven, where Salvador gave him a book in which he was to write the name and punishment of everyone who entered the underworld.

181. When Rocks Were Soft (cf. Texts 130, 170)
Informant: Juan Méndez Tzotzek
Time Level: First Creation
Most Distant Space Category: Chamula hamlets contiguous to sample hamlets

Two men decided to measure their penises and climbed up on a big double rock. Penises were very large and heavy in those days, and the rocks were still soft, so an imprint was left. Both men had the same size penis, so they called the rock Penis Measurer.

182. The Origin of Earth and of Human Cultures (cf.
Texts 95, 133, 137, 156, 169)
Informant: Juan Méndez Tzotzek
Time Level: First Creation
Most Distant Space Category: The whole earth

Long ago, there was no land, only sea. There were no people. Our Father dried up the seas, but there was only flat land—no hills, trees, plants, only land. He made people of clay, but they would not move. He rubbed them and they began to talk, to become flesh and blood. He tried to feed them clay, but they would not eat it. He gave them some of the flesh of his body (maize) and they liked it. He taught them to take care of maize, and the moon taught the women to cook it. The demon taught them to make love, and they were ashamed. The moon taught the women to prepare and weave cotton, to cover themselves. Our Father told them that they could not practice adultery or they would be punished. (Guiteras-Holmes, 1961: 157, 187; Laughlin, 1960: Tale 54; Recinos and Goetz, 1953: 46–47; E.C. Parsons, 1936: 349; Roys, 1967: 117; J.E.S.Thompson, 1930: 150; 1970: 332; Foster, 1945: 236; Madsen, 1960: 126; Cline, 1944: 108–110; La Farge, 1947: 52; Hansen, 1957: Tale Type 798)

183. Infanticide (cf. Texts 63, 130)
Informant: Juan Méndez Tzotzek
Time Level: Before the First Creation
Most Distant Space Category: Unknown

Long ago, people ate their children. They waited six months after they were born and then cooked them in a kettle of hot water. They made tamales and soup of them. Our Father wondered why the population was not increasing and came to see. He asked a pregnant woman when her baby was due and said that he was going to come and see it, which he did. It was a boy, and Our Father was very happy. After only three months they cooked him, but Our Father saw them and asked them why they were cooking their child. They said that they were only bathing him so he would sleep well, but Our Father knew that he was dead and sent a hot water rain that killed all of the first people. (Holland, 1963: 71–72; Laughlin, 1960: Tales 55, 96)

184. The Jews Lose Out (cf. Texts 39, 44, 47, 58, 75, 81, 89, 95, 110, 128, 133, 137, 156, 159, 166, 177, 179)
Informant: Juan Méndez Tzotzek
Time Level: Before the First Creation
Most Distant Space Category: The whole earth
For abstract, see Ch. 7.

Bibliography

Abrahams, Roger D.
  1968a Introductory remaks to a rhetorical theory of folklore.
    Journal of American Folklore 81: 143–158.
  1968b A Rhetoric of everyday life: traditional conversational genres.
    Southern Folklore Quarterly 32: 44–59.
  1970a *Deep down in the jungle: negro narrative folklore from the
    streets of Philadelphia.* Rev. ed. Chicago: Aldine.
  1970b *Positively black.* New York: Prentice-Hall.
  1970c A performance-centered approach to gossip. *Man* (n.s.) 5:
    290–301.
Abrahams, Roger D., and Richard Bauman
  1971 Sense and nonsense in St. Vincent: speech behavior and
    decorum in a Caribbean community. *American Anthropologist* 73:
    762–772.
Anderson, Arabelle
  1957 Two Chol texts. *Tlalocan* 3: 313–316.
Arbuz, Georges
  1963 La construction de la guitare et du violon à Chamula. Unpub. ms.,
    Harvard Chiapas Project, Harvard University.
Arewa, Ojo, and Alan Dundes
  1964 Proverbs and the ethnography of speaking folklore. *American
    Anthropologist* 66, pt. 2: 70–85.
Barlow, R.H., and Valentín Ramírez
  1962 Tonatiw iwan meetstli. *Tlalocan* 4: 55–61.
Bascom, William R.
  1943 The relationship of Yoruba folklore to divining. *Journal of
    American Folklore* 56: 127–131.

1953 Folklore and anthropology. *Journal of American Folklore* 66: 283–290. Also in Dundes, 1965: 25–33.

1954 Four functions of folklore. *Journal of American Folklore* 67: 333–349. Also in Dundes, 1965: 279–298.

1965 The forms of folklore: prose narratives. *Journal of American Folklore* 78: 3–20.

Bauman, Richard

1971 Introduction to Américo Paredes and Richard Bauman, eds., *Towards new perspectives in folklore*. Special number of *Journal of American Folklore 84*, no. 331.

Becerra, Marcos E.

1933 *El antiguo calendario Chiapaneco*. Mexico: Imprenta Mundial.

Beckwith, M.W.

1931 *Folklore in America: its scope and method*. Poughkeepsie, N.Y.: The Folklore Foundation.

Beidelman, T.O.

1961 Hyena and rabbit: a Kaguru representation of matrilineal relations. *Africa* 31: 61–74.

1963 Further adventures of hyena and rabbit: the folktale as a sociological model. *Africa* 33: 54–69.

1970 Myth, legend and oral history: a Kaguru traditional text. *Anthropos* 65: 74–97.

Ben-Amos, Dan

1969a Analytical categories and ethnic genres. *Genre* 2: 275–301.

1969b (ed.) *Symposium on folk genres*, Parts 1 and 2. *Genre* 2, nos. 2–3: 91–301.

Bergson, Henri

1928 *Laughter: an essay on the meaning of the comic*. New York: MacMillan.

Berlin, Brent

1968 *Tzeltal numeral classifiers: a study in ethnographic semantics*. The Hague and Paris: Mouton.

Berlin, Heinrich

1951 The calendar of the Tzotzil Indians. In Sol Tax, ed., *The Civilizations of Ancient America*. Chicago: University of Chicago Press.

Blaffer, Sarah C.

1972 *The black-man of Zinacantan: a Central American legend*. Austin: University of Texas Press.

Boas, Franz

1912 Notes on Mexican folklore. *Journal of American Folklore* 25: 204–241.

Bødker, Laurits

1965 *International dictionary of regional European ethnology and folklore*, vol. 2: *Folk literature (Germanic)*. Copenhagen: Rosenkilde and Bagger.

Boggs, Ralph S.
   1937 Folklore. *Handbook of Latin American Studies* 3: 175–180.
   1938 Folklore. *Handbook of Latin American Studies* 4: 159–165.
Bricker, Victoria R.
   1966 El hombre, la carga y el camino: antiguos conceptos mayas
      sobre tiempo y espacio y el sistema zinacanteco de cargos. In Evon
      Z. Vogt, ed., *Los Zinacantecos*, pp. 355–370. Mexico: Instituto
      Nacional Indigenista.
   1968 The meaning of laughter in Zinacantán: an analysis of the
      humor of a highland Maya community. Ph.D. diss., Harvard
      University.
Brinton, Daniel Garrison
   1883 Folklore of Yucatan. *Folk-lore Journal* 1: 244–256.
Bruner, Jerome S., Jacquelin J. Goodnow, and G.A. Austin
   1967 *A study of thinking*. New York: Wiley, Science Editions.
Bullard, William R., Jr.
   1960 Maya settlement patterns in the Petén, Guatemala. *American
      Antiquity* 25: 355–372.
Bunzel, Ruth
   1940 The role of alcoholism in two Central American cultures.
      Psychiatry 3: 361–387.
Cáceres, Carlos L.
   1946 *Chiapas: síntesis geográfica e histórica*. Mexico.
Cancian, Frank
   1965 *Economics and prestige in a Maya community: a study of the
      religious cargo system in Zinacantán, Chiapas, Mexico*. Palo Alto:
      Stanford University Press.
Chatelain, Heli
   1894 *Folktales of Angola*. Memoirs of the American Folklore
      Society 1. New York and Boston.
Cicco, G. de, and Fernando Horcasitas
   1962 Los cuates: un mito chatiño. *Tlalocan* 4: 75–76.
Cline, Howard
   1944 Lore and deities of the Lacandon Indians. *Journal of American
      Folklore* 57: 108–110.
Coe, Michael D.
   1966 *The Maya*. New York and Washington: Praeger.
Cohen, Percy S.
   1969 Theories of Myth. *Man* (n.s.) 4, no. 3: 337–353.
Colby, Benjamin
   1966 Ethnographic semantics: a preliminary survey. *Current Anthro-
      pology* 7: 3–32.
Collier, George A.
   1968 Land inheritance and land use in a modern Maya community.
      Ph.D. diss., Harvard University.

Collier, Jane F.

1968 *Courtship and marriage in Zinacantan, Chiapas, Mexico.* Middle
American Research Institute, publication 25. New Orleans: Tulane
University Press.

1973 *Law and Social Change in Zinacantan.* Stanford: Stanford
University Press.

Corzo, Angel M.

1943 *Historia de Chiapas: La leyenda de la patria.* Mexico: Editorial
"Protos."

Crumrine, Lynne S.

1968 An ethnography of Mayo speaking. *Anthropological Linguistics*
10, no. 2: 19-31.

Davenport, W.H.

1953 Marshallese folklore types. *Journal of American Folklore*
66: 219-238.

Dégh, Linda

1969 *Folktales and society: storytelling in a Hungarian peasant
community.* Trans. Emily M. Schossberger. Bloomington: Indiana
University Press.

Díaz del Castillo, Bernal

1939 *Historia verdadera de la conquista de la Nueva España.* Mexico:
Editorial Pedro Robredo.

Domínguez, Francisco, Luis Sandi, and Roberto Téllez Girón

1962 *Investigación folklórica en México*, vol. 1: *Materiales.* Intro.
Baltásar Samper. Mexico: Secretaría de Educación Pública, Instituto
Nacional de Bellas Artes.

Douglas, Mary

1966 *Purity and danger.* New York: Praeger.

1970 *Natural symbols: explorations in cosmology.* New York: Pantheon.

Dundes, Alan

1962 From etic to emic units in the structural study of folktales.
Journal of American Folklore 75: 95-105.

1963 Structural typology in North American Indian Folktales.
Southwestern Journal of Anthropology 19: 121-130.

1965 *The study of folklore.* Englewood Cliffs, N.J.: Prentice-Hall.

1967 North American Indian folklore studies. *Journal de la Société
des Américanistes* 56: 53-79.

Durkheim, Emile, and Marcel Mauss

1963 *Primitive classification.* Trans., ed., and intro. Rodney Needham.
Chicago: University of Chicago Press.

Edmonson, Munro S.

1967 Narrative folklore. In Robert Wauchope and Manning Nash,
eds., *Handbook of Middle American Indians*, vol. 6: *Social Anthropology*, pp. 357-368. Austin: University of Texas Press.

1971 *The book of counsel: the Popol Vuh of the Quiché Maya of Guatemala.* Middle American Research Institute, publication 35. New Orleans: Tulane University Press.

Eliade, Mircea
1959 *The sacred and the profane: the nature of religion.* New York: Harcourt, Brace and World, Harvest Books.

Emeneau, M.B.
1966 Style and meaning in an oral literature. *Language* 42: 323–345.

Epstein, Susan
1970 Civil and religious officials in Chamula. Unpub. ms., Harvard Chiapas Project, Harvard University.

Evans-Pritchard, E.E.
1940 *The Nuer.* Oxford: Clarendon.
1967 *The Zande trickster.* London: Oxford University Press.

Finnegan, Ruth
1967 *Limba stories and story-telling.* London: Oxford University Press.

Firth, Raymond
1961 *History and traditions of Tikopia.* Wellington, New Zealand: The Polynesian Society.

Fischer, J.L.
1963 The sociopsychological analysis of folktales. *Current Anthropology* 4: 235–295.

Foster, George M.
1945 Sierra Popoluca folklore and beliefs. *University of California Publications on American Archaeology and Ethnology* 42: 202–236.

Fox, James J.
1971 Semantic parallelism in Rotinese ritual language. *Bijdragen tot de Taal-, Land-, en Volkenkunde* 127: 215–255.
1972 Our ancestors spoke in pairs: Rotinese views of language, dialect and code. Paper prepared for Conference on the Ethnography of Speaking, April, University of Texas, Austin.

Frake, Charles O.
1961 The diagnosis of disease among the Subanum of Mindinao. *American Anthropologist* 63: 113–132.

Fraser, J.T., ed.
1966 *The voices of time: a cooperative survey of man's views of time as expressed by the sciences and by the humanities.* New York: Braziller.

Geertz, Clifford
1965 Religion as a cultural system. In Michael Banton, ed., *Anthropological approaches to the study of religion.* Association of Social Anthropologists Monograph no. 3. London: Tavistock.

Gluckman, Max
1963 Gossip and scandal. *Current Anthropology* 4: 307–316.

1968 Psychological, sociological and anthropological explanations of witchcraft and gossip. *Man* (n.s.) 3: 29–34.

Goetz, Delia, and Sylvanus Morley
1950 *Popol Vuh: the sacred book of the ancient Quiché Maya.* From the Spanish translation by Adrián Recinos. Norman: University of Oklahoma Press.

Goldstein, Kenneth
1964 *A guide for fieldworkers in folklore.* Hatboro, Pa.: Folklore Associates.

Goodenough, Ward
1964 *Explorations in cultural anthropology.* New York: McGraw-Hill.

Gossen, Gary H.
1969 Another look at world view: aerial photography and Chamula cosmology. Paper read at the 68th Annual Meeting of the American Anthropological Association, New Orleans.
1970 Time and space in Chamula oral tradition. Ph.D. diss., Harvard University.
1971a Chamula genres of verbal behavior. In Américo Paredes and Richard Bauman, eds., *Towards new perspectives in folklore.* Special number of *Journal of American Folklore* 84, no. 331: 145–167.
1971b Verbal Dueling in Chamula. Paper read at the 70th Annual Meeting of the American Anthropological Association, New York.
1972 Temporal and spatial equivalents in Chamula ritual symbolism. In William Lessa and E.Z. Vogt, eds., *A Reader in Comparative Religion.* 3rd ed. New York: Harper and Row.
n.d. Chamula (Tzotzil) proverbs: neither fish nor fowl. In Munro S. Edmonson, ed., *Meaning in Mayan Languages.* The Hague: Mouton, in press.

Guiteras-Holmes, Calixta
1961 *Perils of the soul: the world view of a Tzotzil Indian.* Glencoe, Ill.: Free Press.

Hallowell, A.I.
1947 Myth, culture and personality. *American Anthropologist* 49: 544–556.

Hamnett, Ian
1967 Ambiguity, classification and change: the function of riddles. *Man* (n.s.) 2: 379–392.

Hansen, Terrance Leslie
1957 *The types of the folktale in Cuba, Puerto Rico, the Dominican Republic, and Spanish South America.* Berkeley and Los Angeles: University of California Press.

Harrison, Frank and Joan Harrison
1968 Spanish elements in the music of two Maya groups in Chiapas.

Selected Reports 1, no. 2: 1–44. Institute for Ethnomusicology, U.C.L.A. Los Angeles: University of California Press.

Haviland, John B.
1967 *Vob:* Traditional music in Zinacantan. Unpub. ms., Harvard Chiapas Project, Harvard University.
1970 Review of B. Berlin, *Tzeltal numeral classifiers* (1968). *American Anthropologist* 72: 194–196.

Herodotus
1956 *The History of Herodotus.* Trans. George Rawlinson. Ed. Manuel Komroff. New York: Tudor.

Holland, William
1963 *Medicina maya en los altos de Chiapas: un estudio de cambio sociocultural.* Colección de Antropología Social 2. Mexico: Instituto Nacional Indigenista.

Hymes, Dell H.
1962 The ethnography of speaking. In Thomas Gladwin and William Sturtevant, eds., *Anthropology and human behavior.* Washington, D.C.: Anthropological Society of Washington.
1967 Models of the interaction of language and social setting. *Journal of Social Issues* 23, no. 2: 8–28.

Instituto Indigenista Interamericano
1958 *Legislación indígena de México.* Ediciones especiales, no. 38. Mexico.

Jakobson, Roman
1966 Grammatical parallelism and its Russian facet. *Language* 42: 398–429.

Jason, Heda
1969 A multi-dimensional approach to folklore. *Current Anthropology* 10, no. 4: 413–426.

Johnson, Irmgard Weitlander de, and J.B. Johnson
1939 Un cuento mazateco-popoloca. *Revista Mexicana de Estudios Antropológicos* 3: 217–226.

Keesing, Roger
1968 Step kin, in-laws and ethnoscience. *Ethnology* 7: 59–70.
1971 Paradigms lost. Paper read at the 70th Annual Meeting of the American Anthropological Association, New York.

Kiell, Norman, ed.
1963 *Psychoanalysis, psychology and literature: a bibliography.* Madison: University of Wisconsin Press.

Kramer, Fritz
1971 *Literature among the Cuna Indians.* Ethnologiska Studier 30. Gothenberg, Sweden: Göteborgs Etnografiska Museum.

La Farge, Oliver
1947 *Santa Eulalia; the religion of a Cuchumatán Indian town.* Chicago: University of Chicago Press.

La Farge, Oliver, and Douglas Byers
  1931 *The year bearer's people.* Middle American Research Series, publication 3. New Orleans: Tulane University Press.
Laughlin, Robert N.
  1960 Zinacanteco myth and tale texts. Unpub. ms., Harvard Chiapas Project, Harvard University.
  1962 Through the looking glass: reflections on Zinacanteco courtship and marriage. Ph.D. diss., Harvard University.
  1968 The Tzotzil. In Robert Wauchope and E.Z. Vogt, eds., *Handbook of Middle American Indians*, vol. 7: *Ethnology*, pp. 152–194. Austin: University of Texas Press.
Leach, E.R.
  1961a Lévi-Strauss in the Garden of Eden. *Transactions of the New York Academy of Sciences* 23, no. 4: 386–396.
  1961b Two essays concerning the symbolic representation of time. In E.R. Leach, *Rethinking anthropology*, pp. 124–136. London: Athlone Press, University of London.
  1964 Anthropological aspects of language: animal categories and verbal abuse. In Eric H. Lenneberg, ed., *New directions in the study of language.* Cambridge: M.I.T. Press.
  1965 *Political systems of Highland Burma: a study of Kachin social structure.* Boston: Beacon.
  1966 A discussion of ritualization of behavior in animals and men. *Philosophical Transactions of the Royal Society of London*, ser. B, 251, no. 772: 403–408.
  1970 *Claude Lévi-Strauss.* New York: Viking.
León-Portilla, Miguel
  1968 *Tiempo y realidad en el pensamiento Maya.* Mexico: Instituto de Investigaciones Históricas, Universidad Nacional Autónoma de México.
Lévi-Strauss, Claude
  1955 The structural study of myth. *Journal of American Folklore* 28: 428–444.
  1963 *Structural anthropology.* New York: Basic Books.
  1966 *The savage mind.* London: Weidenfeld and Nicolson.
  1969 *The raw and the cooked: an introduction to a science of mythology.* New York: Harper and Row.
Littleton, C. Scott
  1965 A two-dimensional scheme for the classification of narratives. *Journal of American Folklore* 78: 21–27.
Lomax, Alan
  1968 *Folksong style and culture.* American Association for the Advancement of Science, publication 88. Washington, D.C.
Lord, Albert
  1958 *The Singer of Tales.* Cambridge: Harvard University Press.
Madsen, William
  1960 *The Virgin's children.* Austin: University of Texas Press.

Malinowski, Bronislaw
1926 *Myth in primitive psychology.* New York: Norton.
Maranda, Pierre, and Elli Köngäs
1971 *Structural analysis of oral tradition.* Philadelphia: University of Pennsylvania Press.
Mason, J. Alden
1963 Folktales of the Tepecanos. *Journal of American Folklore* 27: 149–210.
Mason, J. Alden, and Aurelio M. Espinosa
1921 Porto-Rican folklore. *Journal of American Folklore* 34: 164–165.
1924 Porto-Rican folklore. *Journal of American Folklore* 37: 249–256.
Maybury-Lewis, David
1969 Review of Claude Lévi-Strauss, *Mythologiques: du miel aux cendres* (1966). *American Anthropologist* 71: 114–120.
McQuown, Norman
1956 The classification of Mayan languages. *International Journal of American Linguistics* 23: 191–195.
Mechling, William H.
1912 Stories from Tuxtepec, Oaxaca. *Journal of American Folklore* 25: 199–203.
Mendelson, E. Michael
1967 Ritual and mythology. In Robert Wauchope and Manning Nash, eds., *Handbook of Middle American Indians*, vol 6: *Social Anthropology*, pp. 392–415. Austin: University of Texas Press.
Menget, Patrick
1968 Death in Chamula. *Natural History* 77: 48–57.
Merkel, Judy
1967 Shamanism in Chamula. Unpub. ms., Harvard Chiapas Project, Harvard University.
Middleton, John
1954 Some social aspects of Lugbara myth. *Africa* 24: 189–199.
1961 *Lugbara religion.* London: Oxford University Press.
Miles, Suzanna W.
1952 An analysis of modern middle-American calendars: a study in conservatism. In Sol Tax, ed., *Acculturation in the Americas*, Selected Papers of the XXIXth International Congress of Americanists. Chicago.
Miller, W.S.
1956 *Cuentos mixes.* Mexico: Instituto Nacional Indigenista.
Mintz, Sidney W., and Eric R. Wolf
1950 An analysis of ritual co-parenthood (compadrazgo). *Southwestern Journal of Anthropology* 6: 341–368.
Molina, Cristóbal
1934 *War of the castes: Indian uprisings in Chiapas, 1867–1870.* Trans. Ernest Noyes and Dolores Morgadanes. Middle American

Research Series, pamphlet 8, publication 5. New Orleans: Tulane University Press.

Morley, Sylvanus
1956 *The ancient Maya.* 3rd ed., rev. George W. Brainerd. Palo Alto: Stanford University Press.

Mülleried, Federico K.G.
1957 *La geología de Chiapas.* Mexico: El Gobierno Constitucional de Chiapas.

Nash, Manning
1957 Cultural persistences and social structure: the Meso-American calendar survivals. *Southwestern Journal of Anthropology* 13: 149–155.

Needham, Rodney
1967 Percussion and transition. *Man* (n.s.) 2, no. 4: 606–614.

Ortiz, Alfonso
1969 *The Tewa world: space, time, being and becoming in a Pueblo society.* Chicago: University of Chicago Press.

Paredes, Américo, and Richard Bauman, eds.
1971 Towards new perspectives in folklore. *Journal of American Folklore* 84, no. 331.

Parsons, E.C.
1936 *Mitla, town of the souls.* Chicago: University of Chicago Press.

Parsons, Talcott, Edward Shils, Caspar D. Naegele, and Jesse R. Pitts
1965 *Theories of society: foundations of modern sociological theory.* New York: Free Press.

Pozas, Ricardo A.
1959 *Chamula: un pueblo indio de los altos de Chiapas.* Memorias del Instituto Nacional Indigenista VIII. Mexico.

1962 *Juan the Chamula: an ethnological re-creation of the life of a Mexican Indian.* Trans. Lysander Kemp. Berkeley and Los Angeles: University of California Press.

Propp, Vladimir
1958 *Morphology of the folktale.* Ed. and intro. Svatava Pirkova-Jacobsen, trans. Lawrence Scott. Indiana University Research Center in Anthropology, Folklore and Linguistics, publication 10. Bloomington: University of Indiana Press. Also in Bibliographical and Special Series of the American Folklore Society 9.

Rattray, R.S.
1930 *Akan-Ashanti folktales.* Oxford: Clarendon.

Recinos, Adrián
1918 Cuentos populares de Guatemala. *Journal of American Folklore* 31: 472–473.

Recinos, Adrián, and Delia Goetz
1953 *The annals of the Cakchiquels.* Norman: University of Oklahoma Press.

Redfield, Margaret Park
  1935 *The folk literature of a Yucatan town.* Carnegie Institution of
  Washington publication 456, no. 14. Washington, D.C.
Redfield, Robert, and Alfonso Villa Rojas
  1962 *Chan Kom: a Maya village.* Chicago: Phoenix.
Reed, Nelson
  1964 *The caste war of Yucatan.* Palo Alto: Stanford University Press.
Reichard, Gladys
  1944 *Prayer: the compulsive word.* Monographs of The American
  Ethnological Society no. 7. New York.
Reid, John Turner
  1935 Seven folktales from Mexico. *Journal of American Folklore*
  48: 107–112.
Remesal, Antonio de
  1908 *1619 historia de la provincia de S. Vicente de Chiapas y
  Guatemala.* Madrid.
Rosaldo, Michelle
  1971 Context and metaphor in Ilongot oral tradition. Ph.D. diss.,
  Harvard University.
Rosaldo, Renato, Jr.
  1964 Some aspects of space and time in the *Popul Vuh.* Paper
  prepared for Anthropology 260, seminar on the Maya, fall, Harvard
  University.
  1968 Metaphors of hierarchy in a Maya ritual. *American Anthropologist* 70: 524–536.
Roys, Ralph L.
  1967 *The Book of Chilam Balam of Chumayel.* Norman: University
  of Oklahoma Press.
Sahagún, Fray Bernardino de
  1957 *The Florentine codex: general history of the things of new
  Spain.* Trans. and anno. A.J.O. Anderson and C.E. Dibble. Monograph no. 14. School of American Research, Santa Fe.
Secretaría de Industria y Comercio
  1963 *VIII censo general de población, 8 de junio, 1960.* Mexico:
  Estado de Chiapas, Dirección general de estadística.
Siegal, Morris
  1943 The creation myth and acculturation in Acatán, Guatemala.
  Journal of American Folklore 56: 123–125.
Siegel, James
  1969 *The rope of God.* Berkeley and Los Angeles: University of
  California Press.
Slocum, M.C.
  1965 The origin of corn and other Tzeltal myths. *Tlalocan* 5: 1–45.
Sydow, C.W. von
  1948 The categories of prose tradition. In Laurits Bødker, ed.,

Selected Papers on Folklore, pp. 60–88. Copenhagen: Rosenkilde and Bagger.

Tedlock, Dennis
1968 The ethnography of tale-telling at Zuni. Ph.D. diss., Tulane University.
1972 *Finding the center: narrative poetry of the Zuni Indians.* New York: Dial Press.

Thompson, J. Eric S.
1930 Ethnology of the Mayas of southern and central British Honduras. *Chicago Natural History Museum Anthropological Series* 17, no. 1: 120–172.
1934 *Sky bearers, color and directions in Maya and Mexican religion.* Carnegie Institution of Washington Publication 436, no. 10. Washington, D.C.
1954 *The rise and fall of Maya civilization.* Norman: University of Oklahoma Press.
1960 *Maya hieroglyphic writing: an introduction.* Norman: University of Oklahoma Press.
1965 Maya creation myths, Part I. *Estudios de Cultura Maya*, V, 13–32. Mexico: Seminario de Cultura Maya, Universidad Nacional Autónoma de México.
1967 Maya creation myths, Part II. *Estudios de Cultura Maya*, VI, 15–43. Mexico: Seminario de Cultura Maya, Universidad Nacional Autónoma de México.
1970 *Maya history and religion.* Norman: University of Oklahoma Press.

Thompson, Stith
1946 *The Folktale.* New York: Holt, Rinehart and Winston.
1955–1958 *Motif index of folk literature.* 2nd ed. 6 vol. Bloomington: University of Indiana Press.
1961 *The types of the folktale: a classification and bibliography.* 2nd rev. Trans. and enl. of Antti Aarne, *Verzeichnis der Märchen typen.* Folklore Fellows Communications, no. 184. Helsinki: Suomalainen Tiedeakatemia.

Tozzer, Alfred M.
1907 *A comparative study of the Mayas and the Lacandones.* New York: Macmillan.
1941 *Landa's relación de las cosas de Yucatán.* Papers of the Peabody Museum of Archaeology and Ethnology 18. Cambridge: Peabody Museum of Harvard University.

Trens, Manuel B.
1957 *Historia de Chiapas*, vol. 1. Mexico: Talleres gráficos de la nación.

Turner, Terrence
n.d. *The fire of the jaguar.* Chicago: University of Chicago Press.

Turner, Victor W.
  1967 *The forest of symbols.* Ithaca : Cornell University Press.

  1968 *The drums of affliction.* London: Clarendon and the International African Institute.

  1969 *The ritual process: structure and antistructure.* Chicago: Aldine.
Tyler, Stephen A., ed.
  1969 *Cognitive anthropology.* New York: Holt, Rinehart and Winston.
Valladares, L.A.
  1957 *El hombre y el maíz.* Mexico: B. Costa-Amic.
Valle, Rafael Heliodoro
  1923 El folklore en la literatura de Centro-América. *Journal of American Folklore* 36: 110–134.
Vansina, Jan
  1965 Oral tradition: a study in historical methodology. Trans. H.M. Wright. Chicago: Aldine.
Villa Rojas, Alfonso
  1968 Los conceptos de espacio y tiempo entre los grupos mayances contemporáneos. Appendix to Miguel León-Portilla, 1968: 119–168.
Vogt, Evon Z.
  1964 The genetic model and Maya cultural development. In Evon Z. Vogt and Alberto Ruz L., eds., *Desarrollo cultural de los Mayas,* pp. 9–48. Mexico: Seminario de Cultura Maya, Universidad Nacional Autónoma de México.

  1966 (ed.) *Los Zinacantecos.* Mexico: Instituto Nacional Indigenista.

  1969 *Zinacantan: a Maya community in the highlands of Chiapas* Cambridge: Harvard University Press.
Wasserstrom, Robert
  1970 Our Lady of the Salt. B.A. honors thesis, Harvard College.
Whelan, Frederick G.
  1967 The passing of the years: calendars, dating and ideas of time in Zinacantan and Chamula. Unpub. ms., Harvard Chiapas Project, Harvard University.
Willey, Gordon R.
  1966 *An introduction to American archaeology,* vol. 1: *North and Middle America.* Englewood Cliffs, N.J.: Prentice-Hall.
Wilson, George Carter
  1966 *Crazy February.* New York: Lippincott.
Wittgenstein, Ludwig
  1968 *Tractatus logico-philosophicus.* London: Routledge and Kegan Paul, International Library of Philosophy and Scientific Method.
Ximénez, Francisco
  1929–1931 *Historia de la provincia de San Vicente de Chiapas y Guatemala de la orden de predicadores.* Guatemala: Tipografía Nacional.

Notes

1. The Community

1. The approximate population of 40,000 for 1968 is based on the 1960 census figure of 26,789 and on the explosive growth rate over the past few decades. The figure includes Chamula hamlets lying in contiguous municipios but retaining ritual affiliation with the main municipio. The municipio is a Mexican political unit, which has no exact English equivalent. Its authority lies just beneath the state organization, analogous to the county in most states of the United States. However, it differs from a county, particularly in those parts of Mexico having Indian populations, where municipio boundaries often coincide with ethnic boundaries, which adds separateness of language and custom to separateness of political entity. This pattern is particularly characteristic of Indian municipios in highland Chiapas.

2. The 1960 census reported that 92 percent of the Chamula population was monolingual in Tzotzil (Secretaría de Industria y Comercio, 1963: 898). However, most men know enough basic Spanish to deal with non-Indian merchants and employers. Women's knowledge of Spanish is generally limited to a very small number of market words. Following is an explanation of the Chamula Tzotzil phonemes used throughout this book:

    a   low, central, open, allophonically fluctuating with [ə]
    e, o   mid, front, and back, open, fluctuating between rounded and unrounded
    i, u   high, front, and back, closed, unsounded
    b   voiced bilabial stop

č   voiceless, aspirated alveopalatal affricate
č' glottalized "č"
h   voiceless velar spirant
H   voiceless, labialized, backed velar fricative.
k   voiceless, aspirated velar stop, more strongly aspirated in final position
k' glottalized "k"
ʔ   glottal stop
l   voiced alveolar lateral with voiceless offglide in final position
m   bilabial nasal
n   alveolar nasal
p   voiceless, aspirated, bilabial stop, more strongly aspirated in final position
r   voiced alveolar flap
s   voiceless alveolar fricative
š   voiceless alveopalatal fricative
t   voiceless, aspirated alveolar stop, more strongly aspirated in final position
t' glottalized "t"
¢   voiceless, aspirated alveolar affricate
¢' glottalized "¢"
v   voiced labiodental fricative freely variable to bilabial "w," with voiceless offglide in final position
y   voiced alveopalatal glide with voiceless offglide in final position

3. For Ancient Maya society, art, and thought, see Coe (1966), León-Portilla (1968), Morley (1956), J.E.S. Thompson (1954, 1960, 1970), Tozzer (1941), Villa Rojas (1968), Willey (1966: 78–177).

4. Material on the colonial period in Chamula is scant. See Trens (1957), Remesal (1908), Ximénez (1929–1931), Díaz del Castillo (1939), Cáceres (1946), Corzo (1943), Pozas (1959: 17–21). For the prehistory and history of the Tzotzil-speaking communities of the Chiapas highlands, see Vogt (1969: 11–31).

5. For the habitat, see Pozas (1959: 11–12), Vogt (1969: 3–10).

6. For detailed surveys of local Chamula industries, see Pozas (1959: 77–110).

7. For Chamula social organization and kinship, see Pozas (1959), Gossen (1970). For analogous data on nearby Zinacantan, see Vogt (1969), Cancian (1965), G.A. Collier (1968).

8. For other experiments to illustrate the nature of Chamula ethnocentrism, see Gossen (1969; 1970: 131–148). Chamula patterns in this regard are not unique, for Herodotus wrote of the Persians: "They honour most their nearest neighbours, whom they esteem next to themselves; those who live beyond these they honour in the second degree; and so with the remainder, the further they are removed, the less esteem in which they hold them. The reason is, that they look upon themselves as very greatly superior in all respects to the rest of

mankind, regarding others as approaching to excellence in proportion as they dwell nearer to them; whence it comes to pass that those who are the farthest off must be the most degraded of mankind" (1956: 52–53).

9. Although the tropical lowlands actually lie mostly south and slightly west of Chamula, the whole lowland area is conceptually united for the Chamulas by the qualities of lowness and association with the setting sun. Thus, Chamulas frequently say that they are going west (*ta ʔolon*, "down" or "below") to the coffee plantations. This is not an error in their directional sense but simply an expression of conceptual equivalences in their cosmology.

10. There is no evidence for the survival of the Ancient Maya Long Count and Short Count cycles among the modern Chamulas. See Coe (1966), Whelan (1967). Chamulas have, however, an immense preoccupation with time. It is as important to them to speak with precision about time as it was to their Ancient Maya forebears. Furthermore, Chamulas are rarely late for work or for any other appointment. If anything, they are usually early. I recall several cases in which informants sent their children on four-hour round-trip errands simply to advise me that an emergency would delay their fathers for a specified period of time.

11. For the civil-religious festivals celebrated in Chamula, see Gossen (1970: 109), Pozas (1959: 171). Of the thirty-two festivals celebrated in 1968, the major ones in terms of duration and intensity of ritual activity and public attendance were: Change of Offices, December 31–January 3; San Sebastián, January 18–20; Carnival or Festival of Games, five days preceding Ash Wednesday; Holy Week; Santa Cruz, May 1–3; San Juan, June 22–24; Santa Rosa, August 28–30; San Mateo, September 19–21; Virgen del Rosario, October 5–7; and Feast of the Dead, October 30–November 1.

12. Time-space categories have been fundamental analytical tools for understanding the Western tradition for millenia, from Aristotle to Einstein. See Fraser (1966). These categories, as defined by other traditions, have been useful to social anthropologists in making non-Western belief systems intelligible. See, e.g., Evans-Pritchard (1940), Middleton (1954, 1961), Leach (1961b), Ortiz (1969). On the cohesion of "equal values" of time and space attributes of events, Jerome Bruner and his associates offered a plausible explanation for the tendency of time, space, and other aspects of symbolism and associational thinking to hang together as logical helpmates. They pointed out that through categorizing the human organism achieves, among other things, a reduction in the complexity of its environment, the identification of objects in the world about it, a reduction in the necessity of constant learning, the direction for instrumental activity, and the opportunity to order and relate classes of events. With reference to the last, they wrote: "We operate . . . with category systems—classes of events that are

related to each other in various kinds of superordinate systems. We map and give meaning to our world by relating classes of events rather than by relating individual events." In Chamula thought, time and space form the principal axes in such a superordinate system for relating classes of events. The categories of such a system also include those that Bruner and his associates called "conjunctive categories," defined by the joint presence of appropriate values of several attributes. These categories explain the tendency for similar values of several aspects of Chamula cosmology and oral tradition to cling together. Bruner and his collaborators observed further: "Once a configuration has been established and the object is being identified in terms of configurational attributes, the perceiver will tend to "rectify" or "normalize" any of the original defining attributes that deviate from expectancy." This helps to explain the Chamula tendency to use the system of attributes in their world view for making associations, as in their association of "biting" with asocial behavior and great social distance. See Bruner et al. (1967: 13, 47).

13. Miguel León-Portilla summarized the diverse symbolic implications of the proto-Maya word root *kinh*, which means "sun," "day," and "time," and concluded that the symbolic presence of time in the diverse conceptual realms of Maya religion makes the ancient belief system intelligible: "From at least the time of the first inscriptions of the Maya Classic [300 A.D.], the concept of time as an abstraction, derived from the cyclical nature of the sun and the related "day" unit, had universal primacy in the sphere of Maya culture. Proof of this comes from the ancient word *kinh*, whose meaning is identical in different groups . . . *kinh* is primordial reality, divine and without limit. *kinh* includes, conceptually, all of the cycles and all of the cosmic ages which have existed . . . The universe of time in which the Mayas lived was an ever-changing stage in which one was able to feel the sum of influence and actions of the various divine forces which coincided in a particular period . . . Since the essence of the nature of *kinh* was cyclical, it was important above all to understand the past in order to understand the present and predict the future . . . The faces of time, that primordial reality which obsessed the Mayas, were objects of veneration . . . The Maya sages invented a cosmovision. Since it was history, measure of, and prediction about the total reality whose essence was time, it would be more appropriate to call the Maya world view a chronovision . . . To ignore the primordial importance of time would be to ignore the soul of this culture" (León-Portilla, 1968: 62–63, 109–110, translation mine). This thesis is illustrated throughout the three most important Maya literary and ethnohistorical works (all transcribed shortly after the Conquest): *The Popol Vuh* (Edmonson, 1971; Goetz and Morley, 1959), *Annals of the Cakchiquels* (Recinos and Goetz, 1954), and *The Book of Chilam Balam of Chumayel* (Roys, 1967).

2. The Nature and Types of Chamula Verbal Behavior

1. Because of the many closely related meanings of *k'op*, it was impossible to find a single best translation to use throughout the book. In almost all instances, however, it is translated either as "word" or "language," depending on the context and sense of the Tzotzil usage.

The contextual interpretation of oral tradition dates roughly from Bronislaw Malinowski's *Myth in Primitive Psychology* (1926), in which he defined myth among the Trobriand Islanders as a "charter for belief" —in a view that may be applied as well to other genres of traditional verbal behavior: "The text, of course, is extremely important, but without the context it remains lifeless . . . the stories live in native life and not on paper, and when a scholar jots them down without being able to evoke the atmosphere in which they flourish, he gives us but a mutilated bit of reality" (Malinowski, 1926: 24). This approach has been adopted in structural and social anthropology, in sociolinguistics, and to a lesser extent in traditional folklore studies. See, e.g., Ortiz (1969), Blaffer (1972), Maranda and Köngäs (1971), Siegel (1969), T. Turner (n.d.), Beidelman (1961, 1963, 1970), Middleton (1961), V. Turner (1968), Leach (1961a, 1965), Lévi-Strauss (1955, 1963, 1966, 1969), Dégh (1969), Abrahams (1970a, 1970b), Evans-Pritchard (1967), Lomax (1968), and Vansina (1965). See also Leach (1967, 1970), Paredes and Bauman (1971), Fischer (1963), Cohen (1969), Jason (1969), Abrahams (1968a, 1968b), Dundes (1962, 1963), Arewa and Dundes (1963), Goldstein (1964). Most of these works deal with traditional narrative genres, particularly myth, whereas a holistic approach should demonstrate that genres other than narrative are also amenable to contextual analysis.

For representative works that deal with "emic" methods of data collection and analysis, see Hymes (1962, 1967), Frake (1964), Goodenough (1964), Colby (1966). Berlin (1968), Haviland (1970), Keesing (1968, 1971), Tyler (1969). For the problem of comparing Western narrative genres with native categories, see Bascom (1965), Littleton (1965), Ben-Amos (1969a). For the standard genre taxonomies of Western Europe, see von Sydow (1948), Bødker (1965). For native genres of oral tradition and related behavior settings, see Chatelain (1894), Malinowski (1926), Rattray (1930), Bascom (1943), Hallowell (1947), Davenport (1953), Firth (1961), Vansina (1965), Crumrine (1968), Arewa and Dundes (1964), Abrahams (1968a, 1968b), Tedlock (1968, 1972), Abrahams and Bauman (1971), Kramer (1970), Finnegan (1967), Dégh (1969). For similar context-conscious treatments of other than narrative genres, see Hamnett (1967), Abrahams (1970c), Gluckman (1963, 1968), M. Rosaldo (1971), Gossen (1971, n.d.). Maranda and Köngäs (1971), Ben-Amos (1969b).

2. For all of the genres of verbal behavior in the taxonomy, I made an effort to elicit a representative corpus. Generally, five methods were used to record texts: notes taken by me or an assistant during actual

in situ performances; tape recordings of actual performances, later transcribed by me or an assistant; special tape performances, hired or requested, which were later transcribed by me or an assistant; direct transcription of texts by me or an assistant in special elicitation sessions; and writing of texts by trained assistants. No one method alone produced the best results. Frequently, only one method could possibly be used to obtain a text. In other cases, several methods of elicitation and transcription were used. When subsequent comparison revealed significant points of variance in the same text obtained by different methods, the version that seemed closest to an actual performance of the genre was used.

For more information on Tzotzil folk genres of verbal behavior in the nearby community of Zinacantan, see Bricker (1968: 30–33). In that community value judgments (good or bad) and degree of seriousness of the subject matter (whether or not people laugh about it), as well as specific content and behavior setting, serve as criteria for classification. Although Bricker found virtually the same super-categories of verbal behavior in Zinacantan as I found in Chamula, the criteria for defining the categories differed considerably there, which shows that even in neighboring communities speaking dialects of the same language, different culturally significant criteria distinguish the same categories.

3. The Marginal Genres

1. The Tzotzil *vaka*, from the Spanish *vaca* ("cow"), signifies both sexes of cattle. Male and female prefixes denote gender. Here it means "bull," shortened from *stot vakaš*.

2. In this text extract and all others throughout the book, indentation and capitalization are used to indicate doubling and other multiples of words, phrases, and semantic units. This convention represents the fundamental repetitive pattern of Tzotzil oral style. The pattern is usually dyadic, forming couplets, but is sometimes expressed in three- and four-part structures. The first part of a multi-unit phrase is set flush with the left margin. The related second, third, and fourth parts are indented below the first, and the first letter of each part is capitalized. A phrase that is not directly related to the immediately preceding phrase is set flush with the left margin and capitalized.

3. For detail on Chamula legal procedure and that of neighboring Zinacantan, see J. Collier (1973), Vogt (1969), and Pozas (1959: 133–155).

4. True Recent Narrative

1. Although crazy talk and recent talk are distinguished from each other by whether they are funny, they share the prose structure. This

chapter deals only with what unifies these two categories. Humorous aspects of the subcategory crazy talk are discussed in the chapter on frivolous language, which subsumes most of the genres of humorous verbal behavior.

2. The dual semantic units used in this text are related to the pattern in emotional language called nonparallel repetition. For a discussion of similar constructions in the Ancient Quiché Maya classic *Popol Vuh*, see Edmonson (1971). He uses the term "metaphoric couplet" for this dual construction and calls it the basic unit of Maya epic composition. I also use this term, but in reference to the more formal kinds of couplets appearing in recent and ancient words. Continuity in Maya style from the pre-Columbian period to the present seems highly probable, according to J.E.S. Thompson (1954: 170–171). For other cross-cultural examples of dyadic construction, see Lord (1958), Fox (1971), Jacobson (1966), and Reichard (1944).

5. Frivolous Language

1. Victoria R. Bricker's work (1968) on the humor of Zinacantan covers some of these subgenres as they occur in that neighboring municipio. Her work has been particularly suggestive to me in the preparation and interpretation of the data in this chapter.

2. This unusual, stylized repetition indicates from the beginning that it is not to be taken as a straight or true story.

3. This text is a standard European folk tale type (Aarne-Thompson Type 1889B). It is significant that it has entered Chamula oral tradition from the Spanish as a genre of humorous language and *not* as a folktale, as it is classified in the European *märchen* tradition. This is one of many cases that call into question the uncritical cross-cultural comparative methods used in European and American folklore scholarship.

4. This competitive aspect of truly frivolous talk is similar to a well-known Mexican genre of verbal dueling called *albur*. It differs from *albur* in that the Chamula genre requires dozens of exchanges for a single performance. An *albur* can be completed with as few as two exchanges.

5. Grinder refers to a hand-cranked corn grinder which is like an ordinary crank-type food grinder. The ground, moist corn resembles excrement as it comes out. Therefore, the grinder is understood here as the anus.

7. True Ancient Narrative

1. This text was supplied by Mateo Méndez Tzotzek, an informant who was a friend of the crier. Méndez Tzotzek claimed that he had heard this version from the crier in a "personal" performance. However, it is almost exactly what the crier says at the Festival of Games. That

it is performed by rote by the official and also known by rote by laymen is curious. For several reasons, then, this text is unique among the narratives in my collection. In the verision presented here, a standard Spanish translation is included with the English, because the Spanish rendition is occasionally unintelligible, being delivered by rote from memory by a monolingual Tzotzil speaker.

2. A reference to Cortéz' Indian mistress, Malinche, whose full name in Chamula is Nana María Cocorina.

3. Squash cooked to a mush with sufficient brown sugar to turn it nearly to syrup.

4. A light brown toffee wrapped in small pieces of corn husk, which is sold in San Cristóbal.

5. The phallic symbolism of this phrase is always uproariously funny to Chamulas. Morcilla sausage, of Spanish origin, is made of coagulated pork blood, onion, and rice.

6. True ancient narrative is used frequently as supporting evidence for an opinion or judgment. The circumstances that prompted this text are typical of the context for tale-telling throughout Chamula.

7. People at this time were made of clay and could not move properly, which is the reason they were destroyed.

8. In other words, the reason for all sexual irregularities is that the demon taught people about sex.

9. The word "Jew" is used as an English gloss for the Tzotzil terms *huraš* and *hurio*, which are used interchangeably. Both are from the Spanish: *huraš* from *Judás* (Judas), and *hurio* from *judio* (Jew). Because of the syncretistic nature of these concepts—partly from Spanish Catholic missionary instruction and partly from a pre-Hispanic notion of forces hostile to the sun deity—there is no precise English gloss for them. "Jew" is therefore used in lieu of a better translation. The Chamula Tzotzil terms do not refer to a living group of people on earth. "Jews" exist only as negative supernaturals, who live outside the universe delimited by the path of the sun deity. The gloss is used with this meaning throughout the book.

8. Language for Rendering Holy

1. The Lacandones are a remnant group of about three-hundred lowland Maya who now live about 150 miles southeast of Chamula. Hardly touched by the Conquest, they remain the most conservative group in the Maya area. Although their language and customs are related to those of Chamula, the Chamulas fear and dislike them.

2. For detail on life crisis rituals in Chamula and nearby Zinacantan, see Pozas (1959: 47–50), Vogt (1969: 195–216), J.F. Collier (1968), and Menget (1967).

3. This single line is only one part of what should be a standard two-part structure. This text is therefore imperfect, though not wrong by

Chamula canons. However, the line may also be considered a third part of the preceding two-part structure. It is semantically, though not syntactically, tied to the preceding couplet.

4. A reference to the arrival of the deceased in the underworld.

5. Note the candle and heat metaphor used in reference to the life cycle.

6. The "monkey assistants" wear costumes that include a red and black waistcoat, snakeskin belt, dark sunglasses, and a high conical hat made of monkey skins. They are associated with the beings who are supposed to have lived on earth before the creation of man. They also serve as policemen who watch the pasiones and other officials to ensure that they do not have sexual access to their wives during the three weeks of the fiesta and its preceding events. To break this prohibition would cause the fiesta to meet with disaster, such as a heavy rain.

7. All regular political cargoholders and some religious officials take office on December 30. Other religious positions (such as mayordomo and alférez) have induction schedules that coincide with the individual fiestas for which each official is responsible.

8. The symbolism of the birth of Christ and the sun is particularly relevant, for Christmas is celebrated only five days before the time of this ritual speech. The blessing specifically likens the new cargoholder to Christ and the sun, which suggests that religious officials are believed to share the burden of the maintenance of order with the deities during their time in office.

9. A reference to the place of oath-taking at the town hall in the Chamula ceremonial center.

10. This and the preceding line refer to the cargoholder's house, which, though humble ("frosty place of wealth"), is to be given over to the service of the deities.

11. "Cause of shame" refers to the ritual meals that the cargoholder must humbly give. This line is the third segment of an unusual three-part structure. It is not imperfect, for there is syntactical parallelism. It may rather be considered an emphatic form of the couplet.

9. Prayer

1. I was never able to secure sample texts because no Chamula would admit familiarity with either priests' or evil persons' knowledge.

2. The colors orange and yellow are associated with the spatial categories of south and the underworld, and with the temporal categories of death in the human life cycle and death of vegetation (October–December) in the annual agricultural cycle. See Fig. 2.

3. The shaman's specialized knowledge actually appears to come as much from informal apprenticeship as from revelation.

4. The junior-senior discrimination of forms or aspects of souls and deities follows the Chamula custom of recognizing junior and senior

aspects of numerous domains, from sibling terminology to topographic features.

5. I transcribed this text from a tape that was not recorded at the curing ceremony itself. The shaman, Mateo Méndez Tzotzek, agreed to make a recording of his prayer the following day under circumstances that were considerably easier for recording than was the ceremony itself.

6. The candle offerings that have been placed before the pine-covered altar.

7. The rope and cord symbolize the place of supernatural communication, that is, the curing ceremony.

8. The thirteen rows and lines refer to the arrangement of candles at the curing ceremony.

9. The "punishment" here and in the following lines refers to the patient's particular illness.

10. Song

1. For technical aspects of Chamula music, see Harrison and Harrison (1968); Arbuz (1963); Domínguez, Sandi and Téllez Girón (1962: 308–312). For a description of instruments, music, and musicians of nearby Zinacantan, see Haviland (1967). Most of the Zinacanteco string instruments (harp, violin, and guitar) are in fact manufactured by Chamulas, who make instruments for themselves and for several other Indian communities in the highlands.

2. The common drum is a cross-section of a hollowed-out log, about thirty centimeters long, which is covered with cowhide. There are six other ceramic drums, called *bahbin*, which are used only at the Festival of Games and other fiestas in the Lenten cycle. These special drums have a separate cult and are classed separately.

3. This text was transcribed from a tape made by a senior musician and his assistants. The tape was not recorded at the fiesta itself but in a separate recording session.

4. Chamulas subscribe to the "homunculus" theory of reproduction, namely, that small beings are present in the male sexual fluid only and are nursed until birth in the mother's womb. This is consistent with the patrifocal nature of Chamula society. It is also one explanation frequently given by Chamulas for their patronymic system, in which men and women keep their father's surname for life.

11. Language, Cosmos, and Social Order

1. Several (two to four) texts were arbitrarily selected for each time period. They included, beginning with the most recent period, Texts 5, 9, 16, 18, 28, 29, 37, 39, 41, 49, 53, 61, 73, 74, 75, 79, 84, 86, 96, 97, 122, 134, 147, 167.

2. *Indigenismo* is part of modern Mexican political and cultural

ideology that emphasizes the nation's ancient and contemporary Indian background.

3. A reference to General Venustiano Carranza, whose troops occupied San Cristóbal for many months during the Mexican Revolution.

12. A Perspective on the Study of Oral Tradition

1. Structural analysis in the tradition of Claude Lévi-Strauss has emphasized the special, even unique, qualities of myth, in comparison with other forms of verbal behavior (Levi-Strauss, 1955: 431; 1966: 130–131). For example, he rejects any important affinities of myth with poetry, saying that these two forms lie at polar extremes of linguistic expression (1955: 431), at least for the purposes of structural analysis.

Index